MATHQUEST SIX

Brendan Kelly
Co-ordinator of Mathematics
Halton Board of Education

Chester Carlow
Associate Professor, Department of Curriculum
Ontario Institute for Studies in Education

Sandra Folk
Supervisor
Leo Baeck School, Toronto

Rudy V. Neufeld
Teacher Specialist, Logo/Mathematics
London Board of Education

J Symington
Mathematics Consultant
York Region Board of Education

Joan Worth
Professor, Elementary Education
University of Alberta

Addison-Wesley Publishers Limited

Don Mills, Ontario • Reading, Massachusetts
Menlo Park, California • Wokingham, England
Amsterdam • Bonn • Sydney • Singapore • Tokyo
Madrid • Bogotá • Santiago • San Juan

EDITORIAL
Dianne Goffin
Lisa Guthro
Mary Martin

DESIGN, ART DIRECTION & ILLUSTRATION
Pronk & Associates

Gord Pronk, Mary Pronk, Faye Arends, Alan Barnard, Cyndy Miller, Gayle Newton, Dave Peden, Steve Pilcher, Grace Salmon, Margo Stahl, Linda Stephenson, Greg Tino, Nelly Toomey

Illustrators

Graham Bardell, Alan Barnard, David Bathurst, Thach Bui, Alan Bunce, Scott Caple, Ian Carr, Bill Chapman, Peter Emslie, Dan Fell, Chuck Gammage, Peter Grau, Rob Johannsen, Danielle Jones, Greg Joy, Kim LaFave, Bernadette Lau, June Lawrason, Barb Massey, David Mazierski, Paul McCusker, Jack McMaster, René Milot, Oni, Angela Parsons, Bill Payne, Steve Pilcher, Paul Rivoche, Greg Ruhl, Cynthia Ward, Carol Watson, Janet Wilson

Photographers

Bryan Alexander/Time-Life Books: 121; Faye Arends: 216; George Bilyk: 24; George Calef/Masterfile: 28–29; Canapress Photo Service: 206, 276; © M.C. Escher Heirs c/o Cordon Art-Baarn-Holland: 350; Indian and Northern Affairs (from a project of the Ojibway and Cree Cultural Centre): 125; 1986 Globus Brothers/Masterfile: 246; Teri Kelly: 312; NASA: 148; Royal Ontario Museum: 128–129; Yale University Press: 130

Cover Illustration
Alan Barnard

ACKNOWLEDGEMENTS
The authors and publishers would like to express their appreciation for the invaluable advice and encouragement received from educators across Canada during the development of this program. We particularly wish to thank the following people: Jan Cornwall, Gordon Jeffery, Ann Maher, Jacquelyn Marrocco, Bill Nimigon, Alexander Norrie, Patrick Ryan, David Simpson, Katherine Willson. Thanks also to Gateway Public School and Wandering Spirit Survival School.

Canadian postage stamps reproduced courtesy of Canada Post Corporation.

Canadian Cataloguing in Publication Data

Kelly, B. (Brendan), 1943–
    MathQuest six

For use in grade 6.
Includes index.

ISBN 0-201-19600-X

1. Arithmetic — 1961–   — Juvenile literature.
I. Title.

QA107.K45 1987   513   C87-094413-4

Printed and bound in Canada.
ISBN 0-201-19600-X

I —BP— 95

Table of Contents

Welcome to MathQuest 6

Some say that mathematics
is the greatest game of all.
It began with early cave dwellers'
Etchings on a wall.

Every human culture
That lives upon this earth
Has inherited some games,
Or to some game has given birth.

Some games may use arithmetic
To count or keep the score,
While others use geometry
To search and to explore.

And measurement is often used
Deciding win or loss,
To determine who is faster, or
Who has the longer toss.

But when the games use strategies
And problem solving skills,
They are most like mathematics
With its challenges and thrills.

And as you tackle MathQuest 6
Just watch your math skills grow!
Every time you win at math
You add to what you know.

PLACE VALUE 1

KO-NO

These players are enjoying a game of Five-Field Ko-No. In this game of logic, each player tries to move pieces to the opposite side of the playing board. Five-Field Ko-No has been played by people in China and Korea for many years. The Korean name for games played on a diagram is Ko-No, and the Chinese name is k'i.

Artist's impression of the Great Wall of China, 3rd century B.C.

PROBLEM SOLVING

Using Logical Thinking

YOUR LIST IS MISSING A VERY IMPORTANT STRATEGY: LOGICAL THINKING.

PROBLEM SOLVING STRATEGIES
- looking for a pattern
- guessing and checking
- making a model
- drawing a diagram
- making a table

BUT ISN'T LOGICAL THINKING USED WITH ALL THE OTHER STRATEGIES?

Problem: What is the mass of cube A?

Fact 1: All cubes with the same letter have the same mass.

Fact 2: The mass of each B cube is 1 kg.

Fact 3: This scale balances.

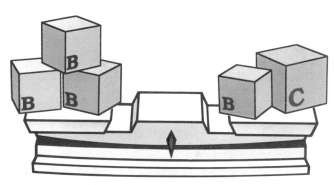

Fact 4: This scale balances.

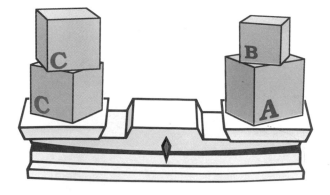

To solve this problem...

A. First, make sure you understand the problem.

Discuss:
- *What is the mass of a B cube?*
- *Do all the B cubes have the same mass?*
- *What do you know about the mass of a C cube?*
- *What do you know about the mass of the A cube?*

B. Then, think of strategies.

Use logical thinking to interpret the facts.

- *What does the 2-pan balance tell us about the masses at opposite ends?*
- *What is the total mass on each pan of the balance in the first picture?*

TRUE, BUT SOMETIMES A PROBLEM CAN BE SOLVED USING ONLY LOGICAL THINKING.

SOUNDS LOGICAL TO ME!

Use logical thinking to solve these problems.

1. How many 1 dollar coins are needed to balance the cylinder? Study both pictures.

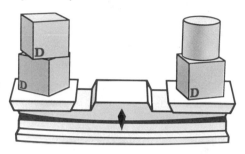

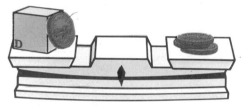

c. Solve the problem and answer the question.

- *Use facts 1 and 2. What is the mass of 3 B cubes?*
- *Use fact 3. What is the mass of 1 C and 1 B cube? What Is the mass of 1 C cube?*
- *Use fact 4. What is the total mass of 2 C cubes? 1 A and 1 B cube? What is the mass of 1 A cube?*

D. Check your answer and discuss your solution.

- *Is the total mass of 1 C cube and 1 B cube the same as the mass of 3 B cubes?*
- *Is the total mass of 1 B cube and 1 A cube the same as the mass of 2 C cubes?*
- *How did each fact help you?*
- *How many A cubes would balance 6 B cubes?*

2. What is the greatest odd number which can be made from these cards?

3. What 2-digit number is a multiple of 7 and 3 and is 1 less than a multiple of 5?

4. Andrew and Rebecca have the same number of coloured pencils. Andrew has 3 full boxes and 4 loose pencils. Rebecca has 2 full boxes and 12 loose pencils. How many pencils are in a box?

5. Mr. Ninevah said that when the digits of his age were reversed, the new number was 10 greater than his age. Was he telling the truth?

3

ESTIMATING

There are 100 stars
in this picture.

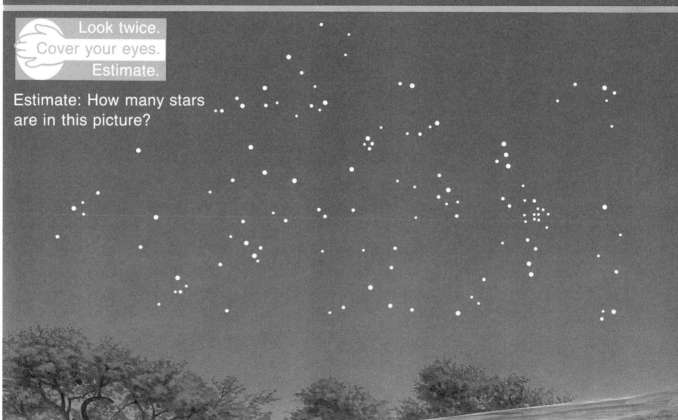

Look twice.
Cover your eyes.
Estimate.

Estimate: How many stars
are in this picture?

4

Estimate: How many stars are in this picture?

Look twice.
Cover your eyes.
Estimate.

Reading and Writing Numbers to 999 999

Earth is 1 of 9 planets in our **solar system**. Of these 9 planets, Earth is the **median** size. That means there are just as many planets that are smaller than Earth as there are larger. The diagram below shows the **diameters** of the planets.

Mercury	Venus	Earth	Mars
4880 km	12 100 km	12 756 km	6794 km

The diameter of Jupiter is **143 200** km.

We think: 143 thousand 200

We say: One hundred forty-three thousand two hundred

Jupiter
143 200 km

Read the diameters of these planets.

1. Venus
2. Mercury
3. Mars
4. Uranus

Write in words the diameter of each:

5. Earth
6. Saturn
7. Neptune
8. Pluto

Write in numerals.

9. sixteen thousand four hundred

10. one hundred thousand ten

11. eighty-three thousand fourteen

12. seven hundred seven thousand

13. two hundred sixty-four thousand

14. eighteen thousand eighty-five

15. nine hundred nine thousand two hundred two

16. four hundred ninety thousand twenty-eight

Uranus
51 800 km

Neptune
49 500 km

Pluto
2600 km

Saturn
120 000 km

17. Write the number that is:

a) 1000 less than 45 682
b) 10 000 greater than 38 417
c) 10 000 less than 112 238
d) 1000 greater than 976 244
e) 100 000 greater than 66 801
f) 100 000 less than 462 176
g) 1000 greater than 299 657
h) 10 000 less than 103 746
i) 10 000 greater than 497 685
j) 10 less than 66 009
k) 100 000 greater than 39 860
l) 1000 greater than 209 343

ESTIMATING

The diameters of the planets in the diagram are drawn to scale.

1. Visually estimate which planet has the diameter that is:

a) the greatest.
b) the least.
c) the closest in size to Earth's diameter.
d) the second greatest.

7

Place Value to 999 999

The earliest calculator was the **abacus**.
It was invented in China over 2000 years ago.

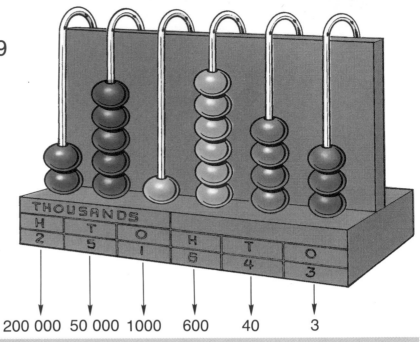

The number shown on this abacus is 251 643.

A place value chart shows the value of each digit in a numeral.

THOUSANDS					
H	T	O	H	T	O
2	5	1	6	4	3
200 000	50 000	1000	600	40	3

Write the value of each coloured digit.

1. 96 **4**53
2. **3**78 503
3. 7**5**4 003
4. **8**76 220
5. **1**49 035
6. 41**6** 820
7. 335 **4**68
8. 409 08**7**
9. 29 **9**29
10. **9**07 **3**09
11. 58 6**1**3
12. **6**74 008

Write the number missing from each mobile.

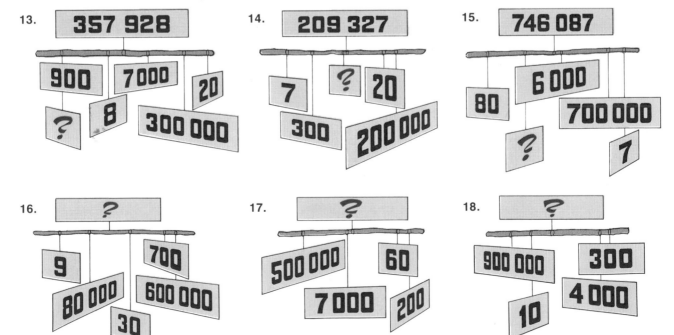

13. 357 928 — 900, 7000, 20, **?**, 8, 300 000

14. 209 327 — 7, **?**, 20, 300, 200 000

15. 746 087 — 80, 6 000, 700 000, **?**, 7

16. **?** — 9, 700, 80 000, 600 000, 30

17. **?** — 500 000, 60, 7 000, 200

18. **?** — 900 000, 300, 4 000, 10

8

Expanded Form

The record for the longest non-stop playing of an accordion is 84 h. If the accordion was squeezed once every second, that would amount to about 302 400 squeezes non-stop!

To write a number in **expanded form**, we add the values of all its digits.

Expanded form   300 000   +   2000   +   400

Another example: 738 459 = 700 000 + 30 000 + 8000 + 400 + 50 + 9

Write each number in expanded form.

1. 68 549
2. 436 985
3. 347 010
4. 119 096
5. 703 860
6. 200 818
7. 98 461
8. 355 008
9. 999 999
10. 16 500
11. 601 001
12. 510 022

Write the numbers that have these expanded forms.

13. 200 000 + 60 000 + 7000 + 80 + 9
14. 40 000 + 3000 + 80
15. 100 000 + 9000 + 500 + 4
16. 20 000 + 200 + 40 + 2
17. 800 000 + 50 000 + 6000 + 80 + 6
18. 500 000 + 40 000 + 4
19. 700 000 + 200 + 70 + 4
20. 100 000 + 90 + 7

Add mentally.

21.	22.	23.	24.
200 000	700 000	500 000	10 000
80 000	6 000	6 000	60
4 000	700	90 000	400
+ 70	+ 8	+ 200	+300 000

9

Comparing and Ordering Numbers to 999 999

Scientists have discovered these facts:

Blond people have up to 149 500 hairs on their heads. Brown-haired people have up to 105 300 hairs on their heads.

Who can have more hair: blonds or brunettes?

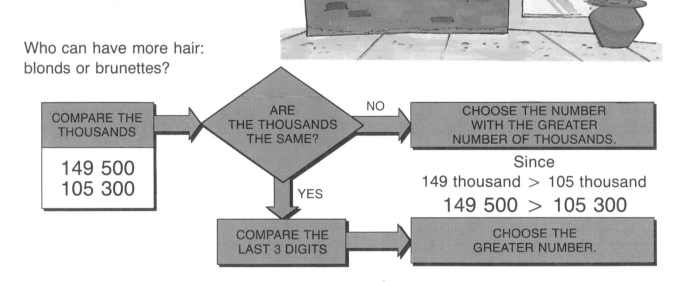

Blond people can have more hair on their heads.

Another example:

Which is greater, 148 927 or 148 932?

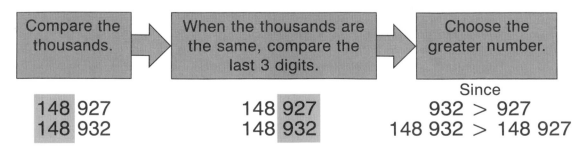

Write > or < for each ▒ .

1. 362 409 ▒ 326 409
2. 43 774 ▒ 43 747
3. 274 582 ▒ 284 582
4. 101 110 ▒ 110 101
5. 412 349 ▒ 412 530
6. 770 595 ▒ 707 959
7. 189 089 ▒ 891 089
8. 972 103 ▒ 927 103

Write the numbers in each set in order from least to greatest.

9. 811 577, 801 597, 810 957
10. 119 989, 191 898, 119 998
11. 346 231, 323 461, 364 231
12. 462 718, 426 719, 462 720
13. 690 050, 690 051, 609 052
14. 973 937, 937 973, 939 737

The **median** in a set of numbers is the middle number when the numbers are arranged in order.

Write the median in each of these sets.

15. 85 217, 58 217, 85 721
16. 201 639, 102 639, 201 963
17. 190 327, 190 237, 190 270
18. 769 008, 679 080, 679 800

19. Use the information on pages 6 and 7 to write the diameters of the planets in order from greatest to least. Is the diameter of Earth the median?

20. Which of these numbers is the best estimate of the number of hairs on this man's head?

190 000
205 000
150 000
730 000
300 000

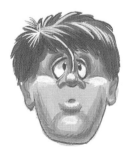

On average, we lose about 45 hairs per day. At this rate, about how many years would it take a blond person with 140 000 hairs to go completely bald?

I DON'T LOSE AS MUCH HAIR PER DAY AS I USED TO!

Does the scalp replace any of the hair it loses? Explain.

Reading and Writing Numbers to 999 999 999

The population of a city is the number of people who live in or around it.
The bar graph shows the 5 cities in the world with the greatest populations.
What city has the greatest population?

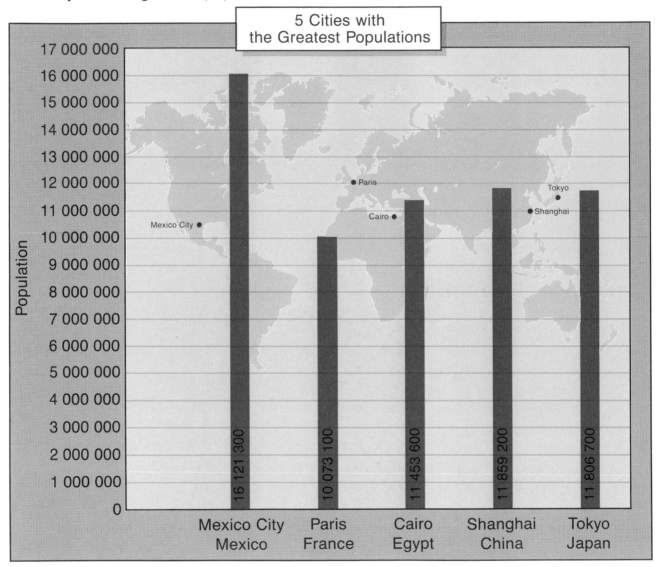

5 Cities with the Greatest Populations

Population values shown on bars:
- Mexico City, Mexico: 16 121 300
- Paris, France: 10 073 100
- Cairo, Egypt: 11 453 600
- Shanghai, China: 11 859 200
- Tokyo, Japan: 11 806 700

Mexico City has the greatest population. The population of Mexico City is 16 121 300.

We see: 16 121 300

We think: 16 million 121 thousand 300

We say: sixteen million one hundred twenty-one thousand three hundred

12

Use the graph to complete
questions 1 to 4.

Write the populations
of these cities in words.

1. Shanghai
2. Paris
3. Mexico City
4. Tokyo

Write in numerals.

5. eighteen million
6. two million forty-seven thousand
7. one hundred sixteen million
8. forty-eight million six thousand
9. two hundred seventy-one million
10. six million two hundred eight thousand
11. ten million nine thousand two hundred
12. seventy million five hundred thousand

13. Write the number that is:
   a) 1000 greater than 18 378 256
   b) 10 000 greater than 6 283 469
   c) 1000 less than 9 684 907
   d) 10 000 less than 15 712 546
   e) 100 000 greater than 6 847 816
   f) 100 000 less than 56 284 907
   g) 1000 greater than 5 929 280
   h) 1000 less than 3 090 421
   i) 100 000 greater than 21 621 011
   j) 1 000 000 greater than 52 713 112

QUESTIONS ABOUT OUR WORLD

Write numerals for the coloured numbers.

14. What language is spoken in the greatest number of countries?

   Answer: English. It is spoken by about **415 million** people spread over about 34 different countries.

15. What language is spoken by the greatest number of people?

   Answer: Mandarin Chinese. It is spoken by about **771 million** people.

16. What is the world's fastest growing city?

   Answer: Mexico City. Some scientists believe its population will reach **31 million 500 thousand** by the year 2000.

EXTENSIONS

The U.S.S.R. has one and one half million kilometres of roads. Canada has twice as many kilometres of roads as the U.S.S.R. How many kilometres of roads does Canada have?

Place Value to 999 999 999

This map shows the populations
of some countries of the world.

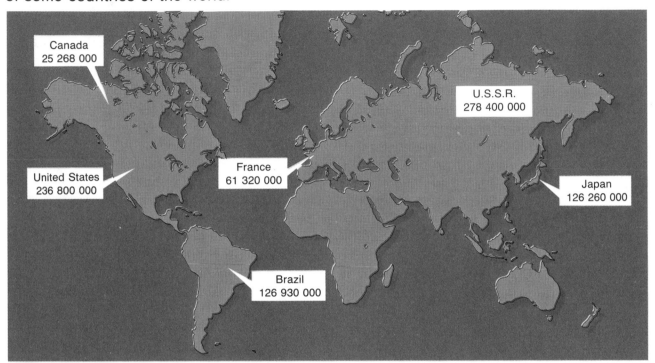

Canada
25 268 000

U.S.S.R.
278 400 000

United States
236 800 000

France
61 320 000

Japan
126 260 000

Brazil
126 930 000

The map shows that the population
of Canada is about 25 268 000.

A place value chart shows the value
of each digit in a numeral.

Millions			Thousands					
H	T	O	H	T	O	H	T	O
	2	5	2	6	8	0	0	0

Make a place value chart.
On it, write the populations of these countries.

1. France   2. United States   3. Japan   4. Brazil   5. U.S.S.R.

Write the value of each coloured digit.

6. 27 389 650   7. 547 938 006   8. 617 805 943
9. 817 364 972   10. 936 405 928   11. 824 667 359
12. 415 692 116   13. 573 899 204   14. 600 726 803
15. 746 993 027   16. 108 773 652   17. 9 335 671
18. 926 008 364   19. 46 589 000   20. 800 073 829

14

Write the number missing from each mobile.

1.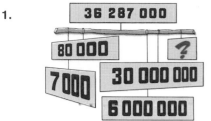

2.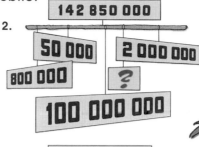

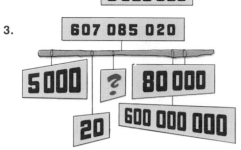

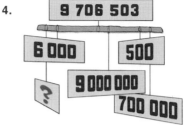

3. 607 085 020

5000   ?   80 000

20   600 000 000

4. 9 706 503

6 000   500

?   9 000 000

700 000

Write the numbers that have these expanded forms.

5. 20 000 000 + 7 000 000
6. 4 000 000 + 30 000 + 200
7. 300 000 000 + 8 000 000
8. 10 000 000 + 8000 + 60
9. 700 000 000 + 40 000 000 + 90 000 + 9
10. 500 000 000 + 2 000 000 + 600 000 + 40 + 7
11. 800 000 000 + 50 000 000 + 7000 + 300 + 9
12. 300 000 000 + 600 000 + 8000 + 10 + 8
13. 1 000 000 + 400 000 + 30 000 + 900 + 70
14. 80 000 000 + 2 000 000 + 500 000 + 90 000 + 4000 + 200 + 1

Write each number in expanded form.

15. 32 500 000
16. 467 300 000
17. 19 680 000
18. 4 827 000
19. 607 900 000
20. 179 306 000
21. 28 000 379
22. 500 154 000
23. 710 600 231

PROBLEM SOLVING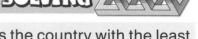

Vatican City is the country with the least population. What is its population?
The thousands digit is:

- an odd number.
- not 3.
- less than 5.

The remaining digits are less than the thousands digit.

15

Comparing and Ordering Numbers to 999 999 999

Country	Population
Brazil	126 930 000
Canada	25 268 000
France	61 320 000
Japan	126 260 000
U.S.S.R.	278 400 000
United States	236 800 000

The approximate populations of 6 countries are given in the table.

Which country has the greater population: the United States or the U.S.S.R.?

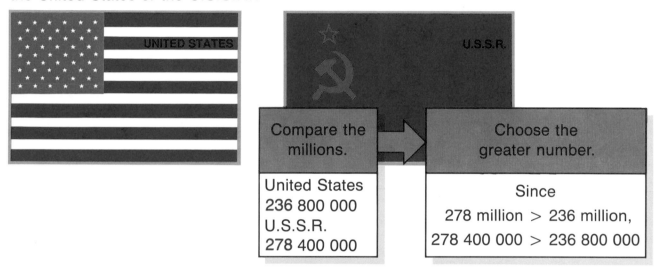

UNITED STATES **U.S.S.R.**

Compare the millions.

United States
236 800 000
U.S.S.R.
278 400 000

Choose the greater number.

Since

278 million > 236 million,

278 400 000 > 236 800 000

The U.S.S.R. has a greater population than the United States.

Another example: Which country has the greater population: Brazil or Japan?

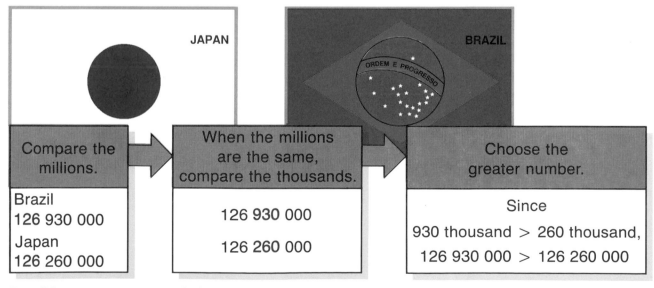

JAPAN **BRAZIL**

ORDEM E PROGRESSO

Compare the millions.

Brazil
126 930 000
Japan
126 260 000

When the millions are the same, compare the thousands.

126 **930** 000

126 **260** 000

Choose the greater number.

Since

930 thousand > 260 thousand,

126 930 000 > 126 260 000

Brazil has a greater population than Japan.

Write > or < for each ▦ .

1. 6 736 000 ▦ 5 800 000
2. 16 887 009 ▦ 51 808 000
3. 128 587 065 ▦ 281 000 000
4. 7 820 000 ▦ 7 503 687
5. 76 307 001 ▦ 158 938 776
6. 83 460 000 ▦ 9 587 693
7. 704 000 967 ▦ 76 847 359
8. 157 284 075 ▦ 157 268 586
9. 29 375 217 ▦ 29 380 000
10. 266 529 381 ▦ 266 529 407
11. 5 007 376 ▦ 15 000 000
12. 72 090 909 ▦ 72 909 090

Write the numbers in each set in order from least to greatest.

13. 27 568 293
    36 302 000
    29 586 200

14. 9 090 900
    9 909 090
    9 090 909

15. 52 784 236
    59 607 300
    52 748 200

16. 467 380 000
    471 270 000
    467 308 500

17. 76 081 887
    102 901 106
    97 000 000

18. 609 060 906
    690 006 609
    609 600 609

Write the median of each set of numbers.

The median in a set of numbers is the middle number when the numbers are arranged in order.

19. 3 107 704
    3 107 407
    3 701 407

20. 97 818 214
    9 781 921
    91 919 214

21. 110 001 010
    110 010 010
    101 010 100

22. List the 6 countries in the table on page 16 from greatest to least population.

23. Write the number that is:

    a) 1 million greater than 907 288.

    b) 1 million less than 414 000 000.

    c) 10 million less than 586 439 121.

    d) 10 million less than 32 609 000.

    e) 100 million less than 846 158 293.

    f) 100 million greater than 59 308 000.

    g) one half million.

PROBLEM SOLVING

The numbers from 1 to 9 are written on large cards. The cheerleaders make 9-digit numbers by displaying the cards.

Write the greatest and least numbers that the cheerleaders can display by changing positions.

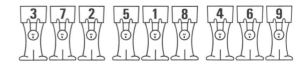

EXTENSIONS

Billions

China has the greatest population of any country in the world. In 1980, the population of China reached the 1000 million mark. To express the number 1000 million, we use the word **billion**.

We see: 1000 million

We say: one billion

We write: **1 000 000 000**

In 1980, the world population was estimated to be 4 415 000 000.

We can show this number on a place value chart.

Billions			Millions			Thousands					
H	T	O	H	T	O	H	T	O	H	T	O
			4	4	1	5	0	0	0	0	0	0

Make a place value chart.
On it, write each of these numbers.
Then read each number.

1. 6 300 000 000
2. 7 058 000 000
3. 8 270 900 000
4. 6 097 080 000
5. 63 525 067 000
6. 103 650 000 000

Choose the number you think best completes each sentence.

7. When you have lived for a billion seconds, you will be about ▒ years old.
   a) 5   b) 15   c) 30

8. In order to travel a billion kilometres, you would make ▒ trips around the earth.
   d) 121   e) 24 954   f) 102 658

9. If you collected $1000 a day, you would have a billion dollars at the end of ▒ years.
   g) 68   h) 432   i) 2740

Check your answers by finding the letters of the correct responses hidden in this picture.

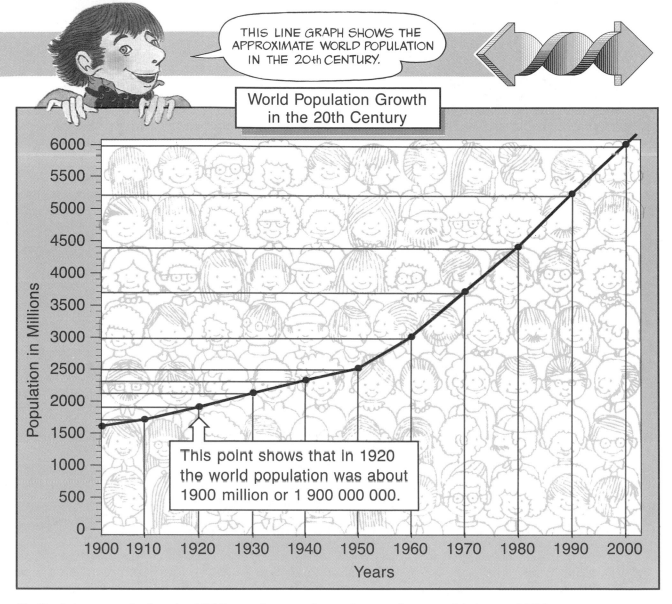

This line graph shows the approximate world population in the 20th century.

World Population Growth in the 20th Century

This point shows that in 1920 the world population was about 1900 million or 1 900 000 000.

To find the population in 1920, we locate the point on the graph above 1920.
Then we read the population of 1900 million from the vertical scale.

1. Write the world population to the nearest 100 million:
   a) in 1900.   b) in 1930.
   c) in 1950.   d) in 1960.
   e) in 1970.   f) in 1980.

2. Estimate the world population in the year:
   a) 1990.   b) 2000.

3. Estimate the year in which the world population reached:
   a) 2 billion.   b) 3 billion.
   c) 4 billion.   d) 5 billion.

4. About how many times as great will the world population be in the year 2000 as it was in 1900?

Inhabitants of the Earth Through the Ages

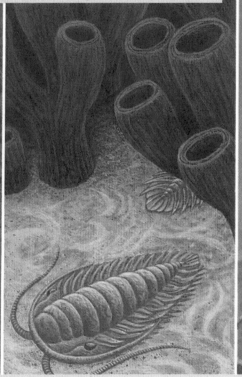

When animals die, their skeletons leave imprints in the sand or mud. These imprints gradually harden into stone. They are called **fossils**.

Using these fossils, scientists can tell approximately when various animals first appeared on the earth.

600 million years ago	500 million years ago	400 million years ago

The first animals appear in the sea

Trilobites first appear

Fish first appear

First animals crawl onto land

Use the time line to answer these questions. Write your answers as numerals.

1. About how many years ago did each of the following animals first appear?
   a) fish
   b) insects
   c) reptiles
   d) humans

2. For about how many years have animals been living on land?

3. Life first appeared on the earth about 3500 million years ago. About how many millions of years later did animals first appear?

20

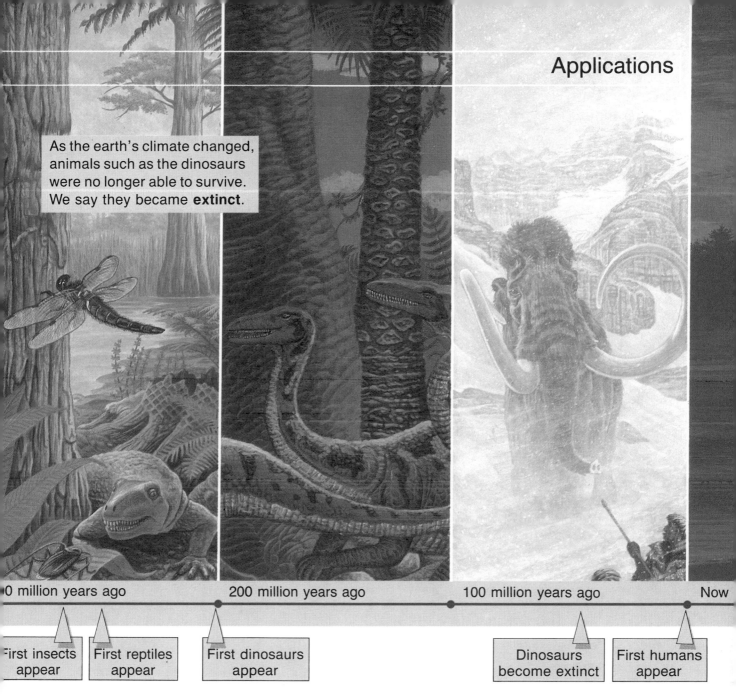

As the earth's climate changed, animals such as the dinosaurs were no longer able to survive. We say they became **extinct**.

0 million years ago   200 million years ago   100 million years ago   Now

First insects appear | First reptiles appear | First dinosaurs appear | Dinosaurs become extinct | First humans appear

4. About how many years ago did dinosaurs:
   a) first appear?   b) become extinct?

5. For about how many years were dinosaurs living on the earth?

6. About how many years after the first reptile appeared did the first dinosaur appear?

7. Did any human ever see a live dinosaur? Explain.

21

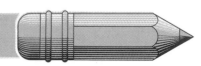

Write as a numeral.

1. seventeen thousand two hundred
2. four hundred seventy-five thousand
3. sixty-three thousand sixty-three
4. eight hundred thirty-four thousand

Write the number that is:

5. 1000 greater than 35 862
6. 10 000 less than 201 394
7. 10 000 greater than 97 235
8. 100 000 less than 372 481

Write the value of each coloured digit.

9. **7**86 202
10. 6**1**4 208
11. 41**9** 780
12. 832 **4**06

Write in expanded form.

13. 58 945
14. 608 681
15. 533 003

Write the number for each expanded form.

16. 300 000 + 70 000 + 8000 + 300 + 6
17. 70 000 + 5000 + 300 + 60 + 2
18. 100 000 + 9000 + 200 + 7

Write > or < for each ▒ .

19. 473 508 ▒ 437 508
20. 614 315 ▒ 614 351
21. 523 845 ▒ 523 485

Write in order from least to greatest.

22. 612 429, 621 249, 621 942
23. 387 542, 387 245, 387 425
24. 914 867, 914 768, 914 876

Write as a numeral.

25. two hundred eighty-three million
26. thirty-eight million six thousand
27. sixty million nine hundred thousand
28. nine hundred million thirty thousand

Write the value of each coloured digit.

29. 3**6** 481 560
30. **7**45 839 000
31. 514 29**6** 611
32. 428 8**5**0 349

Write > or < for each ▒ .

33. 7 842 000 ▒ 7 482 000
34. 18 391 485 ▒ 18 931 485
35. 243 600 000 ▒ 234 600 000
36. 94 576 821 ▒ 94 675 128

Write the number that is:

37. 1 million greater than 9 361 482
38. 100 million greater than 83 721 465
39. 10 million less than 643 572 186
40. 100 million less than 106 583 421

41. What is the smallest even number that can be made from these cards?

Dominoes

Dominoes is a game for 2 to 4 players. Skill and judgement must be used to decide the best piece to play. Dominoes is thought to have been invented in Italy in the 18th century. The name "domino" originally meant a black hood worn by some men of the Church, or a black cloak and mask worn as evening dress at Venetian balls.

Artist's impression of a dominoes game, 18th century Italy.

ESTIMATING

Rounded Numbers

TODO TIMES

Max Beck sets record with beard of 70 000 live buzzing bees!

Sometimes numbers which end in one or more zeros tell exactly how many. Sometimes they are estimates. Such estimates are called **rounded numbers**.

Explain why 70 000 in the headline above is probably a rounded number.

For each of the following headlines, state whether a rounded number is used. Explain your answers.

TODAY TIMES

World Population to reach 6 000 000 000 in year 2000

U.S.S.R. wins 10 000 m relay

TODAY TIMES

Dinosaurs found to be 140 000 000 years old

TODAY TIMES

9 000 000 Canadians watch Pope on television

TODAY TIMES

40 000 Argo Fans attend parade

Prize awarded to 2 000 000th person to attend world's fair

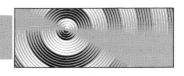

Rewrite each sentence using a suitable rounded number and the word *about*.

1. Jessica is 10 years, 11 months old.
2. Mr. Canton has 79¢ in his pocket.
3. The Johnsons arrived at 5:03.
4. The world's tallest tree is 110 m tall.
5. The Amazon River is 6437 km long.
6. The average honeybee colony has 59 650 members.
7. There are 45 120 thunderstorms in the world every day.
8. The circumference of the earth is 40 017 km.
9. A record crowd of 199 854 attended a soccer game.
10. In 1975, Hong Kong had 190 746 cars and only 1085 km of road.

Write a rounded number for each of these numbers.

11. 39	12. 397
13. 949	14. 4988
15. 9897	16. 14 007
17. 70 388	18. 44 961
19. 129 967	20. 401 387
21. 998 972	22. 1 003 794

A Famous Rounded Number.

In 1852, a team of surveyors measured the height of the highest mountain in the world, Mount Everest.

They measured its height to be exactly 29 000 feet. Fearing that people would think 29 000 was a rounded number and not exact, they recorded the height as 29 002 feet. A later measurement showed that Mount Everest is actually 29 028 feet or 8848 m high.

Use a rounded number to write the approximate height of Mount Everest in metres.

BITS AND BYTES

Calculate the number of hours in one year.

Use rounded numbers to answer these questions.

1. About how many hours are in a year?
2. About how many hours has a 10 year old lived?
3. About how many hours have you lived?

Multiples of 10, 100, 1000

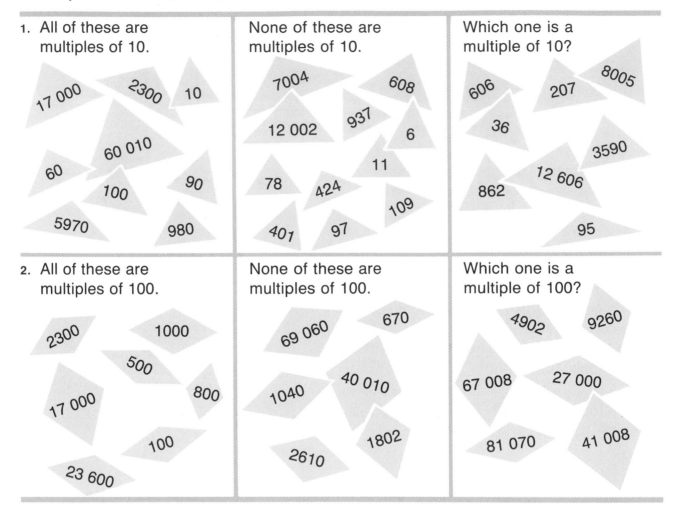

1. All of these are multiples of 10.

   17 000   2300   10   60 010   60   100   90   5970   980

   None of these are multiples of 10.

   7004   608   12 002   937   6   11   78   424   109   401   97

   Which one is a multiple of 10?

   606   207   8005   36   3590   12 606   862   95

2. All of these are multiples of 100.

   2300   1000   500   800   17 000   100   23 600

   None of these are multiples of 100.

   670   69 060   40 010   1040   1802   2610

   Which one is a multiple of 100?

   4902   9260   67 008   27 000   81 070   41 008

3. Write a sentence to explain how to recognize a multiple of:

   a) 10.

   b) 100.

4. Can you write a number which is a multiple of 100 but not a multiple of 10?

5. Use the pattern above to write a sentence explaining how to recognize a multiple of 1000.

6. Which of the following is a multiple of 1000?

   4700   125 000   6380   10 002   9000   28 060

7. Write a number which is a multiple of 10, 100, and 1000.

1. What multiple of 10 does each letter stand for?

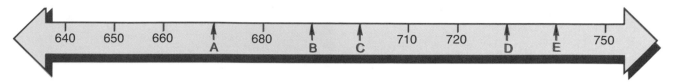

2. Between which 2 multiples of 10 is each letter located?

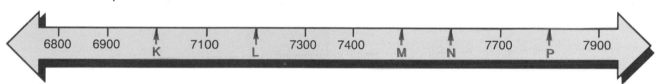

Between which 2 multiples of 10 is each number located?

3. 45   4. 57   5. 82   6. 91   7. 106
8. 327   9. 842   10. 936   11. 709   12. 527

13. What multiple of 100 does each letter stand for?

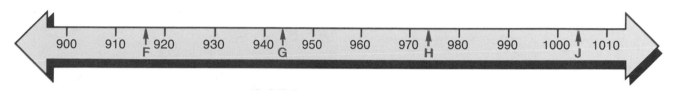

14. Between which 2 multiples of 100 is each letter located?

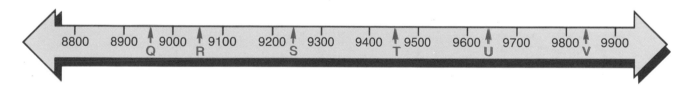

Between which 2 multiples of 100 is each number located?

15. 350   16. 479   17. 687   18. 921   19. 850
20. 1947   21. 2386   22. 4862   23. 14 827   24. 26 592

25. Draw a number line to show multiples
of 1000 from 6000 to 18 000.

Between which 2 multiples of 1000 is each number located?

26. 7386   27. 9927   28. 14 891   29. 11 709   30. 17 926
31. 43 480   32. 26 508   33. 93 500   34. 126 059   35. 387 606

27

Rounding to the Nearest 10, 100, or 1000

This picture shows part of a herd of 6874 caribou.

How many caribou are there to the nearest 10?

We think: On a number line marked in multiples of 10,…

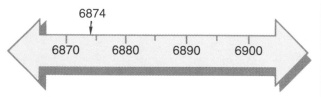

6874 is between 6870 and 6880 but **closer to** 6870.

We write: 6874 rounded to the nearest 10 is 6870.

Round 6874 to the nearest 100.

We think: On a number line marked in multiples of 100,…

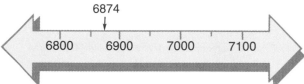

6874 is between 6800 and 6900 but **closer to** 6900.

We write: 6874 rounded to the nearest 100 is 6900.

Round 6874 to the nearest 1000.

We think: On a number line marked in multiples of 1000,…

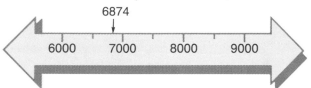

6874 is between 6000 and 7000 but **closer to** 7000.

We write: 6874 rounded to the nearest 1000 is 7000.

Whenever a number is halfway between 2 multiples, **round up**.

For example:

385 rounded to the nearest 10 is 390.
4750 rounded to the nearest 100 is 4800.
9500 rounded to the nearest 1000 is 10 000.

Round to the nearest 10.

1. 57	2. 63	3. 81
4. 142	5. 350	6. 560
7. 825	8. 7994	9. 9296
10. 18 255	11. 72 683	12. 327 485

Round to the nearest 100.

13. 497	14. 648	15. 750
16. 2863	17. 9177	18. 8952
19. 6750	20. 18 792	21. 92 850
22. 416 565	23. 302 816	24. 209 550

Round to the nearest 1000.

25. 6521	26. 8642	27. 6293
28. 38 403	29. 57 409	30. 69 703
31. 52 613	32. 85 500	33. 97 861
34. 611 213	35. 555 000	36. 765 499

37. Copy and complete this table.

	Rounded to the nearest...		
Number	10	100	1000
6 874	6 870	6 900	7 000
8 392			
4 775			
68 528			
72 416			
95 500			
55 550			
287 395			

38. a) Round 3498 to the nearest 100.
   b) Round your answer to the nearest 1000.
   c) Is your new answer the same as 3498 rounded to the nearest 1000? Explain.

PROBLEM SOLVING

A scientist recorded the actual number of caribou in a herd. Rounded to the nearest 1000, there were 8000. Rounded to the nearest 100, there were 8500.

The number of caribou was not a multiple of 100 but was halfway between 2 multiples of 100.

How many caribou were in the herd?

29

A Simple Rule for Rounding

The flow charts show how to round a number without using a number line.

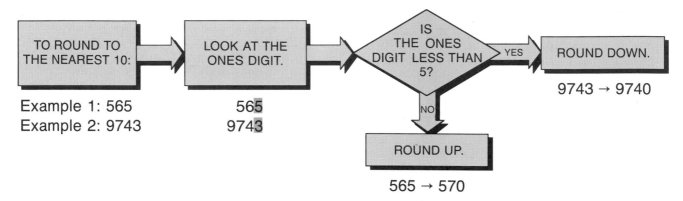

| TO ROUND TO THE NEAREST 10: | → | LOOK AT THE ONES DIGIT. | → | IS THE ONES DIGIT LESS THAN 5? | YES → | ROUND DOWN. |

Example 1: 565
Example 2: 9743

565
9743

9743 → 9740

NO ↓

ROUND UP.

565 → 570

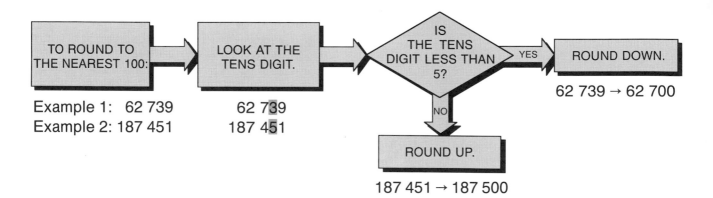

| TO ROUND TO THE NEAREST 100: | → | LOOK AT THE TENS DIGIT. | → | IS THE TENS DIGIT LESS THAN 5? | YES → | ROUND DOWN. |

Example 1: 62 739
Example 2: 187 451

62 739
187 451

62 739 → 62 700

NO ↓

ROUND UP.

187 451 → 187 500

1. Compare the flow charts above. Write a sentence to explain how the 2 flow charts are different.

2. Make a flow chart which shows how to round a number to the nearest 1000.

3. Copy this table. Use the appropriate flow chart to round each number to the nearest 10, 100, or 1000.

Number	Rounded to the nearest...		
	10	100	1000
6 528			
9 455			
13 647			
56 495			
88 009			
368 555			

Rounding to the Nearest 10 000, 100 000, or 1 000 000

This flow chart shows how to round a number to the nearest 10 000.

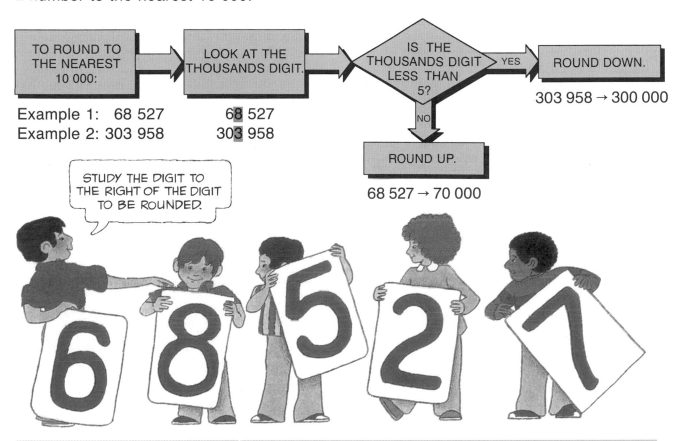

| TO ROUND TO THE NEAREST 10 000: | → | LOOK AT THE THOUSANDS DIGIT. | → | IS THE THOUSANDS DIGIT LESS THAN 5? | YES → | ROUND DOWN. |

303 958 → 300 000

NO ↓

ROUND UP.

68 527 → 70 000

Example 1:   68 527   68 527
Example 2: 303 958   303 958

STUDY THE DIGIT TO THE RIGHT OF THE DIGIT TO BE ROUNDED.

1. Make a flow chart which shows how to round a number to the nearest:

   a) 100 000   b) 1 000 000

2. Copy this table. Use the appropriate flow charts to complete the table.

| | Rounded to the nearest... | | |
Number	10 000	100 000	1 000 000
2 652 000	2 650 000	2 700 000	3 000 000
3 486 000			
13 500 000			
9 326 000			
6 755 000			
8 493 000			
972 000			

31

Adding and Subtracting Rounded Numbers

Canada is the second largest country in the world. It stretches a distance of 5187 km from east to west. We say that 5200 km is the **approximate** distance from east to west.

Canada stretches **approximately** 4600 km from north to south.

About how much further does Canada stretch from east to west than from north to south?

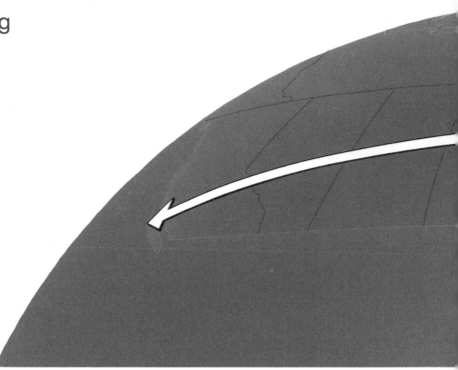

To subtract 4600 from 5200:

Subtract the ones.	Subtract the tens.	Trade a thousand for 10 hundreds.	Subtract the hundreds.
5 20**0** − 4 60**0** **0**	5 2**0**0 − 4 6**0**0 **0**0	⁴ ¹² 5̸ 200 − 4 600 00	⁴ ¹² 5̸ 2̲00 − 4 600 **6**00

Canada stretches about 600 km further in the east to west direction.

Another example:
To add 3500 and 600:

Add the ones.	Add the tens.	Add the hundreds. Trade.	Add the thousands.
3 50**0** + 60**0** **0**	3 5**0**0 + 6**0**0 **0**0	¹ 3 5**0**0 + 6**0**0 **1**00	¹ 3 500 + 600 **4** 100

32

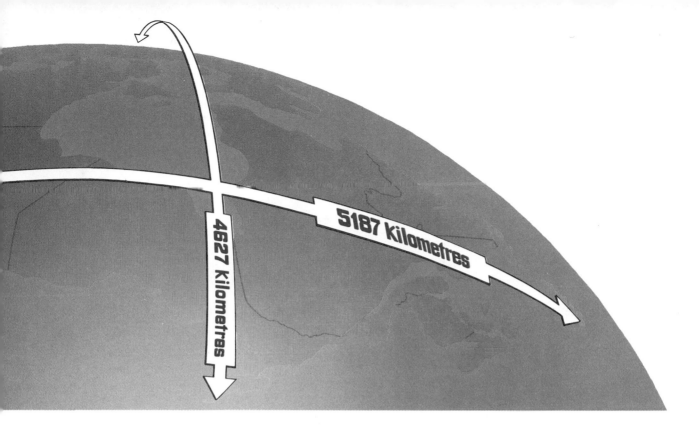

4627 Kilometres

5187 Kilometres

Add or subtract. Watch the signs!

1. 60
  +30

2. 90
  +70

3. 100
  − 60

4. 800
  +900

5. 900
  −400

6. 4 000
  +5 000

7. 12 000
  − 7 000

8. 42 000
  −19 000

9. 70 000
  −56 000

10. 69 000
  +87 000

11. 75 000
  +93 000

12. 40 000
  −27 000

13. 81 000
  −45 000

14. 146 000
  +204 000

15. 100 000
  − 67 000

16. 6 000 + 19 000

17. 7 800 − 900

18. 8 100 − 7 700

19. 62 000 + 15 000

20. 80 000 − 13 000

21. 97 000 − 16 000

22. 72 000 − 69 000

23. 87 000 + 96 000

24. 100 000 − 53 000

25. Write a sentence to explain why approximate numbers are sometimes used when we add or subtract.

26. The Trans-Canada Highway is the longest paved road in the world. When opened in 1962, it was about 7700 km long. Canada's longest river, the Mackenzie River, is about 4200 km long. About how much longer is the Trans-Canada Highway?

ESTIMATING

Estimating Sums by Rounding

Many Canadian birds fly south for the winter.
We say that they **migrate** to warmer climates.

The Arctic tern has the longest migration
route of all birds. One tern was tagged
near the North Pole in July, 1965. It was
discovered in May, 1966 in Australia after
flying about 19 000 km!

An Arctic tern flew from the Arctic to Antarctica
on a route 17 674 km long. It returned to the
Arctic on a route 18 318 km long. Estimate
the length of the entire trip.

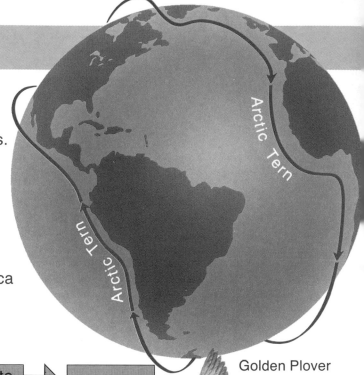

Golden Plover

| To estimate: | ⟹ | Round the addends to the nearest 1000. | ⟹ | Add. |

$$\begin{array}{r} 18\ 318 \\ +17\ 674 \end{array} \qquad \begin{array}{l} 18\ 318 \rightarrow 18\ 000 \\ 17\ 674 \rightarrow 18\ 000 \end{array} \qquad \begin{array}{r} 18\ 000 \\ +18\ 000 \\ \hline 36\ 000 \end{array}$$

The entire trip was about 36 000 km.

Estimate by rounding addends to the nearest 100.

1. $\begin{array}{r} 576 \\ +321 \end{array}$
2. $\begin{array}{r} 632 \\ +489 \end{array}$
3. $\begin{array}{r} 784 \\ +979 \end{array}$
4. $\begin{array}{r} 6\ 382 \\ +5\ 729 \end{array}$
5. $\begin{array}{r} 5\ 341 \\ +2\ 850 \end{array}$

Estimate by rounding addends to the nearest 1000.

6. $\begin{array}{r} 8\ 569 \\ +6\ 397 \end{array}$
7. $\begin{array}{r} 9\ 382 \\ +4\ 699 \end{array}$
8. $\begin{array}{r} 2\ 897 \\ +4\ 281 \end{array}$
9. $\begin{array}{r} 31\ 215 \\ +19\ 686 \end{array}$
10. $\begin{array}{r} 69\ 574 \\ +79\ 808 \end{array}$

Estimate. Decide how to round.

11. $\begin{array}{r} 397 \\ +818 \end{array}$
12. $\begin{array}{r} 886 \\ +175 \end{array}$
13. $\begin{array}{r} 9\ 077 \\ +8\ 862 \end{array}$
14. $\begin{array}{r} 6\ 389 \\ +8\ 450 \end{array}$
15. $\begin{array}{r} 19\ 787 \\ +36\ 266 \end{array}$

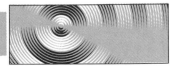

Estimating Sums of Several Addends

A migration route for the Golden Plover has these segments.

Arctic Terns

Spring Migration:		Fall Migration:	
Argentina to United States	7147 km	Labrador to Venezuela	5472 km
United States to Labrador	3203 km	Venezuela to Argentina	4784 km

Estimate the total length of the migration route.

To estimate:	Round the addends to the nearest 1000.	Add.
5 472	5 472 → 5 000	5 000
4 784	4 784 → 5 000	5 000
7 147	7 147 → 7 000	7 000
+3 203	3 203 → 3 000	+3 000
		20 000

The total length of the migration route is about 20 000 km.

Estimate by rounding to the nearest 100.

1.	2.	3.	4.	5.
287	1 428	5 962	683	7 097
596	836	4 387	719	824
+348	+2 850	+2 119	667	4 650
			+409	+5 685

Estimate by rounding to the nearest 1000.

6.	7.	8.	9.	10.
3 785	6 481	12 650	6 684	32 115
7 284	9 686	38 421	9 240	9 732
+2 500	+1 907	+59 716	8 500	27 500
			+4 978	+84 267

Estimate. Decide how to round.

11. 706 + 309 + 555

12. 7 006 + 3 790 + 7 583

13. 28 519 + 9 651 + 22 387

14. 951 + 463 + 1 500

35

Adding Large Numbers

There are several different kinds of Canada geese. One of the most common is the Cackling Canada goose.

Every spring, the Cackling Canada geese migrate north to Canada from the United States. One year, scientists determined that 125 700 Cackling Canada geese had been killed or lost during migration. A total of 178 600 survived the migration and reached the breeding grounds.

How many Cackling Canada geese began the migration that year?

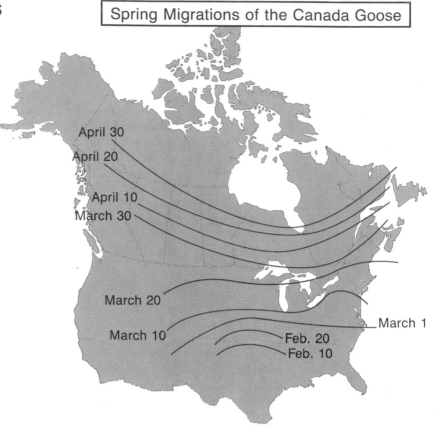

Spring Migrations of the Canada Goose

April 30
April 20
April 10
March 30
March 20
March 10
Feb. 20
Feb. 10
March 1

We think:

Number of surviving geese ⟶	178 600
Number of geese which did not survive ⟶	+ 125 700
Total number of migrating geese ⟶	304 300

We write:

About 304 300 Cackling Canada geese began the migration.

Add.

1. 9 727
+5 216

9 727
+5 216
14 943

2. 2 788
+9 891

3. 8 795
+7 655

4. 8 019
+4 738

5. 16 876
+49 307

6. 81 969
+27 527

7. 74 008
+ 9 993

8. 97 683
+ 8 756

9. 21 514
+ 6 892

10. 49 238
+ 5 692

11. 83 416
+90 875

12. 26 509
+80 950

13. 68 146
+97 352

14. 32 685
+56 172

15. 85 124 + 9 275

16. 3 689 + 21 297

17. 67 007 + 16 238

18. 93 557 + 90 003

Do only those questions
with sums less than 10 000.

1.	6 281 +3 419	2.	5 687 +4 972
3.	8 149 +1 756	4.	2 009 +7 866
5.	3 556 +6 489	6.	5 826 +3 987
7.	367 +8 937	8.	9 738 +1 007
9.	6 500 +3 416	10.	5 735 +4 216
11.	7 913 +2 078	12.	4 967 +5 042

Do only those questions with sums less than 100 000.

13. 21 608 +58 092	14. 75 096 +19 735	15. 36 851 +67 533	16. 93 558 + 8 766	17. 45 661 + 9 383
18. 54 667 +46 551	19. 79 036 +19 868	20. 18 551 +81 420	21. 30 069 +69 338	22. 52 320 +16 943
23. 97 336 + 5 860	24. 26 808 +73 119	25. 47 340 +51 570	26. 62 118 +39 581	27. 10 193 +40 936

28. One year scientists determined that
68 400 Western Canada geese
survived a migration south. They
found that about 16 700 of the geese
had died or been killed during the
migration. About how many Western
Canada geese began the migration?

ESTIMATING

The bar graph on the next page shows
the approximate populations of the
different kinds of Canada geese.
What 2 kinds of Canada geese
have a combined population
of about one million?

37

Sums of Several Addends

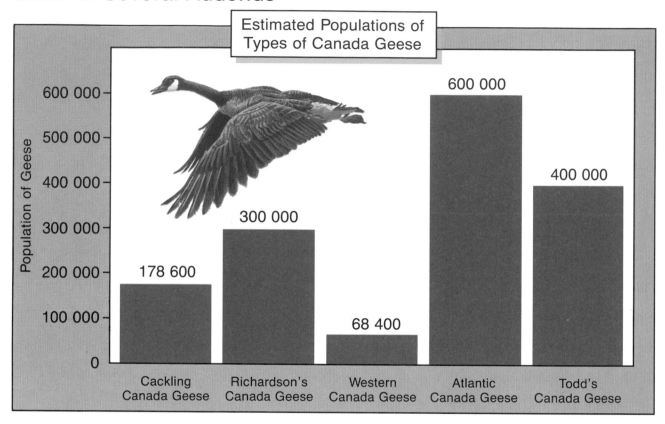

Estimated Populations of Types of Canada Geese

Population of Geese

Cackling Canada Geese	178 600
Richardson's Canada Geese	300 000
Western Canada Geese	68 400
Atlantic Canada Geese	600 000
Todd's Canada Geese	400 000

This bar graph shows estimates of the populations of the major types of Canada geese.

Find the estimated total population of Canada geese.

In all, there are about 1 547 000 Canada geese.

We write:

```
   178 600
   300 000
    68 400
   600 000
 + 400 000
 1 547 000
```

Add.

1.
```
   3 866
   5 027
 +   968
```

2.
```
   6 899
   4 738
 + 9 387
```

3.
```
    4 792
   16 386
 + 45 668
```

4.
```
   76 355
   57 908
    9 076
 + 78 367
```

5.
```
   16 580
    9 730
   68 640
 + 72 860
```

---

6. Find the estimated total population of the 3 most common types of Canada geese.

7. Find the estimated total population of the 4 most common types of Canada geese.

Making Closer Estimates by Compensating

About how many Canada geese were tagged for scientific study reported in the table below?

Types	Number Tagged	Estimates
Cackling	3 625	4 000
Richardson's	5 739	6 000
Western	868	1 000
Atlantic	5 829	6 000
Todd's	1 651	1 000
		18 000

Discuss how the sum was estimated in each example.

A.		B.	
19	20	321	300
28	30	739	700
47	50	648	600
+55	+50	+127	+200
	150		1800

YOU ESTIMATED A TOTAL OF 18 000 CANADA GEESE! HOW DID YOU OBTAIN SUCH A CLOSE ESTIMATE?

THE TOP 4 ADDENDS I ROUNDED UP TO THE NEAREST THOUSAND. I ROUNDED DOWN THE LAST ADDEND TO COMPENSATE.

Estimate by rounding.
Compensate to make closer estimates.

	1.	2.	3.	4.	5.
	453	735	760	713	182
	571	531	559	639	871
	882	529	867	122	450
	+476	+645	+671	+541	+350

Estimate. Compensate when appropriate.

	6.	7.	8.	9.	10.
	56	231	1 583	48	8 310
	29	842	2 963	39	9 415
	49	843	4 736	27	2 326
	+55	+125	+4 512	+15	+9 231

Estimating Differences by Rounding

Canada is bounded by the Atlantic, Pacific, and Arctic Oceans. It also shares, with the United States, the longest undefended border in the world. The total perimeter of mainland Canada including its coastline and the border it shares with the United States is 37 628 km. Canada's coastline is 28 737 km. About how long is the border between Canada and the United States?

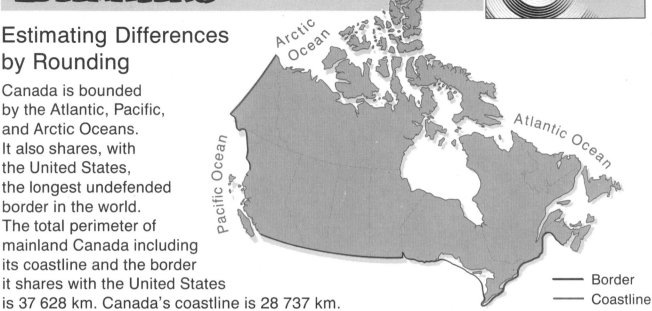

— Border
— Coastline

To estimate:	Round both numbers to the nearest 1000.	Subtract.
37 628 − 28 737	37 628 → 38 000 28 737 → 29 000	38 000 − 29 000 9 000

The Canada-U.S.A. border is about 9000 km long.

Estimate by rounding to the nearest 100.

1. 877
   − 319

2. 1 218
   − 769

3. 2 958
   − 2 692

4. 3 897
   − 1 785

5. 8 042
   − 3 915

Estimate by rounding to the nearest 1000.

6. 7 496
   − 5 208

7. 6 597
   − 3 219

8. 7 396
   − 5 251

9. 12 689
   − 9 102

10. 16 147
   − 12 380

Estimate. Decide how to round.

11. 8 372
   − 5 208

12. 3 520
   − 2 796

13. 4 500
   − 1 168

14. 19 997
   − 9 835

15. 27 996
   − 18 723

BITS AND BYTES

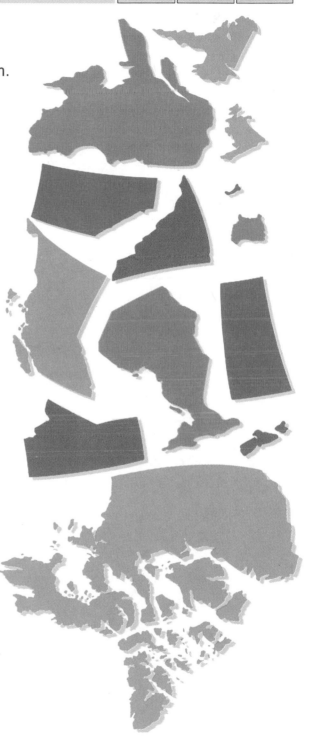

The table below shows the perimeters of the provinces and territories in Canada.

1. Round each perimeter to the nearest 1000 km. Record your answers in a table.

Province or Territory	Perimeter
British Columbia	30 801
Alberta	3 926
Saskatchewan	3 571
Manitoba	4 063
Ontario	6 263
Québec	20 683
New Brunswick	3 078
Prince Edward Island	1 260
Nova Scotia	7 613
Newfoundland and Labrador	33 479
Yukon	4 409
Northwest Territories	165 389

Do these questions in your head.

2. Estimate the difference in the perimeters of:
   a) Manitoba and New Brunswick.
   b) British Columbia and Québec.
   c) Nova Scotia and the Yukon.
   d) Québec and Prince Edward Island.

Do these questions on your calculator.

3. Estimate the difference in the perimeters of:
   a) Ontario and Saskatchewan.
   b) Northwest Territories and Alberta.
   c) Prince Edward Island and British Columbia.
   d) Alberta and Prince Edward Island.

Can you do these faster in your head or on your calculator?

41

Subtracting Large Numbers

The world's largest freshwater lake is Lake Superior. The border between the United States and Canada runs across the length of Lake Superior so that part of the lake lies within Canada and part within the United States.

The total area of Lake Superior is 82 103 km². The part of Lake Superior inside Canada has an area of 28 749 km².

What is the area of Lake Superior that lies inside the United States border?

We think:	We write:
Total area of Lake Superior ⟶	82 103
Area contained in Canada ⟶	− 28 749
Area contained in the United States ⟶	53 354

The area of Lake Superior contained inside the United States is 53 354 km².

Subtract.

1. $\quad$ 4 723 $\quad$ − 3 520	2. $\quad$ 8 685 $\quad$ − 4 369	3. $\quad$ 9 468 $\quad$ − 5 639	4. $\quad$ 8 609 $\quad$ − 7 992	5. $\quad$ 1 015 $\quad$ − 239
6. $\quad$ 27 386 $\quad$ − 9 274	7. $\quad$ 56 738 $\quad$ − 54 829	8. $\quad$ 24 618 $\quad$ − 21 935	9. $\quad$ 57 387 $\quad$ − 56 493	10. $\quad$ 28 170 $\quad$ − 15 688
11. $\quad$ 61 557 $\quad$ − 43 289	12. $\quad$ 50 286 $\quad$ − 9 853	13. $\quad$ 93 081 $\quad$ − 9 893	14. $\quad$ 87 003 $\quad$ − 59 787	15. $\quad$ 63 616 $\quad$ − 13 409

16. 8 258 − 3 139

17. 13 585 − 9 392

18. 24 186 − 19 053

19. 74 932 − 26 876

20. 68 926 − 47 858

21. 93 900 − 87 935

Do only those questions with differences less than 100.

1. 8 246
    − 7 482

2. 9 037
    − 8 975

3. 6 687
    − 6 592

4. 8 179
    − 7 965

5. 9 089
    − 8 990

6. 5 987
    − 5 906

7. 7 368
    − 5 368

8. 8 836
    − 8 778

9. 6 000
    − 5 904

10. 10 000
     − 9 917

Do only those questions with differences less than 1000.

11. 7 658
     − 6 856

12. 8 735
     − 5 826

13. 4 073
     − 3 057

14. 6 907
     − 5 921

15. 9 091
     − 8 102

16. 12 742
     − 11 586

17. 23 526
     − 22 872

18. 59 284
     − 58 520

19. 70 000
     − 69 017

20. 83 526
     − 81 896

Do only those questions with differences less than 10 000.

21. 17 360
     − 9 840

22. 96 326
     − 87 105

23. 92 811
     − 46 722

24. 70 000
     − 65 820

25. 25 000
     − 17 837

26. The largest lakes contained entirely within Canada are Great Bear Lake and Great Slave Lake. The area of Great Bear Lake is 31 339 km². The area of Great Slave Lake is 28 568 km². How much larger is Great Bear Lake?

27. Which of the Canadian lakes named on the list at the right has an area 181 km² less than the Canadian part of Lake Superior?

28. Which of the lakes has an area 22 533 km² less than Lake Superior?

29. Which of the lakes has an area 4170 km² greater than the smallest lake on the list?

30. Is the total area of the 3 smallest lakes greater or less than the area of the largest lake?

ESTIMATING

Which 2 lakes in this list differ in area by less than 1500 km²?

Largest Canadian Lakes	
Lake	Area in square kilometres
Erie	25 693
Great Bear	31 339
Great Slave	28 568
Huron	59 570
Michigan	58 016
Superior	82 103
Winnipeg	24 398

This table lists the world's 6 largest countries in order.

Copy the table.

To complete the table, you must first find the missing numbers in the magic square below.

THE LARGEST COUNTRY IN THE WORLD IS THE U.S.S.R. IT HAS MORE THAN TWICE THE AREA OF CANADA!

	Country	Approximate Area in Square Kilometres
1.	U.S.S.R.	22 500 000
2.	Canada	
3.	China	
4.	United States	
5.	Brazil	8 500 000
6.	Australia	

Use these facts to complete the magic square.
- The sum of the numbers in each **row** is
- The sum of the numbers in each **column** is
- The sum of the numbers along each **diagonal** is

22 500 000

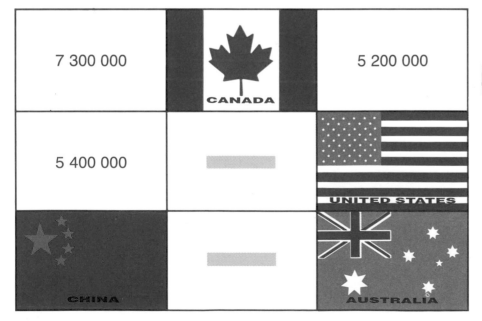

EACH FLAG IS HIDING THE AREA OF ITS COUNTRY IN SQUARE KILOMETRES!

44

WHAT IS THE AREA OF THE NORTH POLE? TRACE THE PUZZLE. WRITE THE DIFFERENCE BETWEEN ANY 2 NUMBERS IN THE CIRCLE BETWEEN THEM. THE ANSWER TO THE RIDDLE WILL APPEAR IN THE CENTRE CIRCLE.

The numbers inside some special circles give the approximate areas of provinces in square kilometres.

Use your completed puzzle to answer these questions. What is the approximate area of
a) Newfoundland and Labrador?   b) New Brunswick?

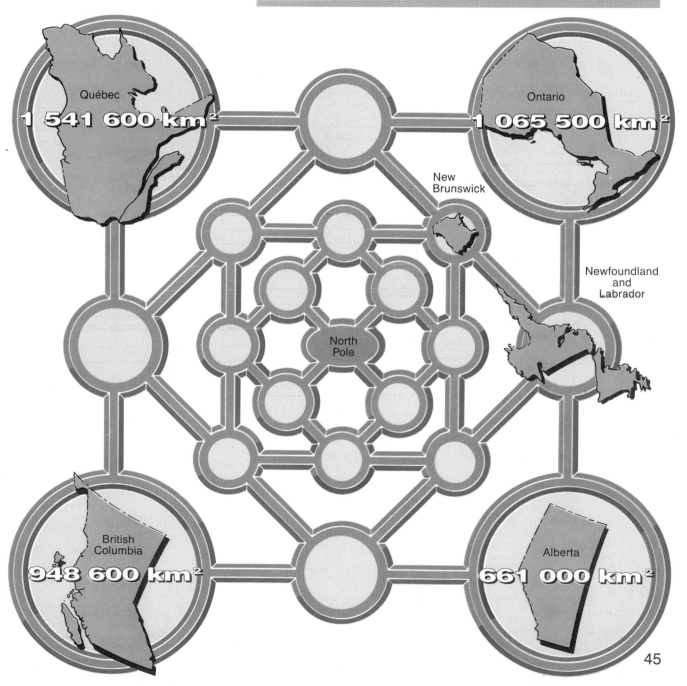

Québec
1 541 600 km²

Ontario
1 065 500 km²

New Brunswick

Newfoundland and Labrador

North Pole

British Columbia
948 600 km²

Alberta
661 000 km²

45

The Changing Caribou Populations

Large herds of migrating caribou are a beautiful scene in northern Canada. For centuries, these rugged travellers have followed special routes through Alaska, Yukon, and the Northwest Territories. However, scientists warn that predators like wolves and human hunters may make the caribou extinct.

The **line graph** shows the number of caribou in the Western Herd between 1965 and 1985.

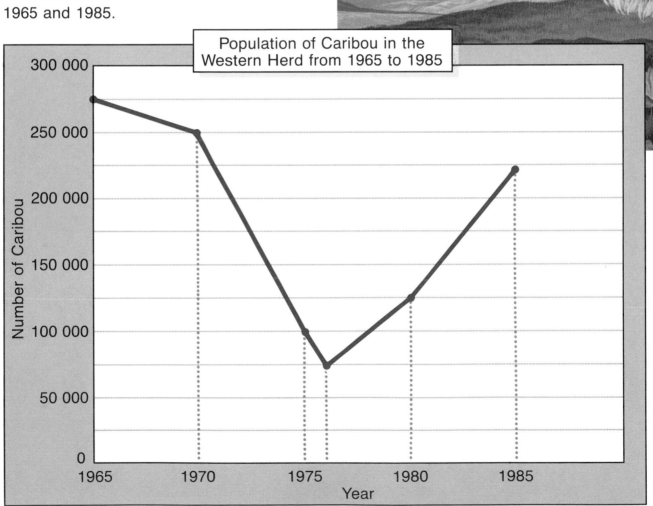

Population of Caribou in the Western Herd from 1965 to 1985

Use the line graph to answer these questions.

1. What was the population of the Western Herd in:

   a) 1965?   b) 1970?   c) 1980?   d) 1985?

2. Estimate the population of the Western Herd in 1976.

3. In what year was the population the greatest?

4. In what year was the population the least?

5. Estimate the present population of the Western Herd.

6. In the early 1970s, hunters began to use snowmobiles instead of dog teams to hunt caribou. How did this affect the caribou population?

The table shows the approximate population of the Nelchina Herd between 1955 and 1985.

Year	1955	1965	1975	1985
Population	40 000	70 000	10 000	30 000

7. Use the information in the table to make a graph. First, label a piece of squared paper like this.

   On your graph, draw 4 points to show the caribou populations in 1955, 1965, 1975, and 1985.

8. Did the use of the snowmobile affect the Nelchina Herd population? Explain.

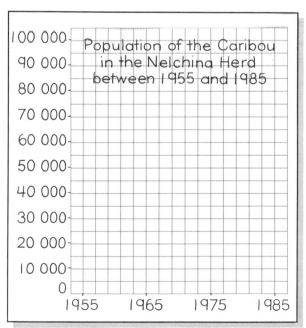

Population of the Caribou in the Nelchina Herd between 1955 and 1985

PROBLEM SOLVING

Looking for a Pattern

TO DISCOVER MATHEMATICAL RELATIONSHIPS, WE OFTEN LOOK FOR PATTERNS.

We ask:

What are the next 3 numbers which continue each pattern?

We think:

A. 3, 5, 7, 9, ■, ■, ■.
   +2 +2 +2

The numbers increase by 2 each time.
The next 3 numbers are 11, 13, and 15.

B. 1, 2, 4, 7, ■, ■, ■.
   +1 +2 +3

The numbers increase by 1 more each time.
The next 3 numbers are 11, 16, and 22.

C. 2, 4, 8, 16, ■, ■, ■.
   ×2 ×2 ×2

Each number is double the previous one.
The next 3 numbers are 32, 64, and 128.

D. 1, 4, 9, 16, ■, ■, ■.

The numbers are 1×1, 2×2, 3×3, 4×4.
The next 3 numbers are 25, 36, and 49.

PROBLEM: FIND THE SUM OF THE ODD NUMBERS FROM 1 TO 25.

$1+3+5+7...$

To solve this problem, . . .

A. First make sure you understand the problem.

Discuss:

- *What are you asked to find?*
- *How many numbers are you finding the sum of?*
- *What are the first 3 odd numbers?*
- *What is the sum of:*
  - *the first 3 odd numbers?*
  - *the first 4 odd numbers?*
  - *the first 5 odd numbers?*

B. Then, think of strategies.

Try making a table and looking for a pattern.

Number of odd numbers	Sum
1	1
2	4
3	9
4	16
⋮	⋮

C. Solve the problem and answer the question.

- *Look at the sequence of numbers you have written.*
- *What is the relationship between 2 and 4? 3 and 9? 4 and 16?*
- *How can you find the sum of the 13 odd numbers from 1 to 25?*

D. Discuss your solution.

- *If this pattern were continued, what would be the sum of the first 25 odd numbers? Of the first 100?*
- *Describe pattern D on page 48 in a different way.*
- *What special kind of numbers do you find by adding consecutive odd numbers?*
- *Look for a pattern in the sum of the even numbers.*

Solve these problems.

1. Write the next 3 numbers to continue each pattern.

   a) 2, 4, 6, 8, ▧ , ▧ , ▧

   b) 3, 5, 9, 17, ▧ , ▧ , ▧

   c) 3, 6, 10, 15, ▧ , ▧ , ▧

   d) 2, 5, 9, 14, ▧ , ▧ , ▧

2. Two cuts through the centre of a pizza divide it into 4 pieces. How many cuts through the centre of a pizza divide it into 32 pieces?

3. In a gathering of 4 people, 6 handshakes are possible if each person shakes hands with each of the others. How many handshakes are possible in a gathering of 9 people?

49

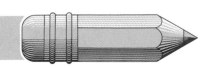

Between which 2 multiples
of 100 is each number located?

1. 460
2. 785
3. 1061
4. 2958

Between which 2 multiples
of 1000 is each number located?

5. 6274
6. 9917
7. 13 653
8. 92 580

Round to the nearest 10.

9. 67
10. 725
11. 8994
12. 17 355

Round to the nearest 100.

13. 650
14. 3873
15. 19 882
16. 309 650

Round to the nearest 1000.

17. 5293
18. 83 304
19. 79 802
20. 765 501

Estimate by rounding.

21. 483
   +511

22. 762
   +895

23. 1 986
   +2 643

24. 4 831
   +2 752

25. 7 632
   8 213
   +5 100

26. 863
   480
   +240

Add.

27. 8 636
   +4 215

28. 3 689
   +9 719

29. 17 686
   +39 408

30. 71 858
   +36 257

31. 94 386
   7 856
   4 612
   +5 342

32. 27 609
   81 490
   48 215
   +34 333

Estimate by rounding.

33. 482
   −375

34. 666
   −491

35. 5 126
   −1 953

36. 19 453
   − 8 377

Subtract.

37. 4 613
   −3 412

38. 7 574
   −3 258

39. 26 275
   − 8 163

40. 25 729
   −21 826

41. 56 276
   −55 382

42. 93 004
   −89 337

43. Lake Superior has an area of
82 103 km². Lake Michigan has an
area of 56 016 km².
   a) What is the total area of the 2 lakes?
   b) How much larger is Lake Superior?

Write the next 3 numbers in each pattern.

44. 3, 7, 11, 15, ▦ , ▦ , ▦

45. 1, 3, 7, 13, ▦ , ▦ , ▦

SENET

Senet is an ancient game of logic involving counting. The 2 players develop strategies, but there is also an element of chance.
Senet was played in Egypt at least 4 500 years ago.

Artist's impression of a wall painting dated 2100 B.C. found in a tomb at Meir in Middle Egypt.

The Peculiar Perils and Perplexing Predicaments of Poly Hedron

POLYHEDRON WAS A PROFESSOR OF POLYNOMIALS, POLYPHONICS, POLYMERS AND POLYPS. POLY WAS NOT JOLLY WITH HER PRESENT PALTRY PREMISES, SO SHE PROCEEDED TO PLAN A PERFECTLY PALATIAL, PROFUSELY PLUSH, NEW PLACE.

AND SO POLY PHONED A PRE-EMINENT PRO, MR. GILDER, THE BUILDER, BY NAME.

PLEASE PREPARE ME A PRISM— A RECTANGULAR PRISM.

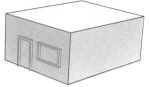

SO GILDER BUILT HER A FRAME.

THROUGH CAULKING AND STRIPPING, THE RAIN KEPT ON DRIPPING. THE FRAME WAS NOT WATERPROOF.

I'VE HAD A VISION—A TRIANGULAR PRISM!...

THE BUILDER CONSTRUCTED A ROOF.

POLY PROMISED TO PLAY POLYPHONIC TUNES ON HER PRODIGIOUS PIPE ORGAN WITH POWER.

A HEXAGONAL PRISM IS WHAT I'LL BE WISHIN'.

SO GILDER BUILT A GLASS TOWER.

THE PIERCING SUN PASSED THROUGH THE POLISHED PLATE GLASS. POOR POLY NEAR PERISHED IN THAT PLACE.

A HEXAGONAL PYRAMID, TO SERVE AS A LID, WILL TOP THE GLASS TOWER WITH GRACE.

WITH HER PALACE IN PLACE, POLY PHONED UP
(IN HASTE)
A YOUNG GARDENER NAMED PATTY PETERS
SAYING "DO BE A DEAR AND PLANT ME SOME SPHERES."
SO POLITE PATTY PLANTED GLOBE CEDARS.

THEN GILDER THE BUILDER AND HIS PARTNER THE
GARDENER WERE INVITED TO TEA AND SOME SCONES.
INTO CYLINDERS THREE, POLY POURED ALL THE TEA,
AND FOR REASONS UNKNOWN, SCONES IN CONES.

THE GARDENER CARVED HER SCONES WITH A FORK
WHILE THE BUILDER WITH HARDLY A CARE SAID,
"SUGAR CUBES THREE WILL PROVE PERFECT FOR ME!"
AND STIRRED HIS TEA WITH HIS T-SQUARE.

THEN POLY PEERED 'ROUND,
FROM THE PEAK TO THE GROUND,
AT THE HOUSE AND THE GROUNDS
FULLY TREED.
HER PAVILION PERFECTED,
OUR POLY REFLECTED:

'TIS A GEOMETRIC
WORLD INDEED!'

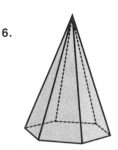

Use the story to help you answer these questions.

1. What geometric solids were mentioned in the story?

2. What geometric solids were used in the construction of Poly's house?

Write the names of these geometric solids.

3.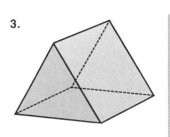

4.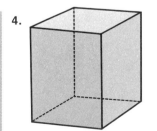

5.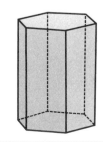

6.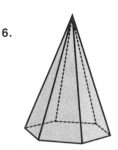

7. Name 3 geometric solids in the story which have curved faces.

8. Name a geometric solid which was not mentioned in the story.

53

Identifying Likenesses and Differences

A polyhedron is a special kind of geometric solid. Prisms and pyramids are special kinds of polyhedra. Study these pictures to discover the meanings of the words **polyhedron**, **prism**, and **pyramid**.

When we speak of more than one polyhedron, we say **polyhedra**.

1. All of these are polyhedra.

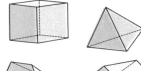

None of these are polyhedra.

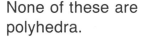

Which one is the polyhedron?

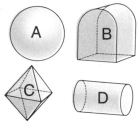

2. All of these are pyramids.

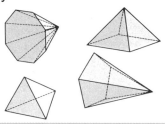

None of these are pyramids.

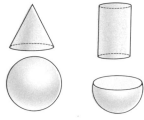

Which one is the pyramid?

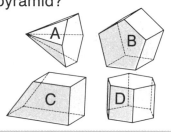

3. All of these are prisms.

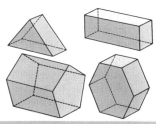

None of these are prisms.

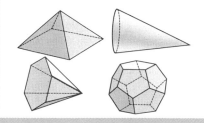

Which one is the prism?

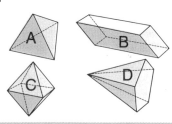

4. Write a sentence to explain how you can tell whether a geometric solid is:

a) a polyhedron. b) a prism. c) a pyramid.

Polyhedra: Prisms and Pyramids

A geometric solid which has only flat surfaces is called a **polyhedron**.

A flat surface of a polyhedron is called a **face**.

These polyhedra are called **prisms**.

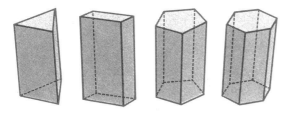

Each of these prisms has 2 congruent faces joined by rectangular faces.

These polyhedra are called **pyramids**.

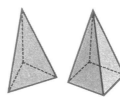

Each of these pyramids has one of its faces bounded by triangular faces which meet at a vertex.

Study the tower of Professor Poly Hedron. Compare the shapes of the faces of the hexagonal prism and the hexagonal pyramid.

Prisms and pyramids are named by the shape of the base.

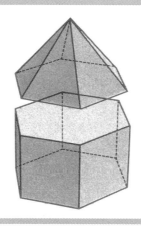

Hexagonal pyramid: triangular faces stand on a hexagonal base and meet at the vertex.

Hexagonal prism: 2 hexagons (top and bottom) are joined by rectangular faces.

Name these prisms and pyramids.

1.

ı. Square Pyramid

2.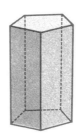

3.

4.

5.

6.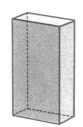

7.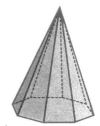

55

A pattern which can be cut out and folded to make a polyhedron is called a **net**.

Follow the instructions to construct a pentagonal prism from this net.

1. When this net is cut and folded, which faces will be joined to the pink face?

A. Trace this net onto stiff paper.

B. Cut along the solid lines of your tracing.

C. Colour the faces of your net as shown here.

D. Fold along the dotted lines.

E. Tape the tabs to make a pentagonal prism.

SAVE YOUR PENTAGONAL PRISM. YOU WILL NEED IT LATER.

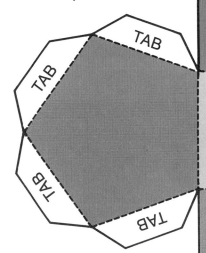

TAB
TAB
TAB
TAB

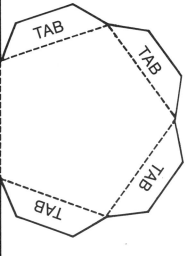

TAB
TAB
TAB
TAB

2. Use this net and a centimetre ruler to find the perimeter of the base of this prism.

   Use your model to check your answers to questions 1 and 2.

ESTIMATING

Collect a shoe box. Estimate the number of these pentagonal prisms your shoe box will hold. Check your estimate.

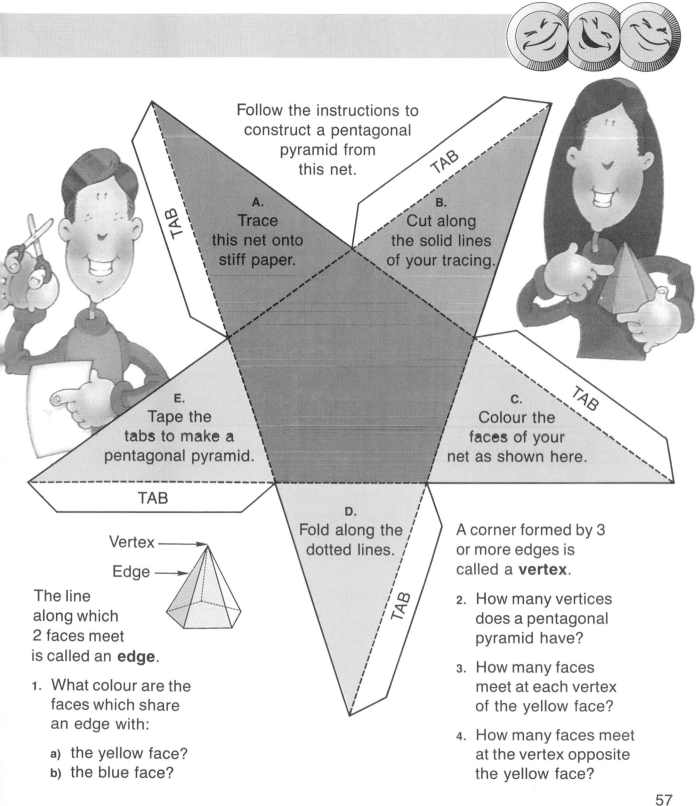

Follow the instructions to construct a pentagonal pyramid from this net.

TAB

TAB

A.
Trace
this net onto
stiff paper.

B.
Cut along
the solid lines
of your tracing.

TAB

E.
Tape the
tabs to make a
pentagonal pyramid.

C.
Colour the
faces of your
net as shown here.

TAB

D.
Fold along the
dotted lines.

TAB

Vertex
Edge

The line
along which
2 faces meet
is called an **edge**.

A corner formed by 3
or more edges is
called a **vertex**.

1. What colour are the
faces which share
an edge with:

a) the yellow face?
b) the blue face?

2. How many vertices
does a pentagonal
pyramid have?

3. How many faces
meet at each vertex
of the yellow face?

4. How many faces meet
at the vertex opposite
the yellow face?

Recognizing Solids From Their Nets

Imagine each of these nets folded into a polyhedron.
Write the name of the polyhedron which could be made
from each net. Then answer the question below that net.

3.

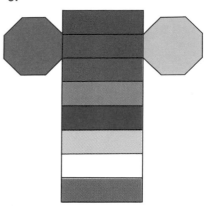

1.

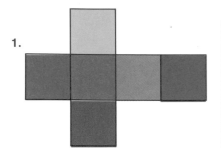

What is the colour
of the face that does
not share an edge
with the blue face?

2.

What is the colour
of the face with the
most vertices?

What is the colour of
the face directly opposite:
• the blue face?
• the yellow face?

4.

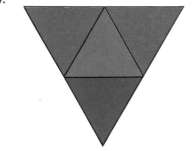

How many faces meet
at each vertex?

5.

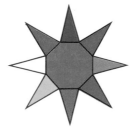

What is the colour
of the face directly
opposite the green face?

6.

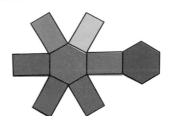

What is the colour
of the face that does
not share an edge
with the red face?

Name the solids which would be formed if
edges with the heavy lines were taped together.

7.

8.

58

To raise money for needy children, St. Mark's School made health bars. Each bar was to be put in a box and placed on a display table.
When the boxes arrived at the school, they were exactly like the net shown here. When the students at St. Mark's School folded this net into a box, they discovered a problem.

TAB

TAB

TAB

TAB

HELP THE NEEDY

VITAMINS ADDED

HEALTH BAR

ST. MARK'S SCHOOL

VITAMINS ADDED

TAB

TAB

TAB

TAB

1. What problem did the students discover?

2. How could the problem be solved?

PROBLEM SOLVING

Making a Model

Any rectangle
can be used as a
net for a cylinder.

Draw the shape of a
net which can be
used to make an
oblique cylinder
like this.

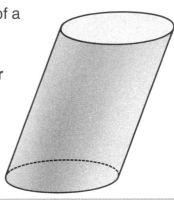

This net can
be rolled into
this cylinder.

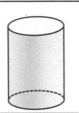

To solve this problem,...

A. First, make sure you understand
the problem.

Discuss:

- *What is a net?*
- *How could you test whether
  a particular shape is a net for
  the oblique cylinder?*

B. Then, think of strategies.
Try making a model.

- *Could an oblique
  cylinder be made
  from a shape like this?*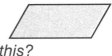

- *How could you make an oblique
  cylinder from a regular cylinder?*

C. Solve the problem and answer
the question.

- *Draw a rectangle and construct
  a paper cylinder.*
- *Cut the cylinder on a slant to get
  an oblique cylinder.*
- *Remove the tape from your cylinder
  and lay it flat.*
- *Trace the shape of the net for
  the oblique cylinder.*

D. Discuss your solution.

- *Draw a net to make a cylinder
  which is tilted even more than
  your first cylinder.*

60

Solve these problems.

1. A dotted line is drawn along the length of a ribbon 4 cm wide and 30 cm long.

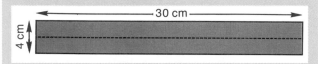

The ribbon is given a half twist and its ends are fastened together.

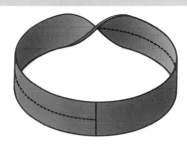

If the twisted ribbon is then cut along the dotted line, how many pieces of ribbon will there be?

2. A piece of paper is folded as shown. A corner is cut off along the dotted line. Sketch the polygon formed when the paper is unfolded.

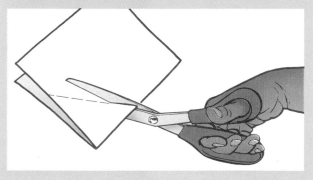

3. Four interlocking cubes are used to make each of these solids. Each solid has one twin. For example solids A and L are twins. Name the other 5 twins.

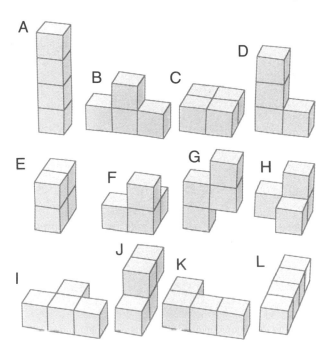

4. The 6 faces of a cube are marked with the letters A through F.

Study the three pictures of the cube. What letter is

- opposite D?

- opposite F?

- opposite C?

Polyhedra: Faces, Vertices, and Edges

A flat surface of a polyhedron is called a **face**.

The line segment where 2 faces meet is called an **edge**.

A corner where 2 or more edges meet is called a **vertex**.

Study these polyhedra. Count and record the number of faces, vertices, and edges for each.

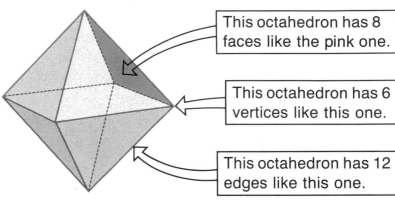

This octahedron has 8 faces like the pink one.

This octahedron has 6 vertices like this one.

This octahedron has 12 edges like this one.

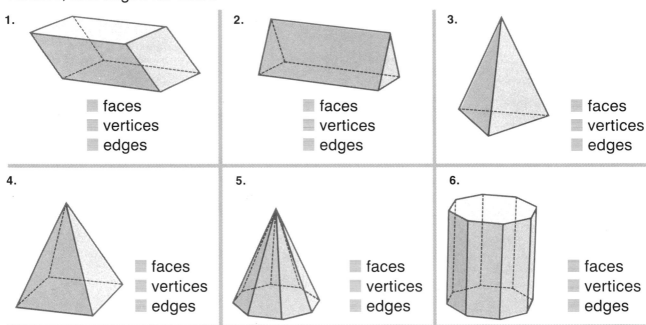

1.
▦ faces
▦ vertices
▦ edges

2.
▦ faces
▦ vertices
▦ edges

3.
▦ faces
▦ vertices
▦ edges

4.
▦ faces
▦ vertices
▦ edges

5.
▦ faces
▦ vertices
▦ edges

6.
▦ faces
▦ vertices
▦ edges

PROBLEM SOLVING

How many faces, vertices, and edges does each of these solids have?

1.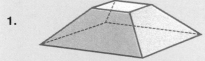

2.

3.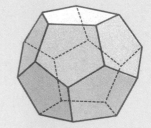

Make a Plasticine model of a square pyramid.
Slice it to check your answers to questions 1 and 2.
Use the net on page 63 to check your answer to question 3.

The net below can be used to make a special polyhedron called a **dodecahedron**.

IT'S EASIER TO MAKE THAN IT IS TO PRONOUNCE!

To construct a dodecahedron from this net, follow the instructions on the net.

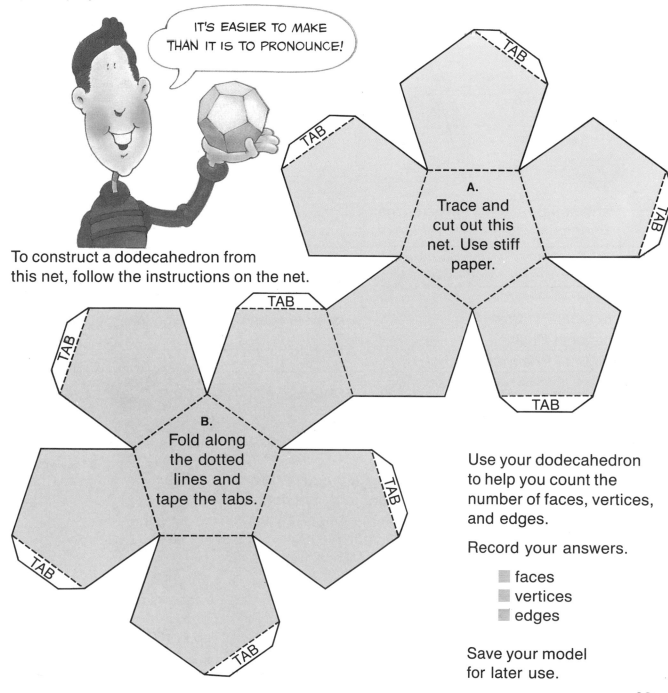

A.
Trace and cut out this net. Use stiff paper.

TAB

B.
Fold along the dotted lines and tape the tabs.

TAB

Use your dodecahedron to help you count the number of faces, vertices, and edges.

Record your answers.

▤ faces
▤ vertices
▤ edges

Save your model for later use.

63

Relating Faces, Vertices, and Edges

1. Use the pictures of these prisms and pyramids to count their faces, vertices, and edges. Complete the table below.

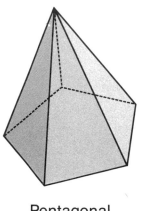 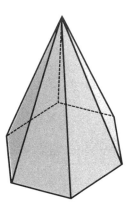 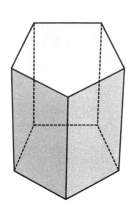 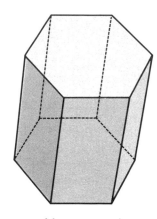

| Pentagonal Pyramid | Hexagonal Pyramid | Pentagonal Prism | Hexagonal Prism |

	Number of Faces (F)	Number of Vertices (V)	Number of Edges (E)	Value of F + V − E
Pentagonal Pyramid				
Hexagonal Pyramid				
Pentagonal Prism				
Hexagonal Prism				

2. Describe any pattern you see in the last column of your table.

PROBLEM SOLVING

Write the name of the polyhedron above which answers each riddle.

1. My faces, they are even,
   And my corners even, too,
   But compared to all my corners,
   My faces number few.
   Who am I?

2. I have a group of faces;
   Of corners, I've not more.
   The number of my edges
   Is a multiple of 4.
   Who am I?

3. I am a bit self-conscious
   When children stare at me
   For my edges and my faces
   Are both quite odd you see.
   Who am I?

EXTENSIONS

A POLYHEDRON WITH ALL FACES CONGRUENT IS CALLED A REGULAR POLYHEDRON.

The Regular Polyhedra

There are only 5 regular polyhedra. All of them were discovered over 2000 years ago by the mathematicians of ancient Greece!

Tetrahedron

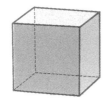
Cube

Octahedron

Dodecahedron

Icosahedron

1. Copy and complete this table. Use the diagrams above to help you count faces, vertices, and edges of the first 3 polyhedra.

2. Use the model of the dodecahedron you constructed to help you complete the last row of your table.

Regular Polyhedron	Number of Faces (F)	Number of Vertices (V)	Number of Edges (E)	Value of F + V − E
Tetrahedron	▦	▦	6	▦
Cube	▦	▦	▦	▦
Octahedron	▦	▦	▦	▦
Dodecahedron	▦	▦	30	▦

PROBLEM SOLVING

It is difficult to count the faces, vertices, and edges of an icosahedron even if you have a model!

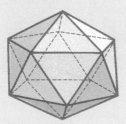

1. Write a sentence to describe any pattern you see in the last column of your table.

2. An icosahedron has 20 faces and 12 vertices. Use the pattern in the table to calculate the number of edges in an icosahedron.

65

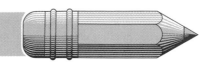
Write the name of each prism.

1.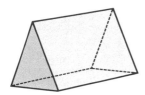

2.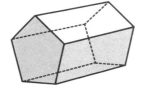

3.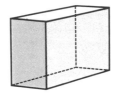

4.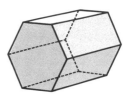

Write the name of each pyramid.

5.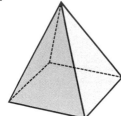

6.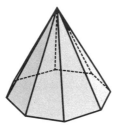

7.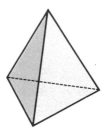

8.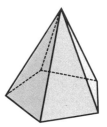

Name the polyhedron that can be made from each net.

9.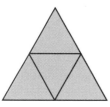

10.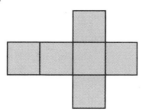

11.

12.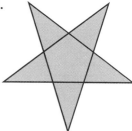

Count and record the number of faces, vertices, and edges for each.

13.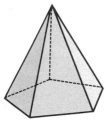

14.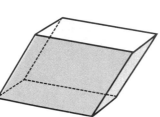

15.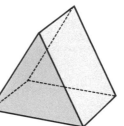

16.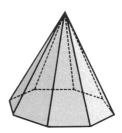

▦ faces
▦ vertices
▦ edges

▦ faces
▦ vertices
▦ edges

▦ faces
▦ vertices
▦ edges

▦ faces
▦ vertices
▦ edges

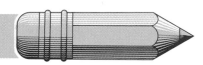

Write as a numeral.

1. fourteen thousand forty
2. fifty-nine thousand fifty-nine
3. eight hundred thousand eighty

Write the number that is:

4. 10 000 less than 204 287
5. 10 000 greater than 93 976
6. 100 000 less than 107 352

Write the value of each coloured digit.

7. 876 303
8. 524 802
9. 518 807
10. 396 714

Write in expanded form.

11. 29 386   12. 518 247   13. 760 308

Write the number for each expanded form.

14. 200 000 + 60 000 + 7000 + 200 + 3
15. 400 000 + 8000 + 300 + 20 + 1
16. 800 000 + 80 000 + 80

Write > or < for each ▒.

17. 284 371 ▒ 248 317
18. 593 462 ▒ 594 362
19. 143 972 ▒ 134 792

Write the value of each coloured digit.

20. 641 692 637
21. 836 437 293
22. 187 938 546

Write > or < for each ▒.

23. 17 294 365 ▒ 17 429 563
24. 265 178 409 ▒ 256 871 904
25. 301 030 605 ▒ 301 003 506

Copy and complete the table.

	Number	Rounded to the nearest...		
		10	100	1 000
26.	786	▒	▒	▒
27.	4 978	▒	▒	▒
28.	29 393	▒	▒	▒
29.	628 751	▒	▒	▒

Write the next 3 numbers in each pattern.

30. 3, 4, 6, 9, ▒ , ▒ , ▒
31. 2, 5, 8, 11, ▒ , ▒ , ▒

Estimate by rounding.

32. 463
   + 521

33. 8 125
   + 1 500

34. 7 821
   + 3 465

Add.

35. 7 545
   + 3 326

36. 4 698
   + 7 919

37. 93 486
   + 8 756

38. 8 006
   + 4 397

39. 16 786
   + 38 507

40. 76 427
   + 89 325

Estimate by rounding.

41. 789
   − 263

42. 8 250
   − 5 499

43. 8 195
   − 7 233

Subtract.

44. 5 613
   − 4 412

45. 8 446
   − 4 617

46. 83 007
   − 79 228

47. 9 508
   − 8 892

48. 22 675
   − 7 532

49. 50 403
   − 36 758

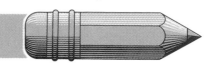

50. A new car costs $11 539. If a dealer takes $950 off the price, what is the sale price of the car?

51. On Friday, 3 681 people came to hear an outdoor concert. 5 039 people attended the concert on Saturday. What was the total number of people who attended that weekend?

52. In a local election, 89 786 votes were cast. 44 882 people voted for John B. Alexander. How many votes were cast for the other candidates?

53. The distance around the world through the poles is 39 997 km. If you travelled that distance twice, how many kilometres would you have travelled?

Write the name of each prism.

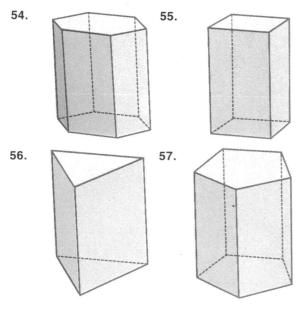

54.   55.

56.   57.

Write the name of each pyramid.

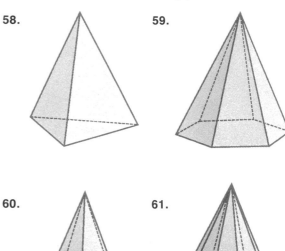

58.   59.

60.   61.

Count and record the number of faces, vertices, and edges for each.

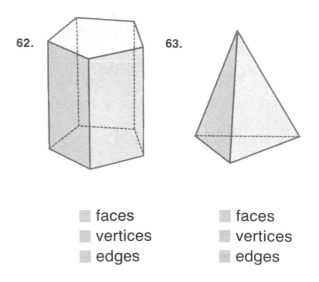

62.   63.

faces	faces
vertices	vertices
edges	edges

Konane

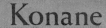

The Hawaiian game of Konane is similar to checkers. Two players move 32 pebbles each horizontally or vertically. Each player tries to position the pebble so the other player's pebbles cannot move. This game was played in Hawaii long before the first European explorers arrived. Wood and stone gameboards have been unearthed from ancient villages. It is said that one of the greatest players was King Kamehameha the Great, ruler of the Hawaiian islands in 1800.

Artist's impression of King Kamehameha, Hawaii 1790-1800

Multiplication Facts: Products to 10 × 10

When 2 **factors** are multiplied together,
the result is called the **product**.

The multiplication table below contains
some products you need to know.
The table also contains the names of some
products invented in the 20th century.

$$3 \times 7 = 21$$

Factors   Product

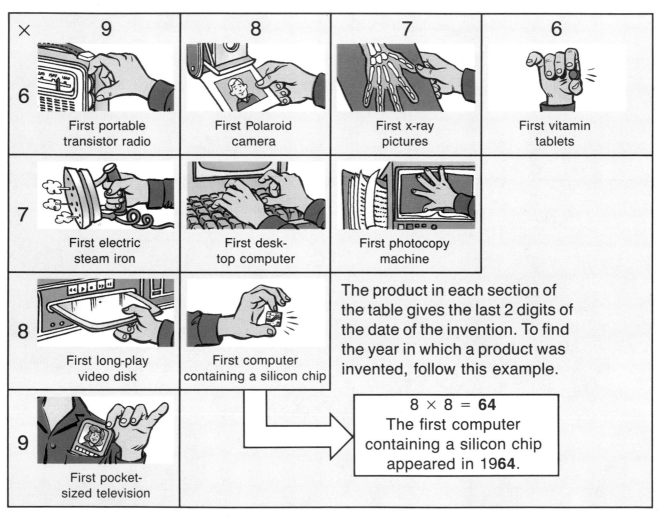

×	9	8	7	6
6	First portable transistor radio	First Polaroid camera	First x-ray pictures	First vitamin tablets
7	First electric steam iron	First desk-top computer	First photocopy machine	
8	First long-play video disk	First computer containing a silicon chip		
9	First pocket-sized television			

The product in each section of
the table gives the last 2 digits of
the date of the invention. To find
the year in which a product was
invented, follow this example.

8 × 8 = **64**
The first computer
containing a silicon chip
appeared in 19**64**.

Use the multiplication table to find the year
when each of these products first appeared.

1. vitamin tablets
2. x-ray pictures
3. Polaroid camera
4. photocopy machine
5. portable transistor radio
6. desktop computer
7. electric steam iron
8. long-playing video disk
9. pocket-sized television

70

Multiply.

1. $\begin{array}{r} 8 \\ \times 2 \\ \hline \end{array}$
2. $\begin{array}{r} 9 \\ \times 0 \\ \hline \end{array}$
3. $\begin{array}{r} 4 \\ \times 2 \\ \hline \end{array}$
4. $\begin{array}{r} 5 \\ \times 6 \\ \hline \end{array}$
5. $\begin{array}{r} 6 \\ \times 7 \\ \hline \end{array}$
6. $\begin{array}{r} 9 \\ \times 3 \\ \hline \end{array}$
7. $\begin{array}{r} 4 \\ \times 6 \\ \hline \end{array}$

8. $\begin{array}{r} 4 \\ \times 10 \\ \hline \end{array}$
9. $\begin{array}{r} 7 \\ \times 2 \\ \hline \end{array}$
10. $\begin{array}{r} 9 \\ \times 5 \\ \hline \end{array}$
11. $\begin{array}{r} 6 \\ \times 9 \\ \hline \end{array}$
12. $\begin{array}{r} 8 \\ \times 8 \\ \hline \end{array}$
13. $\begin{array}{r} 10 \\ \times 6 \\ \hline \end{array}$
14. $\begin{array}{r} 4 \\ \times 7 \\ \hline \end{array}$

15. $\begin{array}{r} 7 \\ \times 5 \\ \hline \end{array}$
16. $\begin{array}{r} 6 \\ \times 8 \\ \hline \end{array}$
17. $\begin{array}{r} 10 \\ \times 8 \\ \hline \end{array}$
18. $\begin{array}{r} 5 \\ \times 10 \\ \hline \end{array}$
19. $\begin{array}{r} 0 \\ \times 6 \\ \hline \end{array}$
20. $\begin{array}{r} 7 \\ \times 3 \\ \hline \end{array}$
21. $\begin{array}{r} 3 \\ \times 6 \\ \hline \end{array}$

22. $\begin{array}{r} 9 \\ \times 9 \\ \hline \end{array}$
23. $\begin{array}{r} 4 \\ \times 8 \\ \hline \end{array}$
24. $\begin{array}{r} 4 \\ \times 9 \\ \hline \end{array}$
25. $\begin{array}{r} 8 \\ \times 5 \\ \hline \end{array}$
26. $\begin{array}{r} 2 \\ \times 9 \\ \hline \end{array}$
27. $\begin{array}{r} 7 \\ \times 8 \\ \hline \end{array}$
28. $\begin{array}{r} 3 \\ \times 8 \\ \hline \end{array}$

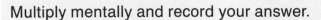

Multiply.

29. 7×7
30. 8×0
31. 0×7
32. 10×10
33. 9×8
34. 10×3
35. 6×6
36. 7×9
37. 8×1
38. 8×4
39. 5×8
40. 1×6

BITS AND BYTES

Use your calculator to complete each pair of products. Look for a pattern in your answers.

1. $\begin{array}{r} 23 \\ \times 1 \\ \hline \end{array}$ $\begin{array}{r} 23 \\ \times 10 \\ \hline \end{array}$
2. $\begin{array}{r} 289 \\ \times 1 \\ \hline \end{array}$ $\begin{array}{r} 289 \\ \times 10 \\ \hline \end{array}$

3. $\begin{array}{r} 3\,756 \\ \times 1 \\ \hline \end{array}$ $\begin{array}{r} 3\,756 \\ \times 10 \\ \hline \end{array}$
4. $\begin{array}{r} 23\,475 \\ \times 1 \\ \hline \end{array}$ $\begin{array}{r} 23\,475 \\ \times 10 \\ \hline \end{array}$

5. Write a rule for multiplying a number by 1.

6. Write a rule for multiplying a number by 10.

Multiply mentally and record your answer.

7. $\begin{array}{r} 49 \\ \times 10 \\ \hline \end{array}$
8. $\begin{array}{r} 52 \\ \times 10 \\ \hline \end{array}$
9. $\begin{array}{r} 293 \\ \times 10 \\ \hline \end{array}$
10. $\begin{array}{r} 124 \\ \times 10 \\ \hline \end{array}$
11. $\begin{array}{r} 509 \\ \times 10 \\ \hline \end{array}$
12. $\begin{array}{r} 317 \\ \times 10 \\ \hline \end{array}$

13. $\begin{array}{r} 6\,032 \\ \times 10 \\ \hline \end{array}$
14. $\begin{array}{r} 4\,266 \\ \times 10 \\ \hline \end{array}$
15. $\begin{array}{r} 3\,841 \\ \times 10 \\ \hline \end{array}$
16. $\begin{array}{r} 10\,730 \\ \times 10 \\ \hline \end{array}$
17. $\begin{array}{r} 47\,812 \\ \times 10 \\ \hline \end{array}$
18. $\begin{array}{r} 79\,842 \\ \times 10 \\ \hline \end{array}$

Multiplication: The Grouping Property

How many boxes are in the stack?

Dara thinks:

Greg thinks:

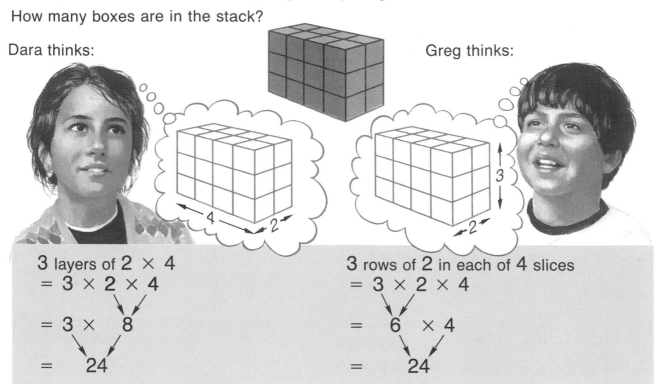

3 layers of 2 × 4
= 3 × 2 × 4

= 3 × 8

= 24

3 rows of 2 in each of 4 slices
= 3 × 2 × 4

= 6 × 4

= 24

Greg and Dara have shown that
3 × 2 × 4 = 3 × 2 × 4.

That is, we get the same product no matter how we group the factors. This is called the **grouping property** of multiplication.

Calculate the number of blocks in 2 ways.
Check that you get the same answer both ways.

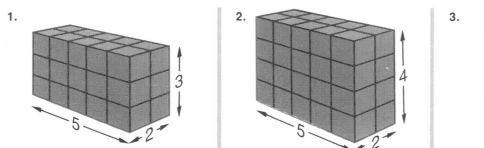

1.

2.

3.

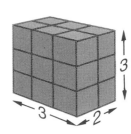

Multiply. Use the grouping property
to calculate each product mentally.

4. 6 × 5 × 2   5. 3 × 2 × 8   6. 4 × 2 × 9   7. 8 × 5 × 2
8. 5 × 4 × 2   9. 9 × 3 × 2   10. 8 × 3 × 3   11. 6 × 3 × 2

Multiplying Multiples of 10, 100, and 1000

The automatic teller at the Money Bank was installed 50 weeks ago. It has operated 7 days a week. How many days has the automatic teller been in use?

TO FIND 7 x 50, I THINK ABOUT $10 BILLS.
7 x $50 = 7 x 5 /$10/
= 35 /$10/
= $350

To multiply:
$$\begin{array}{r} 50 \\ \times\ 7 \\ \hline \end{array}$$

We think:

$$7 \times 50$$
$$= 7 \times 5 \times 10$$
$$= 35 \times 10$$
$$= 350$$

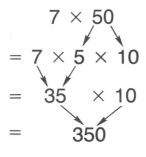

We write:
$$\begin{array}{r} 50 \\ \times\ 7 \\ \hline 350 \end{array}$$

The automatic teller has been in use for 350 days.

Other examples:

$$\begin{array}{r} 40 \\ \times\ 7 \\ \hline 280 \end{array} \qquad \begin{array}{r} 300 \\ \times\ 8 \\ \hline 2400 \end{array} \qquad \begin{array}{r} 6\ 000 \\ \times\ \ \ \ 9 \\ \hline 54\ 000 \end{array} \qquad \begin{array}{r} 70\ 000 \\ \times\ \ \ \ \ 3 \\ \hline 210\ 000 \end{array}$$

Multiply.

1. 3×40
2. 2×80
3. 9×70
4. 8×80
5. 3×200
6. 4×300
7. 5×300
8. 6×800
9. $2 \times 4\ 000$
10. $3 \times 7\ 000$
11. $6 \times 2\ 000$
12. $4 \times 5\ 000$

13. $\begin{array}{r} 80 \\ \times\ 7 \\ \hline \end{array}$
14. $\begin{array}{r} 90 \\ \times\ 3 \\ \hline \end{array}$
15. $\begin{array}{r} 60 \\ \times\ 7 \\ \hline \end{array}$
16. $\begin{array}{r} 700 \\ \times\ 8 \\ \hline \end{array}$
17. $\begin{array}{r} 400 \\ \times\ 9 \\ \hline \end{array}$

18. $\begin{array}{r} 800 \\ \times\ 6 \\ \hline \end{array}$
19. $\begin{array}{r} 800 \\ \times\ 5 \\ \hline \end{array}$
20. $\begin{array}{r} 4\ 000 \\ \times\ \ \ \ 7 \\ \hline \end{array}$
21. $\begin{array}{r} 6\ 000 \\ \times\ \ \ \ 3 \\ \hline \end{array}$
22. $\begin{array}{r} 50\ 000 \\ \times\ \ \ \ \ 5 \\ \hline \end{array}$

Estimating Products: 1-Digit Multipliers

Ocean Travel in Prehistoric Times

The first vehicle used for travel may have been the boat. Scientists have learned that aborigines made primitive boats to cross from the island of New Guinea to Australia over 40 000 years ago! These boats probably carried 3 or 4 people at most.

Ocean Travel Today

Today, large ocean liners have all the comforts of home. One of the largest passenger ships is the Queen Elizabeth II which can carry a total of 2931 people at one time.

About how many people can be transported in 7 trips on the Queen Elizabeth II?

We think: About how many people are in 7 groups of 2931?

To estimate:	Round 2931 to the nearest 1000.	Multiply.

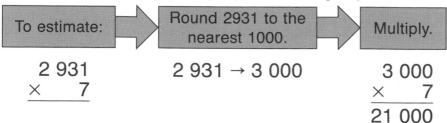

$$\begin{array}{r} 2\ 931 \\ \times \quad 7 \end{array}$$

$$2\ 931 \rightarrow 3\ 000$$

$$\begin{array}{r} 3\ 000 \\ \times \quad 7 \\ \hline 21\ 000 \end{array}$$

The Queen Elizabeth II can transport about 21 000 people in 7 trips.

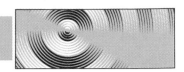

Estimate by rounding to the nearest 10.

1. 25
   × 6

1. 30
   × 6
   180

2. 87
   × 3

3. 91
   × 5

4. 19
   × 8

5. 37
   × 7

6. 94
   × 2

7. 67
   × 4

8. 75
   × 9

9. 82
   × 8

10. 165
    × 7

Estimate by rounding to the nearest 100.

11. 306
    × 4

12. 788
    × 6

13. 931
    × 5

14. 359
    × 6

15. 627
    × 9

16. 528
    × 6

17. 818
    × 7

18. 550
    × 9

19. 229
    × 3

20. 2 350
    × 8

Estimate by rounding to the nearest 1000.

21. 1 196
    × 3

22. 2 785
    × 4

23. 4 209
    × 6

24. 3 985
    × 7

25. 6 897
    × 4

26. 8 275
    × 8

27. 9 682
    × 7

28. 8 193
    × 5

29. 3 500
    × 2

30. 42 750
    × 3

Estimate. Decide how to round.

31. 97
    × 6

32. 63
    × 9

33. 829
    × 5

34. 687
    × 8

35. 4 389
    × 7

36. 6 907
    × 3

37. 2 793
    × 6

38. 9 265
    × 5

39. 59 699
    × 2

40. 43 500
    × 6

41. Which of the products below is greatest?

   9 × 4 708   6 × 7 690

   8 × 5 269   5 × 8 923

   7 × 7 093   4 × 9 989

42. Which of the products below is least?

   8 × 5 395   6 × 7 356

   7 × 6 519   9 × 4 876

   5 × 9 382   8 × 5 472

Multiplying by a 1-Digit Number

Bicycles Then

There were many early designs
for bicycles, but the first bicycle
that worked was made in 1839
by Kirkpatrick Macmillan.
His bicycle had wooden
wheels and iron tires.

Bicycles Now

The superbikes of today are 2-wheeled
enclosed vehicles. Some have motors
and can travel at speeds of up to
140 m/s (metres per second).

During a race, the world's fastest
motorcycle averaged a speed of 137 m/s.
At this speed, how far would it travel in 8 s?

We think: The motorcycle travels 137 m
each second. In 8 s, it travels
8×137 m.

To multiply 137 by 8:

Multiply the ones by 8.	Multiply the tens by 8.	Multiply the hundreds by 8.

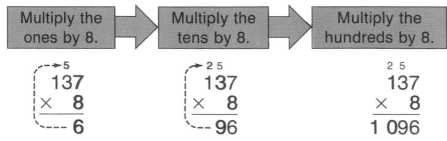

The motorcycle would travel 1096 m in 8 s.

76

Another example:

To multiply 2068 by 9:

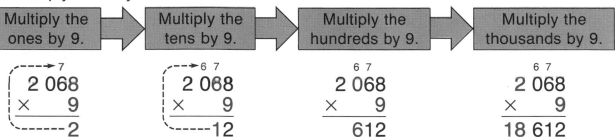

Multiply the ones by 9.	Multiply the tens by 9.	Multiply the hundreds by 9.	Multiply the thousands by 9.

$$
\begin{array}{r} {}^{7} \\ 2\ 068 \\ \times\quad 9 \\ \hline 2 \end{array}
\qquad
\begin{array}{r} {}^{6\ 7} \\ 2\ 068 \\ \times\quad 9 \\ \hline 12 \end{array}
\qquad
\begin{array}{r} {}^{6\ 7} \\ 2\ 068 \\ \times\quad 9 \\ \hline 612 \end{array}
\qquad
\begin{array}{r} {}^{6\ 7} \\ 2\ 068 \\ \times\quad 9 \\ \hline 18\ 612 \end{array}
$$

Multiply. Do only those questions with products greater than 500.

1. 73
    × 8

2. 92
    × 6

3. 96
    × 5

4. 76
    × 6

5. 79
    × 8

6. 83
    × 7

7. 84
    × 6

8. 56
    × 8

9. 44
    × 9

10. 57
    × 9

Multiply. Do only those questions with products greater than 5000.

11. 469
    × 7

12. 685
    × 8

13. 597
    × 4

14. 868
    × 9

15. 907
    × 6

16. 815
    × 8

17. 997
    × 5

18. 832
    × 7

19. 749
    × 7

20. 696
    × 8

Multiply. Do only those questions with products greater than 50 000.

21. 6 809
    ×   8

22. 5 906
    ×   9

23. 7 382
    ×   7

24. 6 066
    ×   8

25. Don Vesco set a motorcycle speed record. He averaged a speed of 135 m/s for a period of 25 s. What was the distance travelled in this time?

BITS AND BYTES

In 1909, W. E. Cook set the world motorcycle speed record with a speed of 34 m/s. The present motorcycle record is about 135 m/s.

About how many times as fast as the 1909 motorcycles are the motorcycles of today?

Multiplication: The Order Property

Write 2 multiplication sentences to
show how many boxes are in the
bottom layer of the stack.

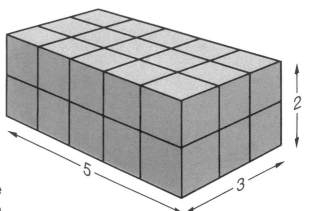

We think: 5 rows of 3   or   3 rows of 5

We write: $5 \times 3 = 15$ or $3 \times 5 = 15$

Changing the order of the factors does not change
the product. We can write 6 different multiplication
sentences to show the total number of boxes in the stack.

2 layers of 15 boxes	3 slices of 10 boxes	5 slices of 6 boxes
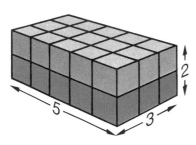	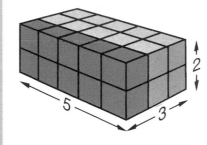	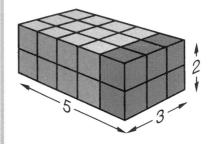
$2 \times \boxed{5 \times 3} = 30$ $2 \times \boxed{3 \times 5} = 30$	$3 \times \boxed{5 \times 2} = 30$ $3 \times \boxed{2 \times 5} = 30$	$5 \times \boxed{3 \times 2} = 30$ $5 \times \boxed{2 \times 3} = 30$

The diagrams above show that when we
change the order of the factors 2, 3, and 5,
the product does not change.

This is called the **order property**
of multiplication.

The order and grouping properties can
be used to compute products mentally.

To multiply $8 \times 7 \times 5$:

Use the order property to switch 7 and 5.	Use the grouping property to group 8 and 5.	Multiply mentally.
$8 \times 7 \times 5$ $= 8 \times 5 \times 7$	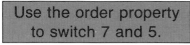 $= \quad 40 \times 7$	$40 \times 7 = 280$

We can use the order and grouping properties to multiply.

We see: 60×29

We write: $60 \times 29 = 6 \times 10 \times 29$ ◀——— Write 60 as 6×10.
$= 6 \times 29 \times 10$ ◀——— Use the order property
to switch 29 and 10.
$= 174 \times 10$ ◀——— Use the grouping property
$= 1\ 740$ to group 6 and 29.

Use the order and grouping properties to
help you multiply mentally. Record your answers.

1. $2 \times 9 \times 5$ 2. $5 \times 7 \times 2$ 3. $5 \times 7 \times 6$ 4. $2 \times 9 \times 5$
5. $4 \times 3 \times 5$ 6. $5 \times 9 \times 4$ 7. $6 \times 9 \times 5$ 8. $2 \times 8 \times 5$
9. $5 \times 9 \times 6$ 10. $6 \times 8 \times 5$ 11. $8 \times 9 \times 5$ 12. $5 \times 9 \times 8$

Multiply. Use the order and grouping properties.

13. 30×19 14. 20×7 15. 63×40 16. 80×123
17. 70×246 18. 90×305 19. 94×30 20. 80×89
21. 20×476 22. 967×80 23. $4\ 156 \times 90$ 24. $70 \times 3\ 595$

EXTENSIONS

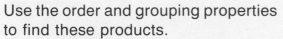

Use the order and grouping properties
to find these products.

1. 70×50 2. 40×90
3. 80×700 4. 90×600
5. $50 \times 8\ 000$ 6. $30 \times 9\ 000$

7. $\begin{array}{r} 30 \\ \times 60 \\ \hline \end{array}$ 8. $\begin{array}{r} 900 \\ \times\ 70 \\ \hline \end{array}$ 9. $\begin{array}{r} 8\ 000 \\ \times\ 800 \\ \hline \end{array}$

10. Use sentences beginning *We see*,
We think, *We write* to show how you
completed questions 1, 4, and 9.

Multiplying by a Multiple of 10

The first gasoline-driven car was invented about a century ago. However, it was not until 1908 that there were enough cars available for public purchase.

The Model T Ford in that year sold for $850. By 1923, the price of a Model T Ford had been reduced to $264. The average price of a new car today is about 60 times the price of the Model T Ford in 1923.

What is the average price of a new car today?

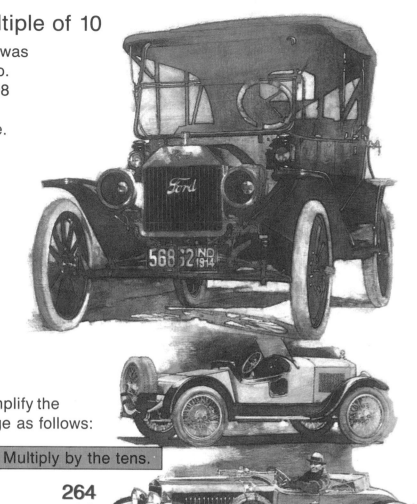

To multiply 264 by 60, we simplify the method on the previous page as follows:

Multiply by the ones.	Multiply by the tens.
264	264
× 60	× 60
0	15 840

The average price of a new car today is about $15 840.

Another example:

To multiply 4086 by 70:

Multiply by the ones.	Multiply by the tens.
4 086	4 086
× 70	× 70
0	286 020

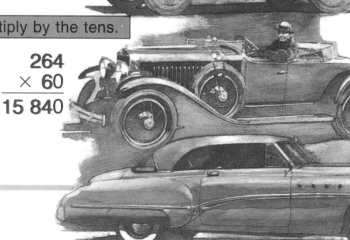

Multiply mentally and record your answer.

1. 40 ×60	2. 60 ×20	3. 50 ×30	4. 70 ×40	5. 700 × 50
6. 300 × 50	7. 500 × 70	8. 600 × 80	9. 4 000 × 60	10. 9 000 × 80

Multiply. Do only those questions
with products greater than 4000.

11. 82 ×70	12. 97 ×30	13. 64 ×70	14. 73 ×50	15. 49 ×90
16. 64 ×60	17. 98 ×40	18. 86 ×50	19. 68 ×60	20. 75 ×70

Multiply. Do only those questions
with products greater than 40 000.

21. 693 × 50	22. 703 × 60	23. 585 × 70	24. 867 × 70	25. 692 × 60
26. 989 × 30	27. 809 × 50	28. 747 × 60	29. 526 × 80	30. 416 × 90

Multiply. Do only those questions
with products greater than 400 000.

31. 5 186 × 80	32. 7 399 × 60
33. 9 665 × 40	34. 8 357 × 70
35. 7 777 × 70	36. 5 896 × 60

37. In 1980, the average price of a car
was about 40 times the price of a
Model T car in 1923. What was the
average price of a car in 1980?

BITS AND BYTES

Use your calculator to find
these products.

1. 300 × 500   2. 400 × 700
3. 600 × 3 000   4. 9 000 × 2 000
5. 800 × 40 000 6. 7 000 × 500

7. How is the number of zeros in the
product related to the total number
of zeros in the factors? Write a rule
to explain.

8. Multiply 5000 by 800. Does your rule
work for this product? Explain.

ESTIMATING

1. Visually estimate the total number of cars in this parking lot. Record your estimate.

To obtain a closer estimate of the total number of cars, complete these questions.

2. Count and record the number of cars inside the coloured rectangle.

3. Calculate the total number of rectangles contained in the picture.

4. Use your answers to questions 2 and 3 to calculate the approximate number of cars in the parking lot.

Using calculations to obtain closer estimates is often called **approximating**.

If there is an average of 2 people per car, about how many people are visiting the mall?

BITS AND BYTES

Using a Calculator to Investigate Patterns

DON'T YOU KNOW YOU CAN'T FIND PRODUCTS WITH MORE THAN 8 DIGITS ON YOUR CALCULATOR?

I JUST USE THE CALCULATOR TO FIND THE PATTERN.

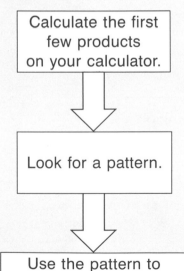

For each question:

Calculate the first few products on your calculator.

↓

Look for a pattern.

↓

Use the pattern to help you complete the remaining products.

Copy and complete.

1. $3 \times 5 =$ ▦
    $30 \times 50 =$ ▦
    $300 \times 500 =$ ▦
    $3\ 000 \times 5\ 000 =$ ▦

2. $11 \times 11 =$ ▦
    $111 \times 111 =$ ▦
    $1\ 111 \times 1\ 111 =$ ▦
    $11\ 111 \times 11\ 111 =$ ▦

3. $5 \times 5 =$ ▦
    $5 \times 55 =$ ▦
    $5 \times 555 =$ ▦
    $5 \times 5\ 555 =$ ▦
    $5 \times 55\ 555 =$ ▦
    $5 \times 555\ 555 =$ ▦
    $5 \times 5\ 555\ 555 =$ ▦
    $5 \times 55\ 555\ 555 =$ ▦
    $5 \times 555\ 555\ 555 =$ ▦

4. $37 \times 3 =$ ▦
    $37 \times 33 =$ ▦
    $37 \times 333 =$ ▦
    $37 \times 3\ 333 =$ ▦
    $37 \times 33\ 333 =$ ▦
    $37 \times 333\ 333 =$ ▦
    $37 \times 3\ 333\ 333 =$ ▦

5. $47 \times 101 =$ ▦
    $407 \times 1\ 001 =$ ▦
    $4\ 007 \times 10\ 001 =$ ▦
    $40\ 007 \times 100\ 001 =$ ▦

6. Use question 5 to predict the product: $5\ 003 \times 10\ 001$

Use your calculator to check your prediction.

83

ESTIMATING

Estimating Products: 2-Digit Multipliers

Between 1900 and 1937, huge airships were used to transport people long distances. In 1937, a large German airship called the Hindenburg, completing a transatlantic flight, exploded into flames. This accident ended the use of the airship as a commercial vehicle.

Between 1910 and 1914, German airships called **Zeppelins** made 1588 safe flights. They carried an average of 21 people per flight.

About how many people were transported safely between 1910 and 1914?

| To estimate: | ➡ | Round both factors to one non-zero digit. | ➡ | Multiply. |

$$
\begin{array}{r}
1\ 588 \\
\times\ \ \ \ 21 \\
\end{array}
\qquad
\begin{array}{l}
1\ 588 \to 2\ 000 \\
21 \to 20 \\
\end{array}
\qquad
\begin{array}{r}
2\ 000 \\
\times\ \ \ \ 20 \\
\hline
40\ 000 \\
\end{array}
$$

About 40 000 people were transported safely.

Other examples:

| To estimate: | ➡ | Round both factors to one non-zero digit. | ➡ | Multiply. |

$$
\begin{array}{r}
83 \\
\times 46 \\
\end{array}
\qquad
\begin{array}{l}
83 \to 80 \\
46 \to 50 \\
\end{array}
\qquad
\begin{array}{r}
80 \\
\times 50 \\
\hline
4\ 000 \\
\end{array}
$$

| To estimate: | ➡ | Round both factors to one non-zero digit. | ➡ | Multiply. |

$$
\begin{array}{r}
684 \\
\times\ \ 53 \\
\end{array}
\qquad
\begin{array}{l}
684 \to 700 \\
53 \to 50 \\
\end{array}
\qquad
\begin{array}{r}
700 \\
\times\ \ 50 \\
\hline
35\ 000 \\
\end{array}
$$

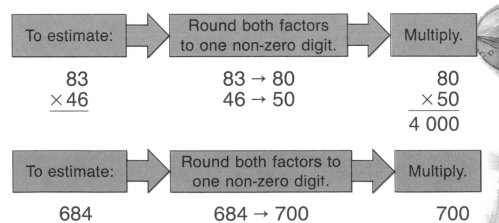

Estimate these products.

1.	89 ×32	2.	61 ×48	3.	76 ×33	4.	82 ×91	5.	68 ×79
6.	98 ×39	7.	47 ×47	8.	79 ×35	9.	64 ×44	10.	90 ×86
11.	239 × 41	12.	306 × 18	13.	209 × 22	14.	587 × 54	15.	953 × 39
16.	550 × 35	17.	650 × 45	18.	3 092 × 58	19.	4 991 × 32	20.	6 500 × 19
21.	5 450 × 45	22.	8 066 × 63	23.	21 006 × 29	24.	14 909 × 51	25.	29 916 × 73

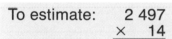

EXTENSIONS

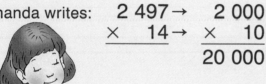

To estimate: 2 497
                 ×   14

Amanda writes:

2 497 →   2 000
×   14 → ×   10
          20 000

Amy writes:

2 497 →   2 000
×   14 → ×   20
          40 000

Whose estimate is closer?

The product is 34 958, so Amy's estimate is closer. Why?

Rounding one factor down and the other factor up is called **compensating**.

1. Estimate these products by compensating.

a)   95
      ×45
    4 275

b)   69
      ×88
    6 072

c)   356
      × 46
    16 376

d)   91
      ×41
    3 731

e)   750
      × 55
    41 250

f)   2 048
      ×   41
    83 968

2. Now estimate the products without compensating.

3. For which products did compensating **not** give better estimates?

Multiplying by a 2-Digit Number

The world's longest railway is the Trans-Siberian railway which stretches across the U.S.S.R. from Moscow to Nakhodka.

The trip from Moscow to Nakhodka takes about 197 h travelling at an average speed of 48 km/h.

What is the length of the Trans-Siberian railway line?

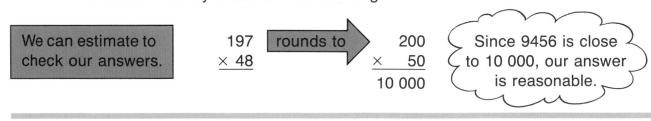

The longest railway in the world

To multiply 197 by 48:

Multiply by the ones.	Multiply by the tens.	Add.
$$\begin{array}{r} 197 \\ \times\ 48 \\ \hline 1\ 576 \end{array}$$	$$\begin{array}{r} 197 \\ \times\ 48 \\ \hline 1\ 576 \\ 7\ 880 \end{array}$$	$$\begin{array}{r} 197 \\ \times\ 48 \\ \hline 1\ 576 \\ 7\ 880 \\ \hline 9\ 456 \end{array}$$

The Trans-Siberian Railway is about 9456 km long.

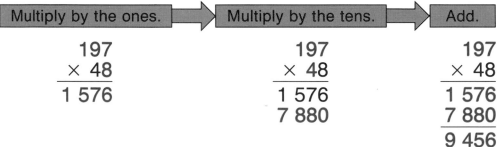

| We can estimate to check our answers. | $$\begin{array}{r} 197 \\ \times\ 48 \end{array}$$ | rounds to | $$\begin{array}{r} 200 \\ \times\ \ 50 \\ \hline 10\ 000 \end{array}$$ | Since 9456 is close to 10 000, our answer is reasonable. |

Other examples:

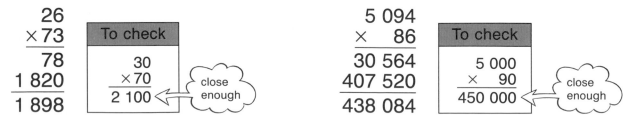

$$\begin{array}{r} 26 \\ \times 73 \\ \hline 78 \\ 1\ 820 \\ \hline 1\ 898 \end{array}$$

To check
$$\begin{array}{r} 30 \\ \times 70 \\ \hline 2\ 100 \end{array}$$ close enough

$$\begin{array}{r} 5\ 094 \\ \times\ \ \ \ 86 \\ \hline 30\ 564 \\ 407\ 520 \\ \hline 438\ 084 \end{array}$$

To check
$$\begin{array}{r} 5\ 000 \\ \times\ \ \ \ 90 \\ \hline 450\ 000 \end{array}$$ close enough

86

Do only those questions with products greater than 3000.

1. 85
   ×42

2. 65
   ×55

3. 38
   ×87

4. 49
   ×72

5. 71
   ×41

6. 92
   ×64

7. 29
   ×86

8. 46
   ×59

9. 87
   ×52

10. 47
   ×65

Do only those questions with products greater than 30 000.

11. 425
   × 82

12. 628
   × 59

13. 509
   × 72

14. 697
   × 46

15. 829
   × 48

16. 987
   × 37

17. 613
   × 54

18. 850
   × 38

19. 529
   × 65

20. 739
   × 43

Do only those questions with products greater than 300 000.

21. 2 589
   ×   82

22. 3 099
   ×   98

23. 4 923
   ×   52

24. 6 899
   ×   42

25. 3 197
   ×   97

ESTIMATING

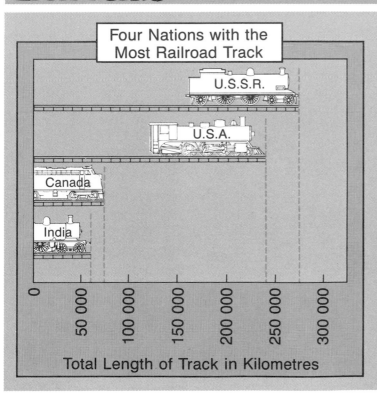

Four Nations with the Most Railroad Track

U.S.S.R.

U.S.A.

Canada

India

0   50 000   100 000   150 000   200 000   250 000   300 000

Total Length of Track in Kilometres

Use visual estimation to complete each sentence.

1. The U.S.A. has about ▨ times as much track as India.

2. The U.S.A. has about ▨ times as much track as Canada.

3. The U.S.S.R. has about ▨ times as much track as Canada.

4. The U.S.S.R. has about ▨ times as much track as India.

Use a ruler to check your answers.

87

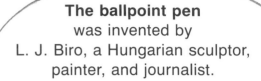

JUST FOR FUN

Many of the objects we use every day have been invented in the last 150 years. To find the year of each invention, calculate the given product.

Which of these everyday objects was invented last?

The ballpoint pen
was invented by
L. J. Biro, a Hungarian sculptor,
painter, and journalist.

Year invented: **2 × 3 × 17 × 19**

The zipper
was patented by
W. L. Judson. It was developed
as a fastener for the shoes of
a friend with a sore back.

Year invented: **3 × 631**

The safety pin
was created by
W. Hunt from a brass wire 20 cm
long. He sold the rights to his
invention for $450.00.

Year invented: **43 × 43**

The pencil eraser
became an everyday
item when H. L. Lipman
patented a pencil with an
eraser glued to one end.

Year invented: **2 × 929**

The shopping bag
was invented by
W. Deubner. Within 3 years,
he had sold over
1 000 000 of them.

Year invented:
2 × 2 × 2 × 239

88

PROBLEM SOLVING

Identifying Relevant Information

To solve these problems, you will need to use information from page 88.

1. In what century were the safety pin, the zipper, and the pencil eraser invented?

2. How long a strip of brass wire would be needed to make 10 000 safety pins identical to the one invented by W. Hunt?

3. How many zippers would be needed for 45 pairs of boots and 84 coats?

4. A store sells 2987 ballpoint pens at an average cost of $1.98. What is the approximate amount of money collected from this sale?

5. How many years after the invention of the zipper was the ballpoint pen invented?

6. How old will you be when the shopping bag has been in use for exactly 100 years?

7. The Rub Out Pencil Company packs 125 pencils in a box and 48 boxes in a case. How many pencils would there be in 10 cases?

8. Walter Deubner sold his shopping bags for 5¢ each. How much would he have collected on the sale of 1 000 000 shopping bags?

Multiplying by a Multiple of 100

The first crossing of the Atlantic Ocean by ship lasted over 2 months.
Today the Concorde jet can fly the Atlantic Ocean in about 3 h!

While the Concorde is the world's fastest passenger plane,
the jumbo jet is the largest of all passenger planes.
A modern jumbo jet can carry up to 500 passengers.

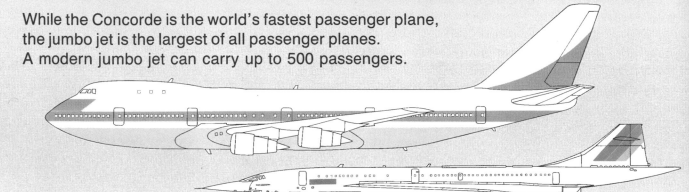

If the 327 jumbo jets in the world today were filled
to capacity, how many people could they transport?

To multiply 327 by 500:

Multiply by the ones.	Multiply by the tens.	Multiply by the hundreds.
327 × 500 —— 0	327 × 500 —— 00	327 × 500 ———— 163 500

We write

327
× 500

instead of

500
× 327

because it simplifies
the multiplication.

The 327 jumbo jets could carry a total of about 163 500 people.

Another example:

To multiply 4239 by 600:

Multiply by the ones.	Multiply by the tens.	Multiply by the hundreds.
4 239 × 600 —— 0	4 239 × 600 —— 00	4 239 × 600 ————— 2 543 400

Multiply mentally and record your answers.

1. 300
×200

2. 800
×300

3. 600
×500

4. 600
×400

5. 700
×600

6. 800
×700

7. 600
×900

8. 800
×500

9. 900
×900

10. 500
×400

Multiply. Do only those questions with products greater than 400 000.

11. 375
×200

12. 685
×700

13. 829
×600

14. 397
×900

15. 587
×700

16. 780
×800

17. 527
×500

18. 669
×700

19. 546
×800

20. 489
×900

Multiply.

21. 8 476
× 200

22. 6 309
× 300

23. 2 879
× 400

24. 5 897
× 600

25. 7 156
× 500

EXTENSIONS

1. Copy and complete this multiplication table.

×	500	80	7
300			

2. Find the sum of the 3 products in your table.

3. Compare this sum with the product of 300 × 587. What do you discover?

4. Use a table like the one above to calculate each of these products.
   a) 800 × 438   b) 700 × 651

5. Copy and complete this multiplication table.

×	500	80	7
300			
20			

6. Find the sum of the 6 products in your table.

7. Use your calculator to compute 320 × 587. Compare your answer to the sum in question 6. What do you discover?

8. Use a table to calculate each of these products.
   a) 280 × 159   b) 450 × 213

ESTIMATING

Estimating Products:
3-Digit Multipliers

Humans have created vehicles to travel over the land, across the sea, and through the air. Only recently, vehicles for space travel have been invented. The power to send these vehicles into space comes from rockets such as Saturn V.

During liftoff, the Saturn V rocket burns 16 400 kg of fuel per second.

About how much does it burn during its 153 s liftoff?

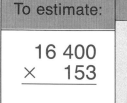

To estimate:	Round both factors to one non-zero digit.	Multiply.
16 400 × 153	16 400 → 20 000 153 → 200	20 000 × 200 4 000 000

The rocket burns about 4 000 000 kg of fuel during liftoff.

Estimate these products.

1. 378
   ×207

2. 526
   ×893

3. 793
   ×504

4. 481
   ×450

5. 392
   ×271

6. 8 686
   × 375

7. 6 091
   × 386

8. 8 327
   × 719

9. 4 861
   × 459

10. 7 777
    × 635

11. 9 846
    × 891

12. 8 903
    × 506

13. 6 521
    × 889

14. 98 462
    × 891

15. 12 240
    × 219

Multiplying by a 3-Digit Number

Calculate the amount of fuel Saturn V actually burns during liftoff.

Multiply by the ones. ⇒	Multiply by the tens. ⇒	Multiply by the hundreds. ⇒	Add.

$$
\begin{array}{r}
16\ 400 \\
\times\quad 153 \\
\hline
49\ 200
\end{array}
\qquad
\begin{array}{r}
16\ 400 \\
\times\quad 153 \\
\hline
49\ 200 \\
820\ 000
\end{array}
\qquad
\begin{array}{r}
16\ 400 \\
\times\quad 153 \\
\hline
49\ 200 \\
820\ 000 \\
1\ 640\ 000
\end{array}
\qquad
\begin{array}{r}
16\ 400 \\
\times\quad 153 \\
\hline
49\ 200 \\
820\ 000 \\
1\ 640\ 000 \\
\hline
2\ 509\ 200
\end{array}
$$

The Saturn V rocket burns 2 509 200 kg of fuel during liftoff.

Multiply.

1. $\begin{array}{r} 380 \\ \times 290 \end{array}$	2. $\begin{array}{r} 490 \\ \times 315 \end{array}$	3. $\begin{array}{r} 695 \\ \times 205 \end{array}$	4. $\begin{array}{r} 590 \\ \times 429 \end{array}$	5. $\begin{array}{r} 705 \\ \times 210 \end{array}$
6. $\begin{array}{r} 119 \\ \times 325 \end{array}$	7. $\begin{array}{r} 216 \\ \times 499 \end{array}$	8. $\begin{array}{r} 2\ 109 \\ \times\quad 210 \end{array}$	9. $\begin{array}{r} 3\ 130 \\ \times\quad 303 \end{array}$	10. $\begin{array}{r} 2\ 467 \\ \times\quad 666 \end{array}$

11. How far would a meteorite moving 42 km/s travel in an hour? There are 3600 s in one hour.

12. Meteorite A has a mass of 113 kg. The mass of Meteorite B is 46 kg greater than the mass of Meteorite A. If Meteorite C is 200 times as heavy as Meteorite B, what is the mass of Meteorite C?

13. Lightning travels to Earth at about 750 km/s. If people could travel at lightning speed, how far could they travel in one hour?

EXTENSIONS

Calculate.

$$
\begin{array}{r}
16\ 400 \\
\times\quad 153 \\
\hline
\end{array}
$$

Compare the product above with the estimate on page 92. Why are they so different?

Estimate the product using compensation. Is the estimate closer?

Solving a Simpler Related Problem

Karl Friedrich Gauss was a mathematical genius. The incident illustrated below occurred in Germany in 1787 when Karl was just 10 years old!

$1+2+3+4$
$+\dots$
$+97+98+99$
$+100=?$

"Karl, what is the sum of all the numbers from 1 to 100?"

Here it is, Professor.

Correct! How did you get it so fast?

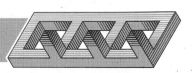

> *What is the sum of all the numbers from 1 through 100?*

To solve this problem...

A. First, make sure you understand the problem.

> *Discuss:*
>
> - *What numbers are to be added?*
> - *How many numbers are there?*

B. Then, think of strategies...
Try solving a simpler, related problem.

> - *Find the sum of the numbers from 1 to 6.*
>   *Write the numbers as shown.*
>   *Then add each pair.*
>
> $$6 + 5 + 4$$
> $$\underline{1} + \underline{2} + \underline{3}$$
>
> - *How many pairs are there?*
> - *What is the sum of each pair?*
> - *What is the sum of all the pairs?*
> - *What is a faster way than adding to find the sum of all the pairs?*

C. Solve the problem and answer the question.

> - *How many pairs of numbers are there in the numbers 1 to 100?*
>
> - *Write the numbers as shown:*
>
> $$1 + 2 + 3 + \ldots + 49 + 50$$
> $$\underline{100} + \underline{99} + \underline{98} + \ldots + \underline{52} + \underline{51}$$
>
> - *What is the sum of each pair?*
> - *What is the sum of all the pairs?*

D. Check your answer and discuss your solution.

> - *Is the sum of all the pairs the same as the sum of all the numbers from 1 to 100? Explain.*
> - *Give the explanation Karl might have given for how he got the answer so quickly.*
> - *How did solving a simpler, related problem help you solve the original problem?*

Use Karl's method to find the sum of the numbers from:

1. 1 to 10
2. 1 to 20
3. 1 to 50
4. 1 to 200

Use only your answers above to find the sum of the numbers from:

5. 11 to 20
6. 21 to 50
7. 51 to 100
8. 101 to 200

9. What is the sum of all the even numbers from 1 to 100?

10. What is the sum of all the odd numbers from 1 to 100?

11. What is the sum of the numbers from 1 to 99?

12. It is now 10:00 a.m. What time will it be 23 999 h from now?

EXPLORING
THE SOLAR SYSTEM

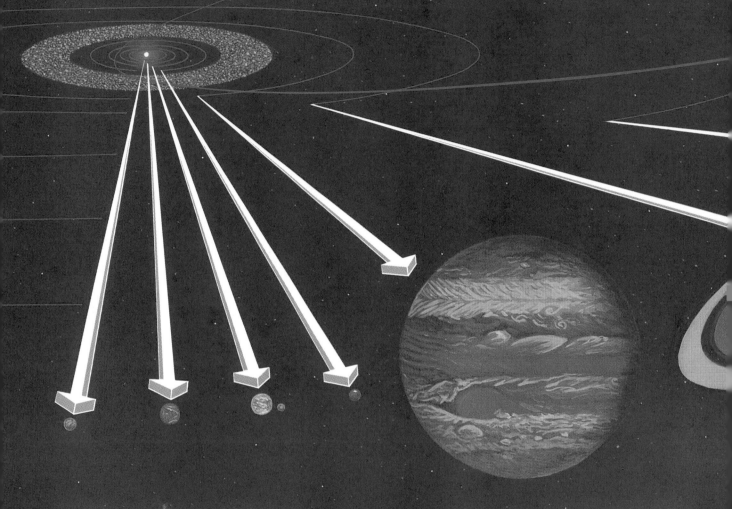

1. On June 13, 1983, the space probe Pioneer 10 became the first vehicle to leave the Solar System. It had been travelling at an average of 416 million kilometres per year for 11 years. How far did Pioneer travel in that time?

2. Halley's comet travels at a speed of about 3 km/s when farthest from the Sun. Its speed is about 50 km/s when nearest to the Sun. About how many times as fast is Halley's comet when nearest to the Sun?

Space probes have enabled us to obtain more information about our Universe.

3. Earth orbits the Sun at a speed of about 30 km/s. How far does Earth travel in one minute?

4. The highest known volcano in the Solar System is Olympus Mons on Mars. It is about 29 km high. The tallest volcano on Earth is about 7 km high. About how many times as tall is Olympus Mons?

5. The diameter of Neptune is about 48 000 km. This is about 4 times the diameter of Earth. What is the approximate diameter of Earth?

6. The diameter of Pluto is about 3000 km. The diameter of Earth is about 13 000 km. About how many times as great is Earth's diameter?

7. Our Solar System is about 4600 million years old. The Universe is about 4 times as old. About how many millions of years old is the Universe?

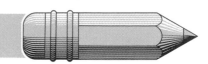

Multiply.

1. 90
   × 6

2. 800
   × 4

3. 600
   × 7

4. 3 000
   × 9

5. 7 000
   × 8

6. 20 000
   × 6

7. 63
   × 8

8. 82
   × 6

9. 709
   × 6

10. 641
    × 7

11. 586
    × 8

12. 1 463
    × 5

Multiply.

13. 50 × 70

14. 60 × 300

15. 70 × 400

16. 80 × 4 000

17. 82
    × 30

18. 63
    × 70

19. 89
    × 40

20. 369
    × 50

21. 625
    × 80

22. 4 168
    × 30

Estimate these products.

23. 62
    × 49

24. 81
    × 92

25. 79
    × 53

26. 578
    × 54

27. 359
    × 38

28. 3 015
    × 49

29. A cruise ship has a capacity of 1237 people. About how many people could be transported in 8 trips on this ship?

30. PCA Motorcycles ordered 65 boxes of motor oil. Each box contains 24 cans of oil. How many cans of oil were ordered?

Multiply.

31. 82
    × 45

32. 37
    × 88

33. 94
    × 62

34. 49
    × 56

35. 83
    × 75

36. 46
    × 29

37. 452
    × 28

38. 826
    × 49

39. 508
    × 63

40. 789
    × 36

41. 631
    × 45

42. 870
    × 37

Multiply.

43. 3 562
    × 28

44. 2 088
    × 89

45. 5 702
    × 43

46. 6 007
    × 36

47. 365
    × 200

48. 892
    × 600

49. 564
    × 800

50. 2 641
    × 300

51. 596
    × 315

52. 507
    × 305

53. Willowby Bikes bought 15 bicycles at a cost of $123 each. What was the total cost?

54. A jet carried 432 passengers from Toronto to Vancouver. On the return flight, 396 passengers were on board. How many more passengers flew from Toronto to Vancouver?

ODD OR EVEN

Odd or Even is a guessing game played in pairs. The players hold beans hidden in their hands. A correct guess of odd or even wins a bean. This game was popular in ancient Greece and Rome. Later, it became well known in England.

Artist's impression of Greece, 100 B.C.

Odd and Even Numbers

All products in the 2 times table are called **multiples of 2**.

×	1	2	3	4	5	6	7	8	9	10	11	12	13	14
2	2	4	6	8	10	12	14	16	18	20	22	24	26	28

Numbers which are multiples of 2 are called **even numbers**.

Numbers which are not multiples of 2 are called **odd numbers**.

The Case of the Numbered Page

ALL THE RIGHT-HAND PAGES OF BOOKS HAVE ODD NUMBERS.

ALL THE LEFT-HAND PAGES OF BOOKS HAVE EVEN NUMBERS.

1. Use the page numbers in this book to make 2 lists showing 10 even numbers and 10 odd numbers. Circle the last digit of each number in each list.

2. In an even number, what digits can be in the ones place?

3. In an odd number, what digits can be in the ones place?

Write *even* or *odd* for each number.

4. 2
5. 17
6. 80
7. 103
8. 369
9. 907
10. 2484
11. 0
12. 9000
13. 11 006
14. 17 285
15. 82 721

Write the smallest even number which is greater than each given number.

16. 21
17. 47
18. 86
19. 99
20. 240
21. 1998

PROBLEM SOLVING

Inspector Sherlock Homely was investigating an important case. A suspect told him that he found a secret note between pages 227 and 228 of the Crimestopper Handbook. How did Inspector Homely know that the suspect was lying?

Addition Properties of Even and Odd Numbers

STUDY THE ADDITION TABLE.

1. The numbers in the pink squares are sums of 2 even numbers. How are they alike?

2. The numbers in the uncoloured squares are sums of 2 odd numbers. How are they alike?

3. The numbers in the blue squares are sums of an even and an odd number. How are they alike?

4. Use your answers to questions 1, 2, and 3 to complete this table.

+	even	odd
even	even	
odd		

+	1	2	3	4	5	6	7	8	9	10
1	2	3	4	5	6	7	8	9	10	11
2	3	4	5	6	7	8	9	10	11	12
3	4	5	6	7	8	9	10	11	12	13
4	5	6	7	8	9	10	11	12	13	14
5	6	7	8	9	10	11	12	13	14	15
6	7	8	9	10	11	12	13	14	15	16
7	8	9	10	11	12	13	14	15	16	17
8	9	10	11	12	13	14	15	16	17	18
9	10	11	12	13	14	15	16	17	18	19
10	11	12	13	14	15	16	17	18	19	20

Without adding, tell whether the sum will be even or odd.

5.   216
   + 320

6.   3 851
   + 2 652

7.   5 105
   + 389

8.   8 208
   + 997

9.   284
   + 93

10. even
   + odd

11. even
   + even

12. odd
   + odd

13. odd
   + even

14. 382
   + 76

15. 327
     423
   + 648

16. 5 892
       620
     7 441
   +   837

17. odd
     even
     odd
   + odd

18. even
     odd
     even
   + odd

19. odd
     odd
     odd
   + odd

101

PROBLEM SOLVING

Using Logical Thinking

On the previous page, we discovered these
simple properties of even and odd numbers.

> The sum of 2 even numbers is an even number.
> The sum of 2 odd numbers is an even number.
> The sum of an even number and an odd number is an odd number.

Use these properties to help you
complete the sentences below.

Map of the Championship Cross Country Ski Tour

Aspen — 13 km → Birch — ? → Canyon — 18 km → Deadly Drop — 17 km → Echo

Aspen — ? → Gliding Glen — 24 km → Frosty Falls — 31 km → Echo

Write *even* or *odd* for each ▦ .

1. The shorter distance from Canyon to Echo is ▦ .

2. The shorter distance from Aspen to Canyon is an even number. The distance from Birch to Canyon is ▦ .

3. The shorter distance from Aspen to Frosty Falls is an odd number. The distance from Aspen to Gliding Glen is ▦ .

Hint: Trace the map and replace each distance with the word *even* or *odd*.

4. Glenna travelled an even number of kilometres from Aspen to Echo. What path did she take?

5. The total length of a round trip through every town exactly once is ▦ .

6. I.M. Turing travelled between 2 towns on the ski tour. He returned by the same route. The total distance travelled is ▦ .

Subtraction Properties of Even and Odd Numbers

STUDY THESE SUBTRACTION QUESTIONS.

Complete each of the following statements.
Write *even* or *odd* for each ▨▨▨ .

1. The difference between 2 even numbers is ▨▨▨ .
2. The difference between 2 odd numbers is ▨▨▨ .
3. The difference between an even and an odd number is ▨▨▨ .

Without subtracting, tell whether the difference will be even or odd.

4.	6 432	5.	9 003	6.	10 000	7.	3 651
	−1 398		−3 675		− 4 391		−2 888

8.	even	9.	odd	10.	odd	11.	even
	−odd		−even		−odd		−even

Copy and complete. Write *even* or *odd* for each ▨▨▨ .

12.	even	13.	▨▨▨	14.	▨▨▨	15.	odd
	−▨▨▨		−odd		−even		−▨▨▨
	odd		even		even		odd

103

Multiples of 3 and 9

All the numbers up to 99 whose digits add to a multiple of 3 are shaded in this chart.

The shaded numbers are also multiples of 3.

A number is a multiple of 3 if the sum of its digits is a multiple of 3.

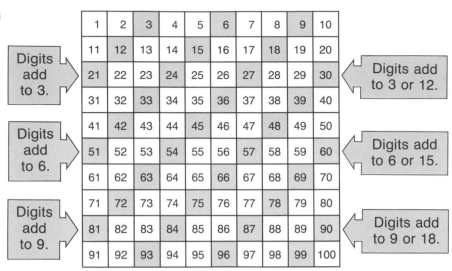

All the numbers up to 99 whose digits add to a multiple of 9 are shaded in this chart.

The shaded numbers are also multiples of 9.

A number is a multiple of 9 if the sum of its digits is a multiple of 9.

Is the number a multiple of 3? Write *yes* or *no* for each.

1. 101   2. 108   3. 113   4. 246   5. 319   6. 512
7. 600   8. 629   9. 729   10. 919   11. 2716   12. 8556

Is the number a multiple of 9? Write *yes* or *no* for each.

13. 109   14. 218   15. 318   16. 495   17. 567   18. 991
19. 1998   20. 3074   21. 5259   22. 6084   23. 7884   24. 8568

Multiples of 5 and 10

NO PENNIES PLEASE!

NO PENNIES PLEASE

A vending machine that accepts only nickels, dimes, and quarters can collect only amounts which are multiples of 5.

The shaded squares show the multiples of 5 up to 100. These are the only possible amounts in cents that can be collected by the machine.

1	2	3	4	5	6	7	8	9	10
11	12	13	14	15	16	17	18	19	20
21	22	23	24	25	26	27	28	29	30
31	32	33	34	35	36	37	38	39	40
41	42	43	44	45	46	47	48	49	50
51	52	53	54	55	56	57	58	59	60
61	62	63	64	65	66	67	68	69	70
71	72	73	74	75	76	77	78	79	80
81	82	83	84	85	86	87	88	89	90
91	92	93	94	95	96	97	98	99	100

This 100-square shows that a number is a multiple of 5 if its last digit is 0 or 5.

Is the number a multiple of 5? Write *yes* or *no* for each.

1. 87
2. 352
3. 501
4. 553
5. 800
6. 455
7. 2495
8. 5503
9. 6300
10. 15 000

---

11. Write a sentence to explain how to recognize quickly whether a number is a multiple of 10.

Is the number a multiple of 10? Write *yes* or *no* for each.

12. 106
13. 200
14. 390
15. 408
16. 1000
17. 6000
18. 8210
19. 9905
20. 19 010

21. What amounts up to $1.00 can be collected by a vending machine that accepts only dimes?

PROBLEM SOLVING

A parking meter accepts only dimes and quarters but no nickels. Can the parking meter collect a total of $24.05?

If so, what is the fewest number of coins required to make this total?

Multiples of 4

Leap years were invented to make the calendar year match one revolution around the sun. The shaded numbers in the table below show all the leap years between 1901 and 1960.

1901	1902	1903	1904	1905	1906	1907	1908	1909	1910
1911	1912	1913	1914	1915	1916	1917	1918	1919	1920
1921	1922	1923	1924	1925	1926	1927	1928	1929	1930
1931	1932	1933	1934	1935	1936	1937	1938	1939	1940
1941	1942	1943	1944	1945	1946	1947	1948	1949	1950
1951	1952	1953	1954	1955	1956	1957	1958	1959	1960

These leap years are all multiples of 4.
We see that the multiples of 4 are:

19**04**,   19**08**,   19**12**,   19**16**,   19**20**,   . . .

4,   **8**,   **12**,   **16**,   **20**,   . . .

Also, the numbers formed by the last 2 digits are multiples of 4.

> A number is a multiple of 4 if the number formed by its last 2 digits is a multiple of 4.

Is the number a multiple of 4?
Write *yes* or *no* for each.

1. 26
2. 80
3. 104
4. 126
5. 180
6. 304
7. 486
8. 595
9. 810
10. 1000
11. 1664
12. 2116

The leap years between 1901 and 1999 are those which are multiples of 4.
Which of these are leap years?

13. 1960
14. 1964
15. 1982
16. 1972
17. 1970
18. 1978
19. 1967
20. 1986
21. 1980
22. 1962
23. 1950
24. 1958

EXTENSIONS

Before 1582, all years divisible by 4 were leap years. But the calendar year still did not match one revolution around the sun.

In 1582, a Vatican librarian calculated that a century year should be a leap year only when it is a multiple of 400. For example, 1600 is a leap year.
            1700 is not a leap year.

Is the year a leap year?
Write *yes* or *no* for each.

1. 1600
2. 1700
3. 1800
4. 1900
5. 2000
6. 3000

Divisibility Rules

There are 2 ways of asking whether 926 is a multiple of 4.

ONE WAY

OR

ANOTHER WAY

We ask:

Is there a whole number such that 926 = 4 × ■ ?

That is, is 926 a **multiple of 4**?

We ask:

Is there a remainder when 926 is divided by 4?

That is, is 926 **divisible by 4**?

For each of the rules for multiples.... there is a divisibility rule.

A number is a **multiple of 2** if its last digit is 0, 2, 4, 6, or 8.

A number is **divisible by 2** if its last digit is 0, 2, 4, 6, or 8.

A number is a **multiple of 3** if the sum of its digits is a multiple of 3.

A number is **divisible by 3** if the sum of its digits is divisible by 3.

A number is a **multiple of 4** if the number formed by its last 2 digits is a multiple of 4.

A number is **divisible by 4** if the number formed by its last 2 digits is divisible by 4.

A number is a **multiple of 5** if its last digit is 0 or 5.

A number is **divisible by 5** if its last digit is 0 or 5.

1. Write a rule to explain how to tell whether a number is divisible by 9.

2. Explain how to tell whether a number is divisible by 10.

3. Write the numbers in the list at the right which are divisible by:
   a) 2   b) 10   c) 4
   d) 5   e) 3   f) 9

4. Which numbers in the list are divisible by both 2 and 3?

   3300 780 80 145 928

   65 1823 42 100 2328

   800 38 4512 26 1600

Common Multiples and the L.C.M.

In this 100-square,
- all the multiples of 6 are shaded.
- all the multiples of 9 are circled.

The numbers 18, 36, 54, 72, and 90 which are shaded and circled are multiples of both 6 and 9. They are called **common multiples** of 6 and 9.

The least of these common multiples is 18. It is called the **least common multiple** (L.C.M.) of 6 and 9.

1	2	3	4	5	6	7	8	9	10
11	12	13	14	15	16	17	18	19	20
21	22	23	24	25	26	27	28	29	30
31	32	33	34	35	36	37	38	39	40
41	42	43	44	45	46	47	48	49	50
51	52	53	54	55	56	57	58	59	60
61	62	63	64	65	66	67	68	69	70
71	72	73	74	75	76	77	78	79	80
81	82	83	84	85	86	87	88	89	90
91	92	93	94	95	96	97	98	99	100

1. a) Write the numbers from 1 to 26. Circle the multiples of 4. Draw a square around the multiples of 6.
   b) Write all the common multiples of 4 and 6 up to 26. Underline the least common multiple of 4 and 6.
2. a) Write all the multiples of 6 up to 100.
   b) Write all the multiples of 8 up to 100.
   c) Write all the common multiples of 6 and 8 up to 100. Underline the least common multiple.

For each pair of numbers,
- write the first 5 common multiples.
- underline the least common multiple.

3. 6 and 8
4. 2 and 3
5. 4 and 7
6. 2 and 5
7. 4 and 5
8. 6 and 10
9. 5 and 8
10. 4 and 10

PROBLEM SOLVING

Three comets, Alpha, Beta, and Gamma, return to our solar system at these times:

Alpha returns every 6 years.
Beta returns every 8 years.
Gamma returns every 9 years.

All 3 comets appeared in the year 1980.
In what year will all 3 comets next appear?

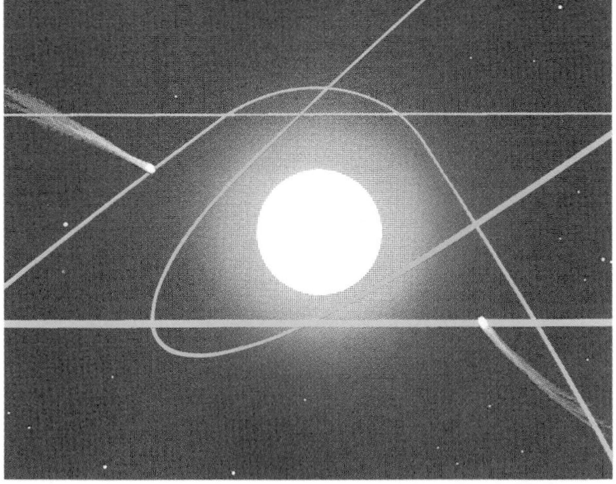

Even with use of leap years, the calendar year still does not match exactly the time for one revolution of the sun. If we did not make further adjustments, eventually summer would be in December!

RIDDLE:

How many years does it take the calendar year to be one full day out of line with the earth's period of revolution?

To answer this riddle, copy and complete the puzzle. Read the pink squares in the direction of the arrow.

HUMANS SURE MAKE LIFE COMPLICATED. THEY USE A FORMULA TO FIGURE OUT IF IT'S A LEAP YEAR.

HOW DO YOU FIND OUT WHETHER IT'S A LEAP YEAR?

I DON'T. I JUST LEAP WHENEVER I FEEL LIKE IT.

ACROSS	DOWN
A. largest multiple of 4 up to 99	A. largest multiple of 5 up to 99
B. last leap year in the 20th century	B. L.C.M. of 3 and 5
D. multiple of 5 between 81 and 89	C. largest 3-digit odd number
E. L.C.M. of 3 and 7	D. multiple of 9 between 80 and 89
F. largest multiple of 9 up to 400	E. L.C.M. of 5 and 25
H. largest multiple of 5 up to 19	F. first leap year in the 31st century
J. L.C.M. of 5 and 6	G. L.C.M. of 3, 4, and 5
K. first leap year in the 21st century	H. the year after the third leap year of this century
L. L.C.M. of 3, 4, and 11	J. L.C.M. of 3 and 10
P. last leap year in the 31st century	K. largest odd number up to 230
Q. L.C.M. of 6 and 8	M. L.C.M. of 2, 3, and 5
	N. largest multiple of 11 up to 50

Common Factors and the G.C.F.

Numbers multiplied together to form a product are called **factors** of the product.

$$3 \times 4 = 12$$

Factor   Factor   Product

The multiplication fact shows that 3 and 4 are factors of 12.

To find all the factors of 12, we think of all the multiplication facts with a product of 12.

Factors of 12

$12 = 1 \times 12 \longrightarrow$ **1, 12**
$12 = 2 \times 6 \longrightarrow$ **2, 6**
$12 = 3 \times 4 \longrightarrow$ **3, 4**

To find all the factors of 30, we think of all the multiplication facts with a product of 30.

Factors of 30

$30 = 1 \times 30 \longrightarrow$ **1, 30**
$30 = 2 \times 15 \longrightarrow$ **2, 15**
$30 = 3 \times 10 \longrightarrow$ **3, 10**
$30 = 5 \times 6 \longrightarrow$ **5, 6**

The factors of 12 are **1, 2, 3, 4, 6**, and **12**.

The factors of 30 are **1, 2, 3, 5, 6, 10, 15**, and **30**.

The numbers **1, 2, 3**, and **6** are factors of both 12 and 30. They are called **common factors** of 12 and 30.

The number 6 is the greatest of the common factors. It is called the **greatest common factor** (G.C.F.) of 12 and 30.

Complete the multiplication facts.
Then list all the factors of each product.

1. $16 = 1 \times$ ▦
$16 = 2 \times$ ▦
$16 = 4 \times$ ▦

2. $24 = 1 \times$ ▦
$24 = 2 \times$ ▦
$24 = 3 \times$ ▦
$24 = 4 \times$ ▦

3. $32 = 1 \times$ ▦
$32 = 2 \times$ ▦
$32 = 4 \times$ ▦

4. $40 = 1 \times$ ▦
$40 = 2 \times$ ▦
$40 = 4 \times$ ▦
$40 = 5 \times$ ▦

Use the facts above to help you find the G.C.F. of each pair of numbers.

5. 16 and 24
6. 32 and 40
7. 12 and 24
8. 30 and 32
9. 16 and 30
10. 24 and 30
11. 12 and 32
12. 16 and 32

List all the factors of each number.

13. 21
14. 36
15. 35
16. 31
17. 60
18. 81
19. 96
20. 41

110

Prime and Composite Numbers

Any number which has only 2 factors (1 and itself) is called a **prime** number.

Any number greater than 1 which has more than 2 factors is called a **composite** number.

The shaded numbers in the 100-square are prime numbers. The remaining numbers (except 1) are composite.

A COMPOSITE NUMBER IS DIVISIBLE BY SOME NUMBER OTHER THAN ITSELF AND 1.

1	2	3	4	5	6	7	8	9	10
11	12	13	14	15	16	17	18	19	20
21	22	23	24	25	26	27	28	29	30
31	32	33	34	35	36	37	38	39	40
41	42	43	44	45	46	47	48	49	50
51	52	53	54	55	56	57	58	59	60
61	62	63	64	65	66	67	68	69	70
71	72	73	74	75	76	77	78	79	80
81	82	83	84	85	86	87	88	89	90
91	92	93	94	95	96	97	98	99	100

Write *prime* or *composite* for each of the following numbers.

1. 8
2. 12
3. 27
4. 37
5. 51
6. 69
7. 81
8. 97
9. 100
10. 105
11. 116
12. 113
13. 125
14. 129
15. 243
16. 290
17. 303
18. 999

19. There were between 20 and 28 people at a birthday party. The people could not be divided into groups of 2, 3, 4 or 5 without leftovers. How many people were at the party?

20. Stacey looked at the calendar. The days of the month were arranged in 4 equal rows. What month was it?

JUST FOR FUN

Find a path from START to FINISH which passes only through spaces containing prime numbers.

Write in order the prime numbers in your path.

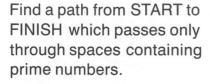

Start	13	213	53	17	83
99	29	77	73	33	79
7	41	63	19	291	101
59	175	23	67	700	61
37	97	103	91	111	Finish

Factor Trees

Every composite number can be written as a product of at least 2 prime numbers. For example,

$$21 = 3 \times 7 \quad \text{and} \quad 12 = 2 \times 2 \times 3$$

To write 20 as a product of primes, we first write 20 as a product of 2 factors.

5 is a prime number so we leave it as is. 4 is a composite number so we write it as 2×2.

Since 5 and 2 are prime factors, we have a completed **factor tree**. The factor tree helps us write 20 as a product of prime numbers.

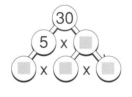

We write: $20 = 5 \times 2 \times 2$

Copy and complete each factor tree. Then use the factor tree to write each number as a product of prime factors.

Note: The number 1 is not used in factor trees.

1.

$21 = 7 \times \blacksquare$

2.

$35 = 5 \times \blacksquare$

3.

$55 = 5 \times \blacksquare$

4.

$14 = \blacksquare \times \blacksquare$

5.

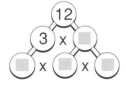

$12 = 3 \times \blacksquare \times \blacksquare$

6.

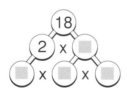

$18 = 2 \times \blacksquare \times \blacksquare$

7.

$30 = 5 \times \blacksquare \times \blacksquare$

8.

$28 = 7 \times \blacksquare \times \blacksquare$

9.

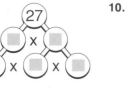

$27 = \blacksquare \times \blacksquare \times \blacksquare$

10.

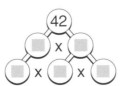

$42 = \blacksquare \times \blacksquare \times \blacksquare$

11.

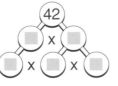

$45 = \blacksquare \times \blacksquare \times \blacksquare$

12.

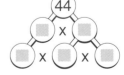

$44 = \blacksquare \times \blacksquare \times \blacksquare$

Copy and complete each factor tree.
Then write each number as a product of prime factors.

1.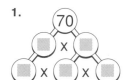

2.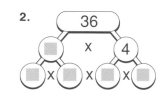

3.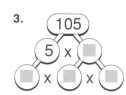

4.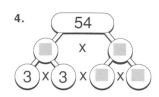

Draw a completed factor tree for each number.
Then write each number as a product of prime factors.

5. 56
6. 64
7. 81
8. 96
9. 72
10. 90
11. 120
12. 125
13. 180
14. 200
15. 250
16. 256

17. A shipment of 105 large boxes are to
be stacked in equal layers on a truck.
If the stack must be less than 5 layers
high, how many boxes are in each layer?

BITS AND BYTES

We can use the calculator
to help us factor large
numbers.

To factor 1989, follow these steps.

A. We think $1 + 9 + 8 + 9 = 27$, so
1989 is divisible by 9.

B. We enter

to obtain the factor 221.

C. Since 221 is not divisible by 2, 3, or 5,
we divide it by 7, 11, and then 13.

D. Division by 13 gives the quotient 17.

E. We write $1989 = 3 \times 3 \times 13 \times 17$.

Use your calculator to help you
write each number as a product
of prime factors.

1. 495
2. 567
3. 1395
4. 4608

113

PROBLEM SOLVING

Guessing and Checking

The 2 stamps shown were issued
to celebrate Expo 86 in Vancouver.
Ms. Esposito bought several of each kind
for a total of $7.45.
If she purchased 20 stamps in all, how
many of each type did she buy?

To solve this problem, . . .

A. First make sure you understand
the problem.

Discuss:

- *How many different types of
  stamps did Ms. Esposito buy?*
- *What was the cost of each type
  of stamp?*
- *How many stamps did she buy?*
- *What was the total cost of the
  stamps?*
- *What are you asked to find out?*

B. Then, think of strategies.

Try guessing and checking.

*Guess: Ms. Esposito bought 10
34¢ stamps and 10
39¢ stamps.*

*Check: Does this total 20 stamps?
Is the total cost equal to $7.45?*

34¢ Stamps	39¢ Stamps	Total Cost
10	10	$3.40 + $3.90 = $7.30

too low

C. Solve the problem and answer
the question.

$7.30 is less than $7.45.

- *Try another guess.*
- *Should you increase the number
  of 39¢ stamps or the number
  of 34¢ stamps?*

D. Check your answer and discuss
your solution.

- *Do you have a total of 20 stamps?*
- *Is the total cost $7.45?*
- *How many guesses did you have
  to make?*
- *How did the total cost change
  when you changed the number
  of each kind of stamp?*

Solve each problem.
Discuss your solutions.

1. Find 2 numbers which have a difference of 7 and a sum of 29.

2. Kim is 4 times as old as Jonathan. The product of their ages in years is 36. How old is Kim?

3. The prime number 41 is the sum of the 3 prime numbers 3, 7, and 31. That is,

$$41 = 3 + 7 + 31$$

Find 3 different prime numbers with the sum 41.

4. Find 3 consecutive whole numbers with a product of 720.

Remember: Whole numbers which differ by 1 are called **consecutive**. For example: 37, 38, and 39 are consecutive.

5. Adrian watched a bikeathon from his window. He counted a total of 14 bicycles and tricycles. These vehicles had a total of 39 wheels. How many tricycles did he count?

6. When the 6 people at a birthday party tried to share the prizes equally there was 1 left over. When another guest arrived they attempted once more to share those same prizes equally but this time there were 3 prizes left over. How many prizes were there?

7. Professor R. K. Ologist discovered some ancient artifacts. When she divided them into groups of 2, there was 1 left over. When she divided them into groups of 3, there was 1 left over. When she divided them into groups of 7, there was 1 left over. How many artifacts did she find?

Exponents

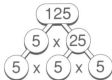

The factor tree for 125 shows that

$$125 = 5 \times 5 \times 5$$

To show that 125 is the product of
3 factors of 5 we use the **exponent 3**.

We write: $125 = 5^3$

Exponents provide a short way to write products with repeated factors.

The exponent tells how many times the factor is used in the product.

3^4 means $\underbrace{3 \times 3 \times 3 \times 3}$

4 factors of 3

Copy and complete.

1. $2 \times 2 \times 2 = 2^{\blacksquare}$
2. $7 \times 7 = 7^{\blacksquare}$
3. $4 \times 4 \times 4 = 4^{\blacksquare}$
4. $5 \times 5 \times 5 \times 5 = 5^{\blacksquare}$
5. $12 \times 12 \times 12 = 12^{\blacksquare}$
6. $10 \times 10 \times 10 = 10^{\blacksquare}$

Write each product using an exponent. Then complete the product.

7. $2 \times 2 \times 2 \times 2$
8. $8 \times 8 \times 8$
9. $6 \times 6 \times 6 \times 6 \times 6$
10. 19×19
11. $10 \times 10 \times 10 \times 10$
12. $3 \times 3 \times 3 \times 3 \times 3$

Use an exponent to tell how many small squares are in each large picture.
Then complete each product.

13.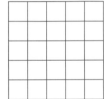

There are 5^2 or 25 squares.

14.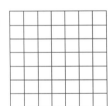

15.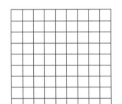

16.

Use an exponent to tell how many small cubes are in each picture.

17.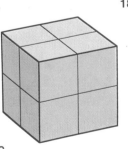

18.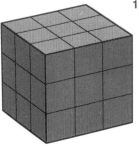

19.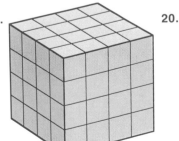

20.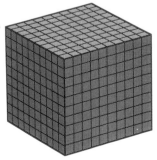

116

Powers of 10

Numbers like 10^2, 10^3, and 10^4 are called **powers** of 10. When we calculate powers of 10 we see a pattern.

$10^1 = 10$
$10^2 = 10 \times 10$ or 100
$10^3 = 10 \times 10 \times 10$ or 1000
$10^4 = 10 \times 10 \times 10 \times 10$ or $10\ 000$

We see that the exponent in a power of 10 tells us how many zeros follow the 1 when the product is calculated.

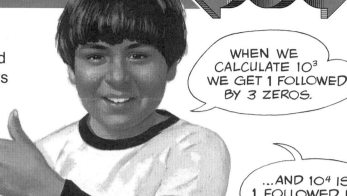

WHEN WE CALCULATE 10^3 WE GET 1 FOLLOWED BY 3 ZEROS.

...AND 10^4 IS 1 FOLLOWED BY 4 ZEROS.

We can write powers of 10 two ways:

the long way		the short way
The diameter of our galaxy is about 1 000 000 000 000 000 000 km.	and	The diameter is about 10^{18} km.

Write each number as a power of 10.

1. 10 000
2. 100 000
3. 10 000 000
4. 1 000 000
5. 100 000 000

Write each power of 10 as a number and in words.

6. 10^5
7. 10^7
8. 10^6
9. 10^{10}
10. 10^8

11. Copy and complete this table.

Name	Numeral	Power of Ten
1 million	1 000 000	▦
▦	1 000 000 000	10^9
1 trillion	1 000 000 000 000	▦
1 quadrillion	▦	10^{15}

EXTENSIONS

Order of Operations

SIR, YOU HAVE WON A FAMILY TRIP TO WONDER WORLD IF YOU CAN ANSWER THIS SKILL-TESTING QUESTION...

...WHAT IS THE VALUE OF TEN MINUS TWO TIMES THREE?

I THINK THE ANSWER IS 24.

NO, IT'S NOT. IT'S...

...FORE!

FORE?

CRASH!!

CONGRATULATIONS! THE ANSWER IS FOUR!

Mathematicians found a problem when they began writing mixed operations like:

$$10 - 2 \times 3$$

Some people thought it meant
"Subtract 2 from 10, then multiply the difference by 3."
They got the answer 24.

Others thought it meant
"Subtract the product of 2 and 3 from 10."
They got the answer 4.

To clarify the meaning of such expressions, mathematicians agreed to these rules for the **order of operations**.

1. First perform all multiplications and divisions in order from left to right:
$$10 - \mathbf{2 \times 3} = 10 - \mathbf{6}$$

2. Then perform all additions and subtractions in order from left to right.
$$10 - \mathbf{6} = \mathbf{4}$$

118

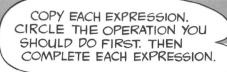

COPY EACH EXPRESSION. CIRCLE THE OPERATION YOU SHOULD DO FIRST. THEN COMPLETE EACH EXPRESSION.

1. $6 + 3 \times 5$

1. $6 + (3 \times 5)$
$= 6 + 15$
$= 21$

2. $9 - 2 \times 3$
4. $8 \div 2 + 2$
6. $27 - 7 \times 3$
8. $8 + 16 \div 4 \times 2$
10. $100 + 10 \times 5 + 2$

3. $8 \times 3 - 2$
5. $2 + 8 \times 3$
7. $15 \div 3 + 2$
9. $40 - 10 \times 3 + 2$
11. $50 - 25 \div 5 + 5$

Write a number expression for each.
Then find the value of each expression.

12. five plus two times four
14. ten minus two times five
16. three more than four times six

13. one plus three times six
15. six times eight minus two
17. two times nine divided by three

BITS AND BYTES

Many calculators are made to follow the order of operations. If you enter the numbers and the operations in order from left to right, the calculator gives the correct answer.

Try these on your calculator.

`1` `2` `÷` `6` `÷` `2` `=`

Is the display 1?

`5` `+` `3` `×` `2` `=`

Is the display 11?

Use your calculator to evaluate these expressions.

A. $231 - 196 \div 49$
B. $109 \times 6 \div 3$
C. $1024 \div 8 \div 4 \div 2$
D. $2187 \div 9 \div 81 - 3$
E. $3600 + 6400 \div 512 \times 2$
F. $375 - 15\,625 \div 5 \div 5 \div 5 \times 3$
G. $312 \times 426 - 312 \times 420$
H. $867 + 246 \div 30 - 75 - 6 \div 5$

If your calculator gave the correct answers, it follows the order of operation rules.

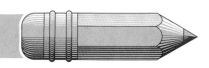

Tell whether each number is *even* or *odd*.

1. 68
2. 319
3. 4650

Which numbers are multiples of 4?

4. 19
5. 36
6. 42
7. 84
8. 532
9. 617
10. 3428
11. 5324
12. 4738

Which numbers are multiples of 9?

13. 72
14. 172
15. 351
16. 1764
17. 8568
18. 9359

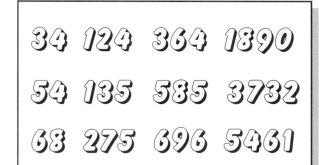

Write the numbers in the above list that are divisible by:

19. 2
20. 4
21. 5
22. 3
23. 9

Which numbers in the list are divisible by:

24. 3 and 9?
25. 3 and 4?

Write the least common multiple for each pair of numbers.

26. 3 and 8
27. 5 and 8
28. 4 and 9
29. 3 and 7

List the factors of each number.

30. 36
31. 28
32. 54
33. 42

Find the greatest common factor of each pair of numbers.

34. 36 and 54
35. 28 and 42
36. 28 and 54
37. 36 and 42

Write *prime* or *composite* for each of the following numbers.

38. 13
39. 21
40. 2
41. 103
42. 131
43. 363
44. 585
45. 233
46. 759

Copy and complete each factor tree.

47.

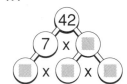

48.

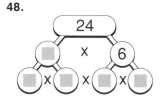

Draw a factor tree for each number. Then write it as a product of prime factors.

49. 63
50. 84
51. 102

Copy and complete.

52. $3 \times 3 \times 3 = 3^{\blacksquare}$
53. $5 \times 5 \times 5 \times 5 \times 5 = 5^{\blacksquare}$

54. Find 2 numbers which have a sum of 18 and a product of 72.

120

6

CAT'S CRADLE

Cat's Cradle is a popular pastime among the Inuit. The game is played with a piece of string tied to form a loop. The players manipulate the string with their fingers to form a variety of designs.

▲ This shows a geometric design.

▲ This is a caribou.

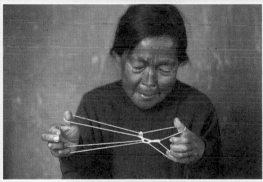

▲ Here a snow bunting "flies" along the string.

▲ This design shows charging musk oxen.

▲ Here is a fox with a bushy tail.

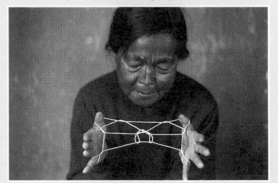

▲ This design shows two houses.

Photographed by Bryan Alexander, at Thule District, Greenland, July/August 1980.

From Multiplication to Division

Each division fact has a related multiplication fact.

The division fact ...   is related to ...   the multiplication fact

$$4\overline{)32}^{\,8}$$

$$4 \times 8 = 32$$

32 books in 4 equal stacks makes 8 in each stack.

4 stacks of 8 books makes 32 books in all.

We can use known multiplication facts to find quotients.

We see: $8\overline{)72}$	We see: $7\overline{)280}$
We think: $8 \times 9 = 72$	We think: $7 \times 40 = 280$
We write: $8\overline{)72}^{\,9}$	We write: $7\overline{)280}^{\,40}$

Copy and complete. Think of a related multiplication sentence.

1. $7\overline{)56}$ 　　2. $9\overline{)63}$ 　　3. $8\overline{)64}$ 　　4. $9\overline{)54}$ 　　5. $7\overline{)560}$

6. $9\overline{)630}$ 　　7. $8\overline{)640}$ 　　8. $9\overline{)540}$ 　　9. $7\overline{)5600}$ 　　10. $9\overline{)6300}$

11. $8\overline{)6400}$ 　　12. $9\overline{)5400}$ 　　13. $6\overline{)480}$ 　　14. $5\overline{)400}$ 　　15. $4\overline{)160}$

16. $3\overline{)90}$ 　　17. $2\overline{)600}$ 　　18. $7\overline{)4900}$ 　　19. $3\overline{)1800}$ 　　20. $4\overline{)8000}$

---

21. A group of 180 sailors is divided into 9 equal crews. How many sailors are in each crew?

22. A colony of settlers travelled 630 km in 7 days. What was the average distance travelled per day?

23. If 560 sled dogs are divided into teams of 8, how many dog teams will there be?

24. A bag of about 2400 seeds were planted in 4 fields. What was the average number of seeds planted in each field?

ESTIMATING

Estimating 1-Digit Quotients

A group of 70 explorers decided to divide into search parties.

If each search party must have at least 9 members, what is the greatest number of search parties possible?

We ask:
How many 9s are in 70?

We think:
$9\overline{)63}$ ← **Largest multiple of 9 up to 70**

We say: There are **exactly** 7 9s in 63.
There are **about** 7 9s in 70.

We write: $9\overline{)70}^{\,7}$ 7 search parties can be formed from 70 explorers.

Estimate.

1. $3\overline{)13}$ 2. $5\overline{)17}$ 3. $7\overline{)24}$ 4. $6\overline{)50}$ 5. $4\overline{)31}$

6. $7\overline{)50}$ 7. $3\overline{)25}$ 8. $4\overline{)30}$ 9. $5\overline{)41}$ 10. $7\overline{)59}$

Estimate.

11. $59 \div 6$ 12. $30 \div 8$ 13. $29 \div 6$ 14. $41 \div 7$ 15. $50 \div 9$
16. $49 \div 8$ 17. $33 \div 7$ 18. $65 \div 9$ 19. $71 \div 8$ 20. $80 \div 9$

21. Each canoe requires 4 paddles. From a collection of 30 paddles, how many canoes can be equipped?

22. A map costs $3.00. How many maps can be bought with $20.00?

23. A search party bought some paddles. Brand A cost $18 and Brand B cost $21. If they saved $24 by buying only Brand A, how many paddles did they buy?

PROBLEM SOLVING

A group of explorers built 6 canoes. When they attempted to divide into 6 equal groups there were 2 people left over.

One canoe was damaged so they divided into 5 equal groups and paddled away in the remaining canoes.
How many explorers were there?

Estimating Quotients: 1-Digit Divisors

Many scientists believe that about 25 000 years ago, people living in Siberia crossed over from Asia to Alaska. They were probably the first people to discover North America, and became the first inhabitants of Canada.

Some of their descendants spread across Canada to the United States and into Latin America. These people are known as Indians. Today there are about 400 000 registered Indians living in Canada.

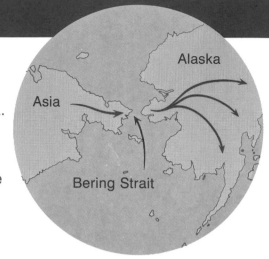

A narrow channel of water called the Bering Strait separates Asia from North America.

In a recent 3-month period, there were 16 200 newly-registered Indians. Estimate the average number registered each month.

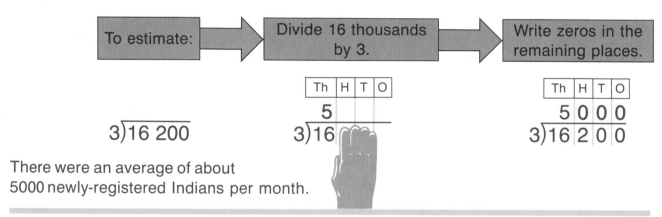

| To estimate: | Divide 16 thousands by 3. | Write zeros in the remaining places. |

$$3\overline{)16\ 200}$$

Th	H	T	O
	5		

$3\overline{)16}$

Th	H	T	O
5	0	0	0

$3\overline{)16\ 2\ 0\ 0}$

There were an average of about 5000 newly-registered Indians per month.

Another example:

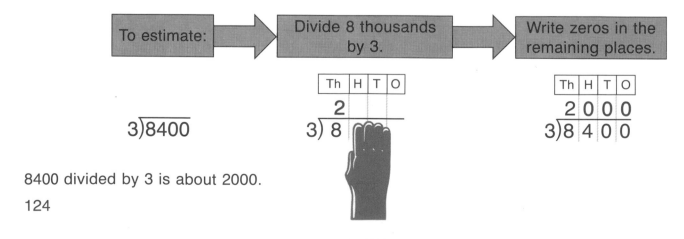

| To estimate: | Divide 8 thousands by 3. | Write zeros in the remaining places. |

$$3\overline{)8400}$$

Th	H	T	O
	2		

$3\overline{)8}$

Th	H	T	O
2	0	0	0

$3\overline{)8\ 4\ 0\ 0}$

8400 divided by 3 is about 2000.

Photographs courtesy of The Ojibway and Cree Cultural Centre.

Estimate.

1. 3)211

$$\frac{70}{3)211}$$

2. 3)62

3. 2)83
4. 5)56
5. 4)85

6. 8)170
7. 6)132
8. 9)183

9. 4)168
10. 5)269
11. 3)281

12. 5)426
13. 9)370
14. 8)500

15. 6)710
16. 6)320
17. 7)497

18. 4)2900
19. 3)2250
20. 5)4125

21. 6)7210
22. 9)5850
23. 8)4930

Estimate.

24. 9309 ÷ 9
25. 25 000 ÷ 8
26. 18 200 ÷ 3
27. 65 000 ÷ 8
28. 64 000 ÷ 3
29. 94 625 ÷ 4

30. Snowshoes vary in shape and size, according to the type of snow they are used on. Cree snowshoes are almost like skis, to walk on the hard, flat snow of the western Prairie. A pair of Cree snowshoes have a total length of 369 cm. Estimate the length of 1 snowshoe.

BITS AND BYTES

1. Use your calculator to find the quotients in questions 26, 27, 28, and 29.

2. Compare the quotients with your estimates. For which question was your estimate:

   a) closest to the quotient?
   b) farthest from the quotient?

PROBLEM SOLVING

Solving Multi-Step Problems

Today's fastest ships travel at speeds of 18 m/s (metres per second). At this rate, about how many days would it take for a ship to travel a distance of 6300 km across the Atlantic Ocean?

To solve this problem,...

A. First make sure you understand the problem.

Discuss:

- *How far must the ship travel to cross the Atlantic Ocean?*
- *What speed can the ship travel?*
- *What are you asked to find?*
- *How many hours are in one day? minutes are in one hour? seconds are in one minute?*
- *How many metres are in one kilometre?*

B. Then, think of strategies. Try to solve the problem by breaking it into steps.

- *First, find the speed of the ship in kilometres per hour.*
- *Then, find the number of hours to go 6300 km.*
- *Then, change the hours to days.*

C. Solve the problem and answer the question.

Use your calculator to help you answer these questions.

- *What is the speed of the ship*
    - *– in metres per second?*
    - *– in metres per hour?*
    - *– in kilometres per hour?*
- *What is the time for the trip*
    - *– in hours?*
    - *– in days?*

D. Check your answer and discuss your solution. Use your calculator to help you answer these questions.

- *Divide 6300 km by the number of days to find the average kilometres travelled per day.*
- *Divide the kilometres travelled per day by 24 to find the kilometres travelled per hour.*
- *Express kilometres per hour as metres per second.*
- *Is your answer close to 18 m/s?*
- *Once you knew kilometres per hour, what 2 different ways could you have finished solving the problem?*

Solve each problem by breaking it into steps. You may use your calculator.

1. Damion bought one magazine for 75¢ and another for $1.08. How much change will he receive from a $2-bill?

2. Write the missing digits in the dividend.

$$\begin{array}{r} 3\ 0\ 7 \text{ R37} \\ 46\overline{)\blacksquare\blacksquare\blacksquare\blacksquare\blacksquare} \end{array}$$

3. Calculate your age to the nearest week.

4. How many years old is a person who has lived for 1 million hours?

5. Express a speed of 9 m/s in kilometres per hour.

6. A Concorde jet crossed the Atlantic Ocean in 3 h at an average speed of 585 m/s. How far did it travel?

Dividing: 1-Digit Divisors

Other descendants of the earliest inhabitants lived in Alaska, northern Canada, and Greenland. They are known as **Inuit**. The Inuit are known for their ability to survive the harsh northern climate. They are also world famous for their art.

A recent census found that there are 27 000 Inuit in Canada. About one quarter of them live in Labrador and northern Québec.

About how many Inuit live in Labrador and Northern Québec?

We think: To find one quarter of 27 000, we divide 27 000 into 4 equal groups.

To divide 27 000 by 4:

| Divide the thousands. | → | Divide the hundreds. | → | Divide the tens. | → | Divide the ones. |

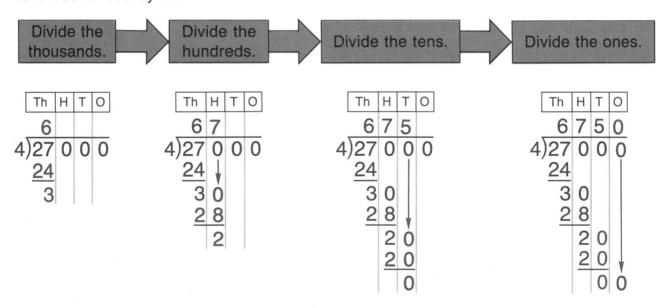

About 6750 Inuit live in Labrador and northern Québec.

Divide.

1. $8\overline{)77}$ 2. $6\overline{)46}$ 3. $9\overline{)84}$

4. $2\overline{)97}$ 5. $3\overline{)103}$ 6. $5\overline{)228}$

7. $7\overline{)369}$ 8. $6\overline{)585}$ 9. $9\overline{)868}$

10. $8\overline{)497}$ 11. $5\overline{)399}$ 12. $4\overline{)387}$

13. $3\overline{)528}$ 14. $4\overline{)769}$ 15. $6\overline{)696}$

16. $8\overline{)927}$ 17. $9\overline{)993}$ 18. $6\overline{)850}$

19. $4\overline{)2168}$ 20. $6\overline{)5036}$ 21. $5\overline{)3062}$

Divide.

22. $4862 \div 7$ 23. $2983 \div 8$ 24. $3766 \div 9$
25. $5874 \div 2$ 26. $9097 \div 4$ 27. $3962 \div 3$

Do only those questions with quotients less than 10 000.

28. $5\overline{)39\,760}$ 29. $6\overline{)57\,286}$ 30. $4\overline{)46\,100}$ 31. $3\overline{)29\,830}$ 32. $5\overline{)62\,951}$

33. $9\overline{)76\,900}$ 34. $8\overline{)72\,180}$ 35. $6\overline{)56\,860}$ 36. $4\overline{)65\,800}$ 37. $5\overline{)45\,555}$

38. On a hunting trip, Avataq caught 1 352 auks over a period of 4 days. What was the average number of auks caught each day by Avataq?

39. In Padlei, 6 women each designed an elaborate beaded coat made from caribou skin. The coats had a total mass of 283 kg. What was the average mass per coat?

PROBLEM SOLVING

The distance across the Bering Strait is about 120 km at one crossing point.

How many hours would it take to cross the Strait in a kayak travelling at 3 m/s?

Dividing: Zero in the Quotient

Probably the first Europeans to discover North America were the **Vikings** or **Norsemen**. They were skilled sailors and warriors from Norway, Sweden, and Denmark. Around the year 1000 A.D., Leif Ericson and his crew sailed from Norway bound for Greenland. However, they missed Greenland and landed in Labrador or Newfoundland.

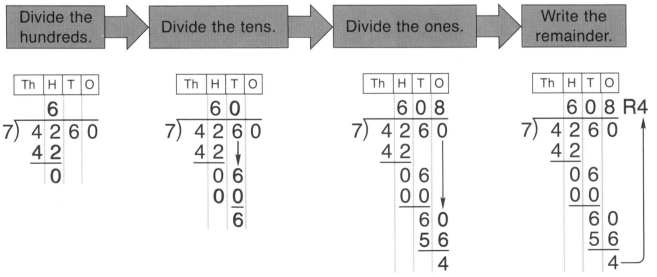

This is the earliest known map showing North America. It was copied over 500 years ago from maps made by the Vikings.

If Leif Ericson sailed 4260 km in 7 weeks, what was the average number of kilometres travelled per week?

To divide 4260 by 7:

| Divide the hundreds. | Divide the tens. | Divide the ones. | Write the remainder. |

Th	H	T	O
	6		

7) 4 2 6 0
   4 2
   ‾‾‾
      0

Th	H	T	O
	6	0	

7) 4 2 6 0
   4 2
   ‾‾‾
      0 6
      0 0
      ‾‾‾
        6

Th	H	T	O
	6	0	8

7) 4 2 6 0
   4 2
   ‾‾‾
      0 6
      0 0
      ‾‾‾
        6 0
        5 6
        ‾‾‾
          4

Th	H	T	O
	6	0	8	R4

7) 4 2 6 0
   4 2
   ‾‾‾
      0 6
      0 0
      ‾‾‾
        6 0
        5 6
        ‾‾‾
          4

Leif Ericson travelled an average of 608 km per week.

Another example: To divide 8033 by 4:

| Divide the thousands. | Divide the hundreds. | Divide the tens. | Divide the ones. |

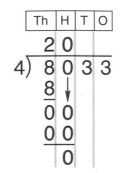

Th	H	T	O
2			

4)8033
8
0

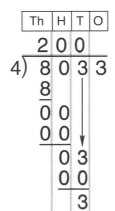

Th	H	T	O
2	0		

4)8033
8
00
00
0

Th	H	T	O
2	0	0	

4)8033
8
00
00
03
00
3

Th	H	T	O
2	0	0	8	R1

4)8033
8
00
00
03
00
33
32
1

Divide.

1. 2)821 2. 3)623 3. 5)650 4. 7)744 5. 6)927

6. 3)9030 7. 4)8315 8. 6)5919 9. 9)2033 10. 7)7420

11. 8)6137 12. 9)6507 13. 4)8037 14. 9)8175 15. 6)5756

Divide.

16. 12 051 ÷ 6   17. 81 923 ÷ 7   18. 39 283 ÷ 4   19. 14 007 ÷ 2

BITS AND BYTES

Find a path from Start which sails only through quotients which contain one or more zeros. On what continent do you finish?

Start	A 3)2428	B 8)5560	C 7)5653	D 6)8570	
			Europe		
E 2)1829	F 7)7695	G 6)4859	H 9)9553	I 5)1990	Africa
J 3)9270	K 4)8925	L 5)5560	M 4)1540	N 2)8237	
		Australia			

131

Short Division

WHEW! I'M READY TO EXPLORE A SHORTER METHOD FOR DOING DIVISION!

USE SHORT DIVISION! IT'S THE SAME AS LONG DIVISION BUT YOU WORK MENTALLY AND RECORD ONLY THE QUOTIENT AND THE REMAINDERS!

To divide:	Divide the hundreds.	Divide the tens.	Divide the ones.
$7\overline{)2\ 3\ 9\ 8}$	$7\overline{)2\ 3^29\ 8}$ quotient 3	$7\overline{)2\ 3^29^18}$ quotient $3\ 4$	$7\overline{)2\ 3^29^18}$ quotient $3\ 4\ 2$ R4

To check:
```
   342  ← Quotient
×    7  ← Divisor
  2394
+    4  ← Remainder
  2398  ← Dividend
```

If the division is correct,

divisor × quotient + remainder = dividend

Use short division to divide. Check each answer.

1. $5\overline{)241}$
2. $6\overline{)372}$
3. $4\overline{)289}$
4. $3\overline{)197}$
5. $7\overline{)549}$

6. $2\overline{)146}$
7. $4\overline{)580}$
8. $3\overline{)682}$
9. $5\overline{)547}$
10. $6\overline{)827}$

11. $8\overline{)2516}$
12. $7\overline{)4175}$
13. $9\overline{)1863}$
14. $3\overline{)8125}$
15. $4\overline{)9664}$

16. $3\overline{)6023}$
17. $5\overline{)1045}$
18. $9\overline{)1413}$
19. $7\overline{)22\ 680}$
20. $6\overline{)12\ 288}$

Use short division to divide. Check each answer.

21. $749 \div 3$
22. $867 \div 6$
23. $4908 \div 8$
24. $5491 \div 5$
25. $8605 \div 2$
26. $19\ 287 \div 6$
27. $54\ 829 \div 9$
28. $6832 \div 6$

JUST FOR FUN

RIDDLE: How did the Vikings communicate?

Divide.

A. $3\overline{)695}$ B. $4\overline{)736}$ C. $9\overline{)357}$ D. $6\overline{)409}$ E. $5\overline{)742}$

F. $2\overline{)499}$ G. $3\overline{)968}$ H. $4\overline{)993}$ J. $8\overline{)667}$ K. $5\overline{)199}$

L. $9\overline{)807}$ M. $8\overline{)671}$ N. $4\overline{)2908}$ O. $7\overline{)5803}$ P. $5\overline{)1697}$

Q. $9\overline{)8186}$ R. $2\overline{)5919}$ S. $4\overline{)9327}$ T. $6\overline{)4099}$ U. $8\overline{)2697}$

V. $2\overline{)8659}$ W. $3\overline{)9178}$ X. $9\overline{)61\ 038}$ Y. $7\overline{)14\ 063}$ Z. $6\overline{)12\ 666}$

To solve the riddle, write the letters of the questions with these answers.

184   2009   727   829   2959 R1   2331 R3   148 R2

39 R6   829   68 R1   148 R2

Dividing: Using Equivalent Division Facts

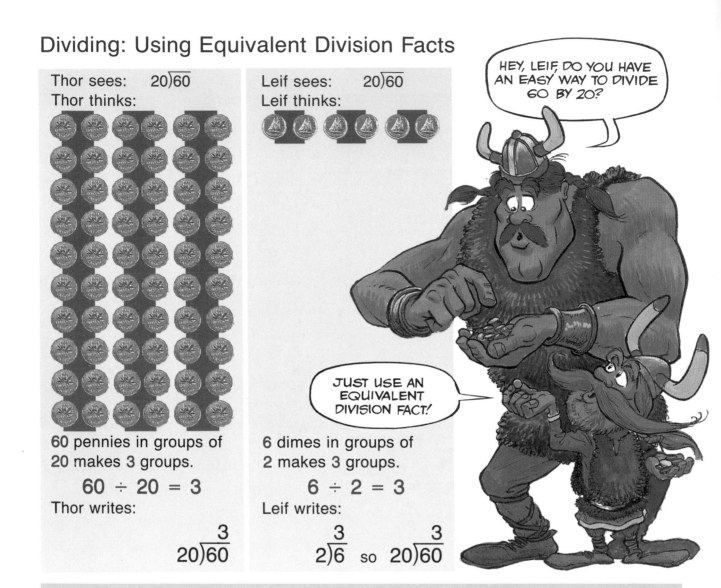

Thor sees: $20\overline{)60}$
Thor thinks:

60 pennies in groups of
20 makes 3 groups.

$$60 \div 20 = 3$$

Thor writes:

$$20\overline{)60}^{\,3}$$

Leif sees: $20\overline{)60}$
Leif thinks:

6 dimes in groups of
2 makes 3 groups.

$$6 \div 2 = 3$$

Leif writes:

$$2\overline{)6}^{\,3} \quad \text{so} \quad 20\overline{)60}^{\,3}$$

HEY, LEIF, DO YOU HAVE AN EASY WAY TO DIVIDE 60 BY 20?

JUST USE AN EQUIVALENT DIVISION FACT!

This example shows that $20\overline{)60}$ and $2\overline{)6}$ have the same quotient. They are called **equivalent division facts**.

We can use equivalent division facts to complete division questions with numbers that end in zero.

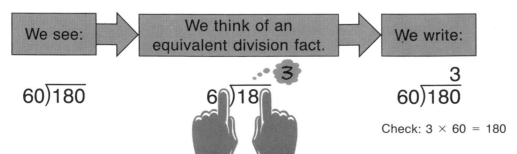

We see: → We think of an equivalent division fact. → We write:

$$60\overline{)180}$$

$$6\overline{)18}^{\,3}$$

$$60\overline{)180}^{\,3}$$

Check: $3 \times 60 = 180$

134

Think of an equivalent division fact.
Then complete the given division question.

Multiply the divisor by the quotient
to check each answer.

1. $20\overline{)80}$

$\quad\quad 4$
$_1 20\overline{)80}$
Check
$4 \times 20 = 80$

2. $30\overline{)90}$

3. $20\overline{)100}$

4. $10\overline{)80}$

5. $70\overline{)210}$

6. $40\overline{)280}$

7. $50\overline{)400}$

8. $80\overline{)400}$

9. $20\overline{)600}$

10. $90\overline{)630}$

11. $60\overline{)240}$

12. $30\overline{)270}$

13. $40\overline{)800}$

14. $20\overline{)6000}$

15. $90\overline{)6300}$

16. $60\overline{)2400}$

17. $30\overline{)2700}$

18. $40\overline{)8000}$

19. $30\overline{)15\,000}$

20. $70\overline{)21\,000}$

21. $40\overline{)16\,000}$

22. $50\overline{)40\,000}$

23. $60\overline{)54\,000}$

Divide.

24. $160 \div 40$

25. $480 \div 80$

26. $3600 \div 90$

27. $4800 \div 60$

28. $2800 \div 70$

29. $30\,000 \div 30$

30. $80\,000 \div 40$

31. $60\,000 \div 60$

32. If 10 people share equally in an inheritance of $100 000, how much does each receive?

33. How many payments of $80 are needed to total $4800?

JUST FOR FUN

The Viking explorers had no compasses. They used the stars for navigation.

The product of the vertices of the star triangle below is $4 \times 9 \times 5 = 180$

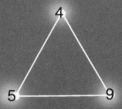

In the star map, the product of the vertices of every triangle is 180.

Write the number which each letter represents.

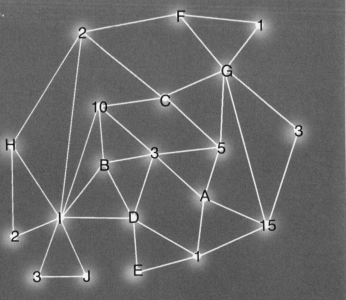

135

ESTIMATING

Estimating Quotients: Divisor a Multiple of 10

Christopher Columbus sailed from Palos, Spain, on August 3, 1492, in search of a route to the East Indies. He landed instead in the West Indies on October 12, 1492.

Following exploration of these islands, he and his crew returned to Spain on March 15, 1493, after a journey of 224 days!

About how many months long was this first voyage of Columbus? (There are about 30 days in a month.)

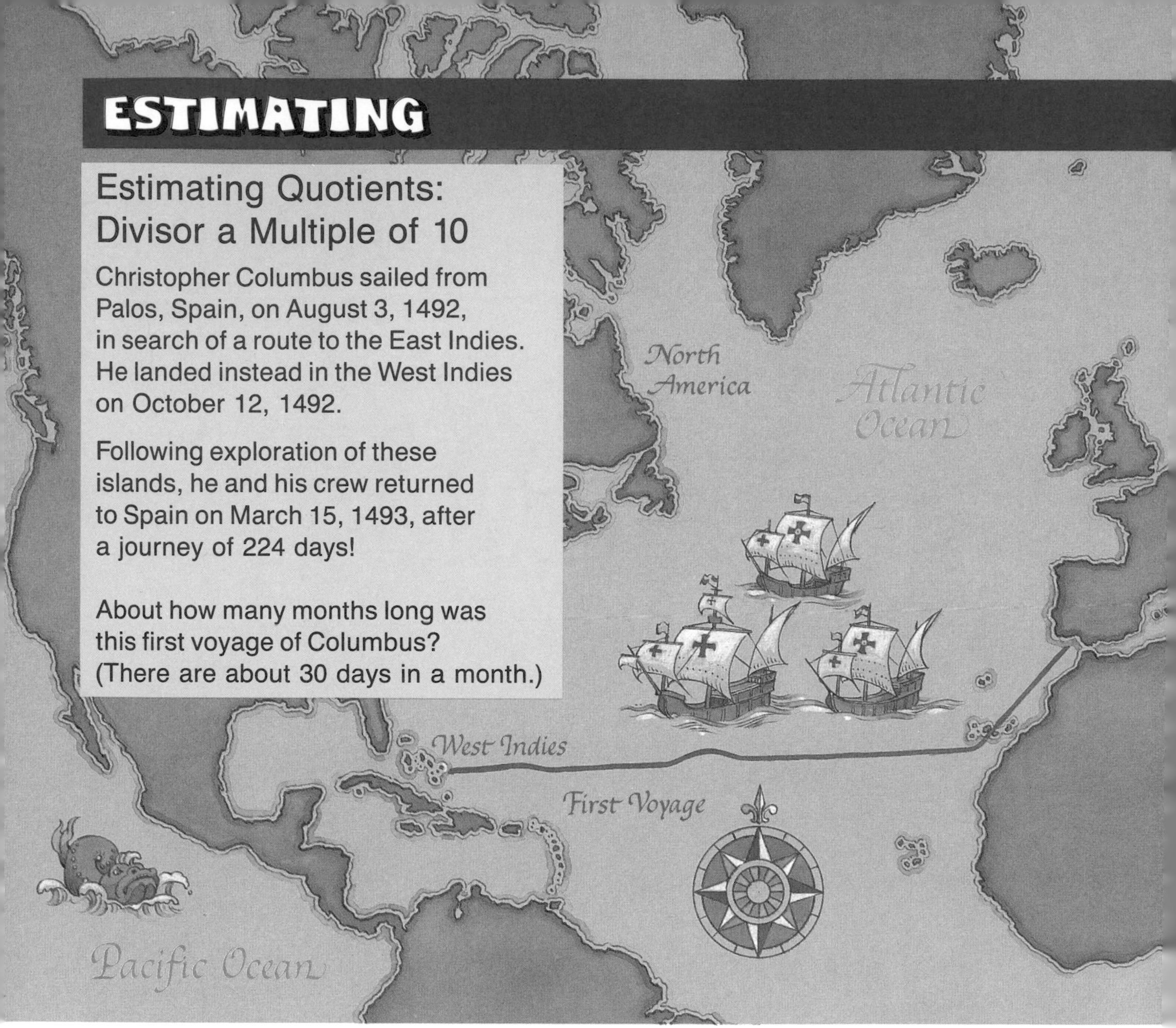

North America

Atlantic Ocean

West Indies

First Voyage

Pacific Ocean

| To estimate: | ⇒ | Think of an equivalent division fact. About how many 3s are in 22? | ⇒ | Write your estimate. |

$$30)\overline{224}$$

$$3)\overline{22} \quad 7$$

$$\overset{7}{30)\overline{224}}$$

Columbus' first voyage was about 7 months long.

136

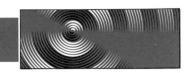

Estimate each quotient.

1. $30\overline{)65}$ 2. $20\overline{)88}$ 3. $40\overline{)93}$ 4. $30\overline{)98}$ 5. $20\overline{)44}$

6. $40\overline{)87}$ 7. $10\overline{)43}$ 8. $30\overline{)82}$ 9. $40\overline{)94}$ 10. $20\overline{)93}$

11. $30\overline{)138}$ 12. $40\overline{)291}$ 13. $70\overline{)561}$ 14. $30\overline{)292}$ 15. $50\overline{)377}$

16. $70\overline{)519}$ 17. $90\overline{)563}$ 18. $40\overline{)362}$ 19. $60\overline{)479}$ 20. $80\overline{)654}$

21. $70\overline{)502}$ 22. $90\overline{)748}$ 23. $30\overline{)164}$ 24. $40\overline{)388}$ 25. $40\overline{)275}$

Estimate.

26. $687 \div 80$ 27. $593 \div 70$ 28. $497 \div 60$ 29. $581 \div 60$
30. $579 \div 60$ 31. $833 \div 90$ 32. $389 \div 50$ 33. $872 \div 90$

34. There are about 30 days in a month. About how many days are there from January 29 to June 2?

35. A recent flight on a Concorde jet from New York to London took 182 min. Estimate the number of hours in the flight.

PROBLEM SOLVING

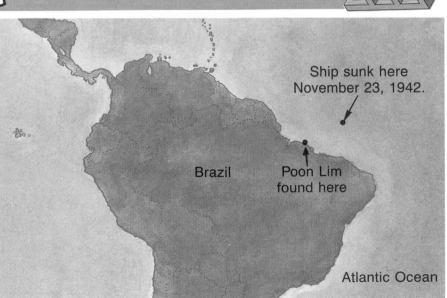

On November 23, 1942, a British ship was sunk in the Atlantic Ocean.

A sailor from that ship was discovered on a raft off the coast of Brazil 133 days later.

The sailor, Poon Lim, had survived alone on the raft all that time.

On what day was he discovered?

Ship sunk here November 23, 1942.

Brazil Poon Lim found here

Atlantic Ocean

ESTIMATING

Estimating Quotients: 2-Digit Divisors

Ferdinand Magellan led the first group to **circumnavigate** the earth. He set sail from Spain on September 20, 1519. He travelled across the Atlantic, around South America and into the Pacific Ocean.

Following 99 days of hardship on the Pacific, Magellan and the survivors of his crew reached the East Indies. Magellan was killed in the Philippine Islands. His associate, del Cano sailed the Vittoria back to Spain on September 8, 1522.

This first circumnavigation of the world took a total of 155 weeks.

About how many years did it take the Vittoria to sail around the world? (There are 52 weeks in a year.)

To estimate:	Think of 52 rounded to the nearest 10.	Think of an equivalent division fact. Divide.	Write your estimate.

$$52\overline{)155} \qquad 50\overline{)155} \qquad 5\overline{)15}\;^{3} \qquad 52\overline{)155}^{\;3}$$

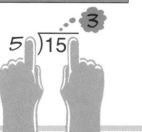

It took the Vittoria about 3 years to sail around the world.

Another example:

To estimate:	Think of 38 rounded to the nearest 10.	Think of an equivalent division fact. Divide.	Write your estimate.

$$38\overline{)2937} \qquad 40\overline{)2937} \qquad 4\overline{)293}\;^{70} \qquad 38\overline{)2937}^{\;70}$$

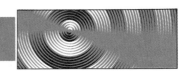

Estimate each quotient.

1. $36\overline{)79}$　　2. $43\overline{)94}$　　3. $19\overline{)59}$

4. $22\overline{)94}$　　5. $31\overline{)84}$　　6. $28\overline{)185}$

7. $37\overline{)863}$　　8. $61\overline{)547}$　　9. $18\overline{)834}$

10. $29\overline{)785}$　　11. $29\overline{)213}$　　12. $46\overline{)298}$

13. $73\overline{)594}$　　14. $54\overline{)831}$　　15. $33\overline{)864}$

16. $57\overline{)423}$　　17. $73\overline{)682}$　　18. $12\overline{)632}$

19. $72\overline{)561}$　　20. $37\overline{)374}$　　21. $68\overline{)494}$

22. $33\overline{)800}$　　23. $35\overline{)2420}$　　24. $42\overline{)3885}$

25. $47\overline{)4051}$　　26. $96\overline{)6989}$　　27. $95\overline{)8426}$

Estimate.

28. $763 \div 82$　　29. $567 \div 76$　　30. $681 \div 31$　　31. $653 \div 27$

32. $1866 \div 93$　　33. $2279 \div 29$　　34. $4565 \div 69$　　35. $4821 \div 35$

36. About how many weeks during a year do you spend in school?

37. About how many years is a period of 84 months?

38. Sir Ranulph Fiennes and Charles Burton took 66 days to travel 4200 km on snowmobiles across Antarctica. About how far did they travel per day?

39. The first circumnavigation of the earth over the North and South Poles was a flight by Captain E.M. Long in 1971. The entire trip took a total of 215 h. Estimate the total number of days for the trip.

40. The first crossing of the continent of Antarctica took 99 days. About how many months did the crossing take?

139

ESTIMATING

Revising Estimates for Division

Captain Bluebeard has found his way home by revising his estimates.

To find an exact quotient, it is often necessary to revise our estimates.

When an estimate is too large, we cannot subtract to get a remainder. It is necessary to **decrease** the estimate by 1 and try again.

To divide 261 by 34:

Estimate.	Check.	Revise the estimate.	Check.
$\begin{array}{r} 8 \\ 34\overline{)261} \end{array}$	$\begin{array}{r} 8 \\ 34\overline{)261} \\ 272 \end{array}$	$\begin{array}{r} 7 \\ 34\overline{)261} \end{array}$	$\begin{array}{r} 7 \\ 34\overline{)261} \\ 238 \\ \hline 23 \end{array}$

Too large. We can't subtract.

$23 < 34$ so the quotient is correct.

When an estimate is too small, the remainder is greater than the divisor. It is necessary to **increase** the estimate by 1 and try again.

To divide 287 by 47:

Estimate.	Check.	Revise the estimate.	Check.
$\begin{array}{r} 5 \\ 47\overline{)287} \end{array}$	$\begin{array}{r} 5 \\ 47\overline{)287} \\ 235 \\ \hline 52 \end{array}$	$\begin{array}{r} 6 \\ 47\overline{)287} \end{array}$	$\begin{array}{r} 6 \\ 47\overline{)287} \\ 282 \\ \hline 5 \end{array}$

Since $52 > 47$, the remainder is too large.

$5 < 47$ so the quotient is correct.

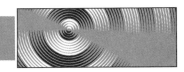

Revise each of these estimates.

1. $\overset{3}{18\overline{)75}}$ 2. $\overset{4}{23\overline{)87}}$ 3. $\overset{4}{17\overline{)94}}$ 4. $\overset{9}{43\overline{)362}}$ 5. $\overset{6}{38\overline{)273}}$

6. $\overset{4}{35\overline{)182}}$ 7. $\overset{5}{54\overline{)264}}$ 8. $\overset{8}{63\overline{)487}}$ 9. $\overset{7}{27\overline{)220}}$ 10. $\overset{6}{33\overline{)192}}$

11. $\overset{8}{54\overline{)416}}$ 12. $\overset{4}{19\overline{)97}}$ 13. $\overset{5}{42\overline{)206}}$ 14. $\overset{6}{73\overline{)430}}$ 15. $\overset{5}{58\overline{)354}}$

Estimate. Revise your estimate until the remainder is less than the divisor.

16. $13\overline{)37}$ 17. $19\overline{)77}$ 18. $38\overline{)79}$ 19. $17\overline{)86}$ 20. $94\overline{)564}$

21. $26\overline{)107}$ 22. $49\overline{)387}$ 23. $61\overline{)529}$ 24. $52\overline{)256}$ 25. $41\overline{)376}$

26. $36\overline{)282}$ 27. $23\overline{)87}$ 28. $47\overline{)410}$ 29. $39\overline{)286}$ 30. $25\overline{)220}$

31. $72\overline{)213}$ 32. $40\overline{)326}$ 33. $69\overline{)487}$ 34. $83\overline{)330}$ 35. $92\overline{)667}$

Estimate and revise.

36. $778 \div 81$ 37. $562 \div 64$ 38. $327 \div 49$ 39. $563 \div 82$

40. $467 \div 78$ 41. $641 \div 61$ 42. $635 \div 74$ 43. $791 \div 93$

BITS AND BYTES

5 of these estimates need revision.
Record the letters of the estimates which need revision.

A $\overset{6}{18\overline{)130}}$ B $\overset{8}{35\overline{)315}}$ C $\overset{8}{21\overline{)179}}$ D $\overset{8}{78\overline{)693}}$ E $\overset{9}{81\overline{)738}}$

F $\overset{5}{92\overline{)457}}$ G $\overset{4}{59\overline{)247}}$ H $\overset{6}{63\overline{)370}}$ I $\overset{7}{76\overline{)625}}$ J $\overset{6}{42\overline{)256}}$

Dividing by 2-Digit Numbers: 1-Digit Quotients

On August 29, 1982, Sir Ranulph Fiennes and Charles Burton became the first people to complete a trip around the world passing through the North and South Poles! We say they were the first people to complete a **polar circumnavigation** of the earth, not counting air or space travel.

The entire trip took about 155 weeks. How long was the trip in years and weeks?

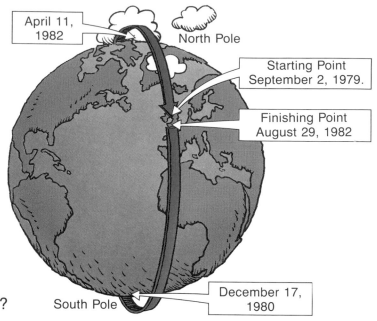

April 11, 1982

North Pole

Starting Point September 2, 1979.

Finishing Point August 29, 1982

December 17, 1980

South Pole

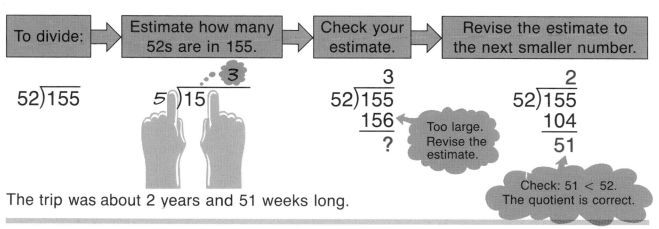

| To divide: | Estimate how many 52s are in 155. | Check your estimate. | Revise the estimate to the next smaller number. |

$52\overline{)155}$

$5\overline{)15}$ ... 3

$\begin{array}{r} 3 \\ 52\overline{)155} \\ 156 \\ \hline ? \end{array}$

Too large. Revise the estimate.

$\begin{array}{r} 2 \\ 52\overline{)155} \\ 104 \\ \hline 51 \end{array}$

Check: 51 < 52. The quotient is correct.

The trip was about 2 years and 51 weeks long.

Another example:

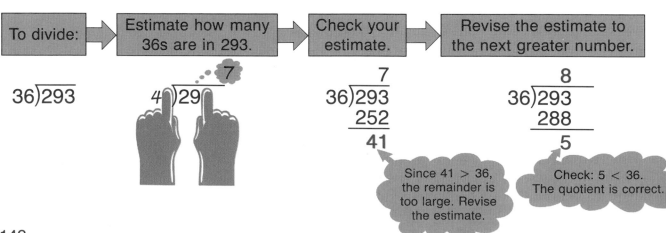

| To divide: | Estimate how many 36s are in 293. | Check your estimate. | Revise the estimate to the next greater number. |

$36\overline{)293}$

$4\overline{)29}$ ... 7

$\begin{array}{r} 7 \\ 36\overline{)293} \\ 252 \\ \hline 41 \end{array}$

Since 41 > 36, the remainder is too large. Revise the estimate.

$\begin{array}{r} 8 \\ 36\overline{)293} \\ 288 \\ \hline 5 \end{array}$

Check: 5 < 36. The quotient is correct.

Copy and complete.

1. 27)164

2. 46)190

3. 51)392

4. 37)341

Divide.

5. 19)69

6. 11)70

7. 29)98

8. 41)93

9. 29)268

10. 39)187

11. 42)377

12. 17)146

13. 52)216

14. 45)320

Divide.

15. 212 ÷ 13

16. 366 ÷ 57

17. 197 ÷ 23

18. 193 ÷ 48

19. 709 ÷ 84

20. 682 ÷ 74

21. 279 ÷ 92

22. 465 ÷ 88

23. How many full weeks are there in a leap year? How many days are left over?

24. How many Sundays are there in a period of 77 full weeks?

25. World Spheres Company sells globes for $46 each. One day the company had $414 in sales. How many globes did the company sell?

PROBLEM SOLVING

Which journey took longer: the first circumnavigation of the earth, or the first polar circumnavigation of the earth?

How much longer was the longer journey?

Dividing by 2-Digit Numbers: 2-Digit Quotients

On October 20, 1911, the Norwegian explorer Roald Amundsen left the Bay of Whales in Antarctica in search of the South Pole. Captain Amundsen and his crew of 4 men travelled by dogsled over more than 1300 km of deep snow and dangerous crevasses.

On December 14, after an overland journey of about 1330 h, Amundsen and his crew became the first people to reach the South Pole!

How many days and hours long was Amundsen's journey to the South Pole?

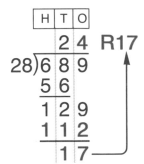

To divide 1330 by 24:

| Divide the tens. | Bring down the ones. | Divide the ones. |

```
      Th  H  T  O               Th  H  T  O               Th  H  T  O
              5                          5                          5  5  R10
   24) 1  3  3  0              24) 1  3  3  0            24) 1  3  3  0
       1  2  0                     1  2  0                   1  2  0
          1  3                        1  3  0                   1  3  0
                                                                1  2  0
                                                                   1  0
```

The overland journey lasted 55 days, 10 hours.

Another example: To divide 689 by 28:

| Divide the tens. | Bring down the ones. | Divide the ones. |

```
    H  T  O              H  T  O              H  T  O
       2                    2                    2  4  R17
  28) 6  8  9         28) 6  8  9         28) 6  8  9
      5  6                 5  6                 5  6
      1  2                 1  2  9              1  2  9
                                               1  1  2
                                                  1  7
```

144

Copy and complete.

1. 43)926

2. 23)386

3. 32)514

4. 13)879

Divide.

5. 24)387

6. 56)784

7. 29)547

8. 71)864

9. 31)842

10. 19)756

11. 84)926

12. 36)866

13. 15)1168

14. 26)1865

Divide.

15. 2138 ÷ 29

16. 1088 ÷ 13

17. 3155 ÷ 39

18. 2556 ÷ 43

19. 3800 ÷ 51

20. 6586 ÷ 72

21. 4660 ÷ 57

22. 3202 ÷ 61

23. 1000 cans of juice are packaged in cases of 24. How many full cases are there? How many cans are left over?

24. A prize of $6000 is to be shared equally among 15 people. How much should each person receive?

25. How many minutes are between 2:45 a.m. and 9:15 a.m.?

26. After Mrs. Henshaw filled 27 cartons with eggs, she had 7 eggs left over. Each carton holds one dozen eggs. How many eggs did she start with?

PROBLEM SOLVING

John Cabot was one of the earliest explorers of Canada. He left Bristol, England, on May 2, 1497, and reached Canada on June 24, 1497.

1. How many days long was his journey?

2. Did Cabot's journey take as long as Amundsen's overland journey to the South Pole?

Dividing by 2-Digit Numbers: 3-Digit Quotients

In 1927, a prize of $25 000 was offered to the first person to fly solo across the Atlantic Ocean.

On May 20, 1927, Charles A. Lindbergh, Jr. left New York in a small aircraft named *Spirit of St. Louis*. With no navigator to guide him and nothing but ocean below, he flew through a night of total darkness.

After 33 sleepless hours on a journey of 5576 km, Lindbergh landed his aircraft in Paris, France. He became an overnight hero.

About how many kilometres did Lindbergh travel per hour?

To divide 5776 by 33:

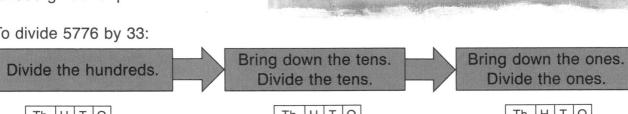

| Divide the hundreds. | → | Bring down the tens. Divide the tens. | → | Bring down the ones. Divide the ones. |

```
   Th H T O                 Th H T O                 Th H T O
        1                        1 7                       1 7 5 R1
33) 5  7 7 6             33) 5  7   6             33) 5  7 7 6
    3  3                      3 3                      3 3
    2  4                      2 4 7                    2 4 7
                             2 3 1                    2 3 1
                               1 6                        1 6 6
                                                         1 6 5
                                                             1
```

Lindbergh travelled about 175 km/h.

146

Copy and complete.

1. 26)5738

2. 31)6598

3. 47)6384

4. 26)8562

Divide.

5. 29)7172

6. 38)7379

7. 54)6422

8. 67)9126

9. 19)8000

10. 55)9042

11. 37)9541

12. 44)7521

13. 83)9739

14. 29)8009

15. 66)8731

16. 30)3482

17. 72)8197

18. 43)9347

19. 39)4732

Divide.

20. 8100 ÷ 37

21. 8367 ÷ 65

22. 5569 ÷ 17

23. 6324 ÷ 18

24. Robert Timm and John Cook flew continuously for about 1558 h. About how many days long was their flight?

25. The first non-stop flight across the Pacific Ocean took 997 min. The distance covered was 7335 km from Japan to the United States.

   a) About how many hours long was the flight?

   b) About how many kilometres per hour did they travel?

26. The first non-stop flight across the Atlantic was in 1919. It took 987 min to travel 3138 km from St. John's, Newfoundland, to Clifden, Ireland. About how many kilometres per hour did they travel?

27. Amelia Earhart was the first woman to fly solo across the Atlantic Ocean. Her flight, in 1932, from Harbour Grace, Newfoundland, to Londonderry, Ireland, took 15 h 18 min. How much shorter was her flight than Lindbergh's transatlantic flight?

Dividing by 2-Digit Numbers: Zero in the Quotient

For thousands of years people have imagined travelling to the moon.

On July 21, 1969, Neil Armstrong became the first human to set foot on lunar soil.

As he took his first step, he announced, "That's one small step for man; one giant leap for mankind."

The journey from the earth to the moon took exactly 6165 min.

How many hours and minutes was the journey from the earth to the moon?

To divide 6165 by 60:

Divide the hundreds.	Bring down the tens. Divide the tens.	Bring down the ones. Divide the ones.

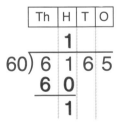

Th	H	T	O
	1		
60) 6	1	6	5
6	**0**		
	1		

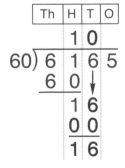

Th	H	T	O
	1	**0**	
60) 6	1	6	5
6	0	↓	
	1	6	
	0	0	
	1	6	

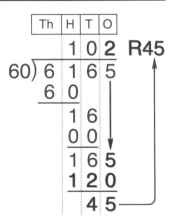

Th	H	T	O	
	1	**0**	**2**	**R45**
60) 6	1	6	5	
6	0			
	1	6	↓	
	0	0	↓	
	1	6	5	
	1	2	0	
		4	5	

The journey lasted 102 h 45 min.

Copy and complete.

1. 27)5 5 3 0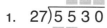

2. 44)8 9 1 2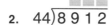

3. 67)7 1 5 9

4. 56)6 1 0 3

Divide.

5. 12)1321

6. 19)2021

7. 34)3592

8. 61)6207

9. 58)6226

10. 43)4899

11. 54)5651

12. 73)7405

13. 86)9302

14. 33)2907

15. 18)1925

16. 56)5826

17. 71)7936

18. 62)5861

19. 83)9766

Divide.

20. 2793 ÷ 26

21. 5687 ÷ 54

22. 7908 ÷ 71

23. 8284 ÷ 83

24. One of Canada's oldest citizens has lived for 1310 months. What is that citizen's age in years?

25. What number when multiplied by 50 yields a product of 5050?

26. A theatre contains 9202 seats arranged in 86 equal rows. How many seats are in each row?

PROBLEM SOLVING

Fill in the missing digits to make a division question with a divisor of 43, a quotient of 109, and a remainder of 41.

$$\begin{array}{r} 1\,0\,9 \text{ R41} \\ 43\overline{)\blacksquare\blacksquare\blacksquare\blacksquare} \end{array}$$

JUST FOR FUN

RIDDLE: Who is Pierre's favorite explorer?

Divide.

A. 16)117	**B.** 61)983	**C.** 56)498	**D.** 9)249	**E.** 84)8682
F. 29)1490	**G.** 38)4790	**H.** 69)1006	**I.** 53)2402	**J.** 93)842
K. 76)7068	**L.** 14)3762	**M.** 75)1579	**N.** 26)4382	**O.** 67)6874
P. 43)4837	**Q.** 59)4062	**R.** 79)3329	**S.** 98)590	**T.** 32)1174
U. 67)3391	**V.** 81)1300	**W.** 23)7397	**X.** 27)5661	**Y.** 32)4169

To solve the riddle, write the letters of the questions with these answers.

8 R50	7 R5	112 R21	36 R22	7 R5	45 R17	168 R14		8 R50	102 R40	102 R40	93

150

Divide.

1. 9⟌72
2. 7⟌630
3. 6⟌5400

4. 8⟌78
5. 6⟌47
6. 8⟌496

7. 6⟌851
8. 3⟌6264
9. 9⟌8163

Use short division.

10. 5⟌242
11. 9⟌1872
12. 6⟌12 828

Estimate.

13. 7⟌53
14. 4⟌91
15. 8⟌154

16. 5⟌693
17. 6⟌8320
18. 3⟌17 243

Divide.

19. 70⟌280
20. 60⟌3600
21. 80⟌32 000

22. 19⟌78
23. 29⟌94
24. 37⟌148

25. 57⟌458
26. 78⟌668
27. 86⟌258

28. 19⟌247
29. 74⟌892
30. 84⟌5312

31. 53⟌2442
32. 47⟌4281
33. 62⟌2294

34. About how many years old is a person who has lived for 1014 months?

35. A crate containing 24 word games cost $312. Estimate the cost of one word game.

Revise each estimate.

36. 24⟌80 (4)
37. 16⟌71 (3)
38. 26⟌78 (2)

39. 37⟌265 (6)
40. 96⟌374 (4)
41. 62⟌429 (7)

42. At a garage sale, Samuel bought 2 records for 55¢ each and an old record player for $4.75. How much change did he receive from a $10 bill?

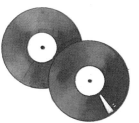

Divide.

43. 36⟌4464
44. 41⟌8741
45. 17⟌5304

46. 86⟌9898
47. 28⟌6141
48. 23⟌9936

49. 18⟌5472
50. 54⟌5565
51. 38⟌7866

52. 12⟌7282
53. 81⟌8350
54. 23⟌8407

55. A school library has about 3500 books. Estimate the number of shelves in the library if each shelf holds about 40 books.

56. A prize of $8125 is to be shared equally by 25 people. How much should each person receive?

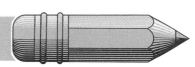
Multiply.

1. $3 \times 4 \times 5$ 2. $7 \times 8 \times 2$
3. 8×40 4. 6×500 5. 3×2000

Estimate.

6. 6×58 7. 3×206 8. 5×4872

Multiply.

9. $\begin{array}{r} 67 \\ \times\ 8 \\ \hline \end{array}$ 10. $\begin{array}{r} 83 \\ \times\ 7 \\ \hline \end{array}$ 11. $\begin{array}{r} 609 \\ \times\ \ 6 \\ \hline \end{array}$

12. $\begin{array}{r} 843 \\ \times\ \ 4 \\ \hline \end{array}$ 13. $\begin{array}{r} 1636 \\ \times\ \ \ \ 5 \\ \hline \end{array}$ 14. $\begin{array}{r} 3587 \\ \times\ \ \ \ 2 \\ \hline \end{array}$

15. A stereo set cost $195. What is the cost of 3 stereo sets?

Estimate.

16. $\begin{array}{r} 32 \\ \times 56 \\ \hline \end{array}$ 17. $\begin{array}{r} 828 \\ \times\ 45 \\ \hline \end{array}$ 18. $\begin{array}{r} 2117 \\ \times\ \ \ 21 \\ \hline \end{array}$

19. $\begin{array}{r} 425 \\ \times 281 \\ \hline \end{array}$ 20. $\begin{array}{r} 801 \\ \times 366 \\ \hline \end{array}$ 21. $\begin{array}{r} 641 \\ \times 777 \\ \hline \end{array}$

Multiply.

22. $\begin{array}{r} 80 \\ \times 30 \\ \hline \end{array}$ 23. $\begin{array}{r} 72 \\ \times 40 \\ \hline \end{array}$ 24. $\begin{array}{r} 396 \\ \times\ 50 \\ \hline \end{array}$

25. $\begin{array}{r} 54 \\ \times 28 \\ \hline \end{array}$ 26. $\begin{array}{r} 87 \\ \times 53 \\ \hline \end{array}$ 27. $\begin{array}{r} 49 \\ \times 26 \\ \hline \end{array}$

28. $\begin{array}{r} 628 \\ \times\ 94 \\ \hline \end{array}$ 29. $\begin{array}{r} 780 \\ \times\ 47 \\ \hline \end{array}$ 30. $\begin{array}{r} 2563 \\ \times\ \ \ 25 \\ \hline \end{array}$

31. Each row at an auditorium seats 22 people. If there are 395 rows, how many people can be seated?

Multiply.

32. $\begin{array}{r} 300 \\ \times 400 \\ \hline \end{array}$ 33. $\begin{array}{r} 825 \\ \times 300 \\ \hline \end{array}$ 34. $\begin{array}{r} 2897 \\ \times\ 600 \\ \hline \end{array}$

35. $\begin{array}{r} 695 \\ \times 135 \\ \hline \end{array}$ 36. $\begin{array}{r} 705 \\ \times 206 \\ \hline \end{array}$ 37. $\begin{array}{r} 273 \\ \times 499 \\ \hline \end{array}$

84	1791	675	348
540	92	3435	813
225	795	711	4136

Write the numbers in the list that are divisible by:

38. 4   39. 5   40. 3   41. 9

Which numbers in the list are divisible by:

42. 2 and 3?   43. 5 and 9?
44. 3 and 4?   45. 3 and 5?

Write the least common multiple for each pair of numbers.

46. 5 and 9
47. 3 and 4
48. 6 and 9

List the factors of each number

49. 40   50. 56   51. 24

Find the greatest common factor of:

52. 40 and 56   53. 24 and 40

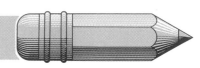

Write *prime* or *composite* for each of the following numbers.

54. 91   **55.** 38   **56.** 19

57. 57   **58.** 87   **59.** 229

Draw a factor tree for each number. Then write it as a product of prime factors.

60. 56   **61.** 60   **62.** 78

63. Marc is 7 years older than Dana. The product of their ages is 60. How old is Marc?

Estimate.

64. $7\overline{)48}$ **65.** $6\overline{)55}$ **66.** $5\overline{)86}$

67. $4\overline{)269}$ **68.** $6\overline{)473}$ **69.** $3\overline{)9308}$

Divide.

70. $8\overline{)92}$ **71.** $6\overline{)815}$ **72.** $4\overline{)2164}$

73. $7\overline{)728}$ **74.** $6\overline{)5432}$ **75.** $9\overline{)7253}$

---

76. Bee's Honey packaged 5688 jars of honey one week. They work 5 days a week. Estimate the number of jars packaged in one day.

77. 4 people shared equally in the cost of renting a car. The bill came to $264. How much did each pay?

Use short division.

78. $5\overline{)284}$ **79.** $9\overline{)936}$ **80.** $4\overline{)8229}$

Estimate.

81. $30\overline{)350}$ **82.** $50\overline{)298}$

83. $80\overline{)629}$ **84.** 737 ÷ 26

85. 585 ÷ 42   **86.** 6438 ÷ 59

Divide.

87. $19\overline{)76}$ **88.** $28\overline{)87}$ **89.** $43\overline{)219}$

90. $18\overline{)247}$ **91.** $74\overline{)893}$ **92.** $91\overline{)4863}$

93. $36\overline{)6444}$ **94.** $41\overline{)8746}$ **95.** $17\overline{)5403}$

96. $18\overline{)5454}$ **97.** $54\overline{)5665}$ **98.** $12\overline{)8436}$

---

99. About how many months old is a person who has lived 2927 days?

100. It cost $8400 to paint the 24 apartments in a building. What was the cost for each apartment?

Revise each estimate.

101. $65\overline{)392}^{\,5}$ **102.** $52\overline{)401}^{\,8}$ **103.** $48\overline{)247}^{\,6}$

---

104. How much change would you receive from a $20 bill if you bought 3 books at $5.95 each?

Nine Men's Morris

Nine Men's Morris is a game of reasoning in which
2 players use strategies to block each other's moves.
This game has a long and interesting history. One gameboard
was cut into roofing slabs of an ancient temple in Karnak, Egypt.
Another was cut into ten-metre wide stairs in the side of a hill
in Sri Lanka. Yet another was discovered in Norway on a ship
which was the burial chamber of a Viking King.

Artist's impression of Nine Men's Morris
in Norway, approximately 1 000 A.D.

Centimetres and Millimetres

Note: The length of the candle does not include the flame.

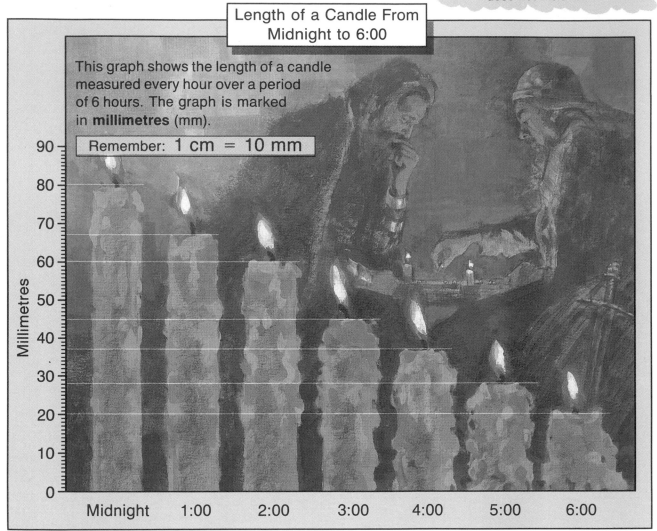

Length of a Candle From Midnight to 6:00

This graph shows the length of a candle measured every hour over a period of 6 hours. The graph is marked in **millimetres** (mm).

Remember: 1 cm = 10 mm

Millimetres: 90, 80, 70, 60, 50, 40, 30, 20, 10, 0

Midnight 1:00 2:00 3:00 4:00 5:00 6:00

Use the graph to help you answer these questions.

1. What was the length of the candle in millimetres at midnight?

2. How many millimetres tall was the candle at 2:00?

3. What was the length of the candle in centimetres at 6:00?

4. What was the approximate length of the candle in millimetres at 4:30?

5. How many millimetres in length did the candle lose in the fourth hour?

6. During which hour did the greatest decrease in length occur?

7. Estimate the length of the candle at 7:00.

8. Estimate the lifetime of a candle with the same diameter as the one shown but measuring 10 cm in length.

156

Millimetres and Centimetres

To estimate lengths in centimetres, think of your baby finger as about 1 cm wide.

Centimetres

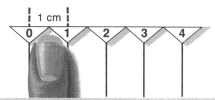

To estimate lengths in millimetres, think of your baby finger as about 10 mm wide.

Millimetres

Estimate the lengths of these candles in centimetres and millimetres.

1. 2. 3. 4. 5.

Record your estimates in a table like this.

Candle Number	Estimated Length in	
	Centimetres	Millimetres
1		
2		
3		
4		
5		

6. Compare your estimates in millimetres with your estimates in centimetres. Explain how they are related.

7. Measure the lengths of the candles above in millimetres. Compare your estimates and measurements.

Copy and complete.

8. 8 cm = ▦ mm
9. 17 cm = ▦ mm
10. 40 mm = ▦ cm
11. 800 mm = ▦ cm
12. 100 mm = ▦ cm
13. 5 cm = ▦ mm
14. 24 cm = ▦ mm
15. 1000 mm = ▦ cm

16.

cm	6	▦	23	▦	30	▦
mm	▦	70	▦	220	▦	1200

BITS AND BYTES

Copy and complete.

1. 27 mm = ▦ cm
2. 385 mm = ▦ cm

3.

cm	▦	▦	72	▦	125	▦
mm	4	8.1	▦	11.5	▦	17.9

Try these without your calculator.

4. 7 mm = ▦ cm
5. 15 mm = ▦ cm
6. 2.4 cm = ▦ mm
7. 13.2 cm = ▦ mm

Measuring Diameters in Millimetres

The picture below shows the **annual rings** of a pine tree cut down in December, 1987. Each ring shows the growth of the tree during a particular year.

The 13 rings show that this tree was 13 years old in December, 1987. This means the tree began growing in 1974.

The width of a tree trunk is called its **diameter**. The picture below shows the diameter of the tree in various years. By measuring the **thickness** of a ring, we can find out how much the diameter increased in a particular year.

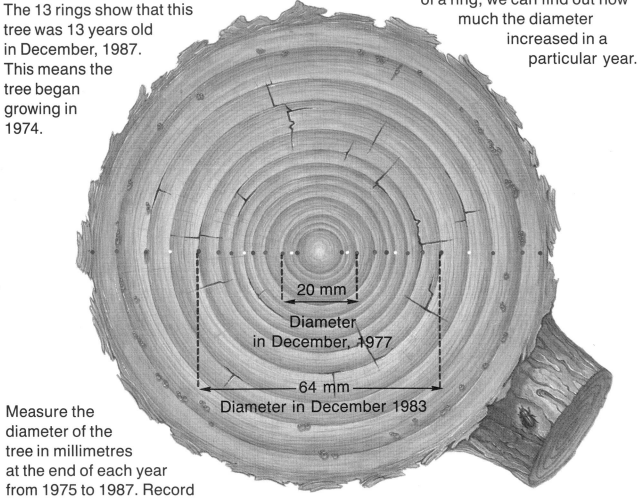

20 mm

Diameter in December, 1977

64 mm

Diameter in December 1983

Measure the diameter of the tree in millimetres at the end of each year from 1975 to 1987. Record your measurements in a table like this.

End of Year	1975	1976	1977	1978	1979	1980	1981	1982	1983	1984	1985	1986	1987
Diameter in Millimetres													

158

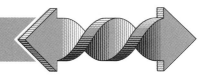
Interpreting and Constructing Line Graphs

This line graph shows the diameter of a poplar tree which began to grow in 1975.

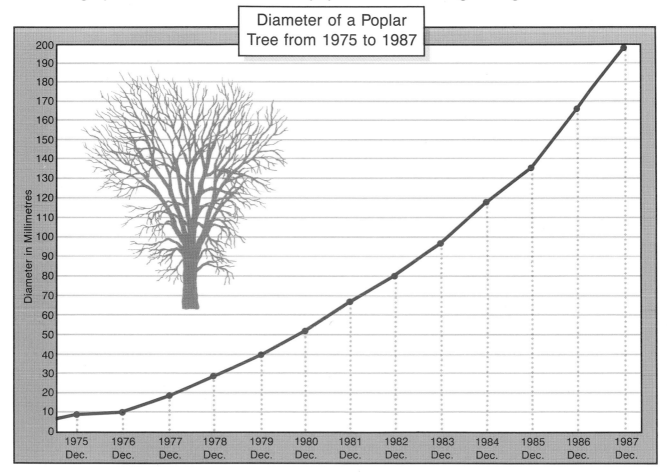

Diameter of a Poplar
Tree from 1975 to 1987

1. What was the diameter of the poplar tree in December, 1979?

2. By how many millimetres did the poplar tree's diameter increase between December, 1979 and December, 1980?

3. In what year did the diameter of the poplar tree reach 10 cm?

4. About how long did it take the diameter to increase from 10 cm to 15 cm?

5. What was the approximate diameter of the poplar tree in June, 1980?

6. Use centimetre paper to make a line graph showing the growth between Dec., 1975 and Dec., 1987 of the pine tree on page 158. Use the table you constructed on the previous page.

Metres

We say: One **metre** is one hundred centimetres.

We write: 1 m = 100 cm

A doorknob is about 1 m above the floor.

1 m

Most people over 5 years old are between 1 m and 2 m in height.

2 m

1 m

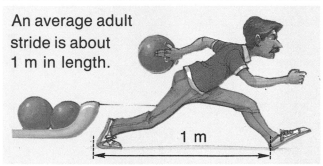

An average adult stride is about 1 m in length.

1 m

A baseball bat is a little shorter than a metre.

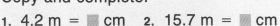

1 m

A golf driver is a little longer than a metre.

Estimate the following measurements in metres.

1. length of a bicycle
2. length of a tennis racket
3. length of a new compact car
4. width of a new compact car
5. height of a doorway
6. height of a table
7. height of your classroom ceiling
8. height of your school

Copy and complete.

9. 6 m = ▓ cm
10. 12 m = ▓ cm
11. 500 cm = ▓ m
12. 1200 cm = ▓ m
13. 8 m = ▓ cm
14. 1000 cm = ▓ m
15. 16 m = ▓ cm
16. 2000 cm = ▓ m

Copy and complete.

17.

m	▓	2	9	▓	13	▓
cm	1500	▓	▓	2700	▓	3000

BITS AND BYTES

Copy and complete.

1. 4.2 m = ▓ cm
2. 15.7 m = ▓ cm
3. 350 cm = ▓ m
4. 1420 cm = ▓ m

5.

m	▓	▓	3.6	▓	▓	12.1
cm	420	690	▓	1380	2150	▓

Try these without your calculator.

6. 2.8 m = ▓ cm
7. 0.5 m = ▓ cm
8. 140 cm = ▓ m
9. 80 cm = ▓ m

JUST FOR FUN

RIDDLE:

What great mathematician invented the first mechanical calculator?

To answer the riddle, find a path up the mountain so that each measurement is greater than the measurement before it. Write in order the letters or blank spaces which you meet in your path.

FINISH!

200 cm

A 120 cm

L 500 mm

N 3 m

C 1 m

S 90 cm

E 1.5 m

200 cm

A 11 cm

P 92 mm

L 8 cm

E 75 mm

R 12 cm

E 10 cm

N 9 cm

S 6 cm

B 5 mm

L 1 cm

A 26 mm

I 50 mm

START

161

Perimeter

The **perimeter** of a figure is the total distance around it.

The sides of this triangle are 2 cm, 3 cm, and 4 cm long.

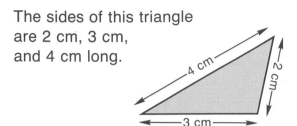

The perimeter of this triangle is

2 cm + 3 cm + 4 cm = 9 cm

This hexagon has 6 equal sides. Each side is 11 mm long.

The perimeter of this hexagon is

6 × 11 mm = 66 mm

These figures are drawn on centimetre paper.

1. Estimate which figure has the greatest perimeter.

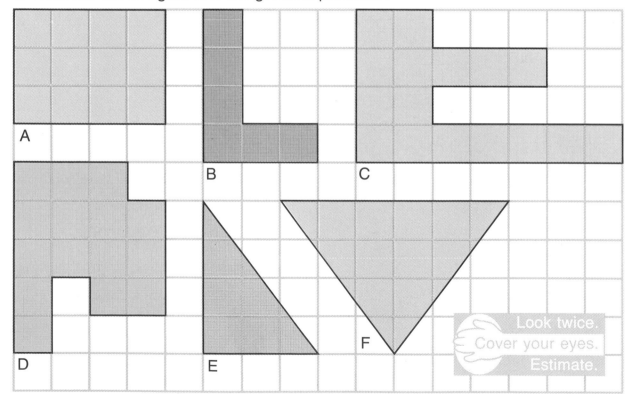

Look twice.
Cover your eyes.
Estimate.

2. Find the perimeter of each figure.
   You may have to measure some
   of the sides.

162

Measure the sides of these figures in millimetres.
Write the perimeter of each figure.

1.

2.

3.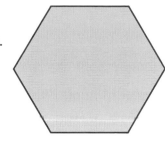

On centimetre paper, draw at least
2 different rectangles for each perimeter.

4. 10 cm
5. 12 cm
6. 14 cm
7. 20 cm
8. 24 cm
9. 26 cm

The diagrams below show the playing
areas for some popular sports. The actual
lengths and widths are 1000 times the
sizes shown here.

Measure the perimeter of each in
millimetres and then calculate the
actual perimeter in metres.

10. TENNIS COURT   11. HOCKEY RINK

12. FOOTBALL FIELD

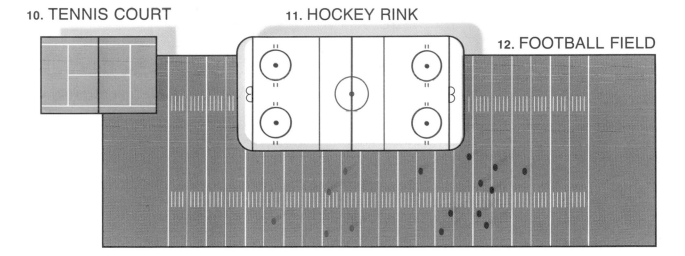

PROBLEM SOLVING

Can you draw a rectangle with a perimeter
of 9 cm that has sides along the ruled
lines of centimetre paper?

Explain your answer.

Not permitted
because all sides
must be along
ruled lines.

Distances Between Parallel Lines

The red lines on this centimetre grid are **horizontal** and the blue lines are **vertical**.

We notice from the grid that:

- Any 2 horizontal lines are parallel.

- Any 2 vertical lines are parallel.

- Any horizontal line is perpendicular to any vertical line.

It is easy to measure the distance between any pair of horizontal or vertical lines.

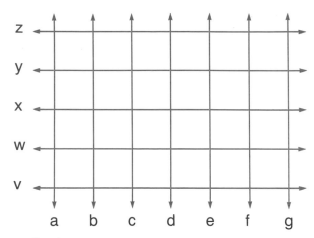

When 2 parallel lines are neither horizontal nor vertical, we can follow these steps to find the distance between them.

STEP 1 Trace the parallel lines onto tracing paper.

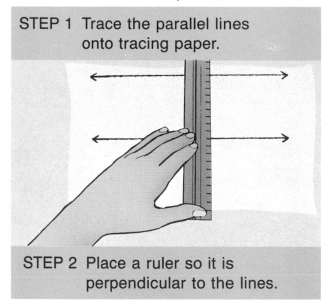

STEP 2 Place a ruler so it is perpendicular to the lines.

STEP 3 Draw a line perpendicular to the parallel lines.

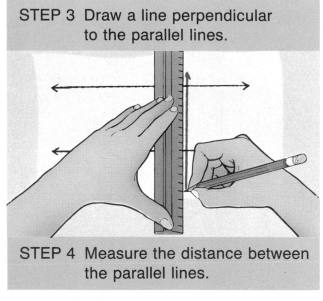

STEP 4 Measure the distance between the parallel lines.

Measure the distance in millimetres between the parallel lines.

1.

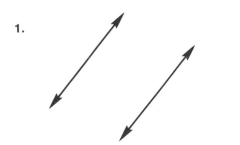

2.

3.

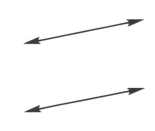

Bases and Heights of Parallelograms and Triangles

A **parallelogram** is a 4-sided figure with 2 pairs of parallel sides.

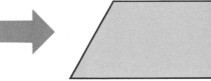

Opposite sides are parallel.

When a parallelogram is positioned so that one pair of sides is horizontal, the bottom side is called the **base**.

The distance from the base to the opposite side is called the **height**.

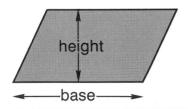

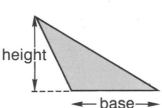

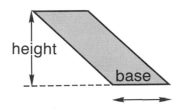

When a triangle is positioned so that one side is horizontal, that side is called the **base**.

The distance from the base to the opposite vertex is called the **height**.

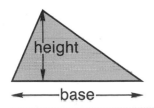

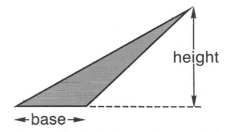

Measure and record the base and height of each figure in millimetres.

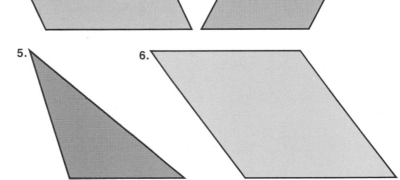

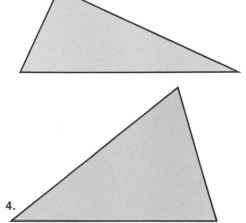

Distances in Kilometres

A distance of 1000 m is called one **kilometre**. We measure long distances in kilometres.

A distance of 1 cm on the map below stands for a real distance of 1 km.

WE USE THE SYMBOL km FOR KILOMETRES!

Museum

WELCOME TO SPACE CITY

Rink

City Hall

School

Theatre

FIFTY MILLION KILOMETRES TO EARTH – NOW SHOWING

1 cm ↔ 1 km

The distance between any 2 buildings can be shown in a table like this.

	School	City Hall	Museum	Theatre	Rink
School	0 km				
City Hall		0 km	8 km		
Museum	10 km		0 km		
Theatre				0 km	
Rink					0 km

This shows that the distance from the museum to the school is 10 km.

1. What does the 8 km in the table mean?

2. What do the zeros mean?

3. Copy the distance table. Use the map of Space City and a centimetre ruler to complete your table.

Use your table to complete these questions.

4. What building is closest to the city hall?

5. What building is farthest from the museum?

6. What 2 buildings are the same distance from the school?

7. What building is 9 km from the museum?

8. How much farther from the city hall is the school than the museum?

9. What is the total distance along the route:
school → museum → rink?

10. What is the total distance along the route:
school → theatre → rink?

11. What is the total distance along the route:
school → theatre → rink → museum?

Choosing the Appropriate Unit

Each picture suggests a length, height, or distance in our everyday world.
Which unit would be used to measure each length, height or distance?

- millimetre
- centimetre
- metre
- kilometre

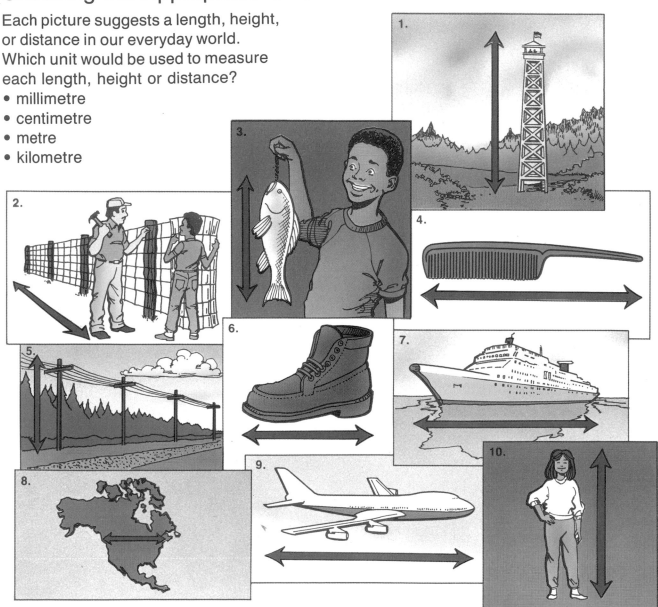

Write the name of the most appropriate unit for measuring each of these things.

11. the length of a hockey stick
12. the height of a tall tree
13. the width of an automobile
14. the width of a pencil
15. the distance from home plate to first base
16. the distance from home to school
17. the depth of a lake
18. the perimeter of a playground
19. the thickness of a guitar string
20. the length of your foot

ESTIMATING

RIDDLE:

What great mathematician, upon solving a mathematical problem, jumped from the bathtub and ran through the streets yelling, "Eureka!" (which means "I have solved it!")?

To answer the riddle, write the letter of the best estimate in each question. Then read the letters in the order they appear.

1. The thickness of a dime is about:
   A. 1 mm   B. 5 mm   C. 1 cm   D. 1 m

2. The height of the CN tower is about:
   P. 550 mm   Q. 550 cm   R. 550 m   S. 550 km

3. The distance from St. John's, Newfoundland to Victoria, B.C. is about:
   A. 5000 mm   B. 5000 m   C. 5000 km   D. 50 000 km

4. The height of the tallest person who ever lived was about:
   G. 200 mm   H. 280 cm   I. 600 cm   J. 600 m

5. The distance from home plate to first base is about:
   I. 30 m   J. 10 cm   K. 90 m   L. 100 km

6. The length of a football field is about:
   J. 150 cm   K. 500 cm   L. 50 km   M. 150 m

7. The thickness of a guitar string is about:
   E. 1 mm   F. 8 mm   G. 1 cm   H. 8 cm

8. In 8 minutes, you can walk a distance of about:
   A. 50 m   B. 100 m   C. 150 m   D. 1 km

9. The longest home run ever hit by a major league baseball player was:
   C. 45 mm   D. 61 cm   E. 179 m   F. 305 km

10. The longest distance a golf ball has been driven in professional competition was:
    P. 100 km   Q. 135 cm   R. 233 mm   S. 311 m

Area: Counting Squares

This square has an area of one **square centimetre**.

We say: one square centimetre

We write: 1 cm^2

The area of a figure is the number of square centimetres it covers.

This square has an area of 2 cm² because 2 half-squares have an area of 1 cm².

Count squares to find the area of each figure in square centimetres.

1.

2.

3.

4.

The figures in questions 1 to 5 can be arranged to form a square.

1. What is the area of the square they form?

2. What is the length of each side of that square?

Trace and cut out the 5 figures. Arrange them into a square. Were your answers correct?

5.

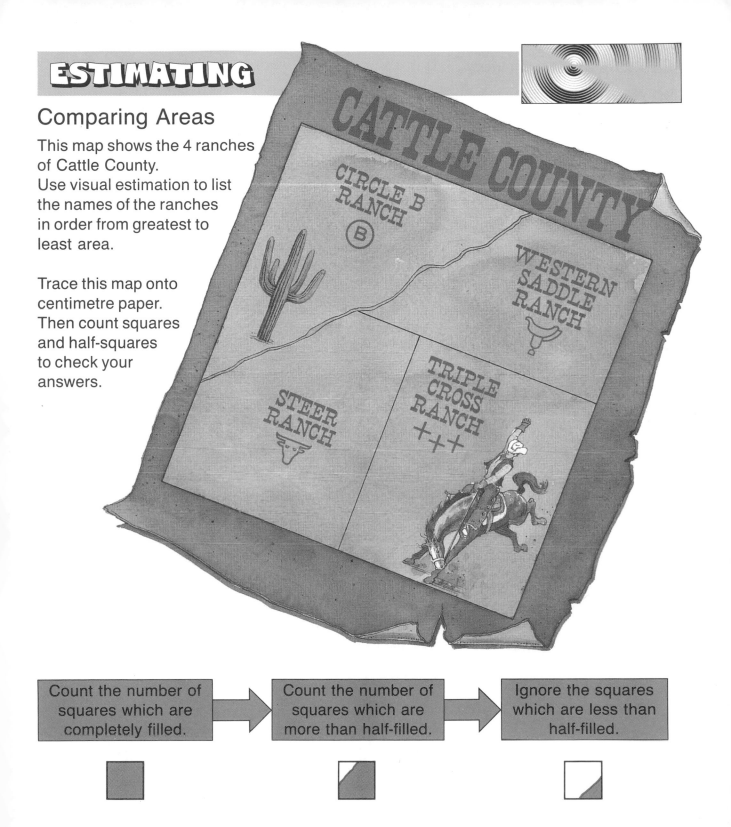

ESTIMATING

Comparing Areas

This map shows the 4 ranches of Cattle County.
Use visual estimation to list the names of the ranches in order from greatest to least area.

Trace this map onto centimetre paper. Then count squares and half-squares to check your answers.

CATTLE COUNTY

CIRCLE B RANCH Ⓑ

WESTERN SADDLE RANCH

STEER RANCH

TRIPLE CROSS RANCH +++

Count the number of squares which are completely filled.	Count the number of squares which are more than half-filled.	Ignore the squares which are less than half-filled.

Areas of Rectangles

We ask: What is the area of this business card?

We think: If we place the card on centimetre paper, it covers 4 rows of 7 squares.

We say: The area of the business card is 28 square centimetres.

We write: The area is 28 cm²

Write a multiplication sentence for the number of centimetre squares covered by each card. Then write the area of the card.

1.

Dangerous Dan

Alias: McGrew
Will Do Any Odd Job
Will Do Some Even Jobs
Terms: Cash on the barrel head

2.

Sam Sly

Used and Misused Cars
Salesperson

Any Colour, Any Shape
(We sell wigs for bald tires)

3.

Granny Smith

FAMOUS AUTHOR

Titles:
Green Apples
Seedy Stories
Life is the Pits

4.

DESIGN-YOUR-OWN-CARD LTD.

NAME: _____
TITLE: _____
LIKES: _____
DISLIKES: _____

5. Copy and complete this table.

Card	1	2	3	4
Length				
Width				
Area				

6. Study your table. Then write a simple rule for finding the area of a rectangle when you know its length and width.

Measure the length and width of each business card in centimetres. Then calculate the area.

1.

Kid Kelly

Occupation: Bully
Role: Bad Guy
Likes: Recess
Dislikes: Detention

2.

Doctor Zorbak
Position: Head Physician
Specialty: Heads
Publications: Headaches in Prehistoric Cave Persons

3.

♪ ♪ Friendly Fred ♪ ♪

INTERESTS: Politics, etc.
AMBITION: Yes
PARTY AFFILIATION: Loves to party, dances to all tunes

4.

ROBERTA ROCK

Occupation: Rock Star
Platinum Records: Shout Out Your Love
Dress: Rhythm is All
Recreation: Loud
Classical Music

On centimetre paper, draw at least 2 different rectangles for each given area.

5. 16 cm²
6. 18 cm²
7. 24 cm²
8. 30 cm²
9. 15 cm²
10. 12 cm²

ESTIMATING

Square A has an area of about 10 cm².

A.

B.

C.

1. Visually estimate the areas of rectangles B and C.

2. Find the approximate length and width of each rectangle using your baby finger. Then calculate the areas.

3. Measure the length and width of each rectangle with a centimetre ruler. Then multiply to find the areas. Which measurement do you think is more accurate?

173

Areas of Parallelograms

To construct a parallelogram from a rectangle, follow these 3 steps:

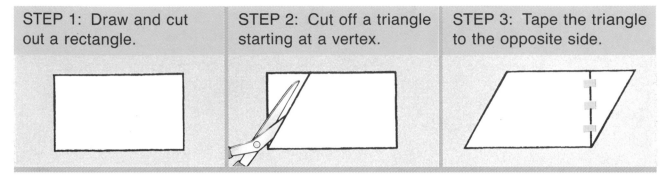

| STEP 1: Draw and cut out a rectangle. | STEP 2: Cut off a triangle starting at a vertex. | STEP 3: Tape the triangle to the opposite side. |

Since the parallelogram was made by rearranging the pieces of the rectangle, the area has not changed.

That is, the area of the parallelogram is the same as the rectangle from which it was made

We think: The area of a parallelogram is the product of its base times its height.

We write: **Area of parallelogram = base × height**

Trace each parallelogram onto centimetre paper. Cut the parallelogram to form a rectangle. Find the area. Then find the area of each parallelogram.

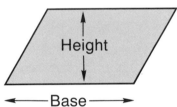

1.

2.

3.

4.

5.

174

In Mathematics Land, all the residents have identification cards shaped like parallelograms.

Measure the base and height of each parallelogram in centimetres. Then calculate the area.

1.

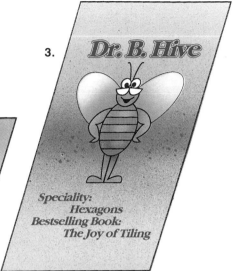

3.

2.

On centimetre paper, draw parallelograms with these areas.

4. 8 cm²
5. 14 cm²
6. 18 cm²
7. 24 cm²
8. 30 cm²
9. 20 cm²

ESTIMATING

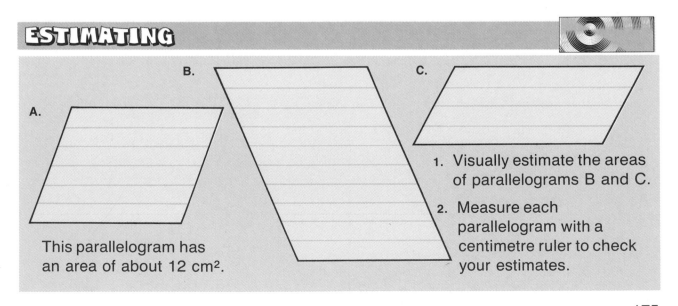

A.

B.

C.

This parallelogram has an area of about 12 cm².

1. Visually estimate the areas of parallelograms B and C.

2. Measure each parallelogram with a centimetre ruler to check your estimates.

Areas of Triangles

To construct a parallelogram from a triangle, follow these steps.

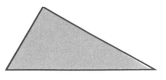

STEP 1: Trace the given triangle.	STEP 2: Cut out the tracing to get 2 congruent triangles.	STEP 3: Fit together to form a parallelogram and tape.

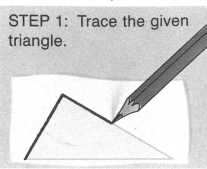

Since the 2 triangles have equal area, each is half the area of the parallelogram.

So the area of the triangle is half the area of the parallelogram having the same base and height.

We think: The area of the triangle is half the product of its base and height.

We write: **Area of triangle** $= \frac{1}{2}$ **base** $\times$ **height**

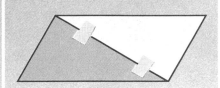

Write the area of each triangle.

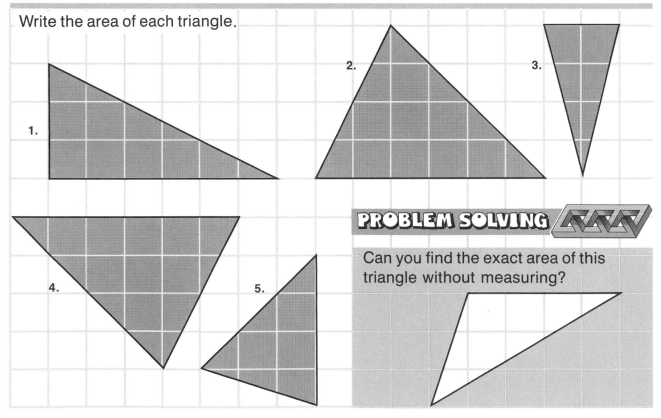

1.

2.

3.

4.

5.

PROBLEM SOLVING

Can you find the exact area of this triangle without measuring?

176

Measure the base and height
of each triangle in centimetres.
Then calculate the area.

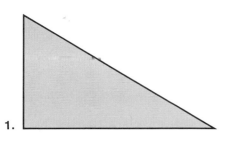
1.

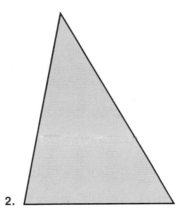
2.

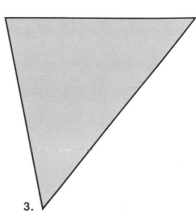
3.

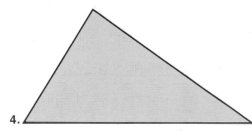
4.

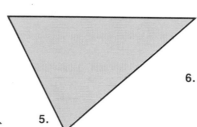
5.

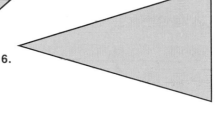
6.

On centimetre paper, draw triangles that have these areas.

7. 3 cm²   8. 5 cm²   9. 8 cm²   10. 12 cm²   11. 15 cm²

12. Use visual estimation to order these
triangles from greatest to least areas.

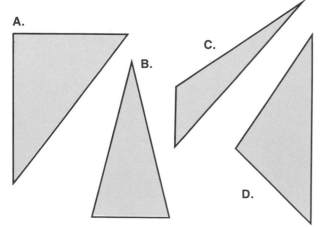

A.

B.

C.

D.

Measure the base and height of each
triangle and calculate the area to check
your estimates.

PROBLEM SOLVING

Calculate the area of this octagon.

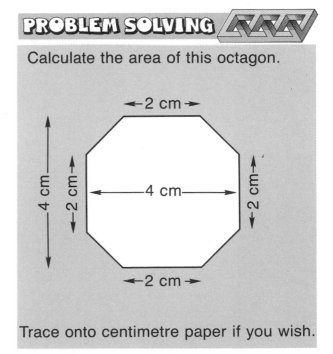

2 cm

4 cm

2 cm

4 cm

2 cm

2 cm

2 cm

Trace onto centimetre paper if you wish.

177

ESTIMATING

Areas of Irregular Shapes

People who travel in the Canadian wilderness learn to recognize animals from their footprints.

Shown here are the footprints of 4 Canadian animals.

The area of the racoon's footprint is about 25 cm².

1. Visually estimate the area of each footprint.

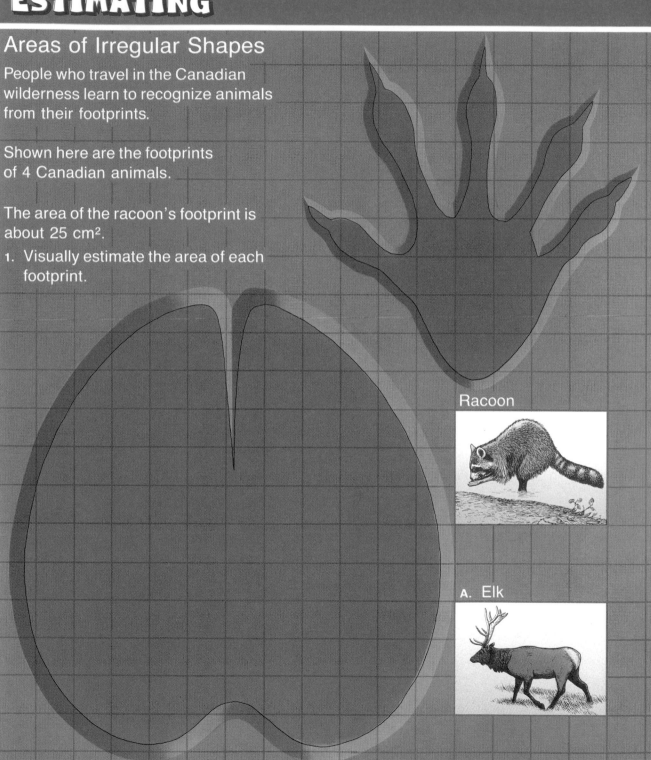

Racoon

A. Elk

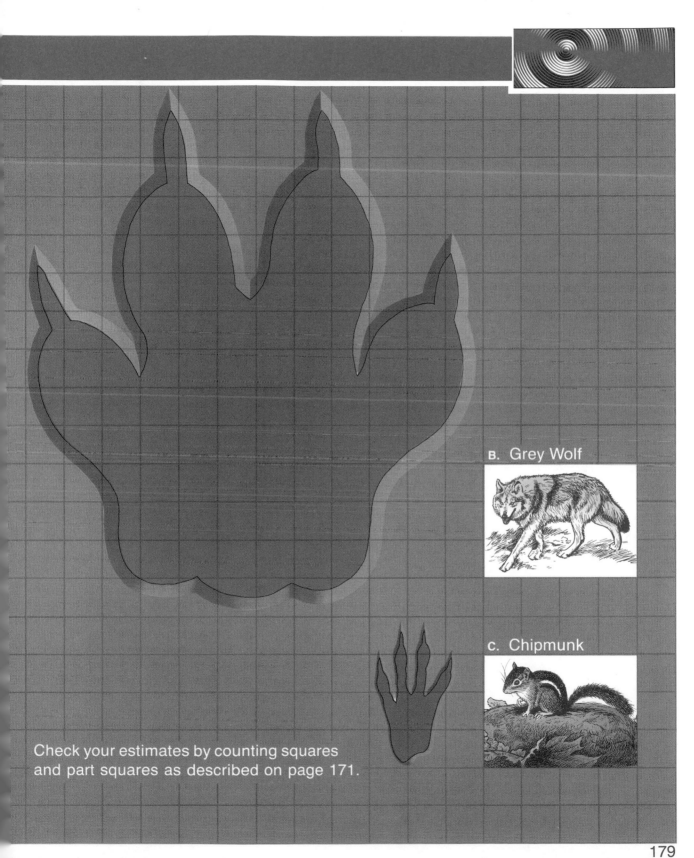

B. Grey Wolf

C. Chipmunk

Check your estimates by counting squares
and part squares as described on page 171.

PROBLEM SOLVING

Selecting a Strategy

SIS, THESE ARE SOME OF THE PROBLEM SOLVING STRATEGIES WE STUDY AT SCHOOL.

OH, YES, WE STUDY THOSE IN HIGH SCHOOL.

- Logical Thinking
- Looking for a pattern
- Making a model
- Solving a simpler related problem
- Guessing and Checking
- Solving multi-step problems

Select one or more strategies to solve each problem.
If one strategy doesn't work, try another.

1. What number when multiplied by itself gives a product of 529?

2. How many squares are there in all?

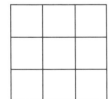

   (There are more than 9 squares.)

3. A rocket is launched at 9:00 a.m. It will return to Earth exactly 2396 h later. At what time of day will it return to Earth?

4. Daryl, Ed, and Frank all met at the library. Daryl visits every 3 days, Ed visits every 4 days, and Frank every 5 days. In how many days will they all meet again at the library?

5. The 6 faces of a cube are marked with the letters from U through Z. Study the two pictures of the cube. What letter is

   • opposite Z?

   • opposite X?

   • opposite Y?

6. The figure shown in the diagram is divided into 9 squares.

   The area of the blue square is 81 square units. The area of the yellow square is 64 square units. What is the area of the pink square?

   Hint: The green square has an area of 1 square unit.

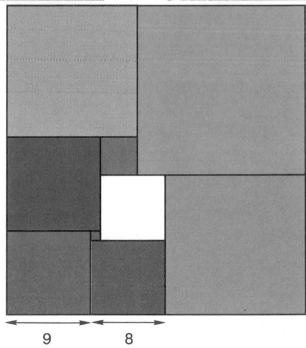

7. If Vince gives Suellen one book, they will both have the same number. However, if Suellen gives Vince one book, he will have twice as many as Suellen. How many books did Vince and Suellen each start with?

8. A computer prints all the numbers from 100 to 200 in order. What is the 138th digit which the computer prints?

181

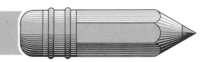

Copy and complete.

1. 7 cm = ▨ mm   2. 18 cm = ▨ mm   3. 400 mm = ▨ cm   4. 300 mm = ▨ cm
5. 8 m = ▨ cm   6. 14 m = ▨ cm   7. 200 cm = ▨ m   8. 5 m = ▨ cm

Find the perimeter of each figure.

9.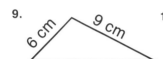
12 cm

10.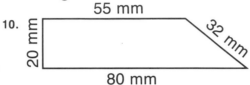
80 mm

11.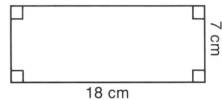

12. Each side of a hexagon is 14 cm long. Find the perimeter.

13. Draw 2 different rectangles with a perimeter of 18 cm.

Write the name of the most appropriate unit for measuring:

14. the height of a hydro pole.

15. the length of a postage stamp.

16. the width of a picture frame.

17. the distance from home to the theatre.

Find the area of each rectangle.

18. 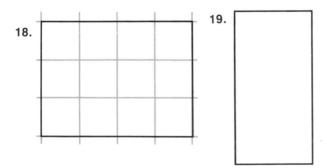   19.

20. A square has an area of 225 cm². What is the length of one side?

Find the area of each parallelogram.

21.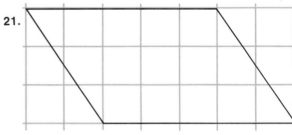

22.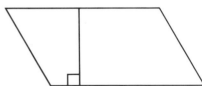

Find the area of each triangle.

23.   24.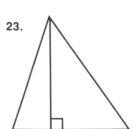

Wari

Wari has been played for thousands of years.
It originated in Egypt, and from there spread
to the rest of Africa, as well as to Asia,
the Philippines, and the West Indies.

Artist's impression of a
Wari game, 18th century Kenya.

Place Value to Tenths

WHO PAINTED THE FENCE?

I PAINTED ONE TENTH OF IT.

I PAINTED THREE TENTHS OF IT.

Mike thinks: 1 out of 10 equal parts
Mike says: 1 tenth
Mike writes: 0.1

Ashley thinks: 3 out of 10 equal parts
Ashley says: 3 tenths
Ashley writes: 0.3

Numbers like 0.1 and 324.5 are called **decimal numbers**.

The values of decimal numbers can be shown in several ways.

We can show 324.5

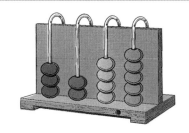

H	T	O	Tenths
3	2	4	5

on an abacus   and   on a place value chart.

Write a decimal number to show how much is shaded.

1.
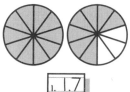

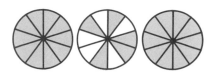
1.7

2.
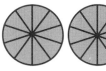

3.

4.
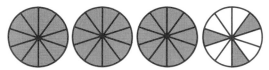

5.

6.

7.
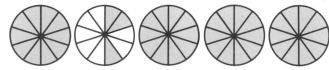 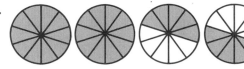

184

Write the number shown on each abacus.

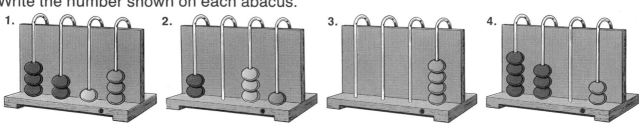

Write each decimal number using words.

5. 1.3 | 5. 1 and 3 tenths | **6.** 4.6   **7.** 0.8   **8.** 5.9   **9.** 0.3

10. 12.5   **11.** 10.6   **12.** 100.2   **13.** 326.1   **14.** 300.3

Write as a decimal number.

15. 8 tenths

16. 24 and 1 tenth

17. 70 and 2 tenths

18. 736 and 5 tenths

Write the number 0.1 greater than:

19. 6.8   **20.** 92.3

21. 0.7   **22.** 208.4

23. 5.0   **24.** 1.9

25. 40.9   **26.** 29.9

Write the value of each coloured digit using words.

27. 27.**4** | 27. 4 tenths | **28.** 8**6**.2   **29.** 4**6**7.1   **30.** **9**38.4

31. **1**330.**9**   **32.** **4**207.8   **33.** **8**23.**5**   **34.** 0.**6**

Write the number missing from each mobile.

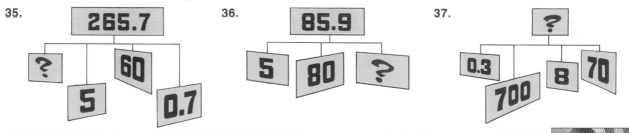

35. 265.7 — ? , 60 , 5 , 0.7

36. 85.9 — 5 , 80 , ?

37. ? — 0.3 , 700 , 8 , 70

Copy and complete.

38. 58.6 = 50 + ▨ + 0.6

39. 309.7 = ▨ + 9 + 0.7

40. 627.4 = 600 + 20 + ▨ + ▨

41. 1050.2 = 1000 + 50 + ▨

42. 891.5 = 800 + ▨ + 1 + 0.5

43. ▨▨▨ = 300 + 7 + 0.1 + 40

44. ▨▨▨ = 0.2 + 80 + 6 + 5000

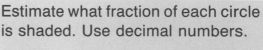

ESTIMATING

Estimate what fraction of each circle is shaded. Use decimal numbers.

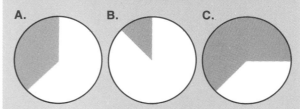

A.   B.   C.

Place Value to Hundredths

The computer screen shows 100 aliens.
What fraction of the 100 aliens are yellow?
What fraction are green?

We see: 23 of the 100 aliens are yellow.

We say: 23 hundredths are yellow.

We write: **0.23** are yellow.

We see: 7 of the 100 aliens are green.

We say: 7 hundredths are green.

We write: **0.07** are green.

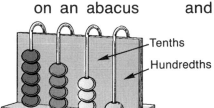

We can show the decimal number **54.31**   on an abacus   and   on a place value chart.

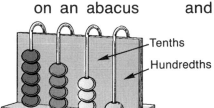

Tenths
Hundredths

T	O	Tenths	Hundredths
5	4	3	1

0.31 may be read as "31 hundredths" or "3 tenths, 1 hundredth."

Write a decimal number to show what fraction of the aliens are yellow.

1.

2.

3.

4.

5.

6.

Write the number shown on each abacus.

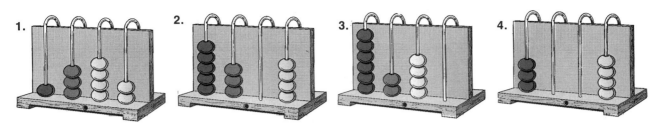

1.   2.   3.   4.

Write each decimal number using words.

5. 16.37   5. 16 and 37 hundredths   **6.** 21.63   **7.** 93.07   **8.** 47.2

9. 0.06   **10.** 203.8   **11.** 0.90   **12.** 80.87

Write as a decimal number. | Write the number 0.01 greater than:

13. 3 tenths, 8 hundredths   **16.** 3.51   **17.** 0.34

14. 14 and 26 hundredths   **18.** 0.02   **19.** 2.60

15. 9 and 6 hundredths   **20.** 7.89   **21.** 14.99

Write the value of each coloured digit using words.

22. 48.**6**   **23.** 58.**7**2   **24.** **8**5.31   **25.** 12**7**.09   **26.** 74.3**8**

27. 27.**3**5   **28.** 2**0**9.8**8**   **29.** 0.3**7**   **30.** 8.**5**4   **31.** **4**20.0**6**

Copy and complete.

32. 76.34 = 70 + 6 + 0.3 + ▦   **33.** 307.96 = 300 + ▦ + 0.9 + 0.06

34. 210.59 = 200 + 10 + ▦ + 0.09   **35.** 73.01 = 3 + ▦ + 70

36. ▦ = 30 + 5 + 0.08   **37.** ▦ = 8000 + 20 + 0.02 + 0.5

EXTENSIONS

An orchestra is composed of 4 different types of instruments: strings, woodwinds, brass, and percussion.

The box graph shows the fraction of the orchestra represented by each type of instrument.

1. Write a decimal number to show what fraction of the instruments in the orchestra are:

     a) strings (S)   **b)** brass (B)

     c) woodwinds (W)   **d)** percussion (P)

Place Value to Thousandths

This computer screen contains 1000 little squares like this ■

We say:
   Each ■ is
   1 thousandth
   of the screen.

We write:
   Each ■ is **0.001**
   of the screen.

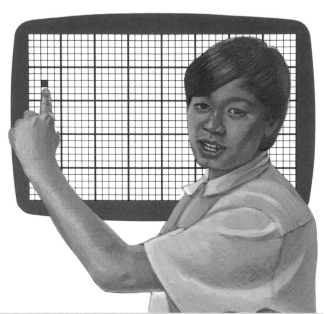

What fraction of each of the following screens is shaded?

We see: 9 of 1000 squares are shaded.	We see: 249 of 1000 squares are shaded.

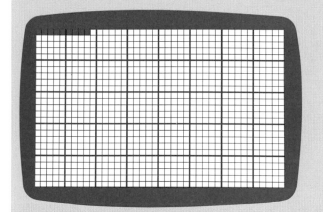

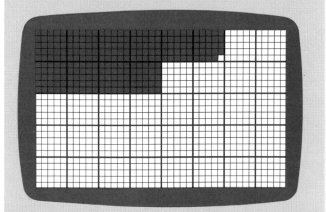

We think:

Ones	Tenths	Hundredths	Thousandths
0 .	0	0	9

We say: 9 thousandths of the
            screen is shaded.
We write: **0.009** of the screen
            is shaded.

We think:

Ones	Tenths	Hundredths	Thousandths
0 .	2	4	9

We say: 249 thousandths of the
            screen is shaded.
We write: **0.249** of the screen
            is shaded.

Write a decimal number to show what fraction of each screen is shaded.

1.
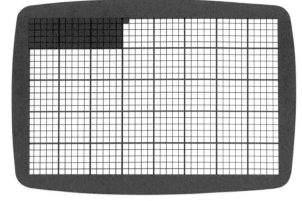

2.
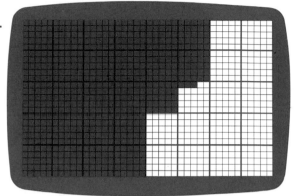

Write each decimal number using words.

3. 6.714 | 3. 6 and 714 thousandths | **4.** 2.836   **5.** 15.600   **6.** 0.492
7. 0.081   **8.** 9.007   **9.** 34.502   **10.** 70.050

Write as a decimal number.

11. 8 thousandths
12. 95 and 412 thousandths
13. 297 and 26 thousandths

Write the number 0.001 greater than:

14. 1.265   **15.** 0.081
16. 27.004   **17.** 0.300
18. 0.659   **19.** 9.899

Write the value of each coloured digit using words.

20. 6.7<mark>2</mark>3   **21.** 0.3<mark>8</mark>5   **22.** 5.61<mark>7</mark>   **23.** 29.30<mark>9</mark>   **24.** 0.47<mark>1</mark>
25. 9.0<mark>4</mark>8   **26.** 0.0<mark>2</mark>9   **27.** 0.00<mark>3</mark>   **28.** 91.0<mark>7</mark>2   **29.** 1<mark>4</mark>.03

Copy and complete.

30. 0.385 = 0.3 + 0.08 + ▇
31. 1.052 = 1 + 0.05 + ▇
32. 2.306 = 2 + ▇ + 0.006
33. 0.752 = ▇ + 0.05 + 0.002
34. 0.898 = 0.8 + 0.008 + ▇
35. 2.003 = 0.003 + ▇
36. 3.107 = 0.1 + 0.007 + ▇
37. ▇ = 0.5 + 0.05 + 0.005

ESTIMATING

Estimate the fraction of the 1000 small squares that are covered by the goose. Write as a decimal number.

189

EXTENSIONS

Ten Thousandths

If 1 thousandth of a computer screen is divided into 10 equal parts, each part is called **1 ten thousandth**.

We say: 1 ten thousandth

We think:

Ones	Tenths	Hundredths	Thousandths	Ten Thousandths
0 .	0	0	0	1

We write: 0.0001

Write as a decimal number.

1. 2 ten thousandths
2. 78 ten thousandths
3. 260 ten thousandths
4. 5476 ten thousandths
5. 8 and 372 ten thousandths
6. 14 and 97 ten thousandths

Write each decimal number using words.

7. 9.0873

7. 9 and 873 ten thousandths
8. 0.8974
9. 2.0517
10. 6.0093
11. 5.0807
12. 0.0009
13. 38.6205
14. 29.0800

Make a place value chart. On it, write each number.

15. 207 ten thousandths
16. 5716 ten thousandths
17. 481 thousandths
18. 600 ten thousandths
19. 17 ten thousandths
20. 890 thousandths
21. 89 hundredths
22. 8 tenths
23. 8000 ten thousandths

Write the value of each coloured digit using words.

24. 6.0007
25. 3.9080
26. 5.6229
27. 0.0536
28. 0.0093
29. 4.1738
30. 8.266
31. 0.5884
32. 21.0079
33. 32.3813

190

Equivalent Decimals

What fraction of this rectangle is shaded?

Jamal says:

> 1 OF 10 EQUAL SQUARES IS SHADED, SO 1 TENTH IS SHADED.

Kevin says:

> 100 OF 1000 LITTLE SQUARES ARE SHADED, SO 100 THOUSANDTHS ARE SHADED.

Jamal writes:

0.1 is shaded.

Kevin writes:

0.100 is shaded.

To find out who is correct, we write both decimal numbers on a place value chart.

	Ones	Tenths	Hundredths	Thousandths
Jamal's answer	0	1		
Kevin's answer	0	1	0	0

Zeros at the end of a decimal number do not change its value.

Both answers show 1 tenth, so both answers are the same.

We write: $0.1 = 0.100$

We say: 0.1 and 0.100 are **equivalent decimals**.

Write an equivalent decimal for each.

1. 0.50
2. 0.7
3. 0.30
4. 0.060
5. 1.050
6. 7.2
7. 0.9
8. 5.81
9. 6.280
10. 27.60
11. 45.02
12. 19.05

Write 2 equivalent decimals for each.

13. 0.700
14. 0.9
15. 1.20
16. 6.10
17. 0.080
18. 9.0
19. 13.8
20. 14.60
21. 0.300
22. 2.7
23. 0.5
24. 8.1
25. 100.0
26. 20.3
27. 16.20

Write 4 equivalent decimals to show what fraction of the rectangle is shaded.

Comparing Decimals to Thousandths

A recent study revealed these facts.

The fraction of Canadian females who reach 85 years of age is 0.336.

The fraction of American females who reach 85 years of age is 0.308.

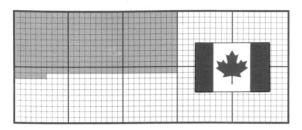

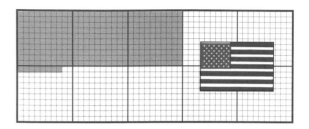

336 out of every 1000 females in Canada reach 85 years of age.

308 out of every 1000 females in the United States reach 85 years of age.

Which country has the greater fraction of women reaching 85 years of age?

To compare 0.336 and 0.308, align the decimal points.

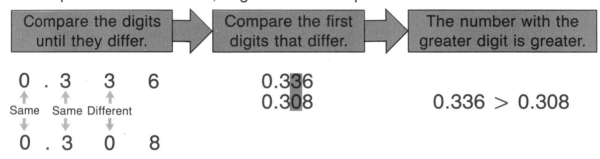

Compare the digits until they differ.	Compare the first digits that differ.	The number with the greater digit is greater.

```
0 . 3   3   6
↑     ↑   ↑
Same Same Different
↓     ↓   ↓
0 . 3   0   8
```

0.336
0.308

0.336 > 0.308

The fraction of females reaching 85 years of age is greater in Canada.

Another example:

To compare 7.34 and 7.304, align the decimal points.

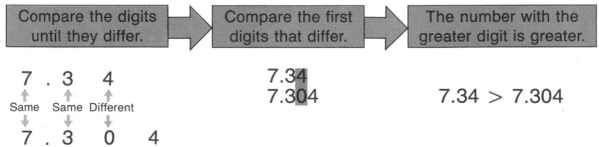

Compare the digits until they differ.	Compare the first digits that differ.	The number with the greater digit is greater.

```
7 . 3   4
↑     ↑   ↑
Same Same Different
↓     ↓   ↓
7 . 3   0   4
```

7.34
7.304

7.34 > 7.304

192

Write >, < or = for each ▓ .

1. 0.24 ▓ 0.02
2. 0.719 ▓ 0.791
3. 41.67 ▓ 41.76
4. 34.645 ▓ 34.564
5. 82.033 ▓ 83.303
6. 336.60 ▓ 336.06
7. 0.075 ▓ 0.705
8. 5827.68 ▓ 5927.98
9. 304.040 ▓ 3040.004
10. 98.65 ▓ 98.650
11. 090.09 ▓ 009.90
12. 716.92 ▓ 761.29
13. 506.025 ▓ 506.250
14. 2391.0 ▓ 4319.2
15. 29.7 ▓ 29.70
16. 43.6 ▓ 3.060
17. 19.700 ▓ 19.09
18. 26.4 ▓ 26.386
19. 46.5 ▓ 46.48
20. 587.50 ▓ 587.5
21. 62.3 ▓ 62.298

22. The fraction of females in Bermuda who reach the age of 85 years is 0.304. Does Bermuda have a greater or lesser fraction of females who reach 85 years of age than Canada?

23. The fraction of females in Hong Kong who reach 85 years of age is 0.303. Is this greater or less than the fraction of females in the United States who reach 85?

EXTENSIONS

This map shows 7 countries where females are most likely to reach 85 years of age. The fraction of females in each country who reach 85 years of age is shown as a decimal number.

List the 7 countries in order from the country with the greatest fraction to the country with the least fraction of females who reach 85.

Norway 0.308

Denmark 0.305

Sweden 0.333

Canada 0.336

Holland 0.320

France 0.316

U.S.A. 0.308

Ordering Decimals

Who was the greatest batter of all time in professional baseball?

This table shows the batting averages of some of the greatest batters in their best seasons.

Write the names of the batters in order from greatest to least average.

Batting Average	=	Number of Hits	÷	Number of Times at Bat

Player	Batting Average	Year
Hugh Duffy	0.438	1894
Ty Cobb	0.420	1911
Babe Ruth	0.378	1924
Ted Williams	0.406	1941
Pete Rose	0.348	1969
George Brett	0.390	1980

We can show these numbers on a number line.

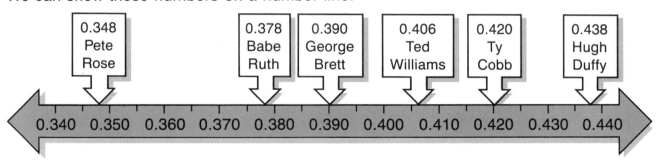

We write: The names of the batters in order from greatest to least batting average are:
Duffy, Cobb, Williams, Brett, Ruth, and Rose.

List from greatest to least.

1. 0.42, 0.24, 0.40
2. 0.385, 0.835, 0.358
3. 1.35, 1.05, 0.53, 1.30
4. 8.780, 7.800, 78.008, 7.780
5. 0.1, 0.110, 0.101, 0.010
6. 6.802, 6.082, 6.82, 6.8

List from least to greatest.

7. 0.680, 0.860, 0.608
8. 2.510, 2.105, 2.501
9. 12.062, 13.1, 12.60, 13.01
10. 10.060, 10.600, 10.006, 10.066
11. 18.3, 18.03, 19.1, 19.01
12. 20.03, 20.3, 20.31, 20.031

---

13. In 1939, Joe DiMaggio had a batting average of 0.381. Between which 2 batters in the list above would this place him?

14. Stan Musial in 1948 had a batting average of 0.376. Between which 2 batters in the list above did Musial place?

Hockey's Highest Goal Scorers

Which N.H.L. hockey player achieved the highest goals per game average during his career?

Average Goals per Game	=	Total Number of Goals	÷	Number of Games Played

The table shows the total number of goals scored by 5 of hockey's highest scorers of the past.

Player	Games Played	Goals	Average Goals per Game
Maurice Richard	978	544	544 ÷ 978 = 0.556
Bobby Hull	1063	610	
Phil Esposito	1282	717	
Richard Martin	685	384	
Guy LaFleur	961	518	

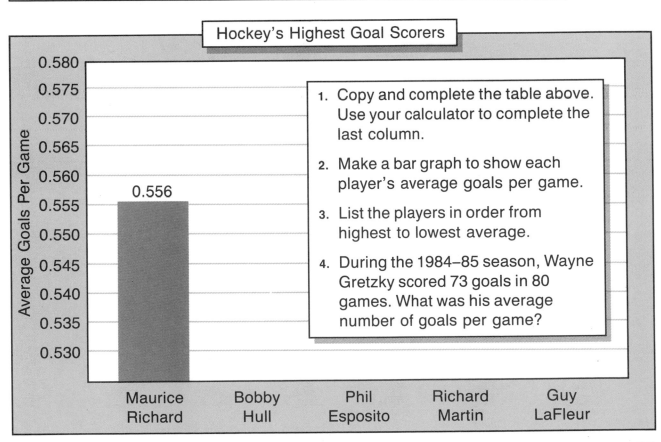

Hockey's Highest Goal Scorers

1. Copy and complete the table above. Use your calculator to complete the last column.

2. Make a bar graph to show each player's average goals per game.

3. List the players in order from highest to lowest average.

4. During the 1984–85 season, Wayne Gretzky scored 73 goals in 80 games. What was his average number of goals per game?

Rounding to the Nearest Whole Number

Round the number in the headline
to the nearest whole number.

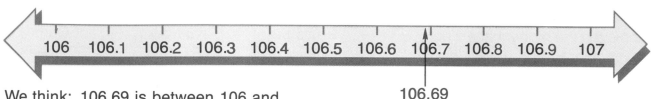

106.69

We think: 106.69 is between 106 and
107 but closer to 107.

We write: **106.69** rounded to the nearest
whole number is **107**.

> If a decimal number is halfway
> between 2 whole numbers, round up
> to the greater whole number.

These headlines use decimal numbers to
report the largest, smallest, fastest, tallest,
longest and highest. Round the number in
each headline to the nearest whole number.

World's Tallest Roller Coaster, Fujikyu Park, Japan.

TODAY TIMES

World's Tallest Roller Coaster is 74.98 m

Smallest TV wrist watch has a 3.05 cm screen

TODAY TIMES

World's Largest Cinema Screen Measures 28.27 m by 21.49 m

TODAY TIMES

World's Longest Bridge Stretches 2.20 km Across Humber Estuary

TODAY TIMES

World's Fastest Car Reaches 1019.251 km / h

Highest Air Speed Ever Recorded: 3528.806 km / h

Round, to the nearest whole number, the temperature shown on each thermometer.

Remember: When the decimal part of a number is 0.5, 0.50 or 0.500, round up.

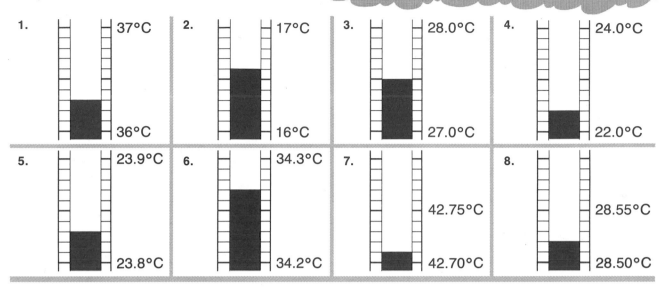

1. 37°C 36°C   **2.** 17°C 16°C   **3.** 28.0°C 27.0°C   **4.** 24.0°C 22.0°C

5. 23.9°C 23.8°C   **6.** 34.3°C 34.2°C   **7.** 42.75°C 42.70°C   **8.** 28.55°C 28.50°C

Round to the nearest whole number.

9. 32.6   **10.** 58.9   **11.** 73.2   **12.** 387.5   **13.** 509.0

14. 9.73   **15.** 17.68   **16.** 87.49   **17.** 227.2   **18.** 438.5

19. 6.918   **20.** 2.099   **21.** 37.690   **22.** 106.500   **23.** 1728.450

Round each amount to the nearest dollar.

24. $2.98   **25.** $3.75   **26.** $16.09   **27.** $0.59   **28.** $18.55

29. $30.85   **30.** $95.99   **31.** $17.50   **32.** $47.51   **33.** $109.02

34. $219.61   **35.** $382.97   **36.** $299.57   **37.** $368.29   **38.** $786.05

39. In 1983, Cody Locke became the world's youngest pilot when he flew solo a Cessna 150 aircraft. At the time, he was only 9 years and 316 days old! What was Cody's age to the nearest year?

40. Write a rule for rounding a decimal to the nearest whole number.

EXTENSIONS

1. Round each decimal number to the nearest whole number.

a) 0.6823   b) 9.7317

c) 2.5555   d) 13.7814

e) 0.8220   f) 85.5002

g) 284.0999   h) 399.0555

2. The thickness of a $10 bill is 0.09 mm. What is the height of a stack of 1000 bills to the nearest centimetre?

Rounding to the Nearest Tenth or Hundredth

On March 17, 1985, Louis Grenier of Canada set a short track world speed skating record. He skated the 1000 m course in 96.55 s.

Round 96.55 to the nearest tenth of a second.

We think:

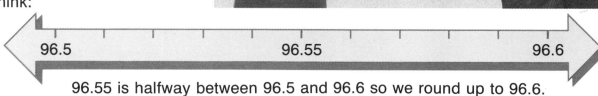

96.55 is halfway between 96.5 and 96.6 so we round up to 96.6.

We write: **96.55** rounded to the nearest tenth of a second is **96.6** s.

Another example:

Round 8.374 to the nearest hundredth.

We think:

8.374 is between 8.37 and 8.38 but closer to 8.37, so we round to 8.37.

We write: **8.374** rounded to the nearest hundredth is **8.37**.

Round each number to the nearest tenth.

1. 7.62	2. 5.49	3. 13.55	4. 21.45	5. 0.79	6. 0.32
7. 10.41	8. 87.86	9. 98.95	10. 100.80	11. 289.64	12. 307.95

Round each number to the nearest hundredth.

13. 3.059	14. 0.073	15. 8.715	16. 5.905	17. 12.007	18. 16.938
19. 21.244	20. 38.771	21. 9.882	22. 92.226	23. 60.555	24. 5.995

Using Rules to Round Numbers

This flow chart shows how to round a decimal number to the nearest whole number.

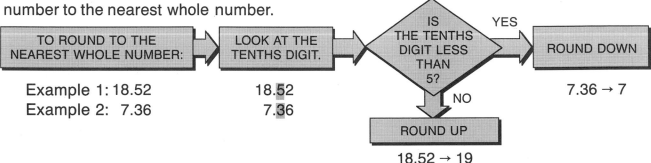

| TO ROUND TO THE NEAREST WHOLE NUMBER: | → | LOOK AT THE TENTHS DIGIT. | → | IS THE TENTHS DIGIT LESS THAN 5? | YES → | ROUND DOWN |

Example 1: 18.52   18.52

Example 2: 7.36   7.36

NO ↓ ROUND UP

18.52 → 19

7.36 → 7

18.52 rounds up to 19

7.36 rounds down to 7

This flow chart shows how to round a decimal number to the nearest tenth.

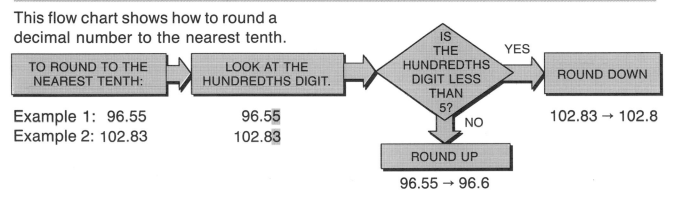

| TO ROUND TO THE NEAREST TENTH: | → | LOOK AT THE HUNDREDTHS DIGIT. | → | IS THE HUNDREDTHS DIGIT LESS THAN 5? | YES → | ROUND DOWN |

Example 1: 96.55   96.55

Example 2: 102.83   102.83

NO ↓ ROUND UP

96.55 → 96.6

102.83 → 102.8

96.55 rounds up to 96.6

102.83 rounds down to 102.8

Round to the nearest whole number.

1. 7.8
2. 3.92
3. 15.41
4. 2.3
5. 86.78
6. 192.55

Round to the nearest tenth.

7. 8.61
8. 5.09
9. 14.05
10. 0.082
11. 99.951
12. 16.486

---

13. Draw flow charts to show how to round a decimal number to the nearest:
    a) hundredth.
    b) thousandth.

Round each number to the nearest hundredth and nearest thousandth.

14. 0.7021
15. 3.8096
16. 5.2055
17. 6.2954
18. 8.0509
19. 9.0045

Making a List

Abbey, Becky, Candice, Daphne, and Elaine were playing tennis in their school tennis tournament. Each girl had to play each of the other 4 girls exactly once.

How many matches were played?

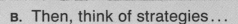

To solve this problem, . . .

A. First, make sure you understand the problem.

Discuss:

- *How many girls are there?*
- *How many matches will each girl play?*
- *What are you asked to find out?*

B. Then, think of strategies . . .

Try making a list of all the matches.

- *Use the first letter of each girl's name to identify the players in each match.*

c. Solve the problem and answer the question.

- *Start by listing all the matches in which Abbey plays.*

> **Abbey's Matches**
> AB ← Abbey vs. Becky
> AC ← Abbey vs. Candice
> AD ← Abbey vs. Daphne
> AE ← Abbey vs. Elaine

- *Then list the games the other girls played.*

D. Check your answer and discuss your solution.

- *How many matches did each girl play?*
- *Did all girls play in the same number of matches?*
- *Did any girl play the same opponent more than once?*
- *What other strategies might you have used to solve this problem?*

1. Six boys, Al, Ben, Carl, Dan, Eric and Frank enter a chess tournament in which each boy plays each of the other boys only once. How many games are played?

2. A computer prints out all the whole numbers from 1 to 100. How many times does the digit 7 appear?

3. How many 4-digit numbers can be made using the cards below?

4. How many whole numbers up to 500 have 9 as the sum of their digits?

ESTIMATING

Estimating Sums and Differences

On April 16, 1983 Silvie Daigle of Canada set short track speed records in the women's 1500 m and 3000 m speed skating races. Her time for the 1500 m race was 161.75 s. Her time for the 3000 m race was 332.31 s.

About how many seconds longer did it take her to complete the 3000 m race?

To estimate:	Round both numbers to the nearest whole number.	Subtract.
332.31 −161.75	332.31 → 332 161.75 → 162	332 −162 170

Silvie's time was about 170 s longer for the 3000 m race.

Estimate by rounding to the nearest whole number.

1. 32.5
   + 6.2

   ```
   1. 33
     +  6
      39
   ```

2. 8.7
   − 1.9

3. 16.58
   − 4.01

4. 12.97
   +45.39

5. 29.728
   − 9.862

6. 75.2
   +54.3

7. 32.1
   −30.8

8. 25.219
   + 8.804

9. 93.76
   − 4.12

Estimate by rounding to the nearest 10.

10. 65.52
    −22.38

    ```
    10. 70
      −20
       50
    ```

11. 126.1
    − 58.3

12. 9.35
    +82.99

13. 11.615
    +73.007

14. 43.086
    + 8.667

15. 93.09
    −19.56

16. 106.7
    + 78.5

17. 212.4
    −186.3

18. 952.68
    −919.05

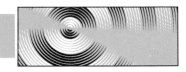

Estimate by rounding to the nearest 100.

19. 519.81
  +357.32

  19. 500
    +400
     900

20. 919.7
  − 109.6

21. 634.38
  − 285.16

22. 1184.369
  +   98.032

23. 2061.5
  + 205.9

24. 784.21
  +296.83

25. 559.826
  − 188.989

26. 1353.2
  − 699.6

27. 907.15
  +634.82

Estimate these sums and differences by rounding each number.

28. 73.9
  − 64.7

29. 198.5
  +286.4

30. $873.50
  + 48.63

31. 87.6
  + 9.5

32. 63.924
  − 45.583

33. $7.88
  − 4.20

34. 665.64
  − 213.85

35. 607.4
  +289.8

36. 2.903
  +45.207

37. 907.3
  − 111.6

PROBLEM SOLVING

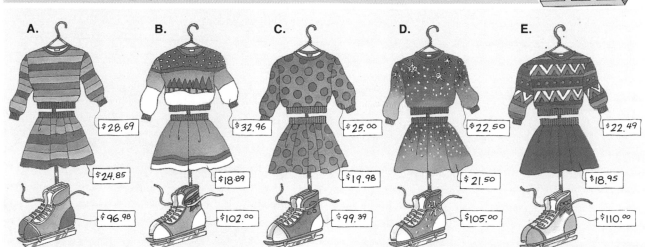

A. $28.69 $24.85 $96.98
B. $32.96 $18.89 $102.00
C. $25.00 $19.98 $99.39
D. $22.50 $21.50 $105.00
E. $22.49 $18.95 $110.00

A shop sells 3-piece figure skating outfits which include a matching sweater, skirt, and pair of skates.

1. Which of the outfits above is:

  a) the least expensive?
  b) the most expensive?

2. How many outfits could be made from those above if an outfit is a sweater, a skirt, and a pair of skates?

3. What is the cost of the least expensive outfit which could be made by selecting a sweater, skirt, and skates from those above?

Adding Decimals

In Olympic slalom skiing, each skier is timed on 2 downhill runs. The skier with the lowest total time is the winner.

Canadian Cathy Kreiner was the gold medalist in the women's giant slalom in the 1976 Olympics. In the 1980 Olympics, her times were 48.06 s and 46.72 s.

What was Cathy's total time in the 1980 slalom?

To add 48.06 and 46.72:

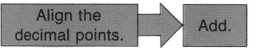

| Align the decimal points. | Add. |

```
  48.06        48.06
+ 46.72      + 46.72
             ──────
              94.78
```

We think:
6 hundredths
+2 hundredths
──────────
8 hundredths

Cathy's total time was 94.78 s.

Another example:

To add $382.73, $8.46, $83.03, and $109.68:

| Align the decimal points. | Add. |

```
  $382.73       $382.73
  $  8.46       $  8.46
  $ 83.03       $ 83.03
+ $109.68     + $109.68
              ────────
               $583.90
```

We think:
3 hundredths
6 hundredths
3 hundredths
+8 hundredths
──────────
20 hundredths
or   2 tenths 0 hundredths

204

Complete only those questions with sums greater than 100.

1. 34.4 + 65.8	2. 29.62 + 74.35	3. 56.079 + 37.926	4. 327.681 + 19.450
5. 19.8 26.4 + 69.5	6. 23.65 48.39 + 24.66	7. 9.082 28.693 52.527 + 13.001	8. 48.201 16.097 9.635 + 30.955

Study the table.

1980 Olympic Slalom Skiing				
Name	Nation	First Run in Seconds	Second Run in Seconds	Total Time in Seconds
Cooper	U.S.A.	44.23	45.05	
Gatta	Italy	44.46	45.48	
Giordani	Italy	44.42	44.70	
Hess	Switzerland	43.50	44.39	
Kinshofer	Germany	42.74	43.76	
Melander	Sweden	44.51	45.31	
Nelson	U.S.A.	44.96	45.89	
Patrakeeva	U.S.S.R.	43.42	45.78	
Wenzel	Lichtenstein	42.50	42.59	

9. Find the total time for each skier.

10. Which skier had a total time 1.57 s greater than Christine Cooper?

11. Write the names of the skiers in order from the skier with the lowest to the skier with the highest total time.

EXTENSIONS

Write your answers to the following questions as decimal numbers.

1. What fraction of the 100-square is shaded?

2. What fraction of the 100-square is not shaded?

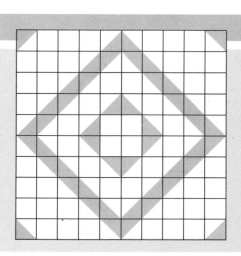

Subtracting Decimals

Are today's Olympic sprinters faster than the sprinters of the past?

Jesse Owens was the fastest human in the 1936 Olympics in Berlin. He ran the 100 m dash in 10.30 s. Carl Lewis, another American, won the 100 m dash in the 1984 Olympics. His time was 9.99 s.

How many seconds faster than Jesse Owens was Carl Lewis?

To subtract 9.99 from 10.30:

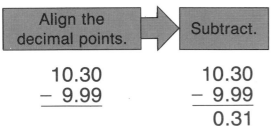

Align the decimal points.	Subtract.

$$\begin{array}{r} 10.30 \\ -\ 9.99 \\ \hline \end{array}$$

$$\begin{array}{r} 10.30 \\ -\ 9.99 \\ \hline 0.31 \end{array}$$

Carl Lewis ran the 100 m race in 0.31 s less than Jesse Owens.

Another example:

To subtract 47.964 from 273.057:

Align the decimal points.	Subtract.

$$\begin{array}{r} 273.057 \\ -\ 47.964 \\ \hline \end{array}$$

$$\begin{array}{r} 273.057 \\ -\ 47.964 \\ \hline 225.093 \end{array}$$

American Jesse Owens in Berlin, 1936

Today's sprinters have slightly lower times in the 100 m dash. Some experts suggest this may be a result of better starting techniques and track surfaces.

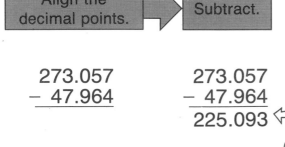

We think:
7 thousandths
−4 thousandths
3 thousandths

Complete only those questions with differences greater than 100.

1. 287.6
    − 179.9

2. 300.2
    − 203.8

3. 579.86
    − 479.78

4. 263.34
    − 185.09

5. 238.57
    − 138.49

6. 2010.00
    − 1909.87

7. 6239.61
    − 5468.09

8. 5000.58
    − 4900.89

9. 298.035
    − 99.903

10. 420.075
    − 320.916

11. 672.007
    − 571.997

12. 780.072
    − 89.348

The table shows how long it took the fastest humans in 6 recent Olympics to run the 100 m dash.

Use the table to help you answer these questions.

Year	Sprinter	Country	Time (seconds)
1984	Lewis	U.S.A.	9.99
1980	Wells	Britain	10.25
1976	Crawford	Trinidad	10.06
1972	Borzov	U.S.S.R.	10.14
1968	Hines	U.S.A.	9.9
1964	Hayes	U.S.A.	10.0

13. How many seconds faster than Crawford was Lewis?

14. Which sprinter took 0.15 s longer than Lewis to run the 100 m race?

15. Which 2 sprinters had times that differed by 0.11 s?

16. What was Lewis' time to the nearest tenth of a second?

PROBLEM SOLVING

Before 1972, the times for the 100 m race were recorded only to the nearest tenth of a second. If the times had been obtained by rounding to the nearest tenth, this would mean that Hines' actual time was somewhere between 9.85 and 9.94 s.

1. Was Lewis faster than Hines? Explain your answer.

2. Who was faster, Lewis or Hayes?

3. Which sprinters named in the table had slower times than Hayes?

4. Can you determine from the data above:

   a) the fastest sprinter?
   b) the slowest sprinter?

Working With Rounded Decimals

Champion athletes understand the importance of proper nutrition in building strong and healthy bodies.

Protein is an important ingredient in the production of muscle tissue. **Carbohydrates** provide the body's major energy.

The table below shows the amount of protein and carbohydrates in popular breakfast foods.

Food (Quantity)	Protein (in grams)	Carbohydrates (in grams)
1 egg	6.58	1.16
1 serving of cereal	6.8	27.2
1 glass of orange juice	1.7	29
1 slice of toast	2	14

About how much protein is there in a breakfast composed of all the foods in the table?

To add 6.58, 6.8, 1.7, and 2:

Align the decimal points.	Write zeros in the empty decimal places.	Add.

$$
\begin{array}{r}
6.58 \\
6.8 \\
1.7 \\
+2. \quad
\end{array}
\qquad
\begin{array}{l}
\text{– Write 6.8 as 6.80} \rightarrow \\
\text{– Write 1.7 as 1.70} \rightarrow \\
\text{– Write 2 as 2.00} \rightarrow
\end{array}
\qquad
\begin{array}{r}
6.58 \\
6.80 \\
1.70 \\
+2.00
\end{array}
\qquad
\begin{array}{r}
6.58 \\
6.80 \\
1.70 \\
+2.00 \\
\hline
17.08
\end{array}
$$

This breakfast has about 17 g of protein.

Is the amount of protein in the breakfast exactly 17.08 g?

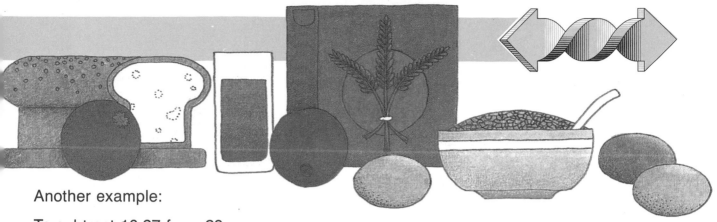

Another example:

To subtract 16.27 from 29:

Align the decimal points.	Write zeros in the empty decimal places.	Subtract.

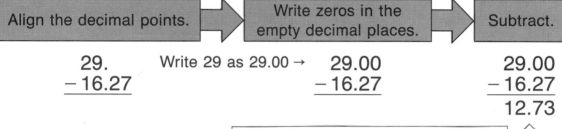

$$\begin{array}{r} 29. \\ -16.27 \end{array}$$ Write 29 as 29.00 → $$\begin{array}{r} 29.00 \\ -16.27 \end{array}$$ $$\begin{array}{r} 29.00 \\ -16.27 \\ \hline 12.73 \end{array}$$

The difference to the nearest whole number is 13.

Since 29 was given to the nearest whole number, we round the answer to the nearest whole number.

Add. Then round each sum to as many decimal places as the addend with the fewest decimal digits.

1. 3.7 + 4.85 + 6.957
2. 18.27 + 9.3 + 34.604
3. 17.3 + 49.27 + 38 + 57.914
4. 6.921 + 25.807 + 8.32 + 19.39

```
1.   3.700
     4.850
  +  6.957
    15.507 → 15.5
```

Subtract. Round each difference appropriately.

5. $$\begin{array}{r} 27.6 \\ -19.75 \end{array}$$

6. $$\begin{array}{r} 81 \\ -29.4 \end{array}$$

7. $$\begin{array}{r} 17.037 \\ -\ 9.6 \end{array}$$

8. $$\begin{array}{r} 40 \\ -17.88 \end{array}$$

9. $$\begin{array}{r} 15.73 \\ -\ 6.9 \end{array}$$

10. How many grams of carbohydrates are there in a breakfast composed of all the foods in the table on page 208?

11. How many more grams of carbohydrates than protein are in the breakfast shown in the table?

12. How much greater is the amount of carbohydrates in a glass of orange juice than the amount of protein?

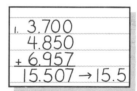

Explain why we round the sum when the addends have different numbers of decimal digits.

Reading Your Receipts

How much change should Tracy receive from $10.00 if she buys a tin of tennis balls and a pair of shoe laces?

This cash register receipt shows the price of each item, the total, the amount **tendered** ($10.00) and the amount of change.

SAM'S SPORTS SPECIALS
ALL PRICES INCLUDE SALES TAX

Tennis Balls	$5.95 per tin
Shoe Laces	$1.29 per pair
Golf Balls	$6.49 per pkg.
Golf Magazine	$2.22 each
Golf Tees	$0.49 per pkg.

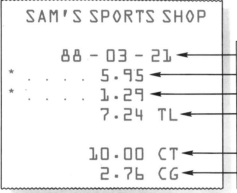

```
SAM'S SPORTS SHOP

      88 - 03 - 21  ◄——  date of purchase
*  . . . . 5.95     ◄——  price of tennis balls
*  . . . . 1.29     ◄——  price of shoe laces
          7.24  TL  ◄——  total price

         10.00  CT  ◄——  cash tendered
          2.76  CG  ◄——  change
```

The cash register adds the prices $5.95 and $1.29 to obtain the total price of $7.24. It then subtracts $7.24 from the $10 which Tracy gave the cashier.

The difference of $2.76 is the change which must be paid to Tracy.

BITS AND BYTES

1. Use your calculator to find the change owing from a $20 bill on each purchase.

   a) 2 tins of tennis balls
   b) a package of golf balls and tees
   c) 2 packages of golf balls and a magazine
   d) 3 tins of tennis balls
   e) 3 tins of tennis balls and 1 pair of laces

Write the missing numbers in these sales receipts.

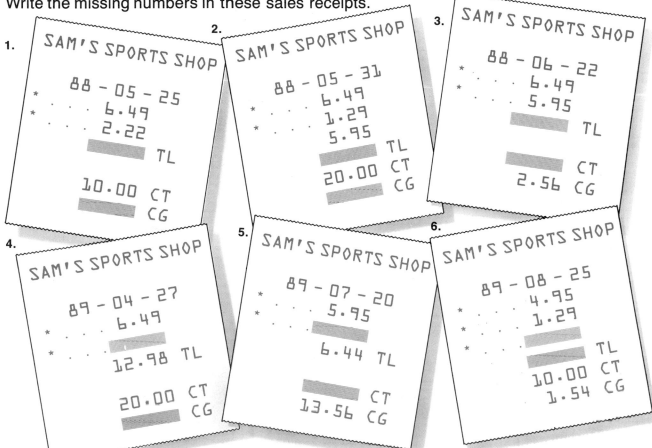

1.

SAM'S SPORTS SHOP

88 – 05 – 25
* · · · · 6.49
* · · · · 2.22
▭▭▭ TL
10.00 CT
▭▭▭ CG

2.

SAM'S SPORTS SHOP

88 – 05 – 31
* · · · 6.49
· · · 1.29
* · · · 5.95
▭▭▭ TL
20.00 CT
▭▭▭ CG

3.

SAM'S SPORTS SHOP

88 – 06 – 22
* · · · · 6.49
· · · · 5.95
▭▭▭ TL
▭▭▭ CT
2.56 CG

4.

SAM'S SPORTS SHOP

89 – 04 – 27
· · · 6.49
* · · ▭▭▭
* · · 12.98 TL
20.00 CT
▭▭▭ CG

5.

SAM'S SPORTS SHOP

89 – 07 – 20
* · · · 5.95
· · · ▭▭▭
6.44 TL
▭▭▭ CT
13.56 CG

6.

SAM'S SPORTS SHOP

89 – 08 – 25
· · · 4.95
· · · 1.29
* · · ▭▭▭
▭▭▭ TL
10.00 CT
1.54 CG

How much change would there be from a $20 bill on each purchase?

7. 3 packages of golf balls
8. 2 magazines and 1 tin of tennis balls
9. 2 packages of golf balls and 1 tin of tennis balls
10. 4 pairs of shoe laces
11. 2 packages of golf balls and 2 packages of golf tees
12. Trevor purchased 2 items from the list of Sam's sports specials. He gave the cashier a $10 bill. What is the smallest amount of change he could receive?

PROBLEM SOLVING

Lynda purchased 3 items from the list of Sam's sport specials. She gave the cashier a $10 bill.

If Lynda received $1.34 change, what items did she purchase?

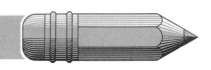

Write as a decimal number.

1. 3 and 5 tenths
2. 28 hundredths
3. 4 and 26 thousandths
4. 67 and 349 thousandths

Write the value of each coloured digit.

5. 3.2**7**6
6. 14.**3**8
7. 0.03**9**

Write the number 0.01 greater than:

8. 5.32
9. 16.09
10. 0.99

Copy and complete.

11. 39.51 = 30 + 9 + ■ + 0.01
12. 0.987 = ■ + 0.08 + 0.9
13. ■ = 1 + 0.7 + 0.003 + 0.04

Write an equivalent decimal for each.

14. 0.600
15. 32.6
16. 116.50
17. 3.620
18. 0.8
19. 5.34

Write > or < for each ■.

20. 6.213 ■ 6.123
21. 10.147 ■ 10.174
22. 136.626 ■ 136.624

List in order from least to greatest.

23. 0.309, 0.390, 0.093
24. 4.061, 4.106, 4.610, 4.016
25. 1.85, 1.805, 5.018, 50.18

Round to the nearest whole number.

26. 23.6
27. 89.5
28. 3.088

Round to the nearest tenth.

29. 3.65
30. 14.083
31. 3.209

Round to the nearest hundredth.

32. 4.039
33. 29.145
34. 19.704

35. List the 4-digit numbers greater than 5000 that can be made using these cards.

Add.

36.	43.3	37.	87.5	38.	3.473
	+56.8		+32.9		+1.089

39.	8.096	40.	65.47	41.	2.56
	17.381		18.80		8.05
	+24.938		+49.09		+7.66

Subtract.

42.	843.7	43.	307.24	44.	64.18
	−267.9		−186.73		−37.44

45.	9.008	46.	4.216	47.	30.06
	−3.759		−2.938		−27.98

Estimate these sums and differences.

48.	36.5	49.	440.68	50.	11.319
	+ 8.2		−239.19		+85.556

Tapatan

Tapatan is a Philippine game of strategy. Each of the 2 players tries to move 3 pieces to form a row. The geometric design of a Tapatan gameboard has been found carved into the roof of an ancient Egyptian temple, as well as into the cloister seats in Canterbury Cathedral and Westminster Abbey.

Artist's impression of Tapatan in the Philippines in the 19th century.

Points, Lines, and Line Segments

Sarah and her friends are playing Capture the Flag.

Sarah is going to draw a map to show the way to the hidden flag.

To show the location of the starting point, she draws a dot and writes the letter A beside it.

We see: A .
We say: **point A**

Sarah draws another dot marked B. She connects A and B with a straight path.

We see:

B
|
A

We say: **line segment AB**
or
line segment BA

We write: AB or BA

Next Sarah draws a dot marked C. She sketches a straight path through A and C with an arrow at both ends.

We see:

We say: **line AC** or **line CA**

We write: $\overleftrightarrow{AC}$ or $\overleftrightarrow{CA}$

The arrows at both ends of the line AC tell us that it extends forever in both directions.

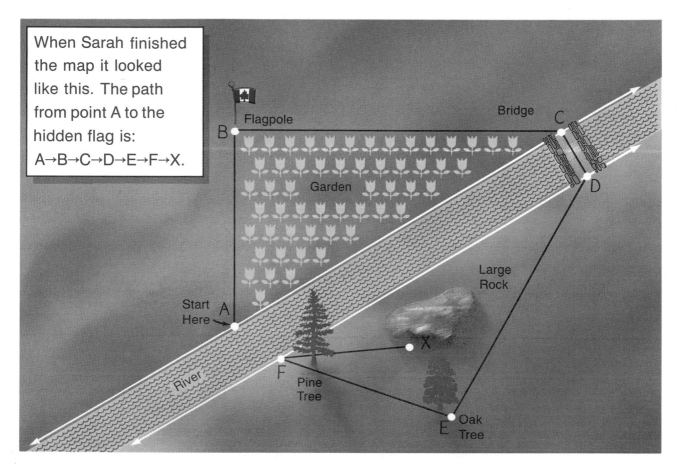

When Sarah finished the map it looked like this. The path from point A to the hidden flag is:

A→B→C→D→E→F→X.

Flagpole

B

Bridge C

Garden

Large Rock

Start Here A

River

F Pine Tree

X

D

E Oak Tree

Use the letters A,B,C,D,E,F, and X to answer these questions.

1. What point marks the location of the:

   a) pine tree?   b) oak tree?
   c) flagpole?   d) hidden flag?

2. What points mark the ends of the bridge?

3. What line segment shows the location of the bridge?

4. Name the line segment which shows the path:

   a) from the oak tree to the pine tree.
   b) from the flagpole to the bridge.
   c) from the bridge to the oak tree.
   d) from the pine tree to the flag.

5. Write the names of the 3 line segments which enclose the garden.

6. Write the names of 2 different line segments which have end point C.

7. Write the names of the lines which show the banks of the river.

8. Which of these line segments is shortest:

   AB, BC, or CD?

9. Which of these line segments is longest:
   BC, CD, or AC?

215

Parallel and Intersecting Lines and Line Segments

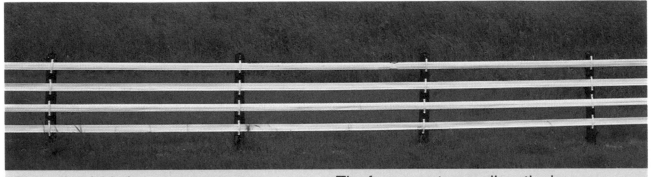

The rails of this fence seem to go on forever without intersecting. The fence rails suggest **parallel lines**.

The fence posts are all vertical. The fence posts suggest **parallel line segments**.

We see:

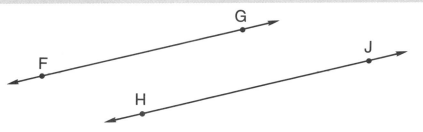

We think: Lines FG and HJ extend forever but do not meet.

We write: $\overleftrightarrow{FG}$ and $\overleftrightarrow{HJ}$ are **parallel lines**.

We think: Line segments FG and HJ are parts of parallel lines.

We write: FG and HJ are **parallel line segments**.

We see:

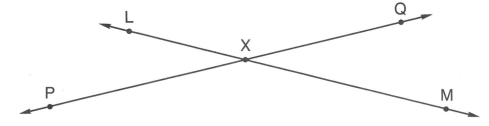

We think: Lines LM and PQ intersect at point X.

We write: $\overleftrightarrow{LM}$ and $\overleftrightarrow{PQ}$ are **intersecting lines**.

We think: Line segments LM and PQ intersect at point X.

We write: LM and PQ are **intersecting line segments**.

Where can you find models of parallel lines or parallel line segments in your classroom?

Is each pair of line segments parallel? Write *yes* or *no*.

1.
2.
3.
4.
5.

Draw each letter with a ruler.
Make parallel line segments the same colour.

Some letters have no
parallel line segments.

6.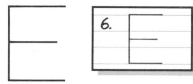
7.
8.
9.

10.
11.
12.
13.
14.

15. Name pairs of parallel line segments
in each figure.

a)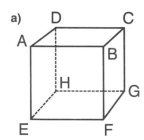

b)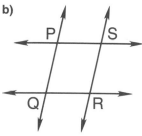

16. For figure b) above name:
   a) the line which passes through
      points P and Q.
   b) the line segment parallel to QR.
   c) a line which intersects $\overleftrightarrow{SR}$.
   d) a line segment which is part of
      line $\overleftrightarrow{QR}$.

JUST FOR FUN

1. Do these train tracks intersect?
2. Do these tracks appear to intersect?
3. Are the train tracks parallel?
4. Explain your answer to question 2.

217

Angles

B   C   BC is a ray.

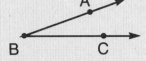

It is a part of a line with one end point. The light from a flashlight suggests a ray.

We see:

A

B   C

We think: Rays BA and BC meet at point B.

We say: Point B is the vertex of angle ABC.

We write: B is the vertex of ∠ABC.

∠CBA and ∠ABC name the same angle. The middle letter names the vertex.

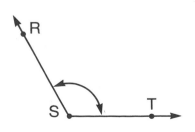

YOU CAN'T CATCH AN ACUTE FISH WITH AN OBTUSE HOOK.

B

A

C

The angle at the corner of a square is a **right angle**.

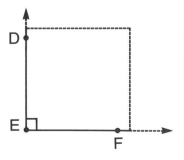

D

E   F

∠DEF is a right angle.

218

An angle smaller than a right angle is an **acute angle**.

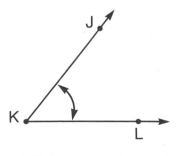

J

K   L

∠JKL is an acute angle.

An angle larger than a right angle is an **obtuse angle**.

R

S   T

∠RST is an obtuse angle.

Name each angle in 2 ways. Then tell whether
it is a right, acute, or obtuse angle.

1.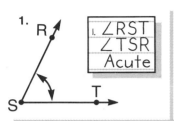
i. ∠RST
∠TSR
Acute

2.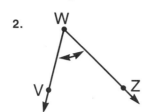

3.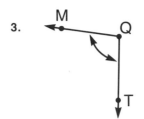

4.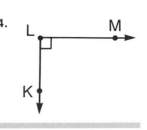

5. Name 8 right angles
in this figure.

6. Name 2 obtuse angles
in this figure.

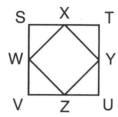

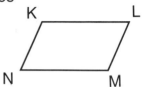

For each triangle, name one acute and one obtuse angle.

7.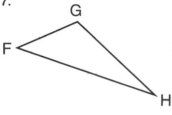

8.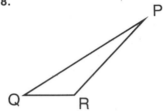

9.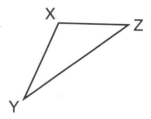

10. Name these angles In order from largest to smallest.

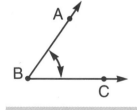 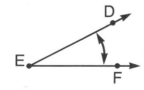 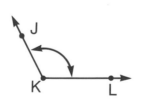 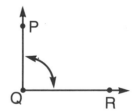

11. Name all the acute angles in the
figure below.

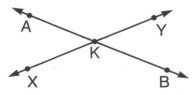

12. Name all the obtuse angles in the
figure above.

PROBLEM SOLVING

1. How many angles are there in all?

2. Name the largest angle.

3. Name the smallest angle.

219

BITS AND BYTES

Angle: A Change in Direction

The computer screen has an invisible circle with 360 equally spaced marks. A turn from one mark to another shows an angle of 1 degree (1°).

We use the symbol ° to show degrees.

The diagram shows angles of 1° and 10°.

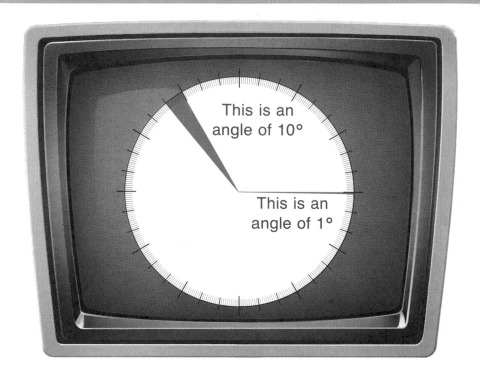

This is an angle of 10°

This is an angle of 1°

When the turtle is given this computer command...

LT 30

...it turns left (counterclockwise) through an angle of 30°.

New Direction   Starting Direction

When the turtle is given this computer command...

RT 50

...it turns right (clockwise) through an angle of 50°.

Starting Direction   New Direction

220

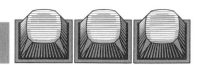

Write a computer command which turns the turtle as shown.

1.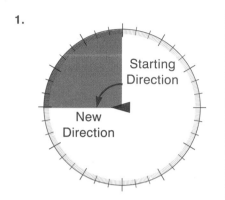

2.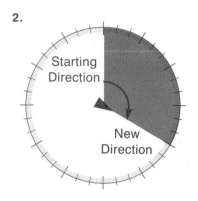

3.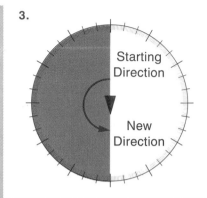

4.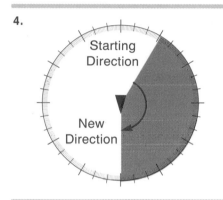

5.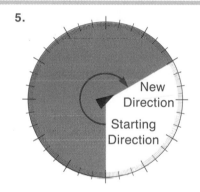

6.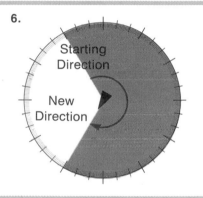

IF YOU START BY FOLLOWING THESE DIRECTIONS, YOU'LL END BY FINDING THE NEW DIRECTION.

Use 8 screens like those above. On each screen, draw a vertical line segment to show the starting direction.

Then draw a line segment to show the new direction given by each command.

7. RT 40   8. RT 120

9. LT 60   10. LT 120

11. RT 180   12. RT 90

13. LT 270   14. RT 360

EXTENSIONS

The Invention of Degrees

Long ago the Babylonians observed that the position of the sun changes by the same amount each day. They thought that the sun revolved around the earth.

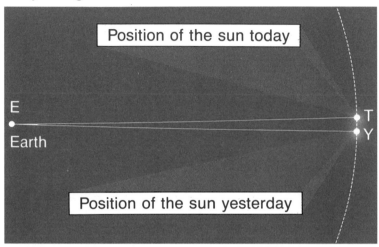

∠YET shows the change in the sun's position in one day.

The Babylonians said the sun moved in one day through an angle of one **degree** (1°).

There were 360 days in the Babylonian year. The sun was therefore observed to revolve through an angle of 360° in a single year.

Today we still use degrees to measure the size of an angle.

We can see from the diagram that:

- An angle of 1° is very small.
- A full turn is 360°.
- A $\frac{1}{2}$ turn is 180°.
- A $\frac{1}{4}$ turn (right angle) is 90°.

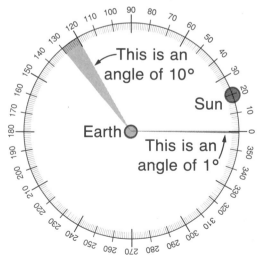

The diagram shows an angle of 10°. About how long does it take for the position of the sun to change by 10°?

On January 1, the sun is observed to be at the 0° position.

Through how many degrees has the sun appeared to move in each of these diagrams?

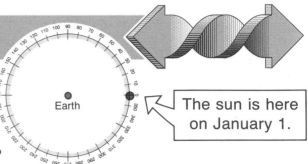

Earth

The sun is here on January 1.

1.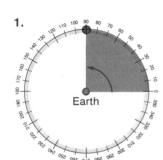

Earth

2.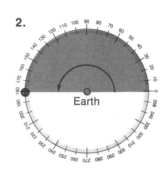

Earth

3.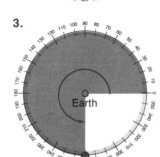

Earth

4.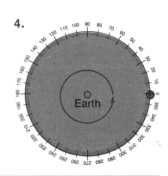

Earth

How many degrees are in each turn?

5. $\frac{1}{4}$ turn

6. $\frac{1}{2}$ turn

7. $\frac{3}{4}$ turn

8. a full turn

9. In how many months would the sun appear to move through:

a) $\frac{1}{2}$ turn?   b) $\frac{1}{4}$ turn?   c) $\frac{3}{4}$ turn?

Remember: It takes about 12 months for the sun to appear to move through a full turn.

ESTIMATING

To estimate the size of this angle...

We think: The angle is a little larger than a $\frac{1}{4}$ turn.

We write: The angle is a little larger than 90°.

Use your answers to questions 1 through 4 to help you estimate these angles in degrees.

A.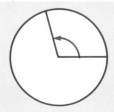

B.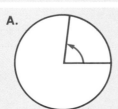

C.

D.

223

Measuring Angles with a Single Scale Protractor

A **protractor** is an instrument used to measure the size of an angle.

This protractor measures angles in degrees. It shows that the measure of ∠ SUN is 60°.

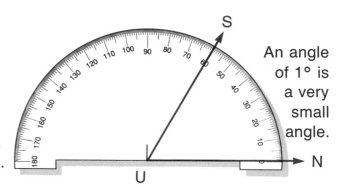

An angle of 1° is a very small angle.

Tell whether each angle is right, acute, or obtuse. Then record the size of each angle.

1.

2.

3.

4.

5.

6.

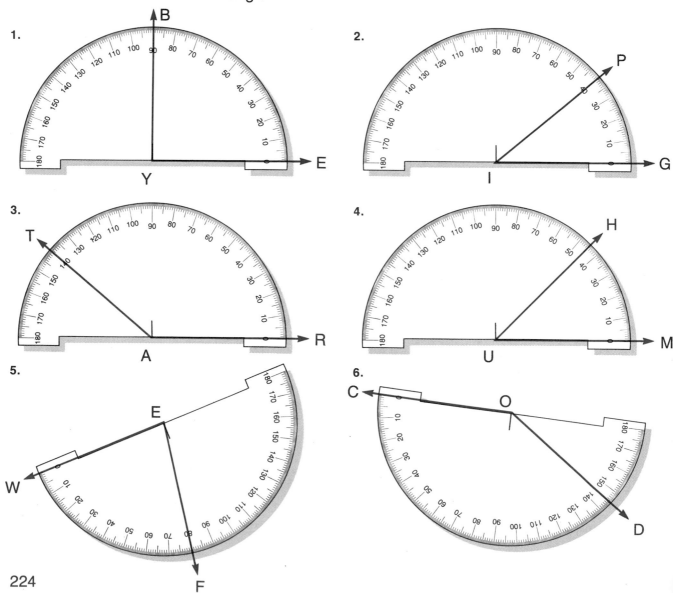

224

Measuring Angles with a Double Scale Protractor

When measuring an angle with a double scale protractor, we must decide which scale to read.

Before we measure an angle, we decide whether the angle is acute or obtuse.

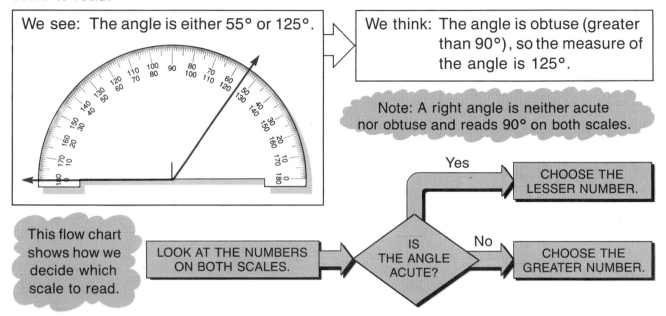

We see: The angle is either 55° or 125°.

We think: The angle is obtuse (greater than 90°), so the measure of the angle is 125°.

Note: A right angle is neither acute nor obtuse and reads 90° on both scales.

This flow chart shows how we decide which scale to read.

LOOK AT THE NUMBERS ON BOTH SCALES. → IS THE ANGLE ACUTE?

Yes → CHOOSE THE LESSER NUMBER.

No → CHOOSE THE GREATER NUMBER.

Tell whether each angle is acute or obtuse. Then write its measure in degrees.

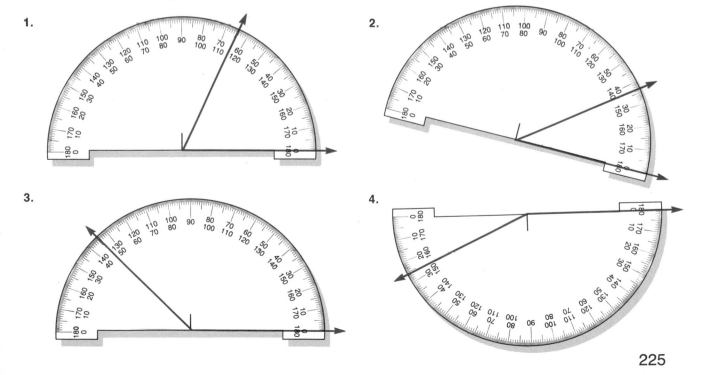

1.

2.

3.

4.

Using a Protractor

To measure an angle with a protractor, follow these steps.

Place the centre of the protractor on the vertex of the angle.

Turn the protractor until its zero degree line lies along one ray. Read the protractor.

The measure of the angle is 120°.

Zero Degree Line

Centre

Tell whether each angle is right, acute, or obtuse. Then use a protractor to measure in degrees.

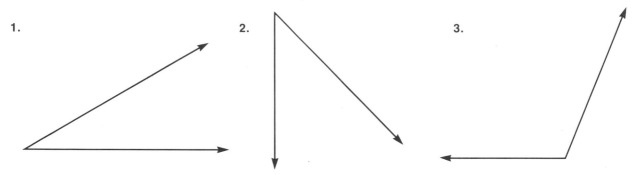

1.

2.

3.

ESTIMATING

Here is a wild turkey's footprint. Estimate the angle between adjacent toes.

Here is a crow's footprint. Estimate each of the 4 angles between adjacent toes.

Use a protractor to check your estimate.

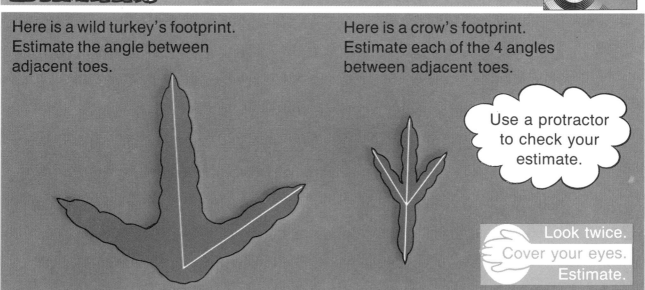

Look twice.
Cover your eyes.
Estimate.

Drawing Angles

We can use a protractor to draw an angle of any given size. To draw an angle of 70°, we follow these steps.

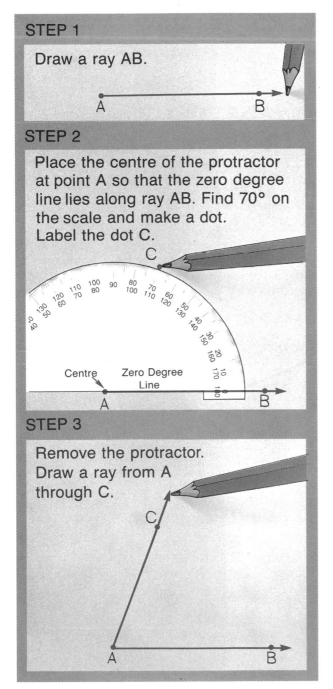

STEP 1

Draw a ray AB.

STEP 2

Place the centre of the protractor at point A so that the zero degree line lies along ray AB. Find 70° on the scale and make a dot. Label the dot C.

Centre   Zero Degree Line

STEP 3

Remove the protractor. Draw a ray from A through C.

Draw an angle with the given measure.

1. 40°	2. 80°	3. 25°
4. 68°	5. 17°	6. 130°
7. 155°	8. 110°	9. 167°
10. 121°	11. 103°	12. 180°

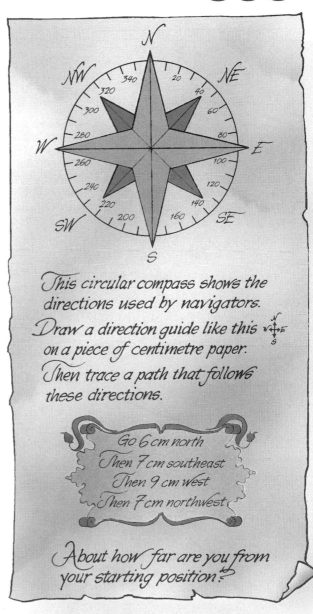

This circular compass shows the directions used by navigators.

Draw a direction guide like this on a piece of centimetre paper.

Then trace a path that follows these directions.

> Go 6 cm north
> Then 7 cm southeast
> Then 9 cm west
> Then 7 cm northwest

About how far are you from your starting position?

WHAT TURTLE TRIP IS DESCRIBED BY THESE COMMANDS?

Turtle Trips

If you want me to travel, you must tell me:

- how far.
- in what direction.

FD 70
RT 120
FD 90

When the turtle is given this computer command...

FD 70

...it moves forward 70 turtlesteps.

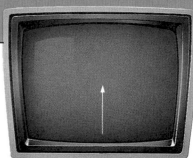

When the turtle is given this computer command...

RT 120

...it turns right (clockwise) 120°.

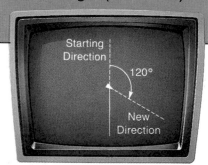

Starting Direction

120°

New Direction

When the turtle is given this computer command...

FD 90

...it moves forward 90 turtlesteps.

MAKE 6 COMPUTER SCREENS LIKE THIS FROM CENTIMETRE PAPER.

Let 10 turtlesteps correspond to a distance of 1 cm on your screen.

For each set of commands:

- Draw the path on your paper screen.
- Use your protractor and ruler.

If you have a computer with Logo, key in each set of commands.

1. FD 10
   RT 53
   FD 50
   RT 90
   FD 40

2. FD 40
   RT 90
   FD 30
   RT 135
   FD 70

3. LT 90
   FD 20
   RT 150
   FD 80
   LT 150
   FD 50

4. FD 30
   RT 127
   FD 50
   RT 143
   FD 40
   RT 90

5. RT 45
   FD 70
   RT 135
   FD 50
   RT 90
   FD 50
   RT 90

6. FD 60
   RT 135
   FD 70
   RT 45
   FD 60
   RT 135
   FD 70
   RT 45

A path which brings the turtle back to its starting position is called a **closed path**.

These are closed paths.

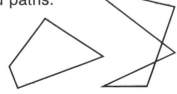

Which of the paths described in questions 1 through 6 are closed? For each closed path, find the total number of degrees through which the turtle has turned.

Explain what you discover.

229

Capture the Flag

Pamela and her friends are playing "Capture the Flag."

The enemy flag is at one of the locations on this map.

To find the enemy flag, you will need to know these words.

- A **clockwise** turn is a turn in the same direction as the hands of a clock.

- A turn in the opposite direction is called **counterclockwise**.

Copy this map onto centimetre paper. Draw on your map the path described in the directions.

Use your protractor and centimetre ruler.

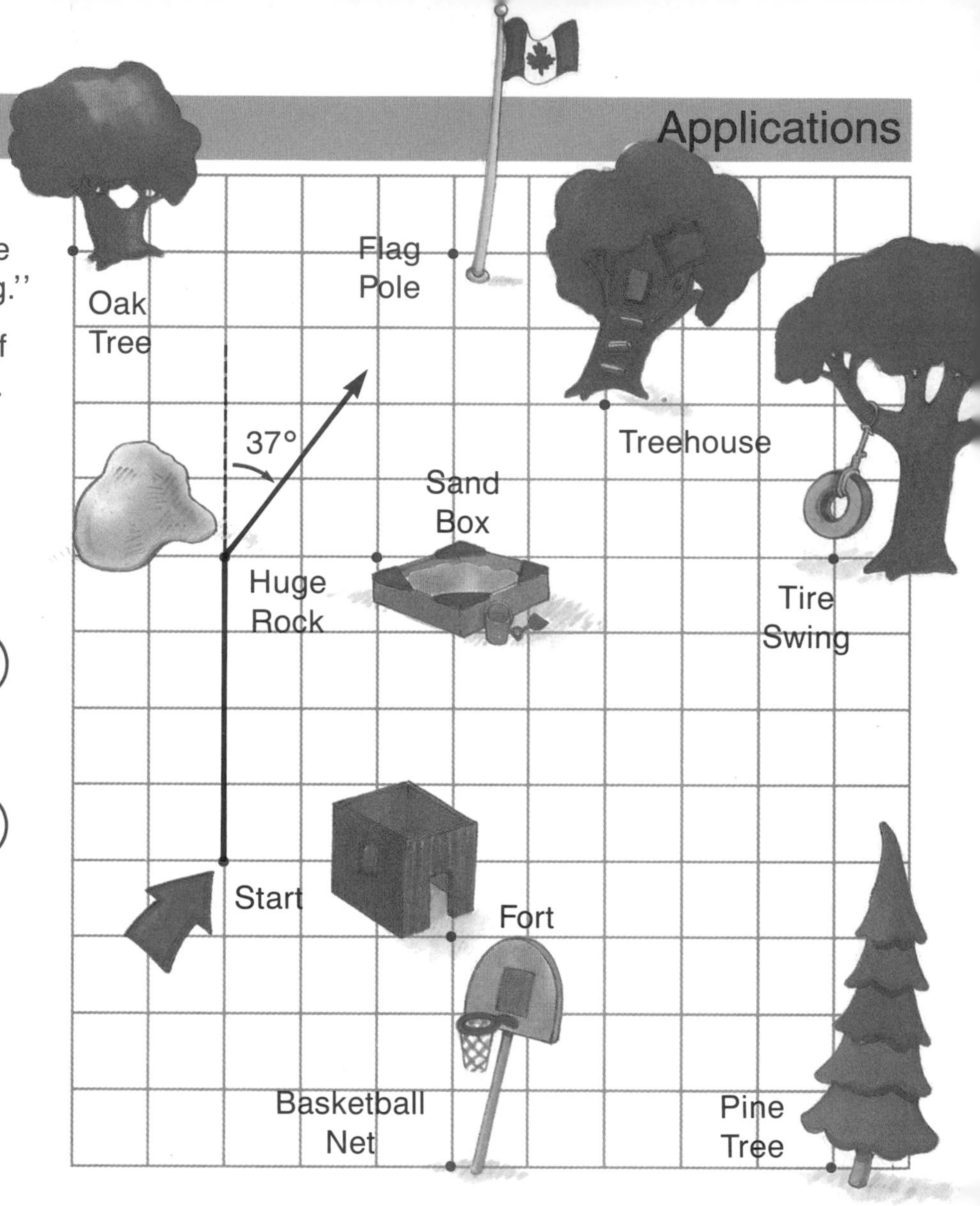

Oak Tree

Flag Pole

Treehouse

37°

Sand Box

Huge Rock

Tire Swing

Start

Fort

Basketball Net

Pine Tree

DIRECTIONS

1. Begin at Start.
2. Travel 4 cm to Huge Rock.
3. Turn clockwise 37°.
4. Go forward 5 cm. (Where are you now?)
5. Turn clockwise 120°.
6. Go forward 13 cm. (Where are you now?)
7. Turn clockwise 166°.
8. Go forward 10 cm. (Where are you now?)
9. Turn counterclockwise 155°.
10. Go forward 5 cm to the enemy flag.

Where is the enemy flag?

230

Sum of the Angles in a Triangle

Measure the 3 angles in each triangle.

1. Record your measurements in a table like this.

Triangle	∠ABC	∠ACB	∠BAC
Blue			
Red			
Green			
Yellow			

2. Use your completed table to calculate the sum of ∠ABC + ∠ACB + ∠BAC for each triangle. Can you find a pattern?

Use your protractor to draw a triangle that has these angles.

3. 30°, 40°, and 110°.
4. 50°, 60°, and 70°.
5. 35°, 75°, and 70°.
6. 120°, 35°, and 25°.

7. A triangle has angles of 35° and 90°. Predict the measure of the remaining angle.

8. Trace the yellow triangle and cut it out. Cut off each vertex and glue in your notebook as illustrated. What do you find?

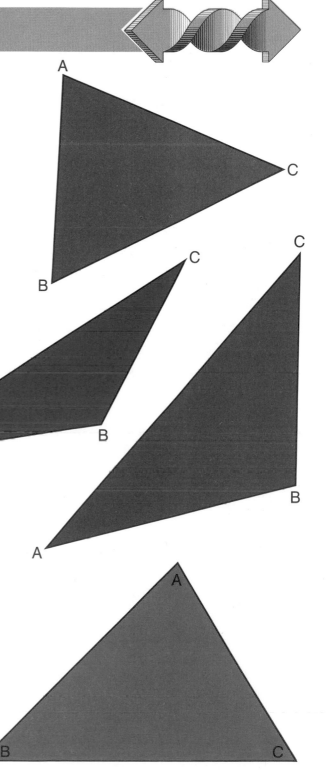

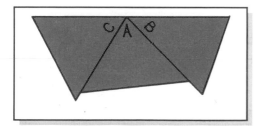

Naming and Classifying Triangles

We use letters to name triangles.

We see:

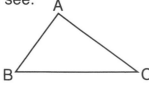

A

B   C

We say: triangle ABC

We write: △ABC

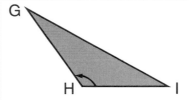

WE COULD ALSO NAME THE TRIANGLE △ACB OR △BCA OR △BAC OR △CAB OR △CBA!

△DEF has a right angle. It is a **right triangle**.	△GHI has an obtuse angle. It is an **obtuse triangle**.	△JKL has 3 acute angles. It is an **acute triangle**.
D E F	G H I	J K L
We use ⌐ to show a right angle.	The angle marked with an arrow is an obtuse angle.	These angles are all acute angles.

Name each triangle. Tell whether it is right, obtuse, or acute.

1.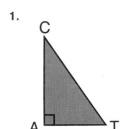
C
A   T

2.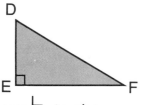
B
O   W

3.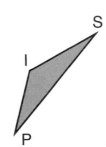
S
I
P

4.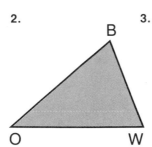
W
A   X

5.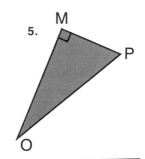
M
P
O

PROBLEM SOLVING

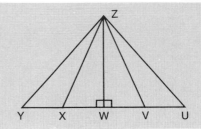

Write the name of every triangle in this figure. Tell whether each is right, obtuse, or acute.

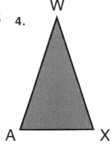

Z

Y   X   W   V   U

232

All 3 angles of this triangle are equal. It is an **equilateral triangle**.	This triangle has 2 equal angles. It is an **isosceles triangle**.	This triangle has no angles of equal size. It is a **scalene triangle**.

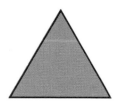

Tell whether each triangle is equilateral, isosceles, or scalene.
You may use your protractor or tracing paper.

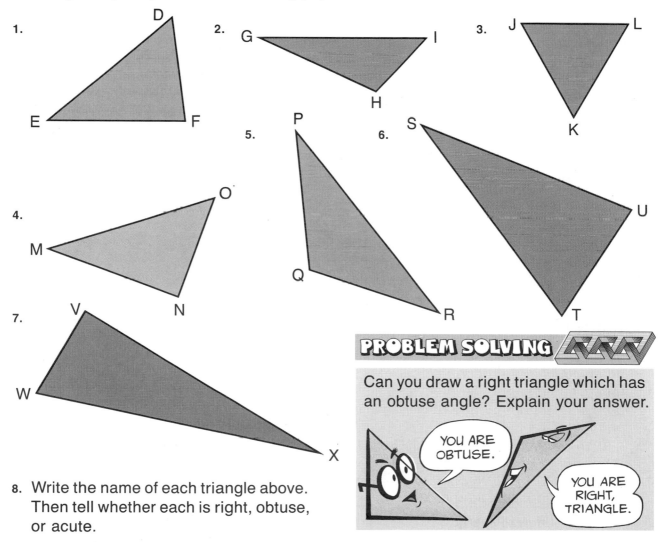

1.

2.

3.

5.

6.

4.

7.

8. Write the name of each triangle above. Then tell whether each is right, obtuse, or acute.

PROBLEM SOLVING

STUDY THESE PICTURES CAREFULLY. THEN WRITE THE ANSWER TO EACH QUESTION.

Identifying Likenesses and Differences

1. All of these are quadrilaterals.	None of these is a quadrilateral.	Which one is the quadrilateral? Why?
		A B C D
2. All of these are parallelograms.	None of these is a parallelogram.	Which one is the parallelogram? Why?
		A B C D
3. All of these are rectangles.	None of these is a rectangle.	Which one is the rectangle? Why?
		A B C D

4. All of these are squares.	None of these is a square.	Which one is the square? Why?
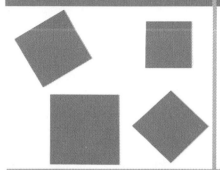		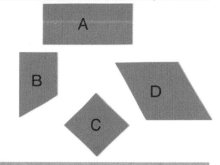

5. Each of these is a rhombus.	None of these is a rhombus.	Which one is the rhombus. Why?
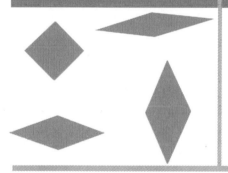		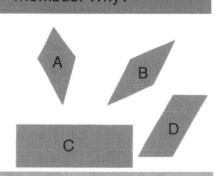

The rectangle, rhombus, and square are all members of the parallelogram family. Copy and complete the table by writing *true* or *false* for each statement.

YOU'RE A SQUARE.

THAT MAKES ME A RHOMBUS, A RECTANGLE, AND A PARALLELOGRAM ALSO.

Statement	Parallelogram	Rectangle	Rhombus	Square
The opposite sides must be parallel.	✓	✓	✓	✓
All sides must be the same length.			✓	✓
All angles must be right angles.		✓		✓

235

The Quadrilateral Family

1. Figure A below is a quadrilateral. It is also a parallelogram and a rhombus.
   Copy and complete the table below.

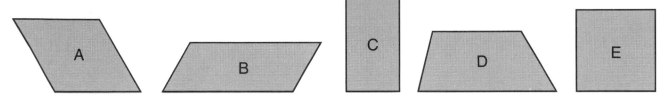

	Is the figure a...				
Figure	Quadrilateral?	Parallelogram?	Rectangle?	Rhombus?	Square?
A	Yes	Yes	No	Yes	No
B					
C					
D					
E					

Copy and complete each sentence.

2. Any quadrilateral containing 4 right angles is a ▭ .

3. Any quadrilateral with 2 pairs of parallel sides is a ▭ .

4. Any parallelogram with all sides of equal length is a ▭ .

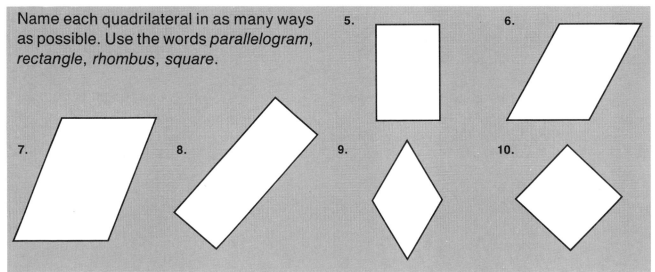

Name each quadrilateral in as many ways as possible. Use the words *parallelogram*, *rectangle*, *rhombus*, *square*.

5. 6. 7. 8. 9. 10.

Write a sentence to explain how to identify each of these figures.

11. quadrilateral   12. parallelogram   13. rectangle   14. square   15. rhombus

Looking for a Pattern

Over 2000 years ago, there lived a secret group of mathematicians called the **Pythagoreans**.

The Pythogoreans believed that number patterns could be used to explain music, science, and geometry. They counted the number of dots in simple polygonal patterns. Some of these **polygonal numbers** are shown below.

Pythagoreans of ancient Greece.

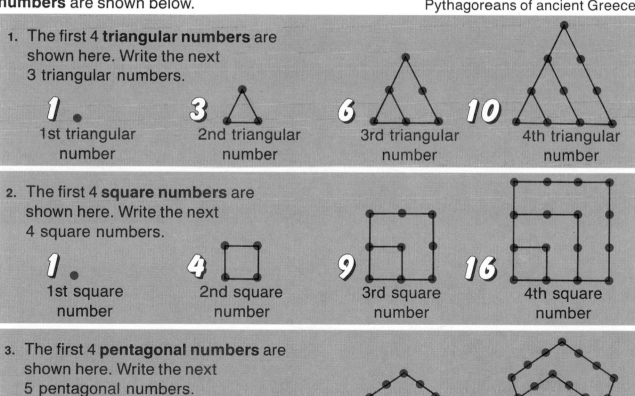

1. The first 4 **triangular numbers** are shown here. Write the next 3 triangular numbers.

1 •   *3*   *6*   *10*

1st triangular number   2nd triangular number   3rd triangular number   4th triangular number

2. The first 4 **square numbers** are shown here. Write the next 4 square numbers.

1 •   *4*   *9*   *16*

1st square number   2nd square number   3rd square number   4th square number

3. The first 4 **pentagonal numbers** are shown here. Write the next 5 pentagonal numbers.

1 •   *5*   *12*   *22*

1st pentagonal number   2nd pentagonal number   3rd pentagonal number   4th pentagonal number

PROBLEM SOLVING

Using Logical Thinking

Sherlock Homely, a master mind,
On a visit to Shapeland was asked to find
The figure who committed a serious crime.

Five suspects stood before him there.
Some were bald and some had hair.
He studied each with special care.

He paused, then spoke, "I will declare
The shape of the guilty one standing there.
But first I will need a generous sum
Of gold and silver from everyone."

They granted his wish.
The money was paid.
His long awaited
announcement was made.

CONSIDER ALL CLUES,
THE CONCLUSION IS NATURAL.
THE GUILTY ONE IS...
...THE QUADRILATERAL!

238

Clues

The guilty figure...

- Is not beside a figure with 4 equal sides.
- Is not beside the rhombus.
- Is a parallelogram.
- Has at least one pair of opposite sides equal.
- Has at least 2 unequal angles.

Look at the 5 suspects. Use the clues and logical thinking to determine the shape of the guilty one.

A. First, make sure you understand the problem.

Discuss:

- *What is wrong with Homely's solution?*
- *What are you asked to find out?*
- *What clues do you have?*

B. Then, think of strategies.

Try deductive thinking.

- *Use the clues to check out each figure.*
- *Record your results in a table.*

C. Solve the problem and answer the question.

- *Number each figure.*
- *Make a table.*

Clue	Could be	Could not be
1st	1, 3, 5	2, 4

D. Check your answer. Discuss your solution.

- *Does your guilty figure satisfy every clue?*
- *Did you need both the "could be" and the "could not be" columns?*

Solve these problems.

1. Al, Beth, Cindy and Don are seated around a square card table. Partners are seated on opposite sides of the table. Al is seated on Don's right. Beth is not seated on Don's left. Who is Cindy's partner?

2. There are 19 girls and 15 boys in Mr. Grant's class. 24 of them ride the bus. What is the fewest number of girls who might ride the bus?

3. Sarah drew a square, a rectangle (which was not a square) and a parallelogram (which was not a rectangle). She coloured 1 blue, 1 red, and 1 green. The red figure had sides of 2 different lengths. The blue one had no right angles. What colour was the rectangle?

4. How many marbles do I have if:

   - all of them are red except 2 and
   - all of them are white except 2 and
   - all of them are blue except 2?

239

From Polygons to Circles

We can use the REPEAT command to carry out the same instructions many times.

REPEAT 3[ ] means "carry out 3 times, the instructions inside the square brackets."

When the turtle is given this computer command...	...it moves forward 70 turtlesteps.

FD 70

When the turtle is given this computer command...	...it turns right (clockwise) through 120°.

RT 120

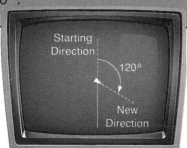

Starting Direction
120°
New Direction

When the turtle is given this computer command...	...it moves forward 70 turtlesteps, and turns clockwise 120° a total of 3 times.

REPEAT 3 [FD 70 RT 120]

1. What polygon does the turtle's path resemble?

2. How many turtlesteps long is each side of the polygon traced by the turtle?

MAKE 3 COMPUTER SCREENS LIKE THIS IN YOUR NOTEBOOK.

For the REPEAT commands in questions 1, 2, 3 below:

- Draw the corresponding path on your paper computer screen.
- Use your protractor to draw required angles.
- Use your centimetre ruler and the scale factor of 10 turtlesteps = 1 cm to draw required line segments.
- Name the polygon you have drawn.

If you have a computer with Logo, key in the commands.

1. REPEAT 4[FD 60 RT 90]   2. REPEAT 5[FD 50 RT 72]   3. REPEAT 6[FD 30 RT 60]

Write a repeat command to draw these regular polygons.

Make all sides 30 turtlesteps long. If you have a computer with Logo, key in your answers.

4.   5.   6.

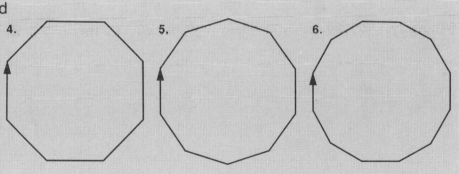

In questions 7 through 9:

- Describe or sketch the polygon which the turtle would trace.
- Write the number of sides in the polygon.

7. REPEAT 8[FD 35 RT 45]

8. REPEAT 9[FD 10 RT 40]

9. REPEAT 360[FD 1 RT 1]

10. Can you name the polygons sketched in questions 4 and 5?

11. What figure does the polygon in question 9 resemble?

CHECK-UP

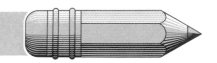

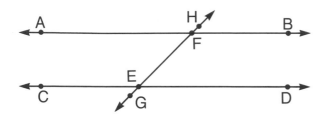

Using the figure above, name:

1. 2 line segments.
2. 2 intersecting lines.
3. 2 parallel lines.
4. 1 acute angle.
5. 1 obtuse angle.

Tell whether each angle below is right, acute, or obtuse.

Use your protractor to measure each angle in degrees.

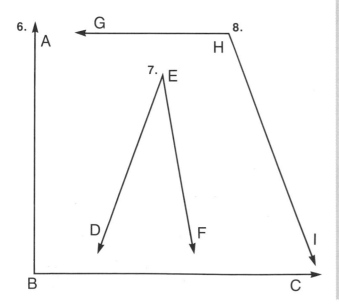

Use your protractor to draw an angle that measures:

9. 40°   10. 75°   11. 135°

12. Name each triangle. Tell whether it is right, acute, or obtuse.

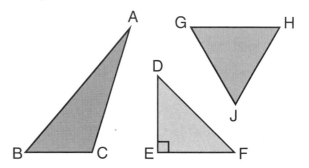

13. Tell whether each triangle in question 12 is scalene, isosceles, or equilateral.

Write the letter of a figure below that is:

14. a quadrilateral.
15. *not* a quadrilateral.
16. a rectangle.
17. a rhombus.
18. a parallelogram.

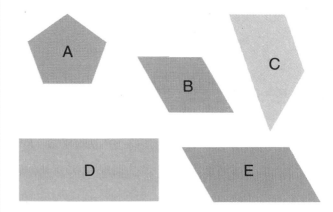

242

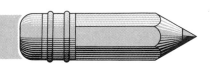
Copy and complete.

1. 6 cm = ▨ mm   **2.** 23 cm = ▨ mm   **3.** 50 mm = ▨ cm   **4.** 600 mm = ▨ cm

5. 2100 cm = ▨ m   **6.** 7 m = ▨ cm   **7.** 20 m = ▨ cm   **8.** 900 cm = ▨ m

Find the perimeter of each figure.

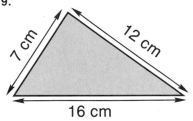

9. 7 cm, 12 cm, 16 cm

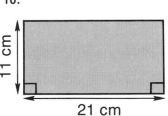

10. 11 cm, 21 cm

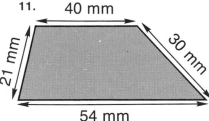

11. 40 mm, 30 mm, 21 mm, 54 mm

Find the area of each figure.

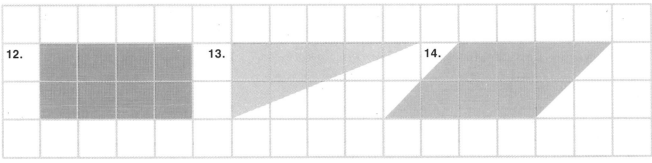

12.   **13.**   **14.**

15.

16.

Write the value of each coloured digit.

17. 4.085   **18.** 17.93   **19.** 137.208

20. 20.7   **21.** 61.387   **22.** 658.392

List in order from greatest to least.

23. 0.483, 0.384, 0.843, 0.834

24. 7.639, 6.936, 9.636, 9.663

Round to the nearest tenth.

25. 18.65   **26.** 5.281   **27.** 3.037

28. 3.073   **29.** 3.37   **30.** 4.39

Round to the nearest hundredth.

31. 5.105   **32.** 5.015   **33.** 5.501

34. 17.395   **35.** 8.496   **36.** 11.374

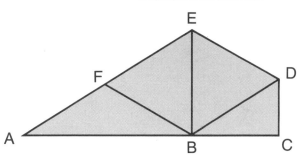

37. List the 4-digit numbers greater than 5000 that can be made using these cards.

Add.

38. 57.9
      +42.8

39. 18.39
      +63.92

40. 4.386
      +2.907

Subtract.

41. 806.9
      −357.2

42. 27.83
      −18.96

43. 7.306
      −5.908

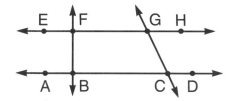

Using the figure, name:

44. 2 intersecting lines.
45. 2 parallel lines.
46. 2 line segments.
47. 1 acute angle.
48. 1 obtuse angle.

Use your protractor to draw an angle with measure:

49. 35°   **50.** 60°   **51.** 125°

Using the figure, name:

52. 2 equilateral triangles.
53. a right triangle.
54. an obtuse triangle that is isosceles.

Use your protractor to measure each angle:

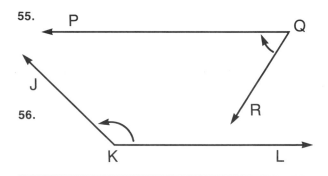

55.
56.

Write the letter of a figure that is:

57. a quadrilateral.
58. a parallelogram.
59. *not* a quadrilateral.
60. a rhombus.
61. a rectangle.

10

MAZDA

Mazda is a game of strategy where 2 players remove coins from 3 piles. Each player tries not to choose the last coin. The game of Mazda was played over 4000 years ago by the people of Babylon. The famous maker of laws, King Hammurabi, was considered to be the greatest Mazda player. He recorded his method of play on the back of the monument where his laws were engraved.

Artist's impression of a private home outside Babylon, 18th century B.C.

Estimating Products: One Decimal Factor

Of all pumps known to science, the human heart is the most reliable. It is estimated that in a lifetime of 70 years, the human heart pumps almost 3 billion times!

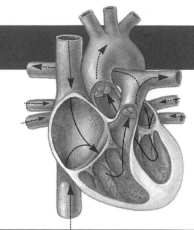

A runner's heart pumps an average of 17.8 L of blood per minute.

Estimate the total volume of blood pumped during a 4 min race.

To estimate:	Round the decimal factor to an appropriate whole number.	Multiply.

$$
\begin{array}{r} 17.8 \\ \times\ \ \ 4 \end{array}
\qquad 17.8 \rightarrow 20 \qquad
\begin{array}{r} 20 \\ \times\ 4 \\ \hline 80 \end{array}
$$

The heart pumps about 80 L
of blood during the 4 min race.

Another example:

To estimate:	Round the dollar amount.	Multiply.

$$
\begin{array}{r} \$14.75 \\ \times\ \ \ \ \ 12 \end{array}
\qquad \$14.75 \rightarrow \$15 \qquad
\begin{array}{r} \$15 \\ \times\ 12 \\ \hline \$180 \end{array}
$$

Is there any other way to estimate this product?

Estimate these sums. (Hint: Write as multiplication sentences.)

1.	24.8	2.	3.1	3.	4.82	4.	$19.98	5.	26.891
	24.8		3.1		4.82		$19.98		26.891
	24.8		3.1		4.82		$19.98		26.891
	24.8		3.1		4.82		$19.98		26.891
	24.8		3.1		+4.82		$19.98		26.891
	+24.8		+3.1				+$19.98		26.891
									+26.891

Estimate these products.

6.	24.8	7.	39.6	8.	9.7	9.	50.3	10.	80.2
	× 7		× 8		×14		× 20		× 35

11.	18.09	12.	3.15	13.	6.95	14.	16.98	15.	30.169
	× 5		× 8		× 7		× 12		× 27

16. 6.1 × 40   17. 8.9 × 60   18. 90 × 7.8

19. 4.16 × 50   20. 80 × 12.93   21. 75 × 8.723

22. Mr. Fraser sponsored Kevin for $1.75 per kilometre in the Terry Fox Run. Kevin ran 12 km. About how much did Mr. Fraser donate to the Terry Fox Fund?

23. Ms. Bradley, the physical education teacher at Bestway School, bought 4 soccer balls at $12.98 each and 5 baseball bats at $8.95 each. About how much did she spend?

Which is the correct product: a, b, or c? Use estimation.

24. 8 × 7.9	a. 6.32	b. 63.2	c. 632
25. 9 × 4.31	a. 0.3879	b. 3.879	c. 38.79
26. 72.4 × 6	a. 4.344	b. 43.44	c. 434.4
27. 6.02 × 63	a. 37.926	b. 379.26	c. 3792.6
28. 0.861 × 9	a. 7.749	b. 77.49	c. 774.9

29. For each of the 5 multiplication sentences above, record the number of decimal places:
   • in the decimal factor.
   • in the correct product.

30. Write a simple rule to explain how you can determine the number of decimal places in the product.

Calculating Products: One Decimal Factor

Randy is 11 years old. He wants to know how tall he will be when he reaches his full adult height.

His baseball coach gave him a table which showed growth factors for boys and girls. The coach told him to multiply his present height by the growth factor for 11 year old boys.

	Growth Factors	
Age	Girls	Boys
10	1.18	1.28
11	1.13	1.23
12	1.08	1.19
13	1.04	1.15

Growth factor for 11 year old boys.

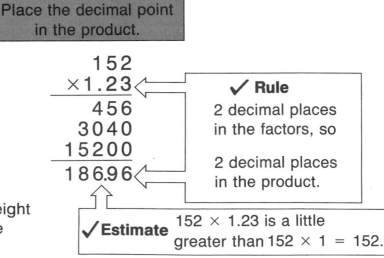

Randy is now 152 cm tall. Use the growth factor to calculate his predicted adult height.

To find the predicted height, we multiply 152 cm by the growth factor, 1.23.

| Multiply as with whole numbers. | ⮕ | Place the decimal point in the product. |

$$\begin{array}{r} 152 \\ \times 1.23 \\ \hline 456 \\ 3040 \\ 15200 \\ \hline 18696 \end{array}$$

$$\begin{array}{r} 152 \\ \times 1.23 \\ \hline 456 \\ 3040 \\ 15200 \\ \hline 186.96 \end{array}$$

✓ **Rule**

2 decimal places in the factors, so

2 decimal places in the product.

Randy's predicted adult height is 186.96 cm, so he may be about 187 cm tall.

✓ **Estimate** 152 × 1.23 is a little greater than 152 × 1 = 152.

The decimal point is missing in each product. Write each product with the decimal point in the correct position.

1.
```
    27.8
×      7
    1946
```
2.
```
     378
×    4.6
   17388
```
3.
```
    903.4
×      86
   776924
```
4.
```
    0.09
×     69
     621
```
5.
```
     7.32
×      29
    21228
```
6.
```
     8.03
×     167
   134101
```
7.
```
      507
×    4.96
   251472
```
8.
```
  $26.45
×      19
  $50255
```
9.
```
    0.891
×      16
    14256
```
10.
```
      1297
×    2.406
   3120582
```

Calculate only those products which are greater than 600.

11.
```
   37.6
×    28
```
12.
```
    179
×   3.8
```
13.
```
    426
×   0.8
```
14.
```
    509
×  0.92
```
15.
```
   7.29
×    96
```
16.
```
   8.19
×    87
```
17.
```
    703
×  1.82
```
18.
```
   5.82
×    47
```
19.
```
  0.939
×    87
```
20.
```
  8.276
×    98
```

Multiply.

21. 56.2×81

22. 7.39×124

23. 587×0.93

24. 439×2.68

25. 0.776×950

26. 237×2.014

27. Marcia is 12 years old and 146 cm tall. Use the growth chart to predict her adult height.

28. Ashley is now 148 cm tall. Using the growth chart, she found her predicted height to be 159.84 cm. Is Ashley 11 or 12 years old?

29. A basketball team averaged 52.5 points per game during its 12 game season. How many points did the team score that season?

30. Measure your height in centimetres. Use the growth chart to predict your adult height.

BITS AND BYTES

When we multiply a whole number by a decimal number, we find:

> The number of decimal places in the product is the same as the number of decimal places in the decimal factor.

Use a calculator to find these products.

1. 785×3.9

2. 8.6×903

3. 0.68×355

4. 287×6.87

5. 3.017×95

6. 76×0.097

7. 2.14×65

8. 0.875×56

Is the rule above true when we use a calculator to compute products? Explain.

PROBLEM SOLVING

Working Backwards

Jennifer bought an antique lamp
at one quarter of the regular price.
The cashier added a sales tax of $1.12.
The total bill was $13.61.

What was the regular price
of the antique lamp?

To solve this problem...

A. First, make sure you understand the problem.

Discuss:

- *What was the total amount that Jennifer paid?*
- *How much did Jennifer pay, not including sales tax?*
- *How is the regular price related to the sale price?*
- *What are you being asked to find?*

B. Think of a strategy to help you solve the problem.

- *Try working backwards.*
- *First, make a flow chart to show how the total bill is calculated from the regular price.*

| regular price | $\Rightarrow$ | sale price $\div 4$ | $\Rightarrow$ | add tax $+ \$1.12$ | $\Rightarrow$ | total bill $\$13.61$ |

- *Then reverse the flow chart to show how the regular price is calculated from the total bill.*
- *To reverse the flow chart, we change addition to subtraction and division to multiplication.*

| regular price | $\Leftarrow$ | $\times 4$ | $\Leftarrow$ | $- \$1.12$ | $\Leftarrow$ | $\$13.61$ |

Total $13.61

Solve each problem.

1. Gary bought 2 records for $6.98 each. The cashier charged him an additional $1.12 in sales tax. After his purchase, Gary had only $4.92 left. How much did he start with?

2. Aaron gave Ben half of his wrestling cards. Ben gave Christie half of the cards he received from Aaron. Christie kept 6 of those cards and gave the remaining 6 to Dana. How many cards did Aaron give Ben?

3. Lauralee was playing Monopoly. Before lunch, she made some money. After lunch, she paid $600 for some property. Then she spent half of what she had left to build some hotels. She paid $75 in taxes, then lost $525 to other players. By that time, she had $600 left. How much did she have when she returned to playing after lunch?

4. A tropical water lily doubles in size each day. It took 30 days for the original plant to completely cover the pond. After how many days was the pond half-covered?

C. Solve the problem and answer the question.

Use the reversed flow chart to work backwards. Then answer these questions.

- *What was the sale price?*
- *How many times as great as the sale price was the regular price?*
- *What was the regular price?*

D. Check your answer and discuss your solution.

- *Start with the regular price that you calculated.*
  Divide by 4.
  Add $1.12.
  Do you get a total bill of $13.61?
- *To reverse the flow chart, why do we change addition to subtraction? division to multiplication?*

251

Multiplying by 10, 100, and 1000

The Ajax Vending Company has a quick way to determine how many coins are in a pile. They weigh them!

From the scales, we see what each set of coins weighs.

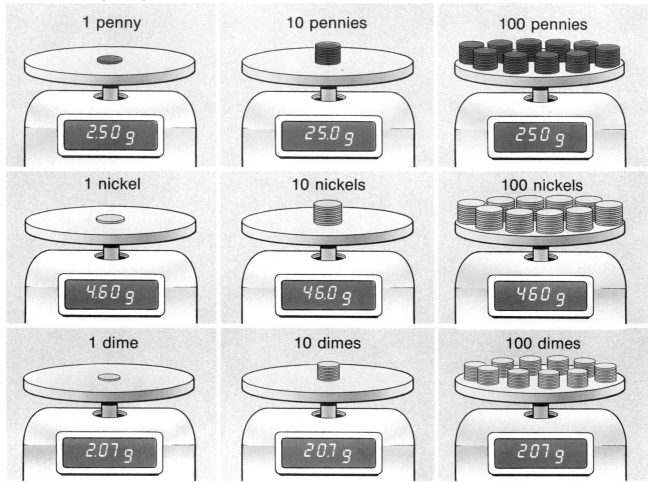

1 penny	10 pennies	100 pennies
2.50 g	25.0 g	250 g

1 nickel	10 nickels	100 nickels
4.60 g	46.0 g	460 g

1 dime	10 dimes	100 dimes
2.07 g	20.7 g	207 g

1. Using the information above, copy and complete this table.

	Mass of		
	1 coin	10 coins	100 coins
Pennies	▓	▓	▓
Nickels	▓	▓	▓
Dimes	▓	▓	▓

2. Study the table. Write a simple rule for multiplying
   a) by 10.   b) by 100.

3. The mass of a quarter is 5.05 g. What is the mass of
   a) 10 quarters?   b) 100 quarters?

4. Look for a pattern in your rules in question 2. Then write a simple rule for multiplying by 1000.

252

Multiply.

1. 3.87 × 10
2. 15.09 × 100
3. 6.854 × 100
4. 10 × 49.8
5. 1000 × 6.07
6. 0.097 × 100
7. 0.386 × 1000
8. 10 × 261.97
9. 100 × 0.079

Multiply.

10.
```
   6.87
×100
```
11.
```
  97.039
×     10
```
12.
```
  15.96
×1000
```
13.
```
  3.093
×  100
```
14.
```
  66.961
×     10
```

15.
```
  4.387
×  100
```
16.
```
  79.68
×1000
```
17.
```
  0.009
×    10
```
18.
```
  86.51
×  100
```
19.
```
  9.106
×1000
```

20.
```
  12.7
×  10
```
21.
```
  5.314
×  100
```
22.
```
  78.12
×1000
```
23.
```
  1.515
×  100
```
24.
```
  17.821
×     10
```

25.
```
  66.6
×100
```
26.
```
  8.382
×    10
```
27.
```
  48.5
×100
```
28.
```
  17.71
×  100
```
29.
```
  8.315
×  100
```

30.
```
  76.15
×    10
```
31.
```
  82.82
×  100
```
32.
```
  82.82
×1000
```
33.
```
  4.831
×1000
```
34.
```
  5.25
×  10
```

Use the information on page 252 to find the mass of each set of coins.

35. a) 10 quarters
    b) 100 quarters
    c) 110 quarters

36. a) 100 dimes
    b) 1 dime
    c) 101 dimes

37. a) 1000 nickels
    b) 101 nickels
    c) 1101 nickels

---

1 kg = 1000 g. Express each of the following masses in grams.

38. 6.8 kg
39. 19.6 kg
40. 27.91 kg
41. 32.84 kg
42. 0.61 kg
43. 0.97 kg
44. 3.712 kg
45. 8.937 kg
46. 0.037 kg
47. 0.069 kg
48. 1.51 kg
49. 4.7 kg
50. 0.15 kg
51. 0.015 kg
52. 15.2 kg
53. 0.46 kg

 **PROBLEM SOLVING**

A pile of quarters has a total mass of 3.03 kg.

What is the total value of the pile of quarters?

You may use your calculator.

Multiplying Tenths

The Carsons are planning to build a swimming pool in their square backyard. The pool is to be 7 tenths the length of the yard and 4 tenths the width of the yard.

What fraction of the yard will be used for the pool?

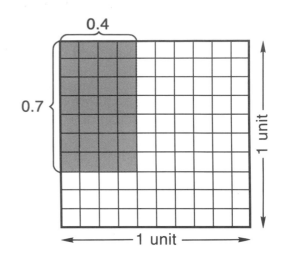

Miguel thinks:
- Length of pool = 0.7 units
- Width of pool = 0.4 units
- Area of pool = 0.7 × 0.4 square units

Sonia thinks:
- The area of the pool is 28 hundredths of the yard or 0.28 square units.

> They write: $0.7 \times 0.4 = 0.28$

Write the multiplication sentence to show what part of each picture is shaded.

1.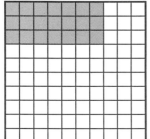

2.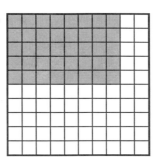

3.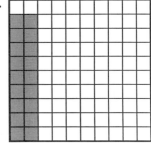

4.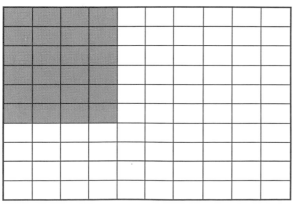

5.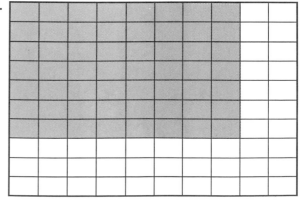

Multiply. Use squared paper if you wish.

1. 0.5
    ×0.6

2. 0.7
    ×0.3

3. 0.9
    ×0.2

4. 0.2
    ×0.6

5. 0.3
    ×0.8

6. 0.7
    ×0.9

7. 0.5
    ×0.3

8. 0.8
    ×0.7

9. 0.6
    ×0.9

10. 0.6
     ×0.7

11. 0.6 × 0.8

12. 0.9 × 0.4

13. 0.5 × 0.5

14. 0.2 × 0.7

15. 0.8 × 0.5

16. 0.8 × 0.8

---

17. Write a multiplication sentence to answer each of these questions. What decimal fraction of the large rectangle is:

   a) rectangle A?   b) rectangle B?
   c) rectangle C?   d) rectangle D?

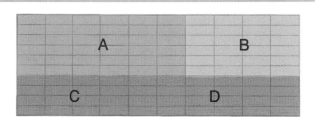

18. About 8 tenths of elementary students will graduate from high school. About half of the high school graduates will continue in school. What decimal fraction of elementary school students will attend school beyond graduation?

19. A farmer has a square field measuring 1 km on each side. He fences a rectangular section 600 m long and 400 m wide. What decimal fraction of the square field is fenced?

ESTIMATING

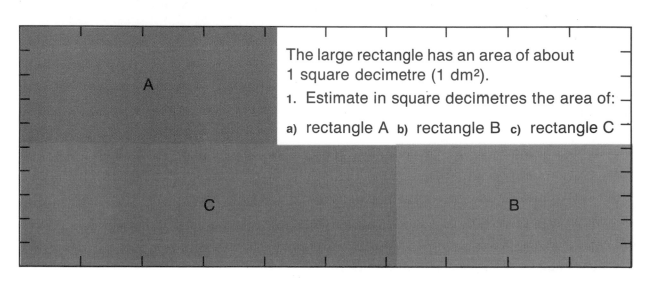

The large rectangle has an area of about 1 square decimetre (1 dm²).

1. Estimate in square decimetres the area of:

   a) rectangle A b) rectangle B c) rectangle C

ESTIMATING

Estimating Products of 2 Decimal Factors

This stamp celebrates the 1988 Winter Olympic Games in Calgary, Alberta.

The stamp is 5.6 cm long and 2.9 cm wide.

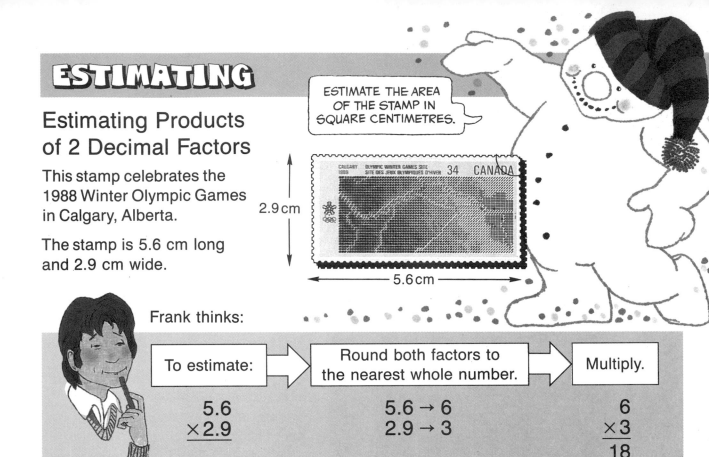

ESTIMATE THE AREA OF THE STAMP IN SQUARE CENTIMETRES.

2.9 cm

5.6 cm

Frank thinks:

To estimate:	Round both factors to the nearest whole number.	Multiply.
5.6 ×2.9	5.6 → 6 2.9 → 3	6 ×3 18

Frank writes: The area of the stamp is about 18 cm².

Laura thinks:

To estimate:	Round only the factor which is closest to a whole number.	Multiply.
5.6 ×2.9	5.6 → 5.6 2.9 → 3	5.6 × 3 16.8

Laura writes: The area of the stamp is about 16.8 cm².

The exact area of the stamp is 16.24 cm².
Which estimate is closer? Why?

Which of the 2 methods above gives a closer estimate of the product on the right? Explain why.

$$\begin{array}{r} 9.3 \\ \times 7.8 \\ \hline 72.54 \end{array}$$

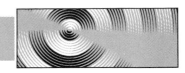

Estimate these products:

a) by rounding both factors.　　**b)** by rounding one factor.

1.　6.84
　　　× 3.3

1. a) 7　b) 3.3
×3　　× 7
21　　23.1

2.　7.12
　　　× 3.4

3.　9.65
　　　× 4.2

4.　2.97
　　　×1.85

5.　0.89
　　　×8.27

6.　15.74
　　　×　0.9

7.　18.03
　　　× 4.02

8.　1.11
　　　×2.22

9.　3.52
　　　×4.41

10. Use your calculator to find the exact products in questions 1 to 9. When does rounding both factors give a closer estimate?

The decimal point is missing in each product.
Write each product with the decimal point in the correct position.
Use estimation.

11.　　7.6
　　　×9.2
　　　6992

12.　　3.64
　　　× 8.8
　　　32032

13.　16.96
　　　×　3.7
　　　62752

14.　10.73
　　　×　9.1
　　　97643

15.　218.6
　　　×　7.5
　　　163950

16.　6.75
　　　×9.34
　　　63045

17.　2.08
　　　×5.37
　　　111696

18.　5.96
　　　×0.87
　　　51852

19.　0.928
　　　×　7.9
　　　73312

20.　5.127
　　　×　8.3
　　　425541

21. Study the factors and products in questions 11 to 20. Write a rule that explains how to decide how many decimal places there are in a decimal product.

22. What is the area in square metres of a piece of paper 0.08 m long and 0.07 m wide?

23. What is the area in square kilometres of a rectangular field 0.85 km long and 0.65 km wide?

Ms. Ching handed a postal clerk $5.00 for a sheet of Winter Olympics stamps. The clerk gave her $1.60 change. What was the approximate area of the sheet of stamps in square centimetres?

Multiplying Tenths and Hundredths

Scientists approximate the height of a prehistoric person by multiplying the length of the footprint by 6.6. What is the approximate height of a prehistoric person who left a footprint 17.9 cm long?

To multiply 17.9 by 6.6:

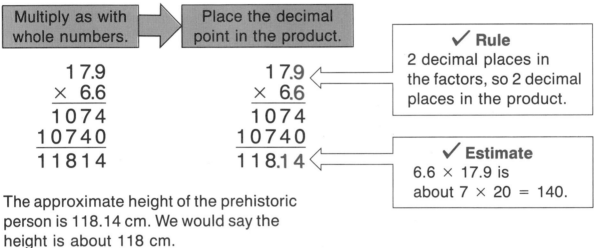

Multiply as with whole numbers.	Place the decimal point in the product.

```
   17.9              17.9
 ×  6.6            ×  6.6
  1074             1074
 10740            10740
 11814           118.14
```

✓ Rule
2 decimal places in the factors, so 2 decimal places in the product.

✓ Estimate
6.6 × 17.9 is about 7 × 20 = 140.

The approximate height of the prehistoric person is 118.14 cm. We would say the height is about 118 cm.

Another example:

To multiply 6.79 by 3.58:

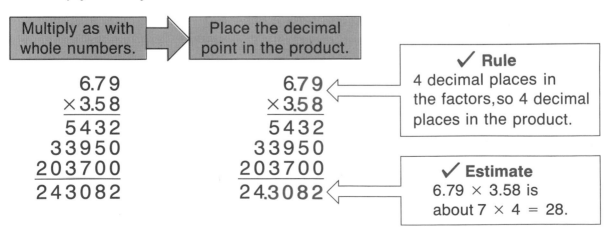

Multiply as with whole numbers.	Place the decimal point in the product.

```
   6.79              6.79
 ×3.58             ×3.58
  5432             5432
 33950            33950
203700           203700
243082           243.082
```

✓ Rule
4 decimal places in the factors, so 4 decimal places in the product.

✓ Estimate
6.79 × 3.58 is about 7 × 4 = 28.

258

The decimal point is missing in each product. Write each product with the decimal point in the correct position.

1.
$$\begin{array}{r} 4.2 \\ \times 3.8 \\ \hline 1596 \end{array}$$

2.
$$\begin{array}{r} 71.8 \\ \times\ 0.9 \\ \hline 6462 \end{array}$$

3.
$$\begin{array}{r} 32.6 \\ \times 2.14 \\ \hline 69764 \end{array}$$

4.
$$\begin{array}{r} 6.82 \\ \times\ 6.9 \\ \hline 47058 \end{array}$$

5.
$$\begin{array}{r} 7.09 \\ \times\ 8.6 \\ \hline 60974 \end{array}$$

6.
$$\begin{array}{r} 5.74 \\ \times 0.65 \\ \hline 37310 \end{array}$$

7.
$$\begin{array}{r} 0.67 \\ \times 1.38 \\ \hline 9246 \end{array}$$

8.
$$\begin{array}{r} 1.43 \\ \times 6.49 \\ \hline 92807 \end{array}$$

9.
$$\begin{array}{r} 0.167 \\ \times\ 9.1 \\ \hline 15197 \end{array}$$

10.
$$\begin{array}{r} 1.209 \\ \times\ 0.98 \\ \hline 118482 \end{array}$$

Calculate only those products which are greater than 50.

11.
$$\begin{array}{r} 7.6 \\ \times 7.8 \\ \hline \end{array}$$

12.
$$\begin{array}{r} 8.92 \\ \times 12.1 \\ \hline \end{array}$$

13.
$$\begin{array}{r} 0.98 \\ \times 48.7 \\ \hline \end{array}$$

14.
$$\begin{array}{r} 10.9 \\ \times\ 5.8 \\ \hline \end{array}$$

15.
$$\begin{array}{r} 42.5 \\ \times 1.08 \\ \hline \end{array}$$

16.
$$\begin{array}{r} 87.6 \\ \times 0.81 \\ \hline \end{array}$$

17.
$$\begin{array}{r} 97.4 \\ \times 0.93 \\ \hline \end{array}$$

18.
$$\begin{array}{r} 39.1 \\ \times 2.07 \\ \hline \end{array}$$

19.
$$\begin{array}{r} 6.39 \\ \times 5.16 \\ \hline \end{array}$$

20.
$$\begin{array}{r} 5.72 \\ \times 9.87 \\ \hline \end{array}$$

Multiply.

21. 17.9×0.87

22. 25.6×2.1

23. 62.8×0.92

24. 0.69×85.6

25. 98.6×0.47

26. 8.38×9.56

27. Find the approximate height of the prehistoric person who made a footprint 18.8 cm long.

28. Today's fossil fuels are made from decomposed plants and animals of prehistoric times. What is the cost of 25.75 L of gasoline when gasoline sells for 52.9¢ per litre?

BITS AND BYTES

When we multiply 2 decimal numbers, we find:

> The number of decimal places in the product is the same as the total number of decimal places in the factors.

Use a calculator to find these products.

1. 0.32×0.7
2. 5.86×3.84
3. 9.8×13.67
4. 25.3×17.06
5. 6.25×8.8
6. 0.04×37.5
7. 0.036×0.05
8. 0.18×3.97

Is the rule true when we use a calculator? Explain.

Calculating Products with Leading Zeros

In one province, the sales tax on an item is found by multiplying the price of the item by 0.08.

What is the sales tax on a pen that sells for $1.09?

$1.18 PLEASE!

THE PRICE TAG SAYS $1.09 AND I HAVE ONLY $1.10.

To multiply $1.09 by 0.08, we follow these steps.

Multiply as with whole numbers.	Count the number of decimal places in the factors.	Place the decimal point in the product. Insert zeros as needed.

$$\begin{array}{r} 1.09 \\ \times 0.08 \\ \hline 872 \end{array} \qquad \begin{array}{r} 1.09 \\ \times 0.08 \\ \hline 872 \end{array} \qquad \begin{array}{r} 1.09 \\ \times 0.08 \\ \hline 0.0872 \end{array}$$

There is a total of 4 decimal places.

Insert a zero to make 4 decimal places in the product.

The sales tax on the pen is $0.0872 which rounds to $0.09 or 9¢.

Other examples:

A. $\begin{array}{r} 0.02 \\ \times 0.3 \\ \hline 0.006 \end{array}$
B. $\begin{array}{r} 0.04 \\ \times 0.02 \\ \hline 0.0008 \end{array}$
C. $\begin{array}{r} 0.45 \\ \times 0.04 \\ \hline 0.0180 \end{array}$
D. $\begin{array}{r} 0.028 \\ \times 0.05 \\ \hline 0.00140 \end{array}$

1. How many zeros were inserted after the decimal point in each product?

2. Use a calculator to find the products in examples A, B, C, and D. Are the calculator answers exactly the same as those above? Explain.

The decimal point is missing in each product.
Write each with the decimal point in the
correct position. Insert zeros as needed.

1. $\begin{array}{r} 0.1 \\ \times 0.7 \\ \hline 7 \end{array}$
2. $\begin{array}{r} 0.26 \\ \times\ 0.9 \\ \hline 234 \end{array}$
3. $\begin{array}{r} 3.02 \\ \times\ 0.8 \\ \hline 2416 \end{array}$
4. $\begin{array}{r} 17.01 \\ \times\ 0.07 \\ \hline 11907 \end{array}$
5. $\begin{array}{r} 0.08 \\ \times 0.07 \\ \hline 56 \end{array}$

6. $\begin{array}{r} 0.29 \\ \times 0.06 \\ \hline 174 \end{array}$
7. $\begin{array}{r} 0.59 \\ \times 0.08 \\ \hline 472 \end{array}$
8. $\begin{array}{r} 0.328 \\ \times\ 0.4 \\ \hline 1312 \end{array}$
9. $\begin{array}{r} 6.05 \\ \times 1.03 \\ \hline 62315 \end{array}$
10. $\begin{array}{r} 0.512 \\ \times\ 0.03 \\ \hline 1536 \end{array}$

Calculate only those products
which are less than 0.1.

11. $\begin{array}{r} 0.84 \\ \times 0.07 \end{array}$
12. $\begin{array}{r} 0.96 \\ \times 0.08 \end{array}$
13. $\begin{array}{r} 1.29 \\ \times 0.3 \end{array}$
14. $\begin{array}{r} 0.06 \\ \times 2.01 \end{array}$
15. $\begin{array}{r} 0.03 \\ \times 1.89 \end{array}$

16. $\begin{array}{r} 2.68 \\ \times 0.01 \end{array}$
17. $\begin{array}{r} 0.034 \\ \times\ 1.7 \end{array}$
18. $\begin{array}{r} 0.046 \\ \times\ 0.9 \end{array}$
19. $\begin{array}{r} 0.215 \\ \times\ 0.8 \end{array}$
20. $\begin{array}{r} 0.099 \\ \times\ 0.9 \end{array}$

Multiply.

21. 0.1×0.9
22. 0.01×9.99
23. 0.2×0.63
24. 0.24×0.69
25. 0.68×0.07
26. 37.9×0.002

27. A fruit fly is about 1 tenth the length
of a mosquito. A mosquito is about
0.8 cm long. About how many
centimetres long is a fruit fly?

28. A human hair has a thickness of
0.05 mm. A red blood cell is only
4 hundredths of this thickness. How
thick is a red blood cell?

29. In one province, the sales tax on an
item is found by multiplying the price
of the item by 0.07. What is the sales
tax on a notebook that sells for $4.95?

PROBLEM SOLVING

In one province, the total cost of an
item, including sales tax, can be found
by dividing the price by 0.926. That is:

Price without sales tax	÷ 0.926 =	Price including sales tax

To purchase a toy, Heather gave the
sales clerk a $10 bill. She received
$2.71 change. What was the price of
the toy without sales tax?

JUST FOR FUN

Help the professor find a route to the
Lost Tombs of the Valley of the Kings.

Find a path which passes through only
multiplication questions with products
greater than 0.01. Use estimation.
Write in order the letters
on your path.

N
1.93
× 0.003

L
5.432
× 0.007

K
0.39
× 0.02

J
0.8
× 0.01

M
410.3
× 0.009

F
1.19
× 0.004

I
9.18
× 0.004

H
7.245
× 0.005

G
11.11
× 0.01

C
2.03
× 0.006

E
0.307
× 0.02

D
0.69
× 0.01

B
0.86
× 0.03

A
1.05
× 0.001

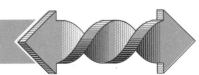

Products of 3 Decimal Factors

Joan was helping Ann with multiplying decimals. She wrote this question on the board for Ann to do.

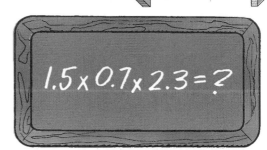

$$1.5 \times 0.7 \times 2.3 = ?$$

When Ann asked Joan for help, Joan showed her the following method.

| To multiply: | ➡ | Multiply any 2 factors. | ➡ | Multiply the product by the remaining factor. |

$1.5 \times 0.7 \times 2.3$

$$\begin{array}{r} 1.5 \\ \times 0.7 \\ \hline 1.05 \end{array}$$

$$\begin{array}{r} 1.05 \\ \times 2.3 \\ \hline 315 \\ 2100 \\ \hline 2.415 \end{array}$$

Find Joan's product beginning with 2 other factors. What did you find out?

Multiply.

1. $0.2 \times 0.2 \times 0.2$
2. $0.1 \times 0.3 \times 3.2$
3. $5.4 \times 0.5 \times 0.1$
4. $0.1 \times 0.1 \times 4.95$
5. $0.25 \times 0.5 \times 4$
6. $3.2 \times 2.5 \times 0.2$
7. $9.0 \times 0.9 \times 0.9$
8. $2.1 \times 3.6 \times 0.25$
9. $0.8 \times 0.5 \times 0.75$

10. In questions 1 to 9, does the order of the factors matter?

11. Copy and complete this table for questions 1 to 9.

12. Write a rule to predict how many decimal places there will be in the product of 3 factors. Is your rule always true when products are computed on a calculator?

	Question Number								
	1	2	3	4	5	6	7	8	9
Total Number of Decimal Places in the Factors	3	▣	▣	▣	▣	▣	▣	▣	▣
Number of Decimal Places in the Product	▣	▣	▣	▣	▣	▣	▣	▣	▣

THE ANIMAL RACES

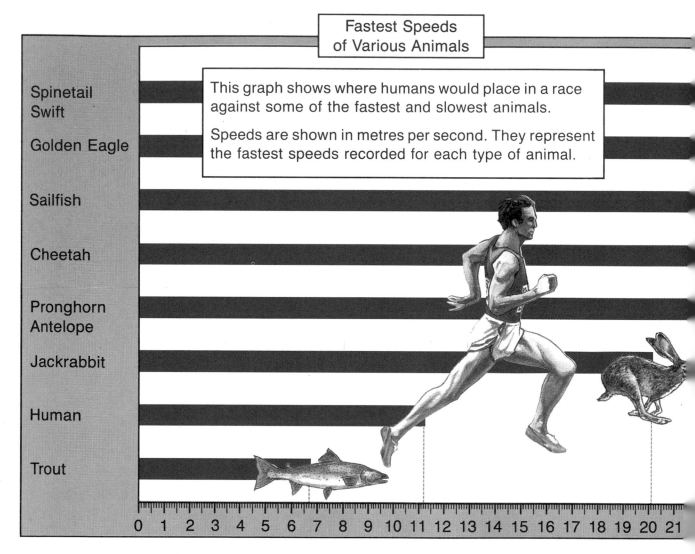

Fastest Speeds of Various Animals

This graph shows where humans would place in a race against some of the fastest and slowest animals.

Speeds are shown in metres per second. They represent the fastest speeds recorded for each type of animal.

Spinetail Swift

Golden Eagle

Sailfish

Cheetah

Pronghorn Antelope

Jackrabbit

Human

Trout

0 1 2 3 4 5 6 7 8 9 10 11 12 13 14 15 16 17 18 19 20 21

1. About how many metres per second can the world's fastest athletes run?

2. About how many more metres does the cheetah cover in one second than the pronghorn antelope?

3. About how fast can the golden eagle fly?

4. Name the 3 fastest animals shown in the graph.

5. About how far could the pronghorn antelope run in 8 s?

6. If a cheetah chased a pronghorn antelope at top speed for 9 s, about how many metres would it gain on the antelope?

264

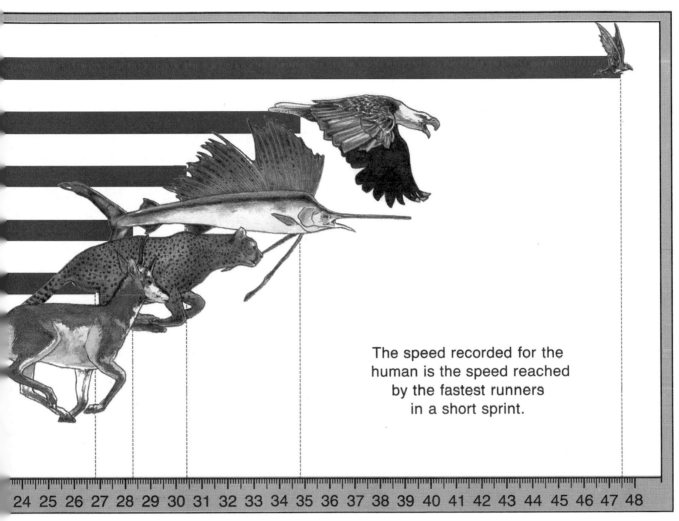

The speed recorded for the human is the speed reached by the fastest runners in a short sprint.

24 25 26 27 28 29 30 31 32 33 34 35 36 37 38 39 40 41 42 43 44 45 46 47 48

7. About how long would it take a sailfish to swim a distance of 100 m?

8. About how many times as fast as a human is the spinetail swift?

9. The giant tortoise travels about 0.076 m/s. Which of the animals in the graph can run about 264 times as fast as the giant tortoise?

10. One day an Olympic runner stumbles upon a jackrabbit. He runs after it as fast as he can but the rabbit runs straight for a thicket.
After running for 10 s, the rabbit reaches the thicket. About how far behind the rabbit is the runner?

265

PROBLEM SOLVING

Adding Missing Information

MATHQUEST 6 CONTAINS MANY INTERESTING FACTS. THIS INDEX SHOWS WHERE SOME OF THESE FACTS CAN BE FOUND.

NAME 2 PLANETS WITH DIAMETERS THAT DIFFER BY 5962 km.

To solve this problem...

A. First, make sure you understand the problem.

Discuss
- *What are you asked to find out?*
- *What do you need to know in order to solve the problem?*
- *What information is missing from the problem?*

B. Then, think of strategies. You need to find the missing information.

Try using the index on page 266 to help you find that information.
- *Study the main headings.*
- *Under which headings will you find the page numbers you need?*

C. Solve the problem and answer the question.

- *Look at the page that contains the information you need.*
- *Estimate which 2 planets have diameters that differ by 5962 km.*
- *Subtract to check your estimate.*
- *Repeat, if necessary.*

D. Check your answer and discuss your solution.

- *Are there other planets with diameters that differ by about 6000 km?*
- *If so, calculate the exact difference. Is it 5962?*
- *Where else could you have found the information you needed to solve this problem?*

Solve these problems.

1. How long after Columbus had returned to Spain in 1493 did Magellan set sail to circumnavigate the earth?

2. About how many times as great as the population of Canada is the population of the U.S.S.R.?

3. How many goals did these hockey players score altogether: Bobby Hull, Maurice Richard, Guy LaFleur, Phil Esposito, and Richard Martin?

4. Compare the time it takes the Concorde to fly across the Atlantic Ocean with Lindbergh's first transatlantic flight.
   a) What is the difference in time?
   b) How many years ago was Charles Lindbergh's flight?

5. Could the first shopping bag have been used to carry home:
   a) some vitamin tablets?
   b) a ballpoint pen?
   c) a pencil with an attached eraser?

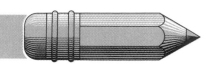

CHECK-UP

Write each product with the decimal point in the correct position.

1. 36.6
    × 7
    ———
    2562

2. 80.73
    × 76
    ———
    613548

3. $9.75
    × 21
    ———
    20475

4. 608
    ×3.74
    ———
    227392

5. 0.918
    × 17
    ———
    15606

6. 2356
    ×1.127
    ———
    2655212

Calculate only those products which are greater than 500.

7. 24.7
    × 22

8. 628
    × 0.94

9. 536
    × 0.8

Multiply.

10. 54.6
     × 7

11. 8.43
     × 13

12. 478
     ×0.94

13. 528
     ×2.56

14. 0.667
     × 840

15. 327
     ×1.016

Write the products.

16. 4.68 × 10
17. 21.08 × 100
18. 5.762 × 100
19. 10 × 53.7
20. 1000 × 7.03
21. 0.086 × 100
22. 0.437 × 1000
23. 10 × 321.86
24. 100 × 0.083
25. 8.207 × 1000

Write the multiplication sentence which shows what part of each picture is shaded.

26.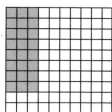

27.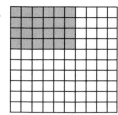

Multiply.

28. 0.4
     ×0.8

29. 0.9
     ×0.3

30. 0.6
     ×0.8

31. 0.7
     ×0.5

32. 0.4
     ×0.9

33. 0.5
     ×0.9

Write each product with the decimal point in the correct position.

34. 5.3
     ×2.8
     ———
     1484

35. 62.6
     × 0.8
     ———
     5008

36. 7.63
     ×5.4
     ———
     41202

37. 6.72
     ×0.53
     ———
     35616

38. 0.263
     × 8.3
     ———
     21829

39. 2.107
     × 0.38
     ———
     80066

Calculate only those products which are greater than 500.

40. 82.2
    × 2.5

41. 51.15
    × 12.3

42. 8.413
    × 68.4

Multiply.

43. 8.3
     ×7.2

44. 6.48
     ×11.4

45. 0.96
     ×0.73

46. 20.5
     ×15.3

47. 36.7
     ×0.04

48. 0.843
     × 0.7

49. Mona spent half of her babysitting money on books. She spent half of the remaining money on lunch. If she went home with $3, how much did she begin with?

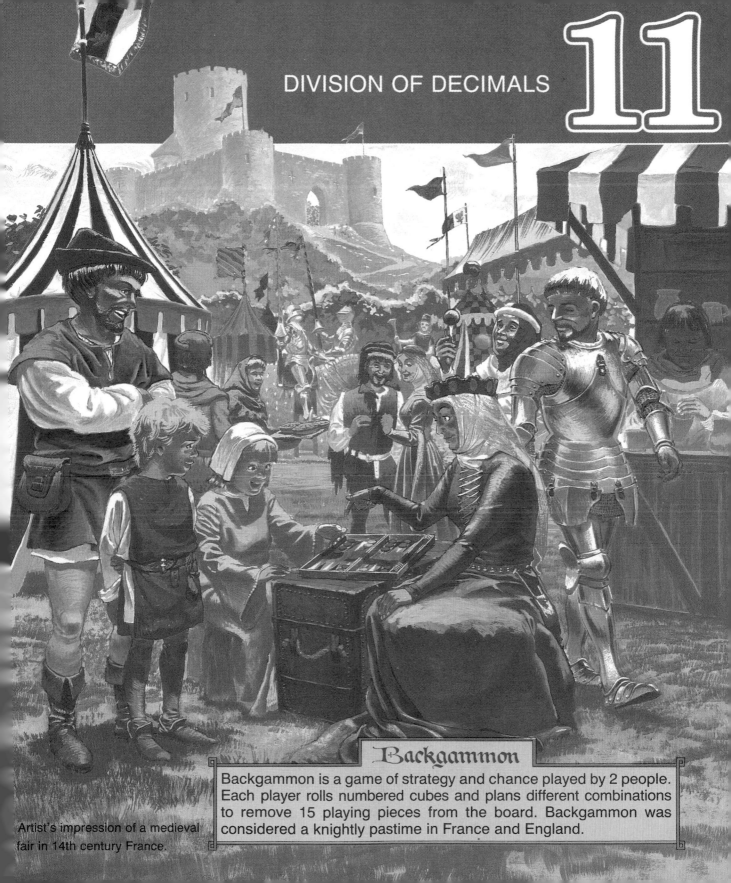

Backgammon

Backgammon is a game of strategy and chance played by 2 people. Each player rolls numbered cubes and plans different combinations to remove 15 playing pieces from the board. Backgammon was considered a knightly pastime in France and England.

Artist's impression of a medieval fair in 14th century France.

Dividing by 10, 100, and 1000

In the previous chapter we discovered
the following rules for multiplying
by 10, 100, and 1000.

To multiply by...	move the decimal point	
10	1 place **right**	$10 \times 9.74 = 97.4$
100	2 places **right**	$100 \times 9.74 = 974$
1000	3 places **right**	$1000 \times 9.74 = 9740$

Sometimes you need to write a zero digit
so you can move the decimal point.

By studying the table below, we can
discover the rules for dividing decimal
numbers by 10, 100, and 1000.

Number	Divided by 10	Divided by 100	Divided by 1000
386.5	38.65	3.865	0.386 5
42.7	4.27	0.427	0.042 7
2.668	0.266 8	0.026 68	0.002 668
419.53	41.953	4.195 3	0.419 53
90.7	9.07	0.907	0.090 7
8462	846.2	84.62	8.462

These are the rules for dividing decimal
numbers by 10, 100, and 1000.

To divide by...	move the decimal point	
10	1 place **left**	$78.3 \div 10 = 7.83$
100	2 places **left**	$78.3 \div 100 = 0.783$
1000	3 places **left**	$78.3 \div 1000 = 0.0783$

Use a division rule to find each quotient.

1. 29.37 ÷ 10
2. 17.6 ÷ 100
3. 79.07 ÷ 10
4. 8.97 ÷ 10
5. 0.23 ÷ 10
6. 2.65 ÷ 100
7. 62.3 ÷ 1000
8. 5.82 ÷ 1000
9. 0.93 ÷ 100
10. 15.6 ÷ 100
11. $700 ÷ 1000
12. $30 ÷ 1000

Divide.

13. $10\overline{)76}$
14. $10\overline{)2.38}$
15. $10\overline{)10.72}$
16. $100\overline{)7.9}$
17. $100\overline{)28.65}$
18. $1000\overline{)279.6}$
19. $1000\overline{)38.9}$
20. $100\overline{)0.6}$
21. $10\overline{)\$12.60}$
22. $100\overline{)\$3.28}$
23. $10\overline{)\$8.60}$
24. $1000\overline{)\$6530}$

---

25. A stack of 100 sheets of paper is 0.85 cm thick. What is the thickness of 1 sheet of paper?

27. A pile of 1000 quarters has a total mass of 5.05 kg. What is the approximate mass of one quarter in kilograms?

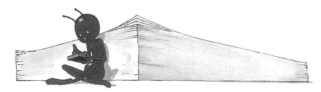

26. If 10 people share equally in a prize of $95.50, how much does each receive?

BITS AND BYTES

Calculate the following quotients in your head using the rules you discovered on the previous page. Record your answers.

1. 6.89 ÷ 10
2. 13.92 ÷ 100
3. 271.8 ÷ 100
4. 810 ÷ 100
5. 2360 ÷ 1000
6. 389 ÷ 10
7. 90.4 ÷ 1000
8. 2.07 ÷ 10

9. Now compute these quotients on a calculator. Record your answers.

10. Compare your answers. For which questions do your quotients look different? Explain why.

Converting Metric Measurements

The scale shows that the leprechaun's height can be measured in centimetres or in millimetres.

To convert a measurement from centimetres to millimetres, we **multiply** by 10 because there are fewer centimetres than millimetres.

5.3 cm = 53 mm

To convert a measurement from millimetres to centimetres, we **divide** by 10 because there are fewer centimetres than millimetres.

53 mm = 5.3 cm

1 cm = 10 mm

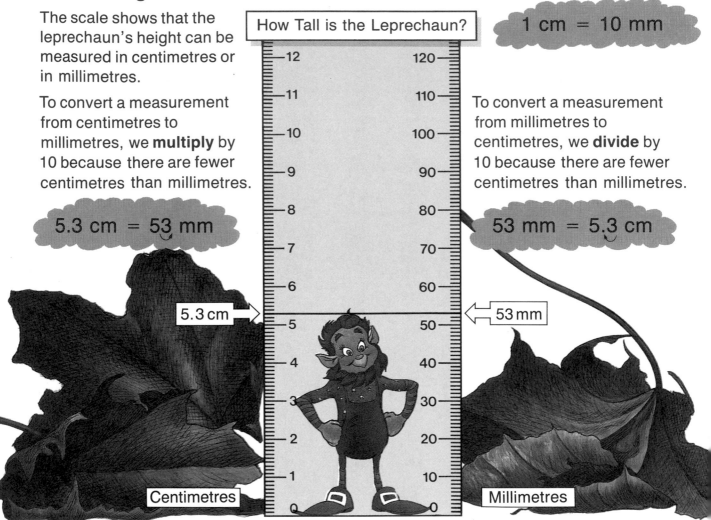

How Tall is the Leprechaun?

5.3 cm → ← 53 mm

Centimetres

Millimetres

Copy and complete. Use the scale above to help you with the first questions.

1. 2.8 cm = ▨ mm
2. 3.9 cm = ▨ mm
3. 0.8 cm = ▨ mm
4. 57 mm = ▨ cm
5. 180 mm = ▨ cm
6. 0.9 cm = ▨ mm
7. 12.68 cm = ▨ mm
8. 2.7 mm = ▨ cm
9. 0.8 mm = ▨ cm
10. 0.28 mm = ▨ cm
11. 15.4 cm = ▨ mm
12. 0.09 cm = ▨ mm

List the lengths in each set in order from greatest to least.

13. 0.3 cm, 0.30 mm, 2.8 mm
14. 1.6 mm, 0.15 cm, 1.5 cm
15. 0.10 mm, 0.020 cm, 0.017 cm
16. 5.2 mm, 0.50 cm, 0.515 mm

This chart shows the average heights in centimetres of boys and girls from 10 to 13 years of age.

Age	Height	
	Boys	Girls
10	137.1 cm	137.1 cm
11	142.2 cm	142.2 cm
12	147.3 cm	147.2 cm
13	152.4 cm	152.2 cm

To express heights in metres,

we recall: **1 m = 100 cm**

So, we divide the height in centimetres by 100.

On average, the height of an 11 year old is 142.2 cm or 1.422 m.

1. Make a table like the one above but record all the heights in metres.

Copy and complete.

2. 147 cm = ▦ m

3. 24.8 cm = ▦ m

4. 92.6 cm = ▦ m

5. 6.8 m = ▦ cm

6. 0.07 m = ▦ cm

7. 150 cm = ▦ m

8. 0.5 m = ▦ cm

9. 18.2 cm = ▦ m

10. 12.4 m = ▦ cm

11. 65.7 cm = ▦ m

12. 253 cm = ▦ m

13. 0.55 m = ▦ cm

Remember: 1 km = 1000 m

Copy and complete.

14. 0.6 km = ▦ m

15. 286 m = ▦ km

16. ▦ m = 0.02 km

17. 45 m = ▦ km

18. 0.23 km = ▦ m

19. ▦ km = 9 m

20. ▦ m = 0.4 km

21. 0.15 km = ▦ m

22. Mount Everest is 8848 m high. Write the height of Mount Everest in kilometres.

23. One strand of human hair has a thickness of 0.05 mm. Write the thickness of a human hair in centimetres.

ESTIMATING

Estimating Quotients

Six people plan to share equally the cost of a $19.75 pizza. About how much will each person pay?

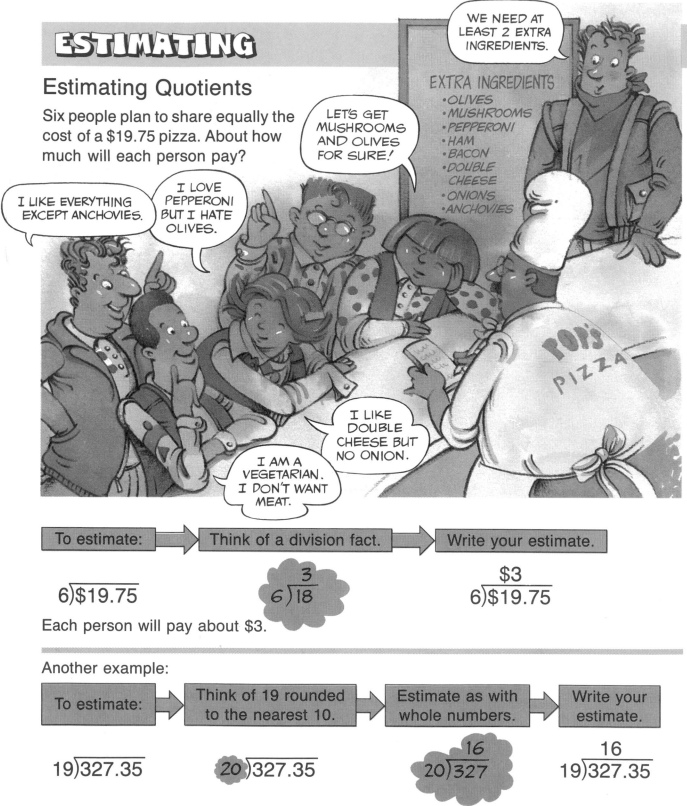

WE NEED AT LEAST 2 EXTRA INGREDIENTS.

EXTRA INGREDIENTS
- OLIVES
- MUSHROOMS
- PEPPERONI
- HAM
- BACON
- DOUBLE CHEESE
- ONIONS
- ANCHOVIES

LET'S GET MUSHROOMS AND OLIVES FOR SURE!

I LIKE EVERYTHING EXCEPT ANCHOVIES.

I LOVE PEPPERONI BUT I HATE OLIVES.

I LIKE DOUBLE CHEESE BUT NO ONION.

I AM A VEGETARIAN. I DON'T WANT MEAT.

To estimate: →	Think of a division fact. →	Write your estimate.

$$6\overline{)\$19.75}$$

$$6\overline{)18}\ \ \ 3$$

$$\begin{array}{r} \$3 \\ 6\overline{)\$19.75} \end{array}$$

Each person will pay about $3.

Another example:

To estimate: →	Think of 19 rounded to the nearest 10. →	Estimate as with whole numbers. →	Write your estimate.

$$19\overline{)327.35}$$

$$20\overline{)327.35}$$

$$\begin{array}{r} 16 \\ 20\overline{)327} \end{array}$$

$$\begin{array}{r} 16 \\ 19\overline{)327.35} \end{array}$$

274

Estimate each quotient.

1. $3\overline{)46.2}$

2. $5\overline{)39.7}$

3. $8\overline{)89.3}$

4. $7\overline{)93.9}$

5. $6\overline{)37.74}$

6. $3\overline{)\$85.68}$

7. $4\overline{)\$129.19}$

8. $2\overline{)38.84}$

9. $12\overline{)89.6}$

10. $29\overline{)93.6}$

11. $41\overline{)286.9}$

12. $19\overline{)768.7}$

13. $23\overline{)94.71}$

14. $37\overline{)\$78.19}$

15. $51\overline{)309.66}$

16. $21\overline{)809.27}$

Estimate.

17. $217.8 \div 9$

18. $309.6 \div 7$

19. $816.23 \div 6$

20. $685.17 \div 8$

21. $597.8 \div 32$

22. $\$902.67 \div 47$

23. These jackpots were shared among 4 people. In which cases did they receive less than $1.00 each?

A. $12.56   B. $3.68   C. $1.96   D. $5.04

24. Write the letters of the quotients which are less than 1.

A. $7.89 \div 8$

B. $9.76 \div 7$

C. $13.9 \div 21$

D. $26.87 \div 31$

E. $261.02 \div 97$

F. $87.658 \div 92$

25. At her summer job, Kim worked 36.5 h during a 5 day week. About how many hours per day did she work?

26. It cost Mrs. Sydney $62.65 to board her dog, Rex, for a full week at Barking Kennels. About how much did it cost per day?

PROBLEM SOLVING

Study the list of extra ingredients available for the pizza on page 274. What choices of extra ingredients would satisfy all 6 of the people ordering the pizza?

(A satisfactory choice would not contain an ingredient which any member does not want. It may leave out items which some members desire.)

Dividing Decimal Numbers: No Remainders

On June 26, 1986, Daniel Goodwin made the longest climb achieved on the vertical face of a building. He climbed a total distance of 624.9 m in 2 successive climbs up the CN tower in Toronto. The total climb took "Spider Man" Goodwin about 3 h.

What was the average distance he climbed per hour?

To divide 624.9 by 3, we follow these steps:

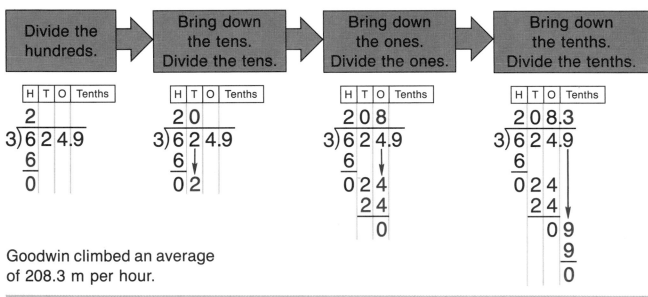

Divide the hundreds.	Bring down the tens. Divide the tens.	Bring down the ones. Divide the ones.	Bring down the tenths. Divide the tenths.

H	T	O	Tenths
2			

```
    2
3)6 2 4.9
  6
  0
```

```
   2 0
3)6 2 4.9
  6↓
  0 2
```

```
   2 0 8
3)6 2 4.9
  6 ↓
  0 2 4
    2 4
      0
```

```
   2 0 8.3
3)6 2 4.9
  6 ↓
  0 2 4
    2 4↓
      0 9
        9
        0
```

Goodwin climbed an average of 208.3 m per hour.

Another example: To divide 4.32 by 48:

Divide the ones. Record zero ones.	Divide the tenths. Record zero tenths.	Divide the hundredths.

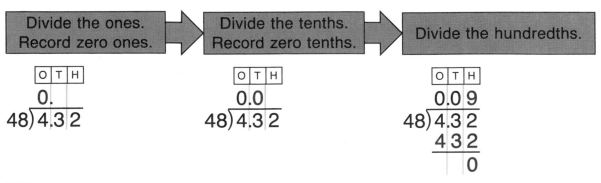

O	T	H
0.		

```
   0.
48)4.3 2
```

```
   0.0
48)4.3 2
```

```
   0.0 9
48)4.3 2
   4 3 2
       0
```

276

Copy and complete.

1. 7)6 8.6

2. 9)4.3 2

3. 6)0.5 0 4

Divide. Do only those questions
with quotients less than 1.

4. 7)49.7

5. 8)14.80

6. 6)2.88

7. 6)46.2

8. 9)4.05

9. 4)1.936

10. 3)2.91

11. 13)7.93

12. 18)95.4

13. 29)26.1

14. 15)7.05

15. 34)25.84

Divide.

16. $63.6 \div 4$

17. $59.2 \div 8$

18. $3.75 \div 5$

19. $9.92 \div 32$

20. $417.6 \div 58$

21. $9.28 \div 16$

ESTIMATING

| To place the decimal point in the quotient. | → | Estimate the quotient. | → | Insert the decimal point. |

$$\begin{array}{r} 1\ 9 \\ 5\overline{)9.5} \end{array}$$

$$\begin{array}{r} 2 \\ 5\overline{)10} \end{array}$$

$$\begin{array}{r} 1.9 \\ 5\overline{)9.5} \end{array}$$

The quotient
is about 2.

The answer 1.9
is close to the
estimated quotient of 2.

Write each quotient with the decimal
point in the correct position.

1. $7.2 \div 4 \rightarrow 18$

2. $38.4 \div 3 \rightarrow 128$

3. $7.74 \div 9 \rightarrow 86$

4. $0.63 \div 7 \rightarrow 9$

5. $62.1 \div 23 \rightarrow 27$

6. $76.8 \div 96 \rightarrow 8$

7. $256.8 \div 8 \rightarrow 321$

8. $24.3 \div 9 \rightarrow 27$

9. $466.4 \div 53 \rightarrow 88$

Writing Zeros in the Dividend

David's uncle sponsored him in the annual fund raising walkathon. His uncle paid the fund $14 for David's 8 km walk. How much per kilometre did David's uncle pay?

To divide 14 by 8:

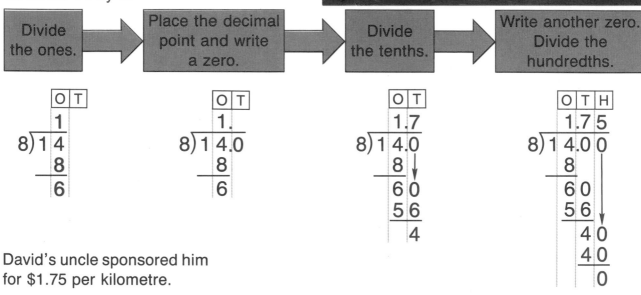

| Divide the ones. | → | Place the decimal point and write a zero. | → | Divide the tenths. | → | Write another zero. Divide the hundredths. |

```
   O T                O T                 O T                O T H
     1                  1.                 1.7               1.7 5
8) 1 4             8) 1 4.0           8) 1 4.0          8) 1 4.0 0
   8                  8                  8                  8
   6                  6                  6 0                6 0
                                         5 6                5 6
                                           4                  4 0
                                                              4 0
                                                                0
```

David's uncle sponsored him for $1.75 per kilometre.

Another example: To divide 102 by 24:

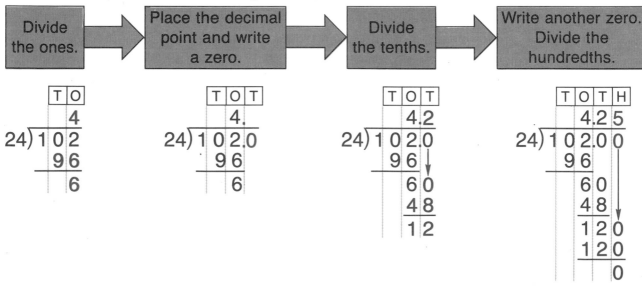

| Divide the ones. | → | Place the decimal point and write a zero. | → | Divide the tenths. | → | Write another zero. Divide the hundredths. |

```
    T O                 T O T               T O T              T O T H
      4                   4.                  4.2                4.2 5
24) 1 0 2           24) 1 0 2.0         24) 1 0 2.0        24) 1 0 2.0 0
    9 6                 9 6                 9 6                9 6
      6                   6                 6 0                6 0
                                           4 8                4 8
                                           1 2                1 2 0
                                                              1 2 0
                                                                  0
```

278

Copy and complete.

1. 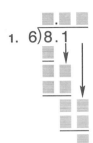 6)8.1

2.  4)9.4 8

3. 4)0.3 8

4. 16)6 1.6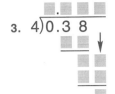

Divide until the remainder is zero.

5. 4)7

6. 6)8.7

7. 8)76

8. 5)24.7

9. 6)106.5

10. 8)0.2

11. 4)0.22

12. 8)55

13. 16)40

14. 12)4.2

15. 18)0.9

16. 14)441

17. 36)99

18. 16)14

19. 46)16.1

20. 16)4.4

21. 5.2 ÷ 8

22. 19.5 ÷ 3

23. 30.42 ÷ 13

24. 103.5 ÷ 6

25. 9.6 ÷ 24

26. 9.1 ÷ 14

27. 179.2 ÷ 7

28. 441 ÷ 18

---

29. During a slapshot, a hockey puck averages a speed of 35 m/s. At this speed, how long does it take a slapshot to travel 21 m?

30. If 6 people paid $2.75 each for a share of pizza, what was the cost of the pizza?

31. A busload of 24 people paid a total of $126 for a tour of the city. How much did each person pay?

32. Jay bought 7 posters for $12.95. What was the cost of 1 poster?

PROBLEM SOLVING

Mrs. Fleming gave the postal clerk $25 for a sheet of 36¢ stamps. She received $1.60 change.

How many stamps were in the sheet?

Finding Averages

Marita practised every day for a week for the cross country cycling tournament at Emmanuel School. The table shows how far she cycled each day.
What was the average distance she cycled per day?

Day	Distance in Kilometres
Sunday	5.8
Monday	6.0
Tuesday	4.9
Wednesday	6.0
Thursday	5.5
Friday	3.9
Saturday	5.0

37.1 km

Total Distance for this Week

To find the average of a set of numbers:

Find the sum of all the numbers.	Divide the sum by the number of addends.

```
  5.8
  6.0
  4.9
  6.0
  5.5
  3.9
+ 5.0
─────
 37.1
```

```
       5.3
   7)37.1
     35
     ──
      2 1
      2 1
      ───
        0
```

Marita cycled an average of 5.3 km per day.

Find the average of each set of numbers.

1. 87, 95, 68, 84, 73
2. 5300, 4400, 5800, 6100
3. $2.10, $5.49, $3.55, $2.99, $4.07
4. 7.5, 9.25, 9.1, 7.75, 11.2, 9.5
5. 11.3, 11.7, 11.1, 11.8, 11.3, 11.2
6. $20.89, $19.97, $22.50, $18.44

7. Simon's running times for the 10 km race are:

   40.6 min, 38.9 min, 41.8 min, 42.0 min, 39.6 min, 40.7 min, and 39.9 min.

   What is Simon's average time for the 10 km race?

This bar graph represents the amount of money earned by 7 children at a garage sale.

Study the graph and estimate the average amount earned per child.

1. These tables show the **annual** rainfall for some of the world's wettest and driest countries.

For each country calculate the average **weekly** rainfall in millimetres.

World's Wettest Countries	
Country	Annual Rainfall
Columbia	4099 mm
Malaysia	3273 mm
Sierre Leone	2829 mm

World's Driest Countries	
Country	Annual Rainfall
Egypt	55.8 mm
Saudi Arabia	73.6 mm
Mauritania	82.8 mm

2. Find the average number of goals scored per game by these famous hockey stars.

Player	Lifetime Totals	
	Goals Scored	Games Played
Gordie Howe	801	1767
Bobby Hull	610	1063
Guy Lafleur	518	961

ESTIMATING

Using Equivalent Division Facts

WE *CAN* FIND THE NUMBER OF DIMES IN A STACK BY MEASURING THE HEIGHT OF THE STACK.

A DIME IS ABOUT 0.1 cm THICK. ESTIMATE THE NUMBER OF DIMES IN A STACK 6 cm HIGH.

Jason thinks:

How many tenths of a centimetre in 6 cm?

A stack 1 cm high contains 10 dimes. A stack 6 cm high contains 6 × 10 or 60 dimes. That is,
6 cm ÷ 0.1 cm = 60

Jason writes:

$$0.1 \overline{)6} \quad 60$$

Allison thinks:

1 cm = 10 mm, so a dime is 1 mm thick and the stack is 60 mm tall.

60 mm ÷ 1 mm = 60

Allison writes:

$$1 \overline{)60} \quad 60$$

There are about 60 dimes in the stack.

The example above shows that $0.1 \overline{)6}$ and $1 \overline{)60}$ have the same quotient. They are called **equivalent division facts**.

To change $0.1 \overline{)6}$ into an equivalent fact $1 \overline{)60}$, we multiply both divisor and dividend by 10.

$0.1 \overline{)6.0}$ becomes $1 \overline{)60}$

282

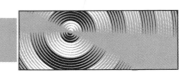

Multiply the divisor and dividend by 10
to obtain an equivalent division fact.

1. $0.3\overline{)1.8}$ $1. \; 3\overline{)18}$ 2. $0.5\overline{)2.5}$ 3. $0.7\overline{)2.8}$ 4. $0.6\overline{)0.42}$

5. $1.2\overline{)4.8}$ 6. $2.5\overline{)7.5}$ 7. $1.6\overline{)0.64}$ 8. $1.1\overline{)0.77}$ 9. $3.5\overline{)10.5}$

Multiply the divisor and dividend by 100
to obtain an equivalent division fact.

10. $0.35\overline{)4.9}$ $10. \; 35\overline{)490}$ 11. $0.49\overline{)9.8}$ 12. $0.19\overline{)5.7}$ 13. $1.64\overline{)11.48}$

14. $0.27\overline{)2.43}$ 15. $0.07\overline{)0.343}$ 16. $0.01\overline{)82.6}$ 17. $2.56\overline{)1.024}$ 18. $5.09\overline{)40.72}$

Write an equivalent division fact which
has a whole number divisor.

19. $1.25\overline{)15}$ $19. \; 125\overline{)1500}$ 20. $0.6\overline{)0.54}$ 21. $2.9\overline{)17}$ 22. $3.8\overline{)51.4}$

23. $0.75\overline{)3.8}$ 24. $4.6\overline{)19.8}$ 25. $3.25\overline{)8.775}$ 26. $1.3\overline{)1.96}$ 27. $2.85\overline{)17}$

BITS AND BYTES

For each of the division questions, follow this flow chart.

Use your calculator to find the quotient. Record it.	→	Multiply divisor and dividend by 10 or 100 to obtain an equivalent fact.	→	Use your calculator to find the quotient. Record it.

1. $0.7\overline{)2.8}$ 2. $0.49\overline{)9.8}$ 3. $1.6\overline{)0.64}$ 4. $0.6\overline{)0.42}$

5. $0.19\overline{)5.7}$ 6. $1.1\overline{)8.8}$ 7. $3.5\overline{)10.5}$ 8. $0.01\overline{)8.6}$

9. $2.56\overline{)1.024}$ 10. $2.5\overline{)6.25}$ 11. $3.25\overline{)8.775}$ 12. $8.75\overline{)49}$

Discuss:

Does multiplication of both the divisor
and dividend by 10 or 100 change
the quotient?

Discuss:

Does multiplication of both the
divisor and dividend by any number
(except zero) change the quotient?

283

ESTIMATING

Decimal Divisors > 1

A ball driven by a professional golfer travels a distance of 238 m in 5.8 s.

Estimate the average number of metres travelled per second by the golf ball during its flight.

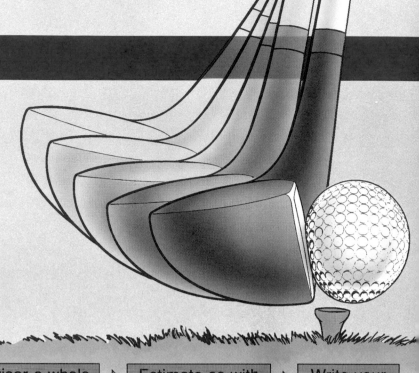

To estimate:	→	Make the divisor a whole number by rounding.	→	Estimate as with whole numbers.	→	Write your estimate.

$$5.8\overline{)238}$$ $$6\overline{)238}$$ $$6\overline{)238}^{\,40}$$ $$5.8\overline{)238}^{\,40}$$

The golf ball travelled an average of about 40 m/s during its flight.

Estimate.

1. $1.9\overline{)38.6}$ 2. $1.8\overline{)17.6}$ 3. $3.1\overline{)89.6}$ 4. $4.9\overline{)9.38}$

5. $9.3\overline{)56.7}$ 6. $7.4\overline{)93.6}$ 7. $8.8\overline{)4.89}$ 8. $1.98\overline{)6.42}$

9. $12.3\overline{)468}$ 10. $5.1\overline{)8.9}$ 11. $29.7\overline{)900}$ 12. $2.05\overline{)16.5}$

13. $27.6 \div 3.9$ 14. $5.07 \div 8.1$ 15. $12.8 \div 6.03$ 16. $48.9 \div 10.5$
17. $228 \div 8.9$ 18. $3.39 \div 9.1$ 19. $45.86 \div 9.4$ 20. $213.2 \div 3.8$

21. Can you use the method above to estimate these quotients?

 a) $0.3\overline{)17.4}$ b) $0.9\overline{)8}$

For which divisors is the method above not useful?

284

Decimal Divisors < 1

During a pitch, a baseball travelled 18.28 m from the mound to home plate in 0.4 s. Estimate the average speed of the baseball.

When the divisor is less than 1, it is usually better to use the following method of estimation.

| To estimate: | → | Make the divisor a whole number by multiplying. | → | Write your estimate. |

$0.4\overline{)18.28}$ $4.\overline{)182.8}$ $4\overline{)182.8}^{\,40}$

We multiply divisor and dividend by 10.

The average speed of the ball is about 40 m/s.

Estimate these quotients by multiplying the divisor and dividend by 10 or 100.

1. $0.4\overline{)7.2}$
2. $1.5\overline{)9.1}$
3. $0.5\overline{)0.84}$
4. $0.25\overline{)6.8}$

5. $0.6\overline{)92.7}$
6. $0.15\overline{)0.93}$
7. $1.2\overline{)14.8}$
8. $0.95\overline{)37.25}$

9. $2.3\overline{)0.97}$
10. $0.02\overline{)9.3}$
11. $0.07\overline{)14.9}$
12. $0.41\overline{)66.58}$

BITS AND BYTES

| Estimate each quotient in 2 different ways. | 1. $0.6\overline{)2.5}$ | 2. $2.9\overline{)6.90}$ |

| Then use your calculator to determine which method gives the better estimate. | 3. $4.5\overline{)0.85}$ | 4. $0.99\overline{)3.98}$ |

| Write a sentence to explain what you discover. | 5. $7.9\overline{)64.5}$ | 6. $1.02\overline{)62.97}$ |

Dividing by Decimal Numbers

To raise money for cancer research, the children at Kilbride School collected quarters. They placed them end-to-end on sticky tape that stretched along the sidewalk around the school.

If the diameter of a quarter is 2.1 cm, how many quarters placed end-to-end are contained along each metre of tape?

We must determine how many lengths of 2.1 cm are contained in a length of 100 cm.

To divide:	Multiply the divisor and the dividend by 10.	Divide.

$$2.1 \overline{)100} \qquad 21_{,} \overline{)1000_{,}} \qquad \begin{array}{r} 47 \\ 21\overline{)1000} \\ \underline{84} \\ 160 \\ \underline{147} \\ 13 \end{array}$$

A maximum of 47 quarters can be placed end-to-end in a length of 1 m.

Another example:

To divide:	Multiply the divisor and the dividend by 100.	Divide.

$$0.35 \overline{)0.805} \qquad 35_{,} \overline{)80_{,}5} \qquad \begin{array}{r} 2.3 \\ 35\overline{)80.5} \\ \underline{70} \\ 10\ 5 \\ \underline{10\ 5} \\ 0 \end{array}$$

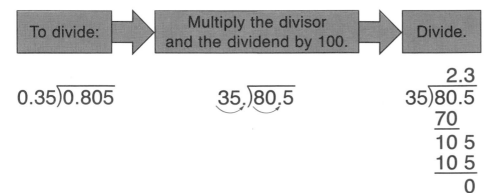

286

Write each quotient with the decimal point
in the correct position.

1. 29.4 ÷ 0.84 → 35
2. 3.102 ÷ 0.47 → 66
3. 130.4 ÷ 1.6 → 815
4. 0.324 ÷ 7.2 → 45
5. 95.06 ÷ 0.98 → 97
6. 0.0336 ÷ 0.7 → 48
7. 0.72 ÷ 0.08 → 9
8. 2.8594 ÷ 0.34 → 841
9. 55.26 ÷ 0.09 → 614

Divide. Calculate only those quotients
which are greater than 1.

10. 0.5)19.5
11. 3.9)2.73
12. 0.3)29.7
13. 5.8)8.12

14. 1.8)13.5
15. 0.35)0.56
16. 6.9)5.175
17. 4.6)14.95

18. 0.65)6.11
19. 0.8)3.4
20. 0.06)8.1
21. 0.24)1.368

Divide.

22. 17.9 ÷ 0.1
23. 7.83 ÷ 0.09
24. 48.1 ÷ 7.4
25. 0.828 ÷ 1.2
26. 55.25 ÷ 0.85
27. 8.46 ÷ 0.9

28. A quarter has a thickness of 1.6 mm.
How many quarters are in a stack
123.2 mm high?

29. A dime has a thickness of 1.16 mm.
What is the total value of a stack of
dimes 13.92 cm high?

30. The Bugatti Royale was the longest
car ever made for road use. Only 6
such cars were ever built. The first
one was built in 1927.

The Bugatti Royale measured 6.7 m
from bumper to bumper. How many
quarters placed end-to-end would
stretch the length of this car?

Rounding Quotients

For Father's Day, Mr. Dunlop's family bought him a dozen golf balls for $28.75.

What was the cost of each golf ball to the nearest cent?

There are 12 golf balls in a dozen. To find the cost of one golf ball using a calculator, we press these keys:

and we obtain the display:

$$2.3958333$$

"Round to the nearest cent" means "Round to the nearest hundredth of a dollar." To do this, we look at the digit which shows thousandths of a dollar.

2.395 rounds up to 2.40, so each golf ball costs $2.40 to the nearest cent.

$$2.3958333$$

Tenths ——————
Hundredths ——————
Thousandths ——————

Copy and complete this table. Use your calculator.

	Quotient Rounded to the Nearest			
	...Whole Number	...Tenth	...Hundredth	...Thousandth
1. 29 ÷ 7				
2. 47 ÷ 13				
3. 53 ÷ 14				
4. 61 ÷ 27				
5. 1.486 ÷ 3				
6. 0.178 ÷ 7				
7. 7.893 ÷ 0.9				

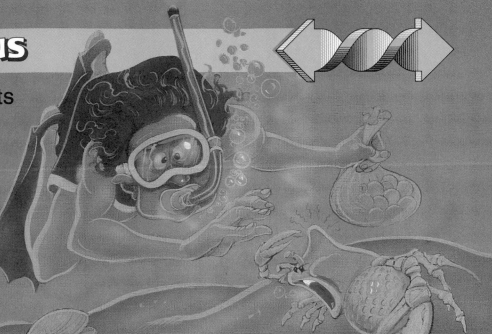

Rounding Quotients

The greenskeeper at the Water Hazard Country Club pays Ryan to retrieve lost golf balls.

Ryan received $7.00 for collecting 16 golf balls. How much did Ryan receive, to the nearest cent, for each golf ball?

To round this quotient to 2 decimal places:	Divide to 3 decimal places, writing zeros as needed.	Round the quotient to 2 decimal places.

$$16\overline{)7.00}$$

$$
\begin{array}{r}
0.437 \\
16\overline{)7.000} \\
6\ 4 \\
\hline
60 \\
48 \\
\hline
120 \\
112 \\
\hline
8
\end{array}
$$

$$0.437 \rightarrow 0.44$$

Ryan received an average of $0.44 for each golf ball (to the nearest cent).

Divide. Round each quotient to the nearest whole number.

1. $4\overline{)7.04}$

2. $7\overline{)38.36}$

3. $0.6\overline{)3.333}$

4. $1.6\overline{)9}$

Divide. Round each quotient to the nearest tenth.

5. $7\overline{)18.13}$

6. $9\overline{)9.63}$

7. $1.2\overline{)8}$

8. $1.6\overline{)0.7787}$

Divide. Round each quotient to the nearest hundredth.

9. $6\overline{)5.8}$

10. $0.8\overline{)0.8392}$

11. $1.2\overline{)0.7867}$

12. $0.35\overline{)12}$

PROBLEM SOLVING

Choosing the Appropriate Operations

To solve this problem...

A. First, make sure you understand the problem.

Discuss:
- *What is the mass of 1 dime? of 1 quarter?*
- *How many grams are in 1 kg?*
- *How many quarters have a mass of 1 kg?*
- *How many dimes have a mass of 1 kg?*
- *Will you be able to solve this problem doing only one operation?*

B. Then, think of strategies.

Try choosing the appropriate operations.

- *How can you find the number of dimes and the number of quarters in 1 kg?*
- *How can you find the value of the dimes and quarters?*
- *What operation is used to find the difference?*

c. Solve the problem and answer the question.

- *Divide to find the number of dimes in 1 kg.*
- *Multiply to find the value of the dimes.*
- *Divide to find the number of quarters in 1 kg.*
- *Multiply to find the value of the quarters.*
- *Subtract to find the difference.*

D. Check your answer and discuss your solution.

- *How many dimes are in 1 kg?*
- *How many quarters are in 1 kg?*
- *What is the value of the dimes? of the quarters?*
- *Were you surprised at the difference in value? Why or why not?*
- *Could you have used different operations or done them in a different order?*

Solve these problems.
You may use your calculator to help you.

1. Light from the sun travels to the earth in 499.012 s. How many minutes is this?

2. A human hair is 0.005 cm thick. How thick will it appear to be under a microscope which enlarges it 1200 times its actual size?

3. The ocean at its deepest point is 10.916 km below sea level. The deepest hole drilled into the earth is 13.716 km below sea level. How many metres deeper than the bottom of the ocean is the world's deepest drilled hole?

4. About 0.27 of the earth's surface is land. The rest is water. About how many times as great as the land area is the water area?

5. One and a half dozen tennis balls have a total mass of 1 kg. What is the mass of one tennis ball in grams?

6. The most poisonous animal venom comes not from a snake but from the skin of a golden arrow-poison frog in South America. An adult frog carries on average 1 mg (milligram) of this venom. This is enough to kill 2000 people. About how many milligrams of this venom would kill one person?

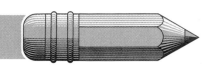

Write each quotient.

1. 36.24 ÷ 10
2. 18.5 ÷ 100
3. 6.58 ÷ 10
4. 0.46 ÷ 10
5. 3.51 ÷ 100
6. 0.83 ÷ 100
7. 625 ÷ 1000
8. 48 ÷ 1000

Find only those quotients less than 1.

9. 7)5.81
10. 12)17.16

11. 8)6.592
12. 14)14.42

Divide.

13. 4)254.4
14. 18)653.4

15. 23)8.51
16. 58)92.8

17. 43)30.96
18. 63)447.3

19. 3)2.241
20. 62)4.96

Divide until the remainder is zero.

21. 5)7
22. 4)9

23. 8)11.6
24. 16)520

25. 24)21
26. 36)12.6

27. 26)110.5
28. 6)0.33

29. 18)4.05
30. 8)1.712

31. A busload of 32 people paid a total of $168 for a tour of the city. How much did each person pay?

Find the average of each set of numbers.

32. 86, 93, 67, 88, 76
33. 7.5, 9.3, 8.6, 7.6, 10.4, 11.8
34. $3.25, $4.16, $3.49, $5.09, $5.01

Write each quotient with the decimal point in the correct position.

35. 31.92 ÷ 0.76 → 42
36. 3.591 ÷ 0.57 → 63
37. 130.05 ÷ 1.7 → 765
38. 2.432 ÷ 6.4 → 38

Divide.

39. 0.6)29.4
40. 2.8)2.24

41. 4.7)7.52
42. 0.8)0.416

43. 0.55)0.99
44. 0.43)32.809

45. 5.8)4.35
46. 0.73)5.986

47. 0.07)8.47
48. 0.27)1.728

49. A quarter has a thickness of 1.6 mm. How many quarters are in a stack 230.4 mm high?

 heckers is considered one of the greatest boardgames of the world. It was probably invented in the south of France about 1100 A·D· In England, the game is usually called draughts.

Artist's impression of the boardgame Checkers in 12th century France.

Volume in Cubic Centimetres

A cube with all edges 1 cm long has a volume of **one cubic centimetre**.

We see:

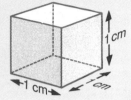

We write: **1 cm³**

We say: one cubic centimetre

We ask: What is the volume of this rectangular prism made from centimetre cubes?

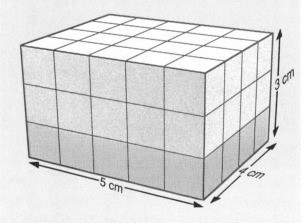

We think: Each layer contains 5×4 or 20 centimetre cubes. There are 3 layers of 20 or 60 centimetre cubes.

We write: 60 cm³

We say: The rectangular prism has a volume of 60 cubic centimetres.

All of these rectangular prisms are made from centimetre cubes.

Write the volume of each in cubic centimetres.

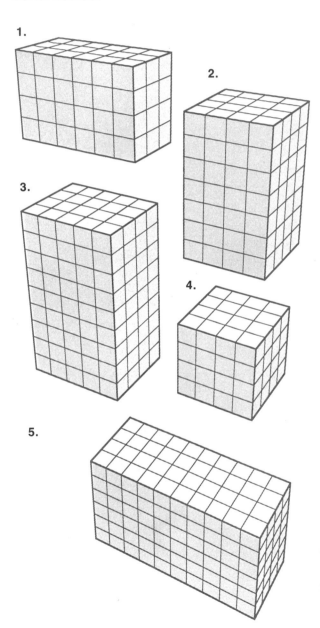

1.

2.

3.

4.

5.

To find the
volume of
this prism,...

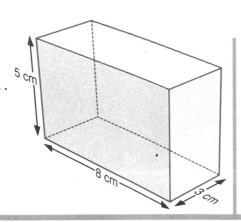
5 cm
8 cm
3 cm

we imagine
it was
made from
centimetre
cubes.

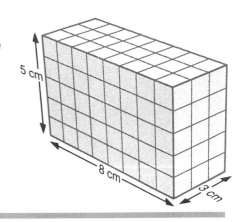
5 cm
8 cm
3 cm

To find the volume of
a rectangular prism,
we calculate:

length × width × height
8   ×   3   × 5 cm³ = 120 cm³
Volume = 120 cm³

Calculate the volume of each box.

1.
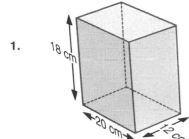
18 cm
20 cm
12 cm

2.
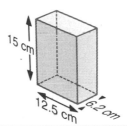
15 cm
12.5 cm
6.2 cm

3.
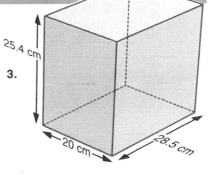
25.4 cm
20 cm
28.5 cm

Calculate the volumes of the rectangular prisms with these dimensions.
Express all volumes in cubic centimetres.

4. length 17 cm
   width 15 cm
   height 6 cm

5. length 9.6 cm
   width   8.5 cm
   height 14.2 cm

6. length 0.6 m
   width 0.4 m
   height 0.3 m

ESTIMATING

Round the dimensions
of these prisms.
Then estimate their
volumes in cubic
centimetres.

A.
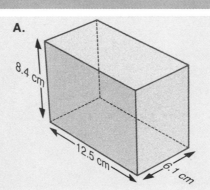
8.4 cm
12.5 cm
6.1 cm

B.
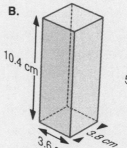
10.4 cm
3.6 cm
3.8 cm

C.
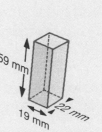
59 mm
19 mm
22 mm

Volume in Cubic Metres

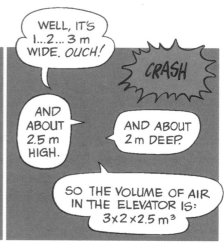

To find the volume of a rectangular prism in **cubic metres**, we calculate the product of the length, width, and height in **metres**.

The elevator is a rectangular prism with dimensions 3 m, 2 m, and 2.5 m.

Its volume is: 3 × 2 × 2.5 m³ or 15 m³

Calculate the volume of each box in cubic metres.

1.

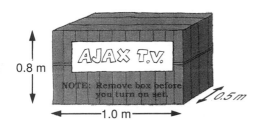

0.8 m

AJAX T.V.

NOTE: Remove box before you turn on set.

1.0 m

0.5 m

2.

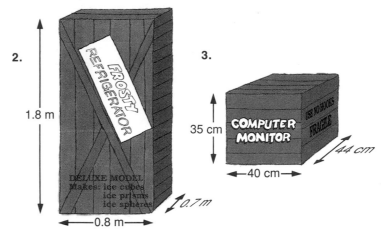

1.8 m

FROSTY REFRIGERATOR

DELUXE MODEL
Makes: ice cubes
ice prisms
ice spheres

0.8 m

0.7 m

3.

35 cm

COMPUTER MONITOR

USE NO HOOKS

FRAGILE

40 cm

44 cm

4.

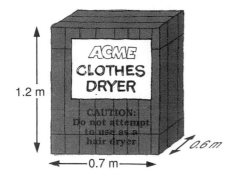

1.2 m

ACME CLOTHES DRYER

CAUTION:
Do not attempt
to use as a
hair dryer

0.7 m

0.6 m

5.

10 cm

COMPUTER

45 cm

30 cm

6. How many of the Frosty refrigerators above could be packed into the truck shown in the picture at the right?

5.6 m

2.4 m

KELLY THE MOVER

1.8 m

KELLY THE MOVER

7. A builder is to excavate a rectangular basement 15 m long, 12 m wide and 2.5 m deep. She must remove the earth from this excavation using a truck with a box measuring 4 m by 3 m by 2 m. How many truckloads will be needed to remove all the earth from the excavation?

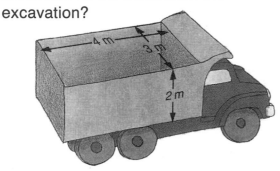

4 m

3 m

2 m

During light activity, the human body burns about 0.02 m³ of oxygen every hour. To obtain this oxygen, the lungs must inhale 5 times that volume of air.

1. How many cubic metres of air must we inhale every hour to survive?

2. About how long would the oxygen contained in the elevator on page 296 last 4 people?

297

Capacity

The **capacity** of a container is the amount of liquid it can hold.

WE USE MILLILITRES, LITRES, AND KILOLITRES TO MEASURE CAPACITY.

1 mL

1 L

1 kL

Millilitres (mL) are used to measure small capacities.

A teaspoon holds about 5 mL of liquid.

A styrofoam cup holds about 180 mL of liquid.

Litres (L) are used to measure capacities as large or larger than a milk container.

Kilolitres (kL) are used to measure capacities of large containers like swimming pools and tanker trucks.

This pitcher of bagged milk has a capacity of about 1 L.

This tanker will hold about 30 kL of gasoline.

ESTIMATING

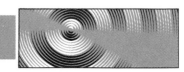

Choose the best estimate for each.

1. How much water is in a typical ice cube?

3 mL   30 mL   1 L

2. How much milk is in a full glass?

200 mL   1 L   2 L

3. How much gas can a car gas tank hold?

50 mL   50 L   50 kL

4. How much toothpaste is in a tube?

2 mL   20 mL   200 mL

5. How much water is in a family swimming pool?

90 kL   90 L   90 mL

6. How much air is contained in a basketball?

8 L   80 L   8 kL

7. How much water will a rain barrel hold?

1.8 L   18 L   180 L

8. How much orange juice is in a small tin?

25 mL   250 mL   1 L

9. How much gas will this container hold?

10 mL   100 mL   10 L

Estimate each of the following in millilitres, litres, or kilolitres.

10. The amount of tomato juice in a family size tin.

11. The amount of fruit punch in a large punch bowl.

12. The amount of water in a small paper cup.

PROBLEM SOLVING

To save hot water, Ms. Miser takes a shower instead of a bath. The shower uses 16 L per minute and a bath requires 200 L. After how many minutes does a shower use more hot water than a bath?

Converting Capacity Units

We can use these relationships to convert a measurement of capacity from one unit to another.

$$1 \text{ L} = 1000 \text{ mL}$$
$$1 \text{ kL} = 1000 \text{ L}$$

We see:　600 mL = ▨ L

We think: To convert from millilitres to litres, we must **divide** by 1000. (The number of litres is less than the number of millilitres.)

We write: 600 mL = 0.600 L

　　　　　　　　　　　divide by 1000

or, 600 mL = 0.6 L

We see:　3 kL = ▨ L

We think: To convert from kilolitres to litres, we must **multiply** by 1000. (The number of litres is greater than the number of kilolitres.)

We write: 3 kL = 3000. L

　　　　　　　　　multiply by 1000

or, 3 kL = 3000 L

Copy and complete.

1. 4 L = ▨ mL
2. 7000 mL = ▨ L
3. 475 mL = ▨ L
4. 0.8 L = ▨ mL
5. 1.6 L = ▨ mL
6. 3000 mL = ▨ L
7. 750 mL = ▨ L
8. 70 mL = ▨ L
9. 3 mL = ▨ L
10. 5000 L = ▨ kL
11. 4 kL = ▨ L
12. 0.65 kL = ▨ L
13. 280 L = ▨ kL
14. 0.05 kL = ▨ L
15. 8 L = ▨ kL
16. 1.34 L = ▨ mL

17. If all 3 juices shown are the same quality, which tin offers:
    - the best value?
    - the least value?

88¢　　　　　$1.15　　　　　$1.80

18. A tap leaks 4 drops every second. Each drop has a volume of 0.2 mL. How much water leaks in:
    a) one second?　　b) one minute?
    c) one hour?　　　d) one day?

PROBLEM SOLVING

HERE ARE 2 UNMARKED PAILS OF CAPACITIES 3 L AND 5 L. TAKE THEM TO THE WELL AND BRING ME BACK EXACTLY 4 L OF WATER, PLEASE.

Explain how to do this using only these 2 containers.

Relating Capacity and Volume

A cubic container with all edges 1 cm long has a **volume** of 1 cm³.

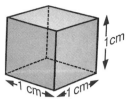

The **capacity** of the cubic container shown is exactly 1 mL. That is,

$$1 \text{ mL} = 1 \text{ cm}^3$$

Since 1 L is 1000 mL, we can write:

$$1 \text{ L} = 1000 \text{ cm}^3$$

Use the relationships above to help you complete these questions.

1. 17 mL = ▥ cm³   2. 210 cm³ = ▥ mL   3. 27.5 mL = ▥ cm³   4. 4 L = ▥ cm³

5. 2000 cm³ = ▥ L   6. 5000 cm³ = ▥ L   7. 8 L = ▥ cm³   8. 1300 cm³ = ▥ L

9. 675 cm³ = ▥ L   10. 250 cm³ = ▥ mL   11. 3.9 L = ▥ cm³   12. 50 cm³ = ▥ L

Calculate the volume of water in litres needed to fill each acquarium.

13.

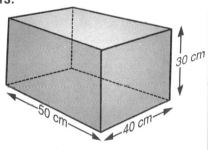

14.

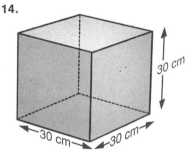

15.

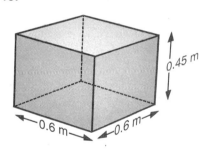

---

16. How many kilolitres of water would it take to fill a swimming pool 8 m long, 6 m wide, and 2 m deep?

17. A champion Holstein cow gave about 50 L of milk every day for a year. About how many kilolitres of milk did the cow give that year?

301

ESTIMATING

Marcie made this net for a cube. Each side is 2 cm long.

Then she made a net with sides that were exactly twice as long as her first net. Each side is 4 cm long.

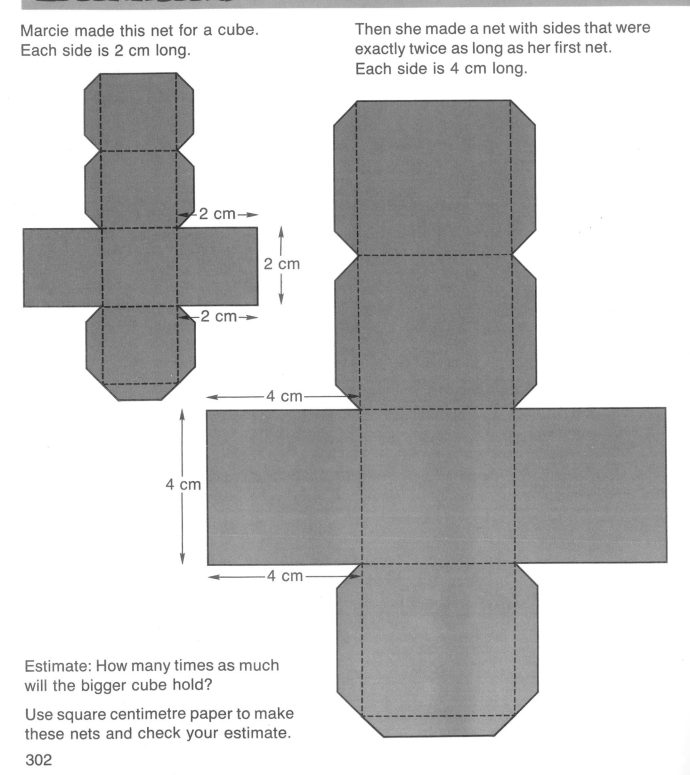

Estimate: How many times as much will the bigger cube hold?

Use square centimetre paper to make these nets and check your estimate.

1. Make a net with sides 3 times as long as Marcie's first net. Estimate how many times as much as the first net it will hold. Then check your estimate.

2. Copy and complete the table below.

3. Study your table. What patterns do you see?

Net	Length of One Side	Perimeter of Net (not including tabs)	Area of Net	Volume of Cube
1	2 cm	■	■	■
2	4 cm	■	■	■
3	6 cm	■	■	■

4. Predict the perimeter and the area of a net with sides 8 cm long. What do you think the volume of a cube made from that net would be? Check your predictions by making a net.

303

Mass

We use grams, kilograms, and tonnes to measure mass.

Grams (g) are used to measure small masses which you can hold in one hand.

A paperclip has a mass of about 1 g.

A dime has a mass of about 2 g.

Kilograms (kg) are used to measure masses as heavy as or heavier than a litre of milk.

A litre of milk has a mass of about 1 kg.

A grade 6 student has a mass of about 35 kg.

Tonnes (t) are used to measure very large masses.

A small car has a mass of about 1 t.

An elephant has a mass of about 5 t.

ESTIMATING

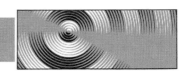

Choose the best estimate for each mass.

1.

20 g   200 g   2 kg

2.

4.6 g   46 g   0.46 kg

3.

750 g   7.5 kg   75 kg

4.

400 g   4 kg   40 kg

5.

80 kg   0.8 t   8 t

6.

30 g   300 g   3 kg

7.

0.5 kg   5 g   50 g

8.

0.8 kg   8 kg   80 kg

9.

6 g   60 g   600 g

Estimate the mass of each of the
following in grams, kilograms, or tonnes.

10. a bunch of 8 bananas

11. a class of 30 grade 6 students

12. a box of 200 paper clips

13. a stack of 50 quarters

14. a package containing 4
    1 L bags of milk

15. the mass of water contained in a bath
    (1 L of water has a mass of 1 kg)

Converting Units of Mass

We can use these relationships to convert a measurement of mass from one unit to another.

> 1 kg = 1000 g
> 1 t = 1000 kg

We see: 300 g = ▨ kg

We think: To convert from grams to kilograms we must **divide** by 1000.

We write: 300 g = 0.300 kg
          divide by 1000

or 300 g = 0.3 kg

We see: 6 t = ▨ kg

We think: To convert from tonnes to kilograms we must **multiply** by 1000.

We write: 6 t = 6000. kg
          multiply by 1000

or 6 t = 6000 kg

Copy and complete.
Use the relationships above.

1. 6 kg = ▨ g
2. 500 g = ▨ kg
3. 825 g = ▨ kg
4. 0.7 kg = ▨ g
5. 3.8 kg = ▨ g
6. 40 g = ▨ kg
7. 250 g = ▨ kg
8. 14 g = ▨ kg
9. 7000 g = ▨ kg
10. 6000 kg = ▨ t
11. 7 t = ▨ kg
12. 0.38 t = ▨ kg
13. 590 kg = ▨ t
14. 0.3 kg = ▨ t
15. 90 kg = ▨ t
16. 1.46 kg = ▨ g

17. Which package contains more cat food: A or B?

A.

B.

18. About how many grams of cat food are in each pouch?

19. A fisherman sold 3.2 t of fish to a processing company for $1200.00. How much did the fisherman receive per kilogram?

20. If gold has a value of $13.20 per gram, what is the value of a gold brick with a mass of 0.4 kg?

comparative shopping

Which is the better buy?

To compare the prices of these 2 items, we calculate the price per kilogram.

We think: 10 groups of 100 g equals 1 kg.
$10 \times 55¢ = \$5.50$

We write: Sara's Corn Snacks at $5.50/kg is the better buy.

When spending your money Be careful and wise. Do comparative shopping To get the best buys.

$5.99/kg   55 cents/100 g

Compare these items.
Which brand is cheaper?

1.

$0.45/100 g $3.85/kg

2.

$1.65/500 g   55¢/100 g

3.

93¢/100 g $8.79/kg

4.

69¢/200 g $3.50/kg

If all 3 brands are the same quality, which is the best buy?

5.
 55¢/200 g    $1.49/500 g    $2.85/kg

307

Using Logical Thinking

All numbers on the masses are kilograms. Use this fact and logical thinking to help you answer each question.

IN THE DIAGRAMS BELOW, ALL CUBES OF THE SAME COLOUR HAVE THE SAME MASS.

1. What is the mass of each cube A?

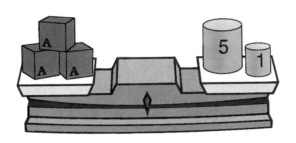

2. What is the mass of each cube B?

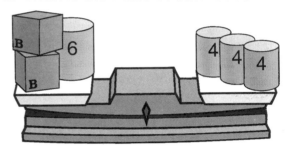

3. What is the mass of each cube C?

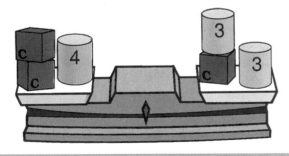

4. What is the mass of each cube D?

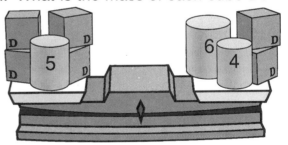

5. All disks of the same colour have the same mass.
   Study both pictures, then answer the question.

   How many green disks would balance 3 pink disks?

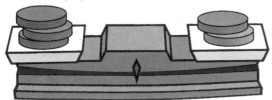
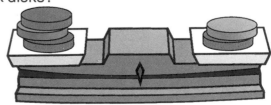

308

Writing Equations

When the arm of a 2-pan balance is horizontal,
the masses on both pans are equal.

We see:

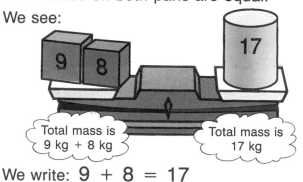

Total mass is
9 kg + 8 kg

Total mass is
17 kg

We write: $9 + 8 = 17$

We see:

We write: $\blacksquare + 6 = 7 + 7$

A number sentence like $9 + 8 = 17$ or $\blacksquare + 6 = 14$ is called an **equation**.
An equation is a number sentence which contains an equal sign.

Write an equation to match each picture.
Use $\blacksquare$ to represent the mass of each cube.

Can you find the mass of each cube?

1.

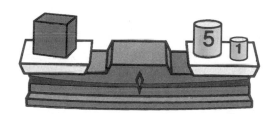

2.

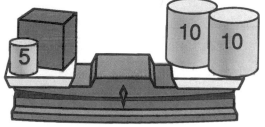

3.

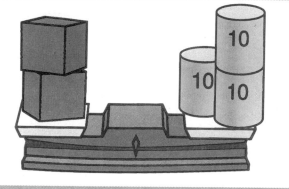

4.

Draw a simple 2-pan balance to show each equation.

5. $\blacksquare = 10 + 10$

6. $\blacksquare + 5 = 7 + 9$

7. $\blacksquare + 3 = 5 + 10 + 1$

8. $6 + 4 = \blacksquare$

9. $\blacksquare + 4 = \blacksquare + 2 + 2$

10. $2 \times \blacksquare = 10$

Checking for Hidden Assumptions

Each of the books in a 2 volume set is 5 cm thick when the covers are included. The front and back covers are each 0.5 cm thick.

A hungry bookworm ate its way from the first page of volume A to the last page of volume B.

How far did it travel?

Solve as many of these problems as you can.

1. Mrs. Gomez registered her daughters, Bonita and Teresa, for swim classes. When the instructor saw that the 2 girls looked very much alike, and that they were born on the same day of the same year, she said, "You must be twins!" "No," explained Bonita, "we're sisters, but we're not twins." How can that be?

2. The day after Mr. Cardinal celebrated his 13th birthday, his daughter, Robin turned 17 years old. What is Robin's birthdate?

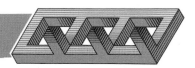

To solve the problem...

A. First, make sure you understand the problem.

> *Discuss:*
> - *What is the thickness of 1 book?*
> - *What is the thickness of 1 cover?*
> - *What are you asked to find?*
> - *Where did the bookworm begin?*
> - *Where did it end?*

B. Then, think of strategies.

> *Check for hidden assumptions. Study the picture.*
> - *Where would the first page of volume A be?*
> - *Where would the last page of volume B be?*
> - *What parts of the books has the worm eaten?*

C. Solve the problem and answer the question.

> - *What operation will you use?*
> - *What numbers will you use?*

D. Check your answer and discuss your solution.

> - *Study the picture again.*
> - *Does your answer make sense?*
> - *What hidden assumption is usually made when first reading this problem?*

3. How is it possible to put 4 speakers in a rectangular room so that each speaker is an equal distance from the other 3? Draw a figure to show your answer.

BE CAREFUL!

4. How can you make 4 equilateral triangles using exactly 6 toothpicks of equal length?

311

WATCHING LIGHTNING GROW

One stormy night in late March, a beautiful mare named Arabian Princess gave birth to a 20 kg colt. The colt was quick and high-spirited from the moment of its arrival, so his owner, Jessica, named him Lightning.

Within a few hours, Lightning was able to walk, and a short time later he was galloping in the fields. For the first few weeks, Lightning stayed close to his mother.

During April, he nibbled the early spring grass that began to sprout in the muddy pasture.

By May, Lightning was grazing on the meadows of the farm.

The more Lightning ate, the larger he grew. By the end of the summer, Lightning was almost fully grown.

The graph below shows Lightning's mass at the end of each month for his first 6 months of life.

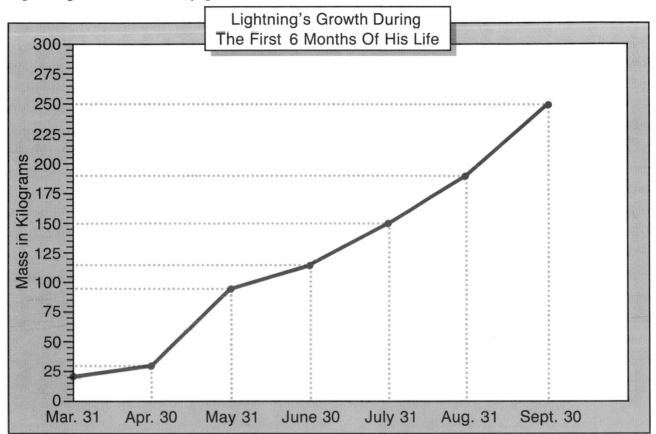

Lightning's Growth During The First 6 Months Of His Life

Use the graph to help answer these questions.

1. What was Lightning's mass at the end of June?

2. What was Lightning's mass at the end of September?

3. How many kilograms did Lightning gain between June 30 and September 30?

4. What was Lightning's mass in tonnes on September 30?

5. About how many kilograms was Lightning on June 15?

6. During which month did Lightning's mass increase the most?

7. Estimate what Lightning's mass would be at the end of October.

8. What was the average mass gained per month:
   a) in kilograms?   b) in tonnes?

313

The Twenty-Four Hour Clock

When we use the 12 h clock...
- Times from midnight to noon are referred to as **a.m.**

We say: 8 o'clock in the morning

We write: **8:00 a.m.**

- Times from noon to midnight are referred to as **p.m.**

We say: 8 o'clock in the evening

We write: **8:00 p.m.**

To avoid using a.m. and p.m., we can use the 24 h clock.

When we use the 24 h clock...
- To read times from midnight to noon we use the inner numbers.

We say: 8 o'clock in the morning

We think: 8 h past midnight

We write: **08:00**

- To read times from noon to midnight, we use the outer numbers.

We say: 8 o'clock in the evening.

We think: 20 h past midnight

We write: **20:00**

Where have you seen 24 h clocks displayed? Make a list.

Study each picture. Then write the time using the 24 h clock.

Write these times using the 24 h clock.

7. 4:00 a.m.   8. noon   9. 12:30 p.m.   10. 2:00 p.m.

11. 6:00 p.m.   12. 12:15 a.m.   13. 9:20 p.m.   14. 11:48 p.m.

Write these times using a.m. or p.m.

15. 08:16   16. 12:20   17. 18:00   18. 19:24

19. 00:10   20. 22:30   21. 19:55   22. 23:59

23. What time is it:
 a) 1 h after 19:25?
 b) 8 h after 22:00?
 c) 1 h before 12:00?
 d) 12 h before 11:59?
 e) 10 min after 11:55?
 f) 15 min before 01:10?
 g) 30 min before 00:00?
 h) 12 h before 06:28?
 i) 4 h 13 min after 19:49?

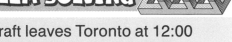

An aircraft leaves Toronto at 12:00 Toronto time. It lands in Halifax, Nova Scotia at 15:30 Halifax time.

How long was the flight if it is noon in Halifax 1 h before it is noon in Toronto?

315

Time Differences

During an airplane flight, Carly and Jessie watched a movie. The movie began at 11:45 and ended at 14:36.

How long was the movie?

To find the difference between 11:45 and 14:36, we follow these steps.

We cannot subtract 45 min from 36 min.	Trade 1 h for 60 min. Subtract the minutes.	Subtract the hours.
14 h 36 min − 11 h 45 min	13 h 96 min − 11 h 45 min 51 min	13 h 96 min − 11 h 45 min 2 h 51 min

The movie lasted 2 h 51 min.

Write the time difference:

1. from 08:32 to 11:41
2. from 04:29 to 09:00
3. from 06:09 to 10:25
4. from 11:28 to 16:00
5. from 14:10 to 22:54
6. from 16:18 to 20:00
7. from 09:25 to 21:10
8. from 12:00 to 16:50
9. from 07:30 to 23:45
10. from 00:46 to 15:25
11. from 00:08 to 17:49
12. from 18:37 to 22:10

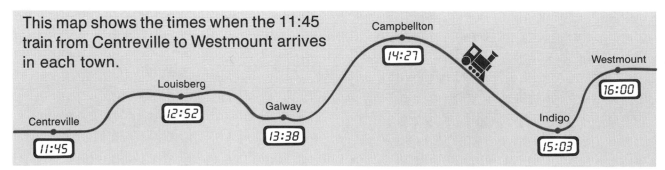

This map shows the times when the 11:45 train from Centreville to Westmount arrives in each town.

Campbellton 14:27
Westmount 16:00
Louisberg 12:52
Galway 13:38
Indigo 15:03
Centreville 11:45

What is the travel time from Centreville to each town?

13. Louisberg
14. Indigo
15. Campbellton
16. Galway
17. Westmount

Time Zones

This map names the 6 time zones into which Canada is divided.

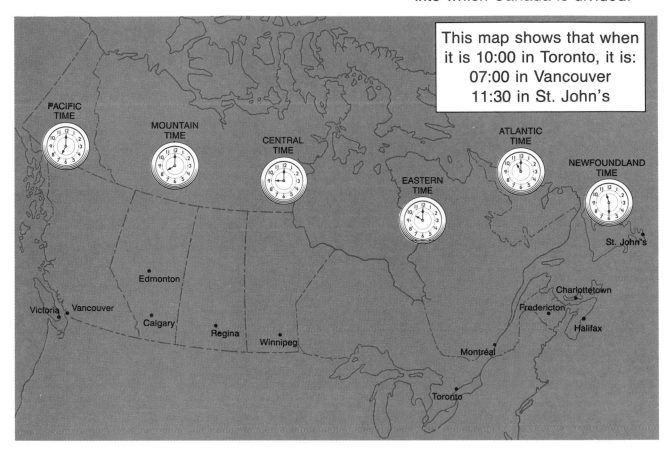

This map shows that when it is 10:00 in Toronto, it is:
07:00 in Vancouver
11:30 in St. John's

Use the map to help you answer these questions.

1. In what time zone is the time 2 h ahead of:
   a) Mountain time? b) Central time?
   c) Pacific time?

2. In what time zone is the time 2 h behind:
   a) Central time? b) Eastern time?
   c) Atlantic time?

3. The Olympic games were broadcast live from Calgary at 17:00. What time were they seen in Fredericton, New Brunswick?

4. An airline flight from Toronto to Halifax takes 2 h 35 min. If it leaves Toronto at 09:55, what time will it arrive in Halifax? Express your answer in Atlantic time.

PROBLEM SOLVING

A direct flight from Winnipeg, Manitoba, to St. John's, Newfoundland, leaves Winnipeg at 13:48 Central time.
It arrives in St. John's at 21:29 Newfoundland time.
How long was the flight?

317

DAYLIGHT HOURS

1. In the winter, Canadian children rise before the sun and fumble for matching socks.

The sun is late to rise.

2. The sun sets early, so it is dark by supper time.

There are fewer daylight hours in winter.

3. In the summer, most Canadian children rise after the sun and rub their eyes.

The sun rises earlier in summer.

4. The sun sets much later, so there is daylight to play after supper.

There are more daylight hours in summer.

The graph below shows the times of sunrise and sunset in a Canadian city on the 21st of each month.
The sunrise times are shown in white boxes.
The sunset times are in black boxes.

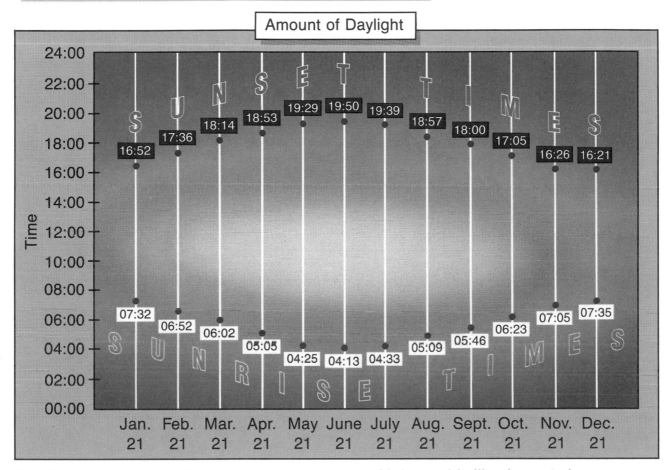

Amount of Daylight

The **daylight** hours are those between sunrise and sunset. To find the number of daylight hours and minutes on a given day, we calculate the time difference between sunrise and sunset.

	Times		
Date	Sunrise	Sunset	Amount of Daylight
Jan. 21	07:32	16:52	9 h 20 min
Feb. 21			

1. Make a table like the one shown. Complete the table for all 12 dates.

2. On which dates in the table is the amount of daylight:
   a) the greatest?   b) the least?

3. Make a bar graph to show the amount of daylight for the 21st day of each month.

Research: Why is the number of hours of daylight greater in summer than in winter?

319

Temperature

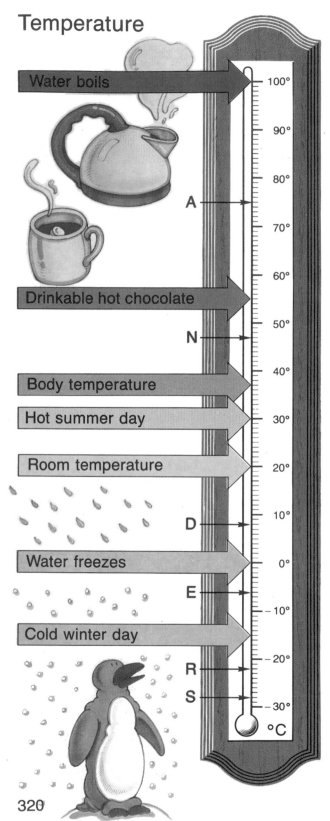

Water boils — 100°

Drinkable hot chocolate

Body temperature

Hot summer day

Room temperature

Water freezes

Cold winter day

A — 70°-80°
N — 50°
D — 10°
E — 0°
R — -20°
S — -30°
°C

This thermometer shows some familiar temperatures on the Celsius scale. Use the thermometer to help you choose the best estimate, A, B, or C, for each question.

1. Temperature on a warm summer day
   (A) −3°C (B) 12°C (C) 28°C

2. Temperature of hot soup
   (A) 10°C (B) 30°C (C) 70°C

3. Temperature of a warm bath
   (A) 45°C (B) 75°C (C) 90°C

4. Temperature inside a freezer
   (A) 10°C (B) 5°C (C) −5°C

5. Temperature of ice cream
   (A) −40°C (B) −5°C (C) 10°C

Write the temperature that matches each of these locations on the thermometer.

6. A 7. N 8. D 9. E 10. R 11. S

12. By how many degrees does the temperature increase during a rise from:
    a) 12°C to 31°C? b) 0°C to 18°C?
    c) −5°C to 0°C? d) −8°C to 7°C?
    e) −12°C to 20°C? f) −9°C to −3°C?

13. By how many degrees does the temperature decrease during a fall from:
    a) 31°C to 16°C? b) 14°C to 0°C?
    c) 0°C to −7°C? d) −6°C to −19°C?
    e) 2°C to −9°C? f) 13°C to −17°C?
    g) −8°C to −14°C? h) −3°C to −16°C?

−20°C is read as 20 degrees Celsius below zero.

Sandra's Skating Rink

Sandra wanted to make a rink to practise her figure skating. She cleared the snow to form a circular region in the yard. Then Sandra flooded her rink.

By 19:00, Sandra finished the rink. The temperature outside was 1° C. The graph below shows the temperature every hour from 19:00 until 07:00 the next morning.

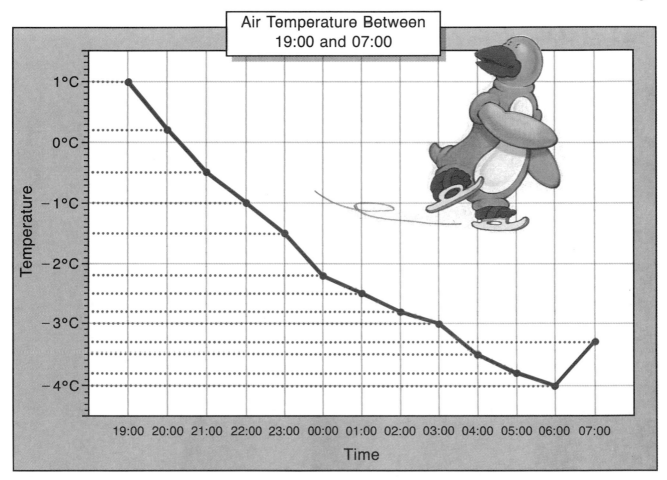

Air Temperature Between 19:00 and 07:00

Use the graph to help you solve these problems.

What was the temperature at each time?

1. 22:00   2. 21:00   3. 01:00

Estimate the temperature at each time.

4. 19:30   5. 03:30   6. 06:30

What was the temperature drop between these times?

7. 19:00 and 22:00   8. 22:00 and 02:00

9. What was the increase in temperature between 06:00 and 07:00?

10. What was the lowest temperature reached? At what time was that?

11. What do you think Sandra discovered when she saw the rink at 07:00?

321

EXTENSIONS

Temperature Range

The Canadian climate is one of the most changing climates in the world. In a recent year, temperatures in Calgary, Alberta rose as high as 35.3° C on July 7 and dropped to −36.2° C on December 29.

The difference between the highest and lowest temperature is called the temperature **range**.

What was the temperature range in Calgary during that year?

Calgary's temperature on July 7.

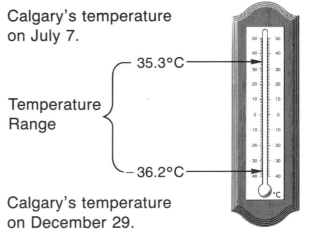

Temperature Range

35.3°C

−36.2°C

Calgary's temperature on December 29.

We ask: How many degrees are there between −36.2° C and 35.3° C?

We think: There are 36.2° C between −36.2° C and 0° C.
There are 35.3° C between 0° C and 35.3° C.

There are 36.2° C + 35.3° C or 71.5° C between − 36.2° C and 35.3° C.

We write: The difference in temperature between −36.2° C and 35.3° C is 71.5° C.

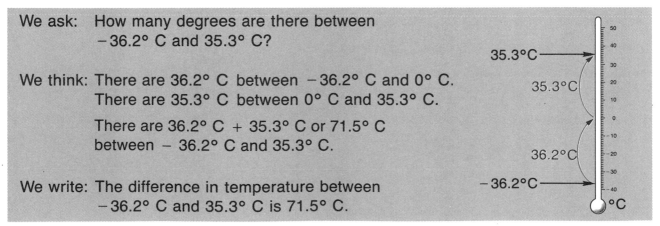

322

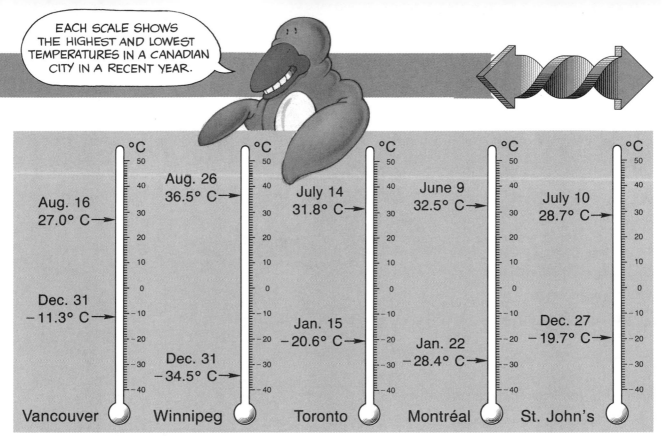

EACH SCALE SHOWS THE HIGHEST AND LOWEST TEMPERATURES IN A CANADIAN CITY IN A RECENT YEAR.

Vancouver:
Aug. 16 — 27.0° C
Dec. 31 — −11.3° C

Winnipeg:
Aug. 26 — 36.5° C
Dec. 31 — −34.5° C

Toronto:
July 14 — 31.8° C
Jan. 15 — −20.6° C

Montréal:
June 9 — 32.5° C
Jan. 22 — −28.4° C

St. John's:
July 10 — 28.7° C
Dec. 27 — −19.7° C

Calculate the temperature range for each city.

1. Vancouver   2. Winnipeg   3. Toronto   4. Montreal   5. St. John's

6. Look at the scales above.
   Identify visually which of the 5 cities had:
   a) the greatest temperature range.
   b) the smallest temperature range.

   Use your answers to questions 1 through 5 to check your answer to question 6.

7. In a recent year, the lowest temperature in Halifax occurred on February 10 when it reached −21.1° C. On July 2 of that year, the highest temperature, 30.6° C, was reached. What was the temperature range in Halifax that year?

8. Verkhoyansk in Siberia (U.S.S.R.) has the greatest temperature range in the world. Temperatures there range from an all time low of −70° C to a high of 36° C. What is the temperature range in Verkhoyansk?

PROBLEM SOLVING

The temperature range on the moon is even greater than the range on Earth When the Sun is overhead, the temperature on the moon reaches 117° C. After nightfall, it drops by 280° C.

What is the temperature on the moon after nightfall?

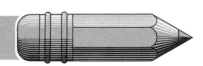

Find the volume of each box.

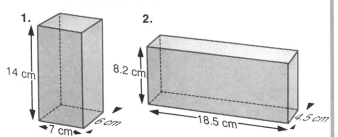

1. 14 cm   7 cm   6 cm

2. 8.2 cm   18.5 cm   4.5 cm

Find the volume of each rectangular prism.

3. length   21 cm
width   30 cm
height   12 cm

4. length   7.4 cm
width   3.5 cm
height   10.6 cm

Find the volume in cubic metres.

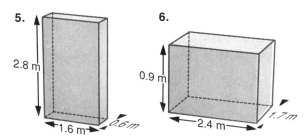

5. 2.8 m   1.6 m   0.6 m

6. 0.9 m   2.4 m   1.7 m

Copy and complete.

7. 3 L = ▧ mL
8. 6000 mL = ▧ L
9. 2.7 L = ▧ mL
10. 0.9 L = ▧ mL
11. 825 mL = ▧ L
12. 55 mL = ▧ L
13. 8000 L = ▧ kL
14. 0.03 kL = ▧ L

15. Find the volume of water in litres needed to fill this aquarium.

1 L = 1000 cm³

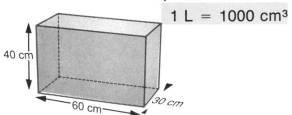

40 cm   60 cm   30 cm

Copy and complete.

16. 8 kg = ▧ g
17. 700 g = ▧ kg
18. 0.6 kg = ▧ g
19. 4.2 kg = ▧ g
20. 35 g = ▧ kg
21. 8500 kg = ▧ t
22. 0.72 t = ▧ kg
23. 0.06 t = ▧ kg

Which is the better buy?

24.

$0.59/100 g $4.95/kg

25. What is the mass of each blue cube?

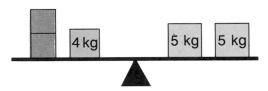

4 kg   5 kg   5 kg

Write, using the 24h clock.

26. 5:30 a.m.
27. 12:45 p.m.
28. 10:46 p.m.
29. 5:15 a.m.

What time is it:

30. 1 h after 18:45?
31. 3 h before 13:50?
32. 25 min before 01:15?

Write the time difference:

33. from 07:42 to 10:53.
34. from 13:15 to 21:25.
35. from 08:35 to 20:20.

Choose the best estimate.

36. Temperature on a hot July day.
  a) −3°C   **b)** 3°C   **c)** 30°C

37. Temperature of an ice cube.
  a) −4°C   **b)** 4°C   **c)** 40°C

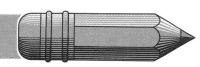

Write each product with the decimal point in the correct position.

1. 47.3
    × 8
    3784

2. 41.26
    × 54
    222804

3. $8.59
    × 19
    16321

4. 0.823
    × 14
    11522

5. 58.4
    × 0.9
    5256

6. 3.214
    × 0.26
    83564

Multiply.

7. 28.7
    × 68

8. 7.41
    ×124

9. 386
    ×0.82

10. 0.538
    × 623

11. 0.6
    ×0.7

12. 0.4
    ×0.7

Write the products.

13. 5.32 × 10
14. 37.06 × 100
15. 6.384 × 100
16. 1000 × 8.02
17. 0.074 × 100
18. 9.315 × 1000

Multiply.

19. 6.7
    ×8.2

20. 5.37
    ×12.3

21. 0.78
    ×46.2

22. 30.7
    ×16.2

23. 53.8
    ×1.06

24. 5.93
    ×4.48

25. 0.3
    ×0.7

26. 0.06
    ×3.43

27. 0.84
    ×0.05

28. 0.06
    ×3.74

29. 4.86
    ×0.02

30. 0.318
    × 0.8

31. 5.3
    ×2.7

32. 21.6
    × 3.4

33. 1.421
    × 3.81

Write each quotient.

34. 27.83 ÷ 10
35. 17.6 ÷ 100
36. 0.74 ÷ 10
37. 2.73 ÷ 100
38. 384 ÷ 1000
39. 53 ÷ 1000

Divide.

40. 3)226.2
41. 17)554.2
42. 32)8.32
43. 54)86.4
44. 46)40.02
45. 3)2.439

Find the average of each set of numbers.

46. 53, 46, 72, 64, 50
47. 2.8, 3.1, 3.8, 4.5, 4.8, 5.6

Divide.

48. 0.7)37.1
49. 3.3)2.64
50. 3.9)6.63
51. 0.9)0.567
52. 0.65)0.78
53. 0.76)5.168

54. A busload of 36 people paid a total of $162 for a tour of the city. How much did each person pay?

55. A quarter has a thickness of 1.6 mm. How many quarters are there in a stack 86.4 mm high?

Find the volume of each box.

56.

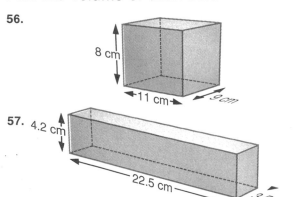

8 cm

11 cm

9 cm

57.

4.2 cm

22.5 cm

3.5 cm

Find the volume of these rectangular prisms.

58. length 1.4 m
width 0.7 m
height 2.3 m

59. length 3.4 m
width 1.6 m
height 0.8 m

Copy and complete.

60. 7 L = ▨ mL

61. 4500 mL = ▨ L

62. 1.6 L = ▨ mL

63. 0.9 L = ▨ mL

64. 7000 L = ▨ kL

65. 0.15 kL = ▨ L

66. Find the volume of water needed to fill this container.

$$1 \text{ L} = 1000 \text{ cm}^3$$

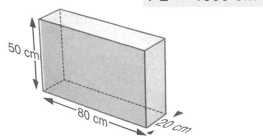

50 cm

80 cm

20 cm

Copy and complete.

67. 6 kg = ▨ g

68. 850 g = ▨ kg

69. 3.8 kg = ▨ g

70. 45 g = ▨ kg

71. 9600 kg = ▨ t

72. 0.15 t = ▨ kg

Which is the better buy?

73.

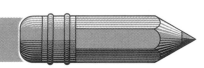

$0.27/200 g $1.19/kg

74.

$1.38/100 g $14.19/kg

75. What is the mass of each red cube?

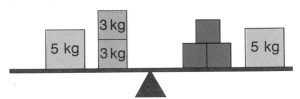

Write using the 24 h clock.

76. 6:45 a.m.

77. 12:50 p.m.

78. 9:35 p.m.

79. 4:55 a.m.

What time is it:

80. 1 h after 19:15?

81. 2 h before 13:10?

82. 35 min. before 01:05?

Write the time difference:

83. from 06:50 to 09:25.

84. from 13:25 to 20:10.

85. from 07:20 to 18:50.

Choose the best estimate.

86. Temperature on a cold January day.
a) $-8°C$ b) $18°C$ c) $80°C$

87. Temperature of a hot cup of tea.
a) $1°C$ b) $10°C$ c) $80°C$

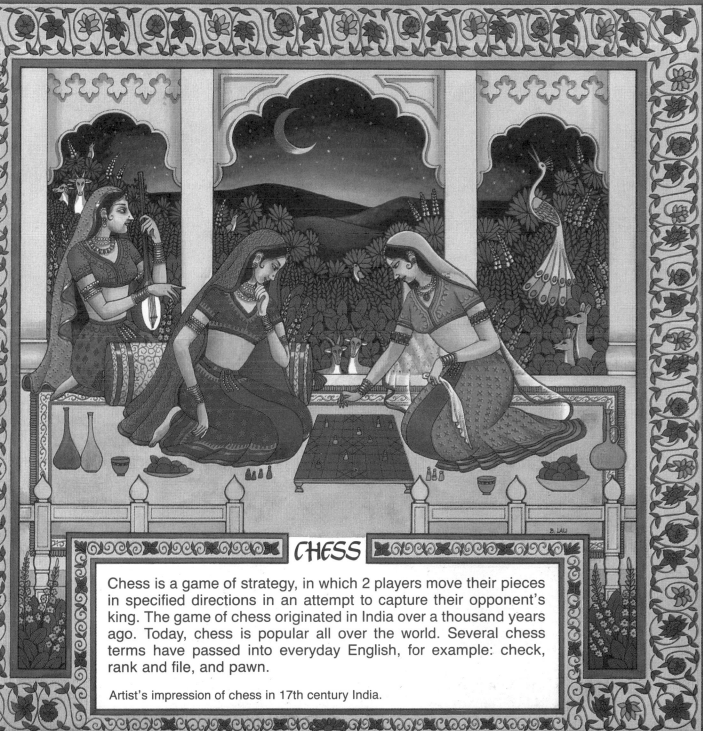

CHESS

Chess is a game of strategy, in which 2 players move their pieces in specified directions in an attempt to capture their opponent's king. The game of chess originated in India over a thousand years ago. Today, chess is popular all over the world. Several chess terms have passed into everyday English, for example: check, rank and file, and pawn.

Artist's impression of chess in 17th century India.

Graphing Ordered Pairs

The parallelogram gang is plotting to cancel summer holidays for all students. Sherlock Homely has learned that their headquarters is at location (3,5).

In what building is their headquarters?

We ask: Where is the location (3,5)?

We think: The **ordered pair** (3,5) is used to name the point 3 units right and 5 units up from the origin.

We count:

(3,5) Government House

5 units up

3 units right

The gang headquarters is in Government House.

Write the names of the buildings in these locations.

1. (5,3)   2. (9,2)   3. (2,1)

4. (7,1)   5. (0,2)   6. (4,0)

Write an ordered pair to give the location of each building.

7. Fire Hall   8. Arena   9. Museum   10. Theatre

Graph each set of ordered pairs on grid paper. Join all the points in each set so they form the vertices of a polygon. Name each polygon.

11. (8,6)   12. (7,10)   13. (3,3)   14. (0,3)
    (6,8)   (4,7)   (4,11)   (4,0)
    (6,6)   (5,4)   (12,11)   (6,0)
    (8,8)   (9,4)   (11,3)   (2,3)
            (10,7)

PROBLEM SOLVING

Using Logical Thinking

Who are the members of the parallelogram gang?
The parallelogram gang has 4 members.
Their pictures in the Crime Stoppers scrapbook
are located at the vertices of a parallelogram.

Use the clues below
to find the 4 gang members.

Clues

- One of the gang members is 2 units
  above the person at (2,1).
- One of the gang members is between
  the person at (2,0) and the person at (0,2).

- If you reverse the ordered pair that
  names Tough Guy, you get the location
  of a gang member.
- Sherlock Homely is not a member of
  the parallelogram gang.

329

Slides

Last week, Sly Dee lived at location (2,5). Then she moved 3 streets right and 4 streets down as seen on the map. Sherlock Homely is tracking her movements.

He thinks: Start at (2,5). Move 3 streets right and 4 streets down.

He writes: Sly Dee moved to the location (5,1).

Sly Dee's new location is 5 streets right of the origin and 1 street up.

The point (5,1) to which Sly Dee moved is called the **slide image** of the point (2,5) from which she started.

Graph each point and its slide image on squared paper. Write the ordered pair for each slide image. Draw an arrow from each point to its slide image.

1. point: (2,3)
   slide: 3 units right
          1 unit down

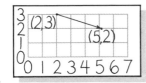

2. point: (3,1)
   slide: 2 units left
          3 units up

3. point: (6,1)
   slide: 1 unit left
          3 units up

4. point: (4,0)
   slide: 0 units right
          2 units up

5. point: (0,2)
   slide: 1 unit right
          4 units up

6. point: (4,2)
   slide: 4 units left
          0 units down

7. point: (3,7)
   slide: 2 units right
          4 units down

8. point: (6,8)
   slide: 3 units left
          3 units down

We can draw a **slide arrow** to show the length and direction of a slide.

Draw a slide arrow on dot paper to show each of these slides.

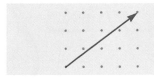

right 4 units
up 3 units

1. right 4 units
   up 5 units

2. left 2 units
   down 4 units

3. right 5 units
   down 0 units

4. left 0 units
   up 3 units

Describe in words the slide which moves the pink figure to the location of the green figure.

Copy each diagram onto dot paper. Draw a slide arrow from a vertex to its slide image.

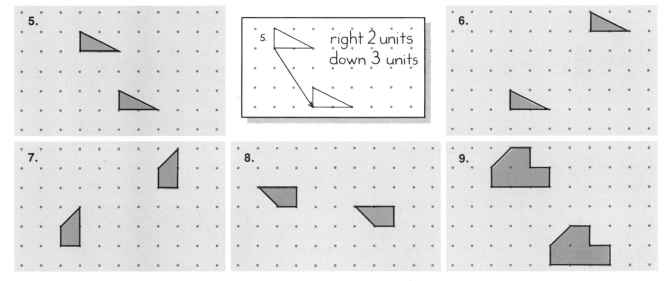

5.

5. right 2 units
   down 3 units

6.

7.

8.

9.

Graph the quadrilateral with the given vertices. Then graph its slide image.

10. vertices: (8,4), (8,6), (10,4), (10,8)
    slide: 8 units left and 1 unit up

11. vertices: (3,5), (3,7), (4,8), (8,8)
    slide: 2 units left and 4 units down

12. vertices: (1,1), (4,0), (5,2), (2,3).
    slide: 2 units right and 2 units up

13. Sly Dee once moved 4 streets right and 3 streets up, to the location (6,7). From what location did she start?

PROBLEM SOLVING

Sly Dee lived at (3,5). She then performed 3 slides shown by the arrows below. At what location does she live now?

Does the order in which the slides are performed change Sly Dee's final location?

Turtle Slides

This program teaches
the turtle how to
draw a hotel.

```
TO HOTEL
FD 20    RT 90
FD 20    LT 60
FD 20    RT 120
FD 20    RT 30
FD 20    RT 90
FD 40    RT 90
END
```

When the turtle is given
these commands...

...it draws this hotel and
then turns right 60 degrees.

HOTEL
RT 60

When the turtle is given
these commands...

...it draws the slide arrow and
then turns left 60 degrees.

FD 50
LT 60

When the turtle is given
this command...

...it draws another hotel.

HOTEL

HOTEL
RT 80
FD 70
LT 80
HOTEL

THESE COMMANDS TELL THE TURTLE TO DRAW THE HOTEL AND ITS IMAGE AFTER A SLIDE.

Make computer screens like this from square centimetre paper. Label your screens in multiples of 10 turtlesteps.

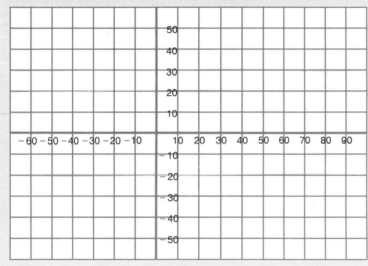

For each set of commands in questions 1 to 5 follow these steps:

- Draw the path on one of your paper screens.

- Use your protractor to draw the given angles.

- Use your centimetre ruler and the scale factor *10 steps* = **1 cm** to draw the given distances.

1. HOTEL
   RT 90
   FD 80
   LT 90
   HOTEL

2. HOTEL
   RT 120
   FD 80
   LT 120
   HOTEL

3. HOTEL
   RT 180
   FD 80
   LT 180
   HOTEL

4. HOTEL
   RT 240
   FD 80
   LT 240
   HOTEL

5. HOTEL
   RT 300
   FD 80
   LT 300
   HOTEL

6. Teach the turtle to draw another figure.
   Repeat questions 1 to 5 using your new figure in place of HOTEL.

IF YOU HAVE A COMPUTER WITH LOGO, CHECK YOUR ANSWERS ON THE COMPUTER.

Turns

The Ferris wheel below is seen to turn in a **counterclockwise** direction, as shown by this arrow.

From the other side, the Ferris wheel would appear to turn in a **clockwise** direction.

1

Turn Centre

AT LAST!

Adrian and Lisa waited an hour for their turn on the Ferris wheel.

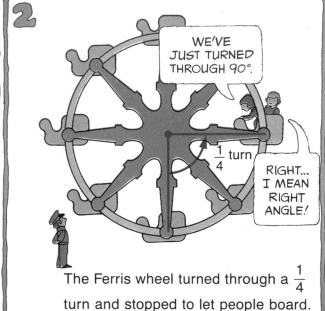

2

WE'VE JUST TURNED THROUGH 90°.

$\frac{1}{4}$ turn

RIGHT... I MEAN RIGHT ANGLE!

The Ferris wheel turned through a $\frac{1}{4}$ turn and stopped to let people board.

3

WE'VE JUST TURNED THROUGH 180°.

STRAIGHT!...I MEAN STRAIGHT ANGLE.

$\frac{1}{2}$ turn

The wheel completed a $\frac{1}{2}$ turn. Adrian and Lisa reached the top.

4

WHAT A LET-DOWN! WE WAITED AN HOUR FOR A TURN.

AND ALL WE GOT WAS A $\frac{3}{4}$ TURN!

$\frac{3}{4}$ turn

EVERYBODY OFF!

When it completed a $\frac{3}{4}$ turn, there was a power failure.

The Fairfax Fair Ferris wheel starts with the **F** in the upright position.

Write $\frac{1}{4}$ **turn**, $\frac{1}{2}$ **turn**, $\frac{3}{4}$ **turn**, or **full turn** to describe the *counterclockwise* turn in each picture.

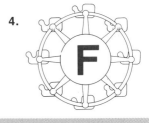

1.

2.

3.

4.

Write $\frac{1}{4}$ **turn**, $\frac{1}{2}$ **turn**, or $\frac{3}{4}$ **turn** to describe the *clockwise* turn of each letter.

All letters begin in the upright position.

5.

6.

7.

8.

Copy each figure onto dot paper. Draw its **turn image** for the indicated turn about turn centre C. Use tracing paper if you wish.

9.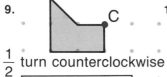
$\frac{1}{2}$ turn counterclockwise

10.
$\frac{3}{4}$ turn counterclockwise

11.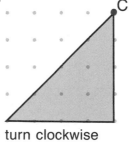
$\frac{1}{4}$ turn clockwise

12.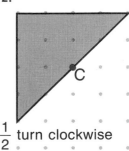
$\frac{1}{2}$ turn clockwise

PROBLEM SOLVING

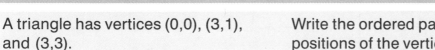

A triangle has vertices (0,0), (3,1), and (3,3).

Write the ordered pairs which give the positions of the vertices of the turn image after a $\frac{1}{4}$ turn around the point (3,3).

Flips

The image of the house seen in the water is the **mirror image** or the **flip image** of the real house.

Jacqueline traced this diagram.

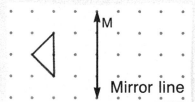

Mirror line

Then she folded her tracing along the mirror line and pressed her pencil on each vertex.

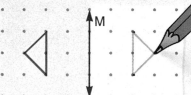

Then she joined the dots to draw the flip image of the figure onto her paper.

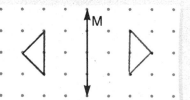

A polygon and its flip image are drawn on dot paper. Record the distance of each vertex and its flip image from the mirror line.

1.

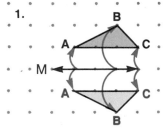

1. Point	Distance from Mirror Line
Vertex A	1 unit
Image A	1 unit
Vertex B	2 units

2.

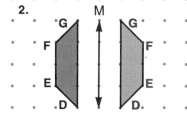

3.

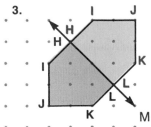

4.

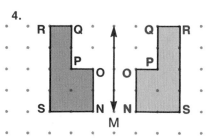

5. Study your tables. What do you discover?

336

Copy each diagram onto dot paper.
Then draw the flip image of each polygon.

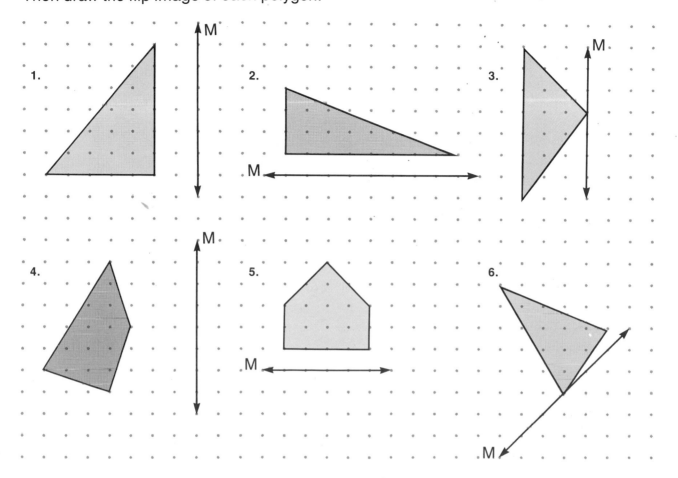

1.
2.
3.
4.
5.
6.

Copy each diagram onto 1 cm squared paper. Sketch
the flip image of each polygon. Then write the ordered
pairs for the vertices of the image polygon.

7.
8.
9.

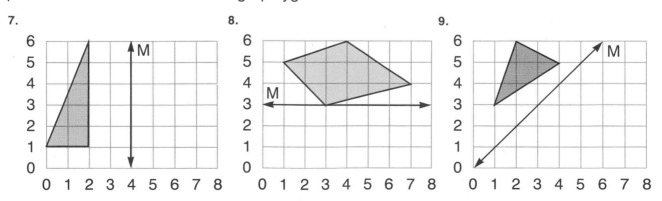

PROBLEM SOLVING

Drawing a Diagram

After they scored the winning goal, all 6 players of the Swift Skaters hockey team shook hands with each other.

How many handshakes were made if each player shook hands exactly once with each of the other players?

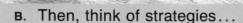

To solve this problem...

A. First, make sure you understand the problem.

Discuss:
* *How many players shook hands?*
* *With how many players did each player shake hands?*
* *If player 1 shakes hands with player 2, does player 2 need to shake hands with player 1?*
* *What are you asked to find out?*

B. Then, think of strategies...

* *Try drawing a diagram.*
* *Draw a dot for each of the players and label each dot.*
* *Join the dots with line segments to show player 1's handshakes.*
* *How many handshakes did player 1 have?*

338

C. Solve the problem and answer the question.

- *Join the dots to show each of the other player's handshakes and keep a record for each player.*
- *How many line segments are there in all?*
- *How many handshakes are there in all?*

D. Check your answer and discuss your solution.

Look at your diagram.
- *Is each dot joined to all the other dots?*
- *How many handshakes are there for each player?*
- *How many new lines did you draw for player 6?*
- *What other strategy could you have used to solve this problem?*

Solve each problem.

1. In a 200 m race, Andy finished 7 m behind Bob. Carl was 8.6 m behind Andy. David was 14.2 m in front of Carl. Who won the race and by how much? Who came last?

2. A square garden of perimeter 48 m is enclosed by a fence with posts 2 m apart. How many posts are there?

3. Alexis, Brad, Carol and Dana are of different ages. Brad is older than Dana. Carol is younger than Alexis but Dana is older than Alexis. Which person is oldest? youngest?

4. There are 8 chairs in a rectangular classroom. How can the chairs be placed along the walls so there are three chairs along each wall?

Successive Flips

1. **a)** Graph triangle T and lines M and N.

   b) Graph the flip image of T in the mirror line M. Call it T(1).

   c) Graph the flip image of T(1) in the mirror line N. Call it T(2).

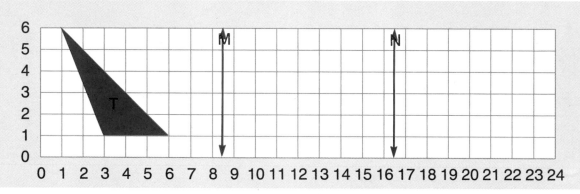

2. Write the ordered pairs for the vertices:
   a) of T(1)   **b)** of T(2)

3. Write **slide**, **flip**, or **turn** to describe the motion that would move triangle T into the position of T(2).

4. Follow the instructions in question 1 for trapezoid T below.

5. Write the ordered pairs for the vertices:
   a) of T(1)   **b)** of T(2)

6. Describe a single motion which could move T into the position of T(2).

A triangle R with vertices (1,5), (0,2), and (4,0) has a flip image R(1) with vertices (6,2), (4,6), and (1,5).

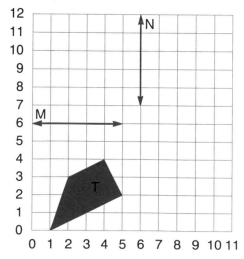

WRITE 2 ORDERED PAIRS WHICH NAME 2 DIFFERENT POINTS ON THE MIRROR LINE.

340

Slides, Flips, and Turns

In each question, write **slide**, **flip**, or **turn** to indicate how the green figure can be moved into the position of the pink figure.

Describe each motion by giving one of the following pieces of information:
- length and direction of the slide, or
- 2 points on the flip line, or
- turn centre and amount of turn.

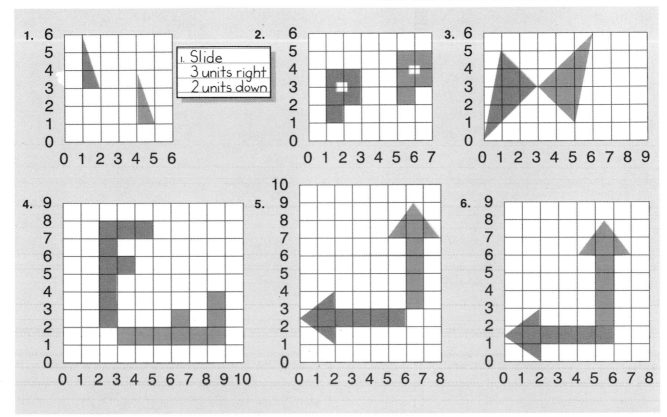

PROBLEM SOLVING

Renowned sculptor, I. Luv Welding made this iron sculpture.

When Mr. Welding first saw the sculpture in the gallery, it was partly hidden.

Sketch the sculpture as it would appear when in full view.

341

Congruent Figures

The Congruent Cookie Company cuts cookies using a computer-controlled cookie cutter.

All the cookies are identical. They all have the same size and shape.

Geometric figures which have the same shape and size are said to be **congruent**.

THE COOKS AT THE CONGRUENT COOKIE COMPANY CUT CONGRUENT COOKIES.

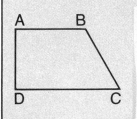 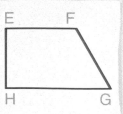 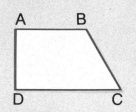 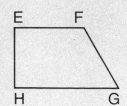

To make a congruent copy of △ABC, we trace it.
We label our tracing △DEF.

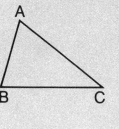

△ABC and △DEF are congruent.

The symbol ↔ shows matching vertices and sides.

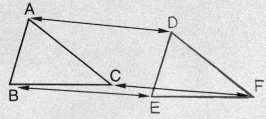

Matching Vertices	A ↔ D	Matching Sides	AB ↔ DE
	B ↔ E		BC ↔ EF
	C ↔ F		AC ↔ DF

To determine whether 2 geometric figures are congruent, trace and cut out one of the figures.

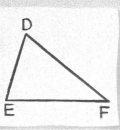

Slide, flip, or turn your cutout to see if it matches the other figure.

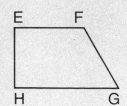

If the figures match, they are congruent.

1. Use tracing paper to determine which of the cookies below was made from this cookie cutter.

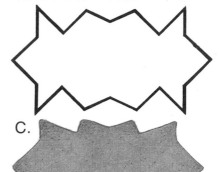

A.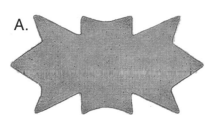

B.

C.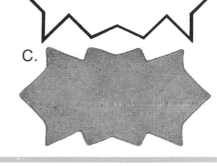

Estimate whether a, b, or c is congruent to the given polygon.

Check by tracing and matching. List matching vertices.

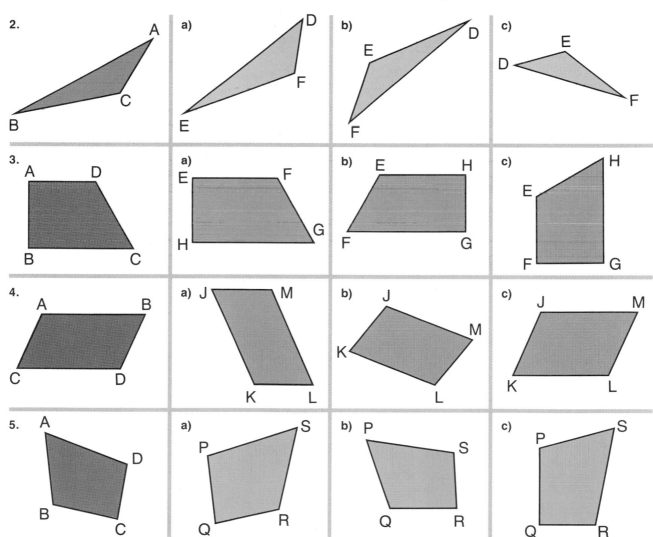

2.

a)

b)

c)

3.

a)

b)

c)

4.

a)

b)

c)

5.

a)

b)

c)

343

Line Symmetry

To make a shamrock, Shamus drew half a shamrock on a folded piece of paper.

fold line

Then he cut out the half shamrock and unfolded it to obtain a full shamrock.

The fold line is called a **line of symmetry** of the shamrock.

Trace and cut out the shamrock. Fold it to find more lines of symmetry.

1. How many lines of symmetry does the shamrock have?

2. Trace the triangles shown. Draw all lines of symmetry. Then copy and complete the table below.

Type of Triangle	Number of Lines of Symmetry
Equilateral	▦
Isosceles	▦
Scalene	▦

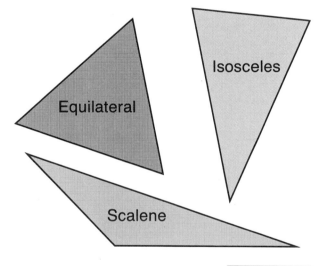

Isosceles

Equilateral

Scalene

3. The diagonal line divides the parallelogram into 2 congruent parts.

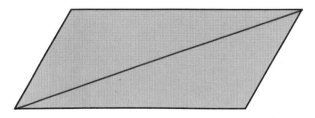

Is the diagonal a line of symmetry of the parallelogram? Explain.

344

PROBLEM SOLVING

How many lines of symmetry has:
a) a square?   b) a regular hexagon?

What kind of figure has more lines of symmetry than any polygon?

Point Symmetry

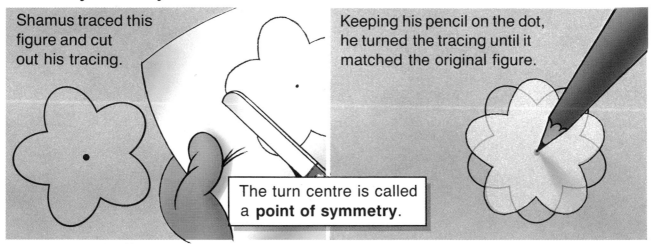

Shamus traced this figure and cut out his tracing.

Keeping his pencil on the dot, he turned the tracing until it matched the original figure.

The turn centre is called a **point of symmetry**.

Since the tracing matches the original figure in less than a full turn, the figure has **point symmetry** or **turn symmetry**.

Trace and cut each of these figures. Use Shamus' method to determine if a figure has point symmetry.

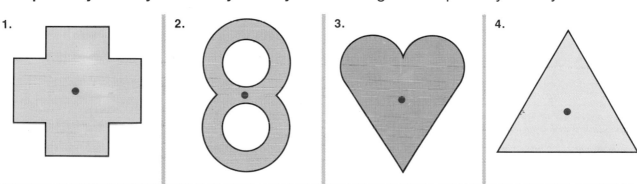

1.

2.

3.

4.

5. Which of these letters have point symmetry?

A N F E

M Z O H

PROBLEM SOLVING

Trace and cut out this template. Use it to sketch a shamrock. How many degrees did you turn your template about turn centre C to trace each leaf?

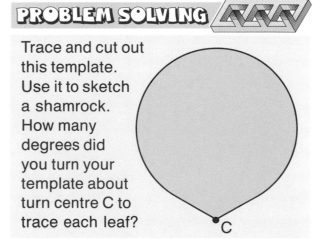

C

Circles and Symmetry

Geometric solids with turn symmetry can be formed on a lathe.

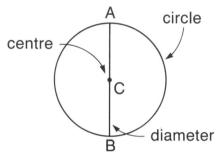

We can trace around an edge of any of these solids to draw a **circle**.

This diagram shows a **circle**, its **centre** (point C), and a **diameter** (line segment AB). Line segment CA is called a **radius** of the circle.

> A diameter of a circle is twice the length of a radius.

To draw a circle using a paper clip:

Step 1 Place the tip of a pencil at one end of the paper clip.	**Step 2** Turn the paper clip with a pencil while holding the first pencil fixed.
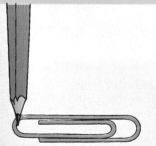	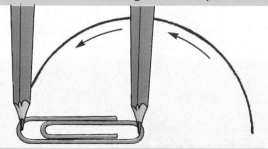
The fixed pencil marks the centre of the circle.	This construction shows that all points on a circle are the same distance from its centre.

We can use a protractor as a template to draw a circle.

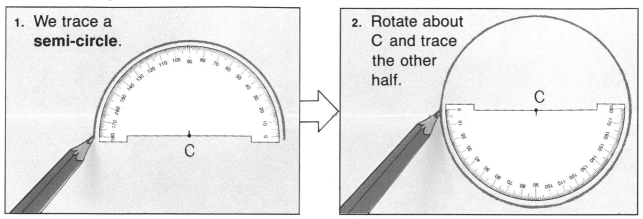

1. We trace a **semi-circle**.

2. Rotate about C and trace the other half.

The protractor construction shows that:
The centre is a point of
symmetry of a circle.

Cut out the circle and fold to find lines
of symmetry. What do you discover?

Discuss:

- *How many lines of symmetry
  does a circle have?*
- *How many diameters does a circle have?*

- *Do all diameters of a circle
  have the same length? Why?*

1. For circles A, B, C, and D write:

   - the ordered pair for the centre,
   - the length of the radius and
     diameter, and
   - the ordered pair for the point of
     symmetry.

   Record your answers in a table.

2. Use a paper clip to draw a circle.
   Measure the paper clip to find the
   approximate radius and diameter.

3. Trace around an edge of a cylinder or
   cone to make a circle. Cut out the
   circle and fold it to find a diameter.
   Measure the diameter and calculate
   the radius.

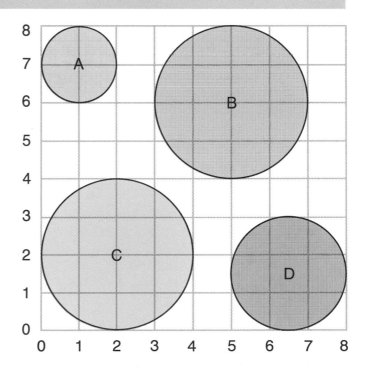

EXTENSIONS

Constructing Circles with Compasses

For thousands of years, people have drawn circles using some kind of compasses.

Explain why the peg and rope didn't produce a circle.

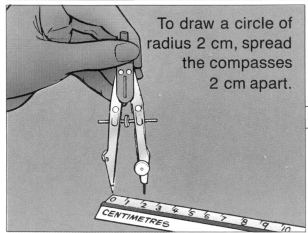

To draw a circle of radius 2 cm, spread the compasses 2 cm apart.

Hold the sharp end fixed at the centre and draw the circle.

CENTIMETRES

CENTRE

Use compasses to draw a circle with:

1. radius 2 cm
2. radius 4 cm
3. diameter 6 cm
4. diameter 5 cm

The **circumference** is the distance around a circle.

5. Use a string to measure the circumferences of the circles in questions 1 through 4.

Use compasses to construct a shamrock like this one.

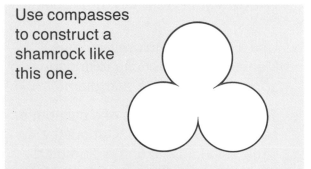

Make each circle of radius 3 cm.

348

Planes of Symmetry

| A **line of symmetry** divides a figure into 2 halves so that each half is the mirror image of the other. | A **plane of symmetry** divides a geometric solid into 2 halves so that each half is the mirror image of the other. |

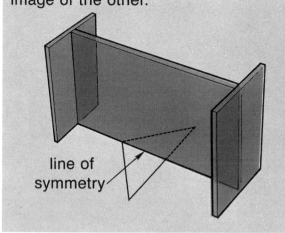

line of symmetry

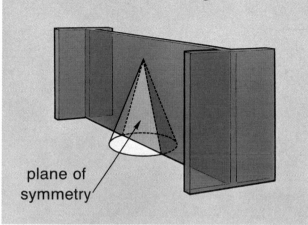

plane of symmetry

1. Which of these items has at least one plane of symmetry?

A.

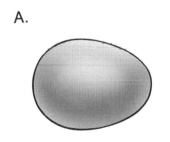

B.

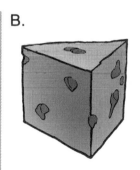

C.

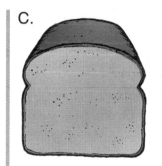

D.

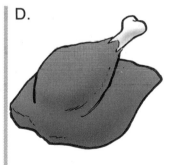

2. Study these geometric solids. Then copy and complete this table.

Solid	Number of Planes of Symmetry
A	▦
B	▦
C	▦
D	▦
E	▦

A.

B.

C.

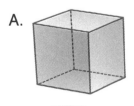

D.

E.

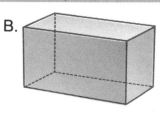

349

Tessellations

This work of art is titled "Study of Regular Division of the Plane with Human Figures."

It was created by the famous Dutch artist Maurits Escher in 1938.

At first glance many people see a repeating pattern with a boy dressed in a yellow outfit. Others see a repeating pattern with a boy dressed in red. A few people see the pattern with a boy dressed in blue.

This Escher work is a tiling pattern in which all tiles (yellow, red, and blue) are congruent.

Such a tiling pattern is called a **tessellation**.

A **tiling pattern** is a covering of a surface with tiles so that:
- the tiles do not overlap.
- there is no gap between tiles.

To create a tessellation from a given figure, we follow these steps.

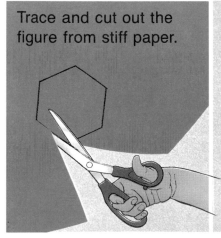

Trace and cut out the figure from stiff paper.

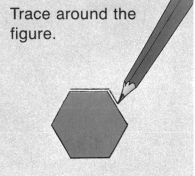

Trace around the figure.

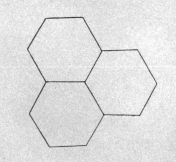

Slide, flip, or turn the figure so there is no gap or overlap. Then trace again.

ESTIMATING

Estimate: How many figures like the one shown in question 3 on page 351 would it take to cover your MathQuest book? Work with several classmates to check your answer.

Trace and cut out each figure to draw a tessellation.

1.
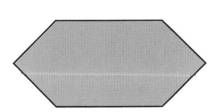

2.

3.
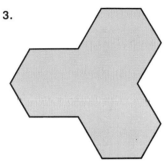

Copy each figure onto dot paper. Then draw a tessellation by forming the slide, flip, or turn image of each figure.

4.

5.
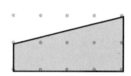

6.

PROBLEM SOLVING

The pattern shown has been created using only tiles formed into a shape like this:

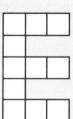

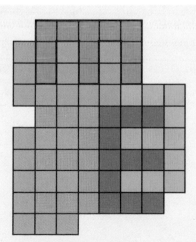

Name the motion or motions needed to move the orange tile so that it matches the:

a) blue tile.
b) green tile.
c) pink tile.
d) purple tile.

Could this pattern be continued to cover without gaps a sheet of centimetre paper?

Can this tile be used to create a tessellation?

Similar Figures

These crackers have the same shape. Each side of cracker A is twice as long as each side of cracker B.

B

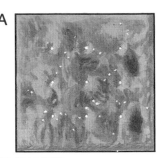
A

We can say these crackers are **similar** because one is a magnification of the other.

These figures are also similar. Each side of figure C is 3 times as long as the corresponding side of figure D.

D

C

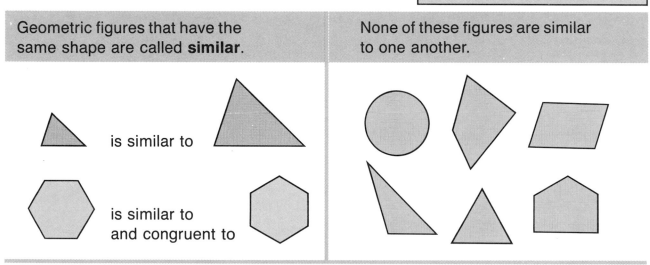

Geometric figures that have the same shape are called **similar**.	None of these figures are similar to one another.
is similar to	
is similar to and congruent to	

Which figure, a, b, or c, is similar to the given figure?

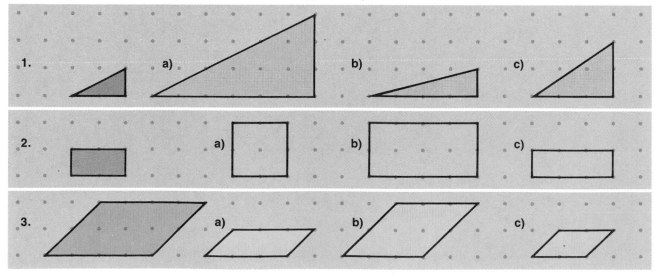

1. There are 6 pairs of similar figures shown below.
   Use the letters to name all 6 pairs.

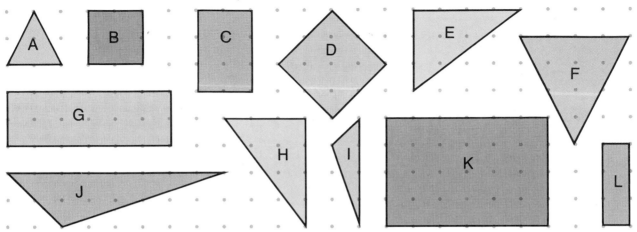

2. All 3 triangles are similar.
   Measure ∠A, ∠B, and ∠C
   in each triangle and record
   in a table like the
   one below.

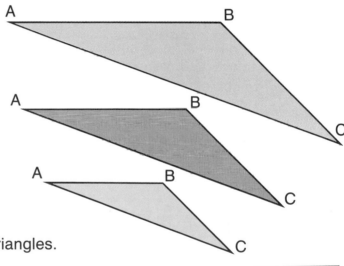

Triangle	∠A	∠B	∠C
Blue			
Yellow			
Green			

Can you see a pattern in your table?
Describe a relationship between similar triangles.

PROBLEM SOLVING

Which of these cheeses can be cut into slices which are:
a) similar but not congruent?   b) congruent?

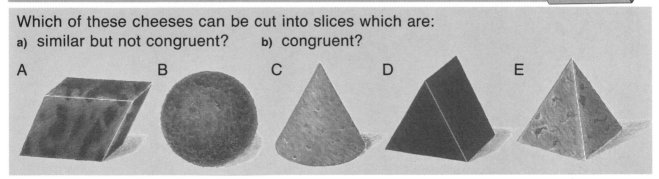

A   B   C   D   E

Drawing Similar Figures

Andrea drew a map of Newfoundland for her geography project.

She pressed *reduce* on the photocopy machine and made a copy.

Then she pressed *enlarge* on the photocopy machine and made a copy.

A photocopy machine may change the size of a figure but not the shape. Photocopy machines make similar figures.

Another way to make similar figures is to use a grid.

We start with this cartoon.

To reduce the cartoon, we copy it onto a smaller grid.

To enlarge the cartoon, we copy it onto a larger grid.

When we reduce or enlarge a figure, the new figure is similar to the original figure.

Reduce each figure by copying onto centimetre paper.

1.

2.

Enlarge each figure by copying onto centimetre paper.

3.

4.

5.

6. Plot the triangles with these vertices on centimetre paper.

A. (1,1), (2,3), and (4,1).

B. (2,2), (4,6), and (8,2).

C. (3,3), (6,9), and (12,3).

Measure the lengths of the sides of the triangles and record in a table.

Triangle	Length of...		
	longest side	shortest side	remaining side
A	▨	▨	▨
B	▨	▨	▨
C	▨	▨	▨

7. Describe a pattern in your table. Are the triangles similar?

355

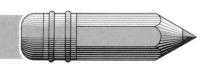

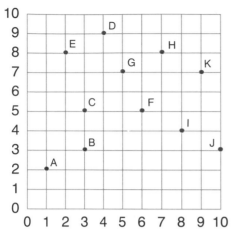

1. Write the ordered pair that locates:
   a) D   b) J   c) B   d) H   e) K

2. Write the letter located by:
   a) (3,5)   b) (1,2)   c) (5,7)   d) (8,4)

3. Graph each set of ordered pairs.
   Join the points to form a polygon.
   Name the polygon.
   a) (1,2), (1,5), (6,5), (6,2)

   b) (1,5), (3,8), (7,8) (5,5)

4. Graph the quadrilateral with the given
   vertices. Then graph its slide image.
   a) vertices: (2,5), (2,8), (5,8), (5,5)
      slide: 3 units right and 2 units down

   b) vertices: (5,1), (6,3), (10,3), (9,1)
      slide: 2 units left and 5 units up

5. Which of these letters have:
   a) line symmetry?   b) point symmetry?

Copy each figure on dot paper. Then draw
its image after a counterclockwise
turn as indicated.

a) $\frac{1}{4}$ turn   b) $\frac{1}{2}$ turn   c) $\frac{3}{4}$ turn

6.   7.

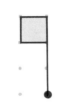

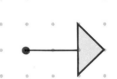

Copy each figure on dot paper.
Then draw its flip image.

8.   M   9.   M

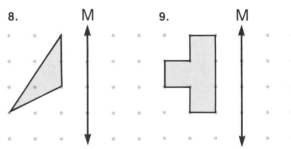

10. Write the numbers of the figures:
    a) congruent to A.
    b) similar to A.

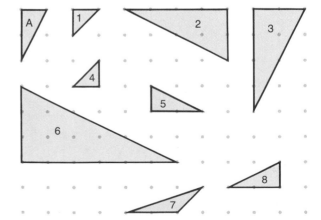

The Peach Stone Game

The Peach Stone Game is a game of probability enjoyed by people of many Indian tribes. In this game, 6 or 8 peach stones which have been scorched on one side are shaken in a wooden bowl and tossed into the air. Points are scored by counting the stones which land scorched side up.

Artist's impression of a Peach Stone Game, 17th century Canada.

Fraction Concepts

A fraction may be used to name a part of an area...	OR	A fraction may be used to name a part of a set.

What fraction of the net is grey?

We think: The net is made of 6 **equal** squares of which 4 are grey.

We write: $\dfrac{4}{6}$ ← number of grey parts
← total number of equal parts

We say: 4 sixths of the net is grey.

What fraction of the faces have even numbers?

We think: 3 out of 6 faces have even numbers.

We write: $\dfrac{3}{6}$ {number of faces with even numbers
← total number of faces

We say: 3 sixths of the faces have even numbers.

Parts of a fraction
$\dfrac{4}{6}$ ← **numerator**
← **denominator**

Draw and label a net for a cube so that $\dfrac{1}{2}$ of the faces are red and $\dfrac{2}{3}$ of the red faces have even numbers.

358

Write a fraction to tell what part is coloured.

1.

2.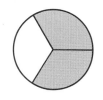

3.

4.

5.

6.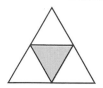

7.

8.

What fraction of each carton of tin cans is left?

9.

10.

11.

12.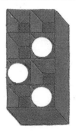

Use this picture to answer the questions below.

What fraction of the animals:

13. have antlers?   14. have stripes?

15. do not have stripes?   16. have long tails?

17. have short tails?   18. are brown?

19. are grey?

 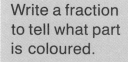
Write a fraction
to tell what part
is coloured.

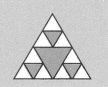

359

ESTIMATING

Estimating Fractions of a Region

Write A, B, C, or D to answer each question below.

1. Which of these figures has about half of its area shaded?

A.

B.

C.

D.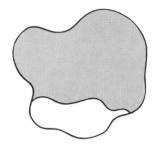

---

2. Which of these circles has about $\frac{3}{4}$ of its area shaded?

A.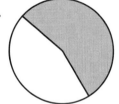

B.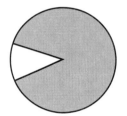

C.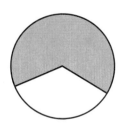

D.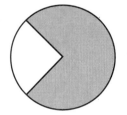

---

3. Which of these circles has about $\frac{2}{3}$ of its area shaded?

A.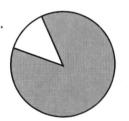

B.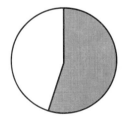

C.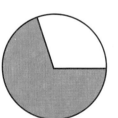

D.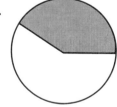

---

4. Trace this figure onto centimetre paper. Colour about one quarter of its area. Then count squares to find the approximate area of the figure and its coloured part.

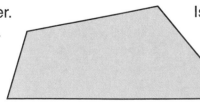

Is the area of this figure about 4 times the area of the part you coloured?

Estimating Fractions of a Set

Look twice.
Cover your eyes.
Estimate.

1. Which circle contains about:
   a) one half of the dots? b) one quarter of the dots?

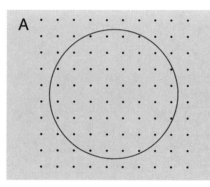

A

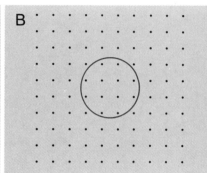

B

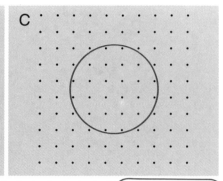

C

2. About what fraction of each set is ringed?

a)
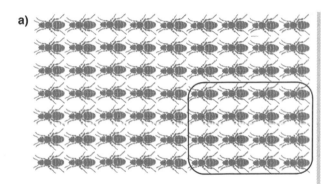

b)
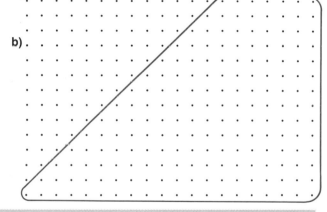

3. Estimate the fraction of birds which are:

   a) blue.   b) red.   c) green.   d) not red.   e) neither blue nor red.

Equivalent Fractions

What fraction of the pawns are red?

Len says: 6 out of 9 pawns are red.

Len writes: $\frac{6}{9}$ are red.

Teresa says: 2 out of 3 equal rows are red.

Teresa writes: $\frac{2}{3}$ are red.

Both fractions name the same part of the set.

We say: $\frac{6}{9}$ and $\frac{2}{3}$ are **equivalent fractions**.

We write: $\frac{6}{9} = \frac{2}{3}$

Copy and complete the equation suggested by each picture.

1.

$\frac{1}{2} = \frac{3}{6}$

2.

$\frac{1}{2} = \frac{\blacksquare}{8}$

3.

$\frac{1}{3} = \frac{\blacksquare}{\blacksquare}$

4.

$\frac{\blacksquare}{2} = \frac{5}{10}$

5.

$\frac{\blacksquare}{\blacksquare} = \frac{3}{9}$

6.

$\frac{\blacksquare}{\blacksquare} = \frac{4}{10}$

7. Draw 15 pawns so that 1 in every 3 is red. Write 2 equivalent fractions which indicate what fraction of the pawns are red.

8. Draw a square and divide it into quarters. Divide each quarter in half. Colour one quarter of the square. Write 2 fractions for the shaded part.

Write 2 equivalent fractions for each coloured area.

1.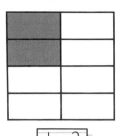

$\dfrac{1}{4} = \dfrac{2}{8}$

2.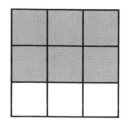

3.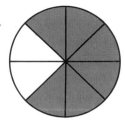

4.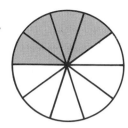

5.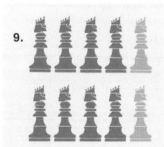

6.

7.

8.

Write 2 equivalent fractions for the red part of each set.

9.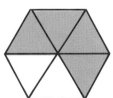

10.

11.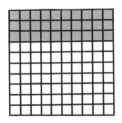

12.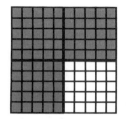

Draw and colour an area or a set to show each equation.

13. $\dfrac{1}{2} = \dfrac{2}{4}$

14. $\dfrac{4}{5} = \dfrac{8}{10}$

15. $\dfrac{2}{3} = \dfrac{8}{12}$

16. $\dfrac{3}{4} = \dfrac{9}{12}$

Copy and complete these questions.
Draw a diagram if you wish.

17. $\dfrac{2}{3} = \dfrac{\blacksquare}{12}$

18. $\dfrac{3}{8} = \dfrac{\blacksquare}{16}$

19. $\dfrac{3}{5} = \dfrac{\blacksquare}{10}$

20. $\dfrac{5}{6} = \dfrac{\blacksquare}{12}$

21. $\dfrac{3}{4} = \dfrac{15}{\blacksquare}$

22. $\dfrac{1}{3} = \dfrac{5}{\blacksquare}$

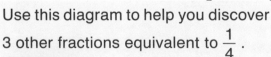

Use this diagram to help you discover
3 other fractions equivalent to $\dfrac{1}{4}$.

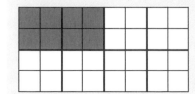

363

Multiplying to find Equivalent Fractions

WE DON'T LIKE OLIVES!

WE LOVE OLIVES!

When the Olivers order pizza, they order half with olives and half without.

When cut in 4 equal slices, the pizza has 2 pieces with olives.	When cut in 6 equal slices, the pizza has 3 pieces with olives.	When cut in 8 equal slices, the pizza has 4 pieces with olives.

$\frac{2}{4}$ of the pizza has olives.	$\frac{3}{6}$ of the pizza has olives.	$\frac{4}{8}$ of the pizza has olives.

$\frac{2}{4}$, $\frac{3}{6}$, and $\frac{4}{8}$ are all equivalent to $\frac{1}{2}$.

We write: $\frac{1}{2} = \frac{2}{4} = \frac{3}{6} = \frac{4}{8}$

To find an equivalent fraction...	⟹	Multiply the numerator and the denominator by the same number.

$\frac{1}{2}$

$$\overset{\times 2}{\underset{\times 2}{\frac{1}{2} = \frac{2}{4}}}$$

Other examples:

$$\overset{\times 3}{\underset{\times 3}{\frac{1}{5} = \frac{3}{15}}} \qquad \overset{\times 5}{\underset{\times 5}{\frac{3}{4} = \frac{15}{20}}} \qquad \overset{\times 4}{\underset{\times 4}{\frac{5}{8} = \frac{20}{32}}}$$

364

Multiply to find an equivalent fraction.

1. $\dfrac{3}{5} = $ (×2)(×2)

2. $\dfrac{1}{3} = $ (×5)(×5)

3. $\dfrac{2}{3} = $ (×6)(×6)

4. $\dfrac{7}{10} = $ (×10)(×10)

5. $\dfrac{3}{4} = $ (×4)(×4)

6. $\dfrac{5}{8} = $ (×3)(×3)

7. $\dfrac{2}{5} = $ (×7)(×7)

8. $\dfrac{3}{10} = $ (×9)(×9)

9. $\dfrac{1}{6} = $ (×3)(×3)

10. $\dfrac{7}{12} = $ (×4)(×4)

11. $\dfrac{3}{8} = $ (×8)(×8)

12. $\dfrac{4}{5} = $ (×12)(×12)

Write the missing multiplier.

13. $\dfrac{1}{2} = \dfrac{6}{12}$ (×☐)(×☐)

14. $\dfrac{3}{8} = \dfrac{15}{40}$ (×☐)(×☐)

15. $\dfrac{5 \times \blacksquare}{9 \times \blacksquare} = \dfrac{35}{63}$

16. $\dfrac{6 \times \blacksquare}{7 \times \blacksquare} = \dfrac{18}{21}$

Write the missing numerator.

17. $\dfrac{1}{3} = \dfrac{\blacksquare}{6}$

18. $\dfrac{2}{5} = \dfrac{\blacksquare}{15}$

19. $\dfrac{3}{4} = \dfrac{\blacksquare}{20}$

20. $\dfrac{7}{10} = \dfrac{\blacksquare}{100}$

21. $\dfrac{2}{3} = \dfrac{\blacksquare}{12}$

22. $\dfrac{3}{4} = \dfrac{\blacksquare}{24}$

23. $\dfrac{3}{8} = \dfrac{\blacksquare}{40}$

24. $\dfrac{7}{12} = \dfrac{\blacksquare}{36}$

Copy and complete.

25. $\dfrac{5}{6} = \dfrac{15}{\blacksquare}$

26. $\dfrac{3}{5} = \dfrac{12}{\blacksquare}$

27. $\dfrac{5}{6} = \dfrac{20}{\blacksquare}$

28. $\dfrac{2}{10} = \dfrac{20}{\blacksquare}$

29. $\dfrac{7}{8} = \dfrac{\blacksquare}{64}$

30. $\dfrac{4}{5} = \dfrac{16}{\blacksquare}$

31. $\dfrac{7}{10} = \dfrac{\blacksquare}{60}$

32. $\dfrac{\blacksquare}{5} = \dfrac{12}{20}$

PROBLEM SOLVING

Write the next equivalent fraction in each pattern.

A. $\dfrac{2}{3}, \dfrac{6}{9}, \dfrac{18}{27}, \dfrac{\blacksquare}{\blacksquare}$

B. $\dfrac{3}{4}, \dfrac{15}{20}, \dfrac{75}{100}, \dfrac{\blacksquare}{\blacksquare}$

C. $\dfrac{5}{6}, \dfrac{20}{24}, \dfrac{80}{96}, \dfrac{\blacksquare}{\blacksquare}$

Common Factors and the G.C.F.

We recall from unit 5 that:

> A number that is a factor of 2 given numbers is said to be a **common factor** of both numbers.

CAN YOU NAME OUR COMMON FACTORS?

THERE'S NOTHING COMMON ABOUT MY FACTORS!

Factors of 12: 1, 2, 3, 4, 6 and 12

Factors of 18: 1, 2, 3, 6, 9 and 18

Common factors of 12 and 18: 1, 2, 3, 6

6 is called the **greatest common factor (g.c.f.)** of 12 and 18.

Other examples:

Factors of 6: 1, 2, 3 and 6
Factors of 10: 1, 2, 5, and 10

Common factors: 1, 2
    g.c.f.: 2

Factors of 21: 1, 3, 7 and 21
Factors of 16: 1, 2, 4, 8 and 16

Common factors: 1
    g.c.f.: 1

List the common factors and the g.c.f. of each pair of numbers.

1. 6
    10

2. 12
    15

3. 18
    24

4. 12
    20

5. 4
    12

6. 8
    20

7. 18
    30

8. 9
    24

9. 14
    21

10. 10
    30

11. 42
    64

12. 30
    42

Find the g.c.f. of the numerator and denominator of each fraction.

13. $\dfrac{6}{8}$

14. $\dfrac{18}{32}$

15. $\dfrac{24}{36}$

16. $\dfrac{15}{20}$

17. $\dfrac{18}{42}$

18. $\dfrac{36}{90}$

PROBLEM SOLVING

List pairs of numbers with greatest common factor 6. Find a pair of numbers with greatest common factor 6 and least common multiple 72.

Simplifying Fractions

To find an equivalent fraction with **greater** numerator and denominator, we **multiply** both by the same number.

$$\frac{2}{5} \overset{\times 3}{\underset{\times 3}{=}} \frac{6}{15}$$

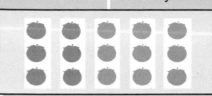

To find an equivalent fraction with **smaller** numerator and denominator, we **divide** both by a common factor.

$$\frac{6}{15} \overset{\div 3}{\underset{\div 3}{=}} \frac{2}{5}$$

Finding an equivalent fraction by division is called **simplifying** or **reducing to simpler form**.

$\frac{2}{5}$ is in simpler form than $\frac{6}{15}$

Other examples:

$$\frac{15}{25} \overset{\div 5}{\underset{\div 5}{=}} \frac{3}{5} \qquad \frac{18}{24} \overset{\div 6}{\underset{\div 6}{=}} \frac{3}{4} \qquad \frac{32}{48} \overset{\div 4}{\underset{\div 4}{=}} \frac{8}{12} \qquad \frac{10}{16} \overset{\div 2}{\underset{\div 2}{=}} \frac{5}{8}$$

Divide to find an equivalent fraction:

1. $\frac{6}{8} \overset{\div 2}{\underset{\div 2}{=}} \frac{}{}$

2. $\frac{9}{12} \overset{\div 3}{\underset{\div 3}{=}} \frac{}{}$

3. $\frac{18}{27} \overset{\div 9}{\underset{\div 9}{=}} \frac{}{}$

4. $\frac{30}{36} \overset{\div 6}{\underset{\div 6}{=}} \frac{}{}$

Copy and complete.

5. $\frac{16}{24} \overset{\div 8}{\underset{\div ?}{=}} \frac{}{}$

6. $\frac{25}{40} \overset{\div 5}{\underset{\div ?}{=}} \frac{}{}$

7. $\frac{35}{42} \overset{\div ?}{\underset{\div ?}{=}} \frac{5}{}$

8. $\frac{18}{81} \overset{\div ?}{\underset{\div ?}{=}} \frac{}{9}$

9. $\frac{32}{40} = \frac{4}{}$

10. $\frac{70}{80} = \frac{7}{}$

11. $\frac{14}{35} = \frac{2}{}$

12. $\frac{25}{80} = \frac{}{16}$

Divide by a common factor to find an equivalent fraction.

13. $\frac{6}{10}$

14. $\frac{4}{12}$

15. $\frac{12}{16}$

16. $\frac{10}{16}$

17. $\frac{9}{24}$

18. $\frac{21}{28}$

19. $\frac{30}{70}$

20. $\frac{75}{100}$

21. $\frac{35}{56}$

22. $\frac{42}{48}$

23. $\frac{45}{54}$

24. $\frac{13}{52}$

367

Reducing Fractions to Simplest Form

A fraction such as $\frac{2}{3}$ cannot be reduced to simpler form because 2 and 3 have no common factor except 1.

We say $\frac{2}{3}$ is in **simplest form**.

Randy used repeated division to reduce $\frac{60}{90}$ to simplest form.

Sarah reduced $\frac{60}{90}$ to simplest form using only one division! She divided by the g.c.f. of 60 and 90.

Another example:

To reduce to simplest form.	Find the g.c.f. of the numerator and denominator.	Divide by the g.c.f.

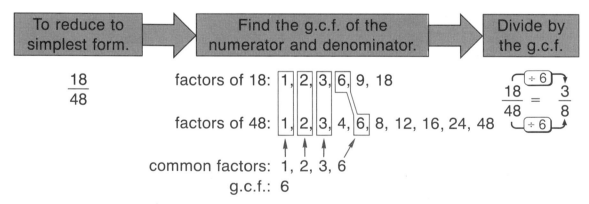

$\frac{18}{48}$

factors of 18: 1, 2, 3, 6, 9, 18

factors of 48: 1, 2, 3, 4, 6, 8, 12, 16, 24, 48

common factors: 1, 2, 3, 6

g.c.f.: 6

$$\frac{18}{48} = \frac{3}{8} \quad (\div 6)$$

Record the fractions which are in simplest form.

$\frac{29}{58}$　　$\frac{21}{43}$　　$\frac{17}{35}$　　$\frac{30}{72}$　　$\frac{13}{52}$　　$\frac{27}{64}$　　$\frac{7}{91}$　　$\frac{14}{53}$

Reduce to simplest form. Use Randy's or Sarah's method.

1. $\dfrac{6}{8}$ 2. $\dfrac{9}{12}$ 3. $\dfrac{12}{18}$ 4. $\dfrac{16}{24}$ 5. $\dfrac{30}{40}$ 6. $\dfrac{16}{20}$

7. $\dfrac{50}{75}$ 8. $\dfrac{20}{45}$ 9. $\dfrac{21}{63}$ 10. $\dfrac{25}{35}$ 11. $\dfrac{32}{56}$ 12. $\dfrac{8}{32}$

13. $\dfrac{120}{210}$ 14. $\dfrac{300}{1000}$ 15. $\dfrac{125}{1000}$ 16. $\dfrac{450}{600}$ 17. $\dfrac{875}{2000}$ 18. $\dfrac{260}{390}$

Express as a fraction in simplest form.

19. 15 min as a fraction of an hour
20. 80¢ as a fraction of a dollar
21. 18 h as a fraction of a day
22. 20 cm as a fraction of a metre
23. 4 months as a fraction of a year
24. 9 slices of a 12-slice pizza
25. 8 donuts as a fraction of a dozen
26. 125 m as a fraction of a kilometre

The tiling pattern shown on the far right is made by repeating the basic pattern 8 times.

Basic Pattern

Tiling Pattern
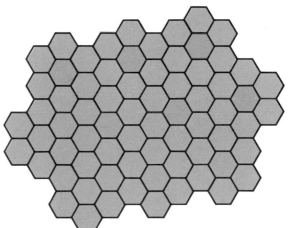

27. What fraction of the tiles in the basic pattern are green?

28. What fraction of the tiles in the tiling pattern are green?

29. Are the fractions in questions 27 and 28 equivalent? Explain.

30. What fraction of the tiles in the tiling pattern are pink? (Express in simplest form).

BITS AND BYTES

Reduce $\dfrac{3750}{4375}$ to simplest form using:

A. Sarah's method
B. Randy's method

Which method is faster? Explain.

A common factor of 2 numbers is also a factor of their difference.

Use this fact to reduce $\dfrac{3750}{4375}$ to simplest form.

Decimal Numbers as Fractions in Simplest Form

The Earth's Surface by Area

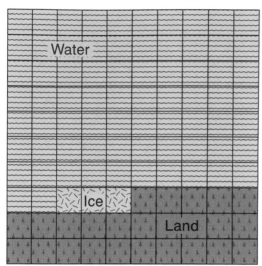

The box graph shows that the land area is 25 hundredths of the earth's total surface area.

What fraction of the earth's surface is land?

$$0.25 \qquad \frac{25}{100} \qquad \frac{1}{4}$$

Which answer is correct?

We can write 25 hundredths as 0.25 or $\frac{25}{100}$. Since $\frac{1}{4}$ is $\frac{25}{100}$ in simplest form, then all answers are correct.

To write a decimal number as a common fraction in simplest form:	→	Write as a common fraction.	→	Reduce the common fraction to simplest form:

$$0.25 \qquad\qquad \frac{25}{100} \qquad\qquad \frac{25}{100} \overset{\div 25}{\underset{\div 25}{=}} \frac{1}{4}$$

Other examples:

$$0.75 = \frac{75}{100} \overset{\div 25}{\underset{\div 25}{=}} \frac{3}{4} \qquad 0.6 = \frac{6}{10} \overset{\div 2}{\underset{\div 2}{=}} \frac{3}{5} \qquad 0.875 = \frac{875}{1000} \overset{\div 125}{\underset{\div 125}{=}} \frac{7}{8}$$

Write each shaded part as a decimal number and as a common fraction in simplest form.

1.

2.

3.

4.

5.

6.

7.

8.

370

Write each decimal number as
a fraction in simplest form.

1. 0.4   2. 0.75   3. 0.8
4. 0.05   5. 0.15   6. 0.65
7. 0.125   8. 0.375   9. 0.015
10. 0.075   11. 0.625   12. 0.0625

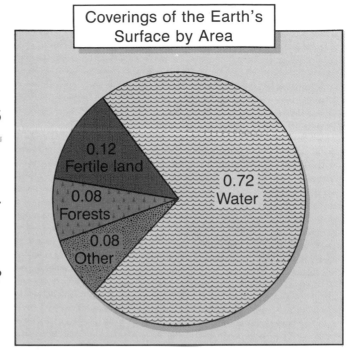

Coverings of the Earth's
Surface by Area

0.12
Fertile land

0.08
Forests

0.08
Other

0.72
Water

The approximate fractions of the earth's
surface covered by water, fertile land,
and forests are shown on the **circle graph**.

13. What fraction of the earth's surface
    in simplest form is covered by:
    a) water?   b) forest?   c) fertile land?

14. What fraction of the earth's surface
    is not covered by water, forest,
    or fertile land?

ESTIMATING

Study these
pictures.

0.1   0.2   0.3   0.4

0.9   0.8   0.7   0.6

Estimate: What fraction of each square is shaded?

A.   B.   C.   D.   E.   F.

Study these pictures.

Estimate: What fraction   G.   H.   I.
of each circle is shaded?

Decimal Equivalents of Special Fractions

Above the surface of the earth is a blanket of gases which we call air. Air is composed of nitrogen, oxygen, and other gases.

Nitrogen is about $\frac{4}{5}$ of our air by volume.

Write this fraction as a decimal number.

To write $\frac{4}{5}$ as a decimal number:	Find a fraction equivalent to $\frac{4}{5}$ with a denominator of 10, 100, or 1000.	Write as a decimal number.
$\frac{4}{5}$	$\frac{4}{5} \overset{\times 2}{\underset{\times 2}{=}} \frac{8}{10}$	$\frac{8}{10} = 0.8$

Another example:

To write $\frac{27}{30}$ as a decimal number:	Find a fraction equivalent to $\frac{27}{30}$ with a denominator of 10, 100, or 1000.	Write as a decimal number.
$\frac{27}{30}$	$\frac{27}{30} \overset{\div 3}{\underset{\div 3}{=}} \frac{9}{10}$	$\frac{9}{10} = 0.9$

To change a fraction to a decimal number, it is sometimes necessary to divide and multiply.

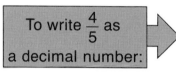

$$\frac{24}{75} \overset{\div 3}{\underset{\div 3}{=}} \frac{8}{25} \overset{\times 4}{\underset{\times 4}{=}} \frac{32}{100} \text{ or } 0.32$$

Write an equivalent fraction with a denominator of 10. Then write as a decimal number.

1. $\frac{3}{5}$ 2. $\frac{1}{2}$ 3. $\frac{6}{20}$

4. $\frac{1}{5}$ 5. $\frac{24}{40}$ 6. $\frac{15}{25}$

Write an equivalent fraction with a denominator of 100. Then write as a decimal number.

1. $\frac{3}{50}$ 2. $\frac{7}{25}$ 3. $\frac{3}{4}$

4. $\frac{9}{20}$ 5. $\frac{17}{50}$ 6. $\frac{21}{75}$

Write an equivalent fraction with a denominator of 1000. Then write as a decimal number.

7. $\frac{9}{500}$ 8. $\frac{1}{250}$ 9. $\frac{17}{200}$

10. $\frac{3}{125}$ 11. $\frac{1}{8}$ 12. $\frac{7}{8}$

Write as a decimal number.

13. $\frac{2}{5}$ 14. $\frac{1}{4}$ 15. $\frac{40}{50}$

16. $\frac{7}{50}$ 17. $\frac{19}{25}$ 18. $\frac{11}{50}$

19. $\frac{3}{10}$ 20. $\frac{3}{8}$ 21. $\frac{35}{500}$

22. $\frac{9}{125}$ 23. $\frac{13}{250}$ 24. $\frac{6}{8}$

Write each statement using a decimal number.

25. Air is about $\frac{1}{5}$ oxygen.

26. Swim class lasts about $\frac{3}{4}$ of an hour.

27. $\frac{13}{25}$ of Christian's classmates are boys.

28. A kilometre is about $\frac{5}{8}$ of a mile.

RIDDLE: What is a sea monster's favorite food?

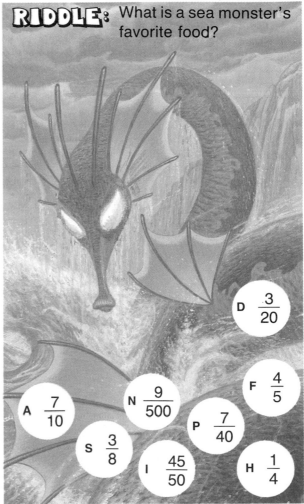

D $\frac{3}{20}$

F $\frac{4}{5}$

A $\frac{7}{10}$ N $\frac{9}{500}$ P $\frac{7}{40}$

S $\frac{3}{8}$ I $\frac{45}{50}$ H $\frac{1}{4}$

To answer the riddle, write the letters of the fractions equivalent to these decimal numbers.

▨   ▨   ▨   ▨
0.8   0.9   0.375   0.25

▨   ▨   ▨
0.7   0.018   0.15

▨   ▨   ▨   ▨   ▨
0.375   0.25   0.9   0.175   0.375

Writing Fractions as Decimal Numbers

To express $\frac{5}{8}$ as a decimal number, Sarah changed $\frac{5}{8}$ to an equivalent fraction with a denominator of 1000.

$$\frac{5}{8} \overset{\times 125}{\underset{\times 125}{=}} \frac{625}{1000} = 0.625$$

Sarah's method is not always easy to apply.

To express $\frac{5}{8}$ as a decimal number, Randy thought:

$\frac{5}{8}$ means 5 divided by 8.

He wrote:

$$\begin{array}{r} 0.625 \\ 8\overline{)5.000} \\ \underline{4\,8} \\ 20 \\ \underline{16} \\ 40 \\ \underline{40} \\ 0 \end{array}$$

Stop dividing at zero remainder.

$$\frac{5}{8} = 0.625$$

Randy's method can always be applied.

DO YOU LIKE MY SHORT METHOD?

SURE, IT'S GREAT IF YOU REMEMBER THAT THERE ARE 125 8'S IN 1000.

> We can express a fraction as a decimal number by dividing the numerator by the denominator.

Use division to express these fractions as decimal numbers.

1. $\frac{1}{4}$
2. $\frac{1}{2}$
3. $\frac{3}{4}$
4. $\frac{7}{50}$
5. $\frac{4}{5}$
6. $\frac{12}{15}$

7. $\frac{3}{8}$
8. $\frac{5}{8}$
9. $\frac{1}{20}$
10. $\frac{27}{75}$
11. $\frac{1}{16}$
12. $\frac{5}{32}$

BITS AND BYTES

Use your calculator to express these fractions as decimal numbers.

A. $\frac{7}{8}$
B. $\frac{9}{16}$
C. $\frac{3}{64}$
D. $\frac{17}{125}$
E. $\frac{23}{80}$
F. $\frac{23}{800}$

EXTENSIONS

Repeating Decimals

To express $\frac{16}{99}$ as a decimal, Rip Van

Wrinkle divided 16 by 99. He kept on dividing for 99 years but he never got a zero remainder.

Some fractions, when expressed as decimal numbers, have digits which repeat forever. Such decimal numbers are called **repeating decimals**.

Sometimes we use a bar to show repeating digits.

We write: $\frac{16}{99} = 0.\overline{16}$ Other examples: $\frac{1}{3} = 0.\overline{3}$ $\frac{17}{18} = 0.9\overline{4}$ $\frac{1}{7} = 0.\overline{142857}$

Write each decimal number using a bar to show repeating digits.

1. 0.262626...
2. 0.66666...
3. 0.472472472...
4. 0.5383838...
5. 0.95121212...
6. 0.020202...

Express each fraction as a repeating deoimal number. Use a bar to show repeating digits.

7. $\frac{2}{3}$
8. $\frac{4}{9}$
9. $\frac{5}{6}$
10. $\frac{1}{11}$
11. $\frac{7}{11}$
12. $\frac{51}{99}$

BITS AND BYTES

Use a calculator to help you express each fraction as a repeating decimal.

Use a bar to show the repeating digits.

1. a) $\frac{2}{9}$ b) $\frac{2}{99}$ c) $\frac{2}{999}$

   d) $\frac{1}{24}$ e) $\frac{5}{27}$ f) $\frac{128}{999}$

2. Write a fraction which has 4 repeating digits when in decimal form.

3. Can your calculator be used to express $\frac{10}{81}$ as a repeating decimal?

   Explain.

Mixed Numbers

How many pies are shown?

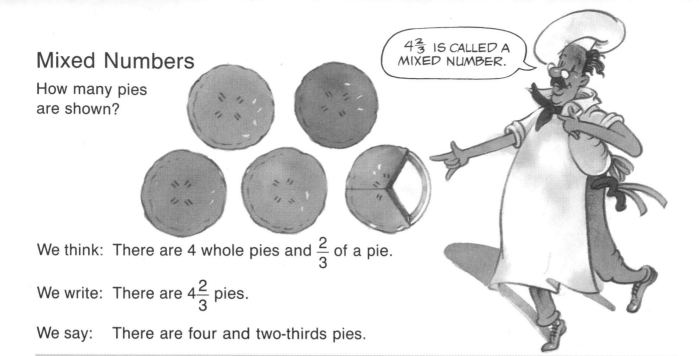

We think: There are 4 whole pies and $\frac{2}{3}$ of a pie.

We write: There are $4\frac{2}{3}$ pies.

We say: There are four and two-thirds pies.

Write a mixed number to show how many pies.

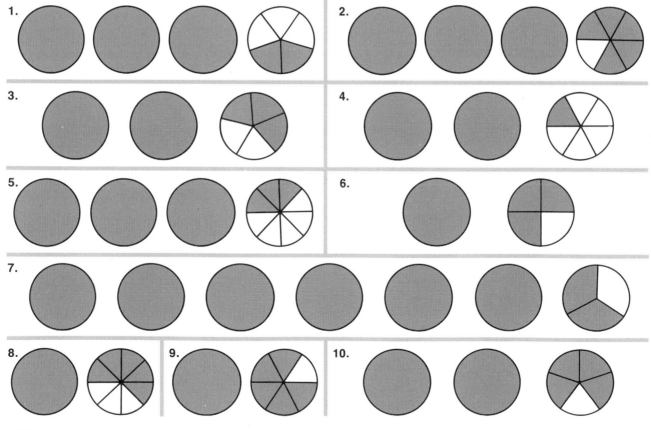

1.

2.

3.

4.

5.

6.

7.

8.

9.

10.

376

Fraction Numbers on a Number Line

We can show fractions and mixed numbers on a number line.

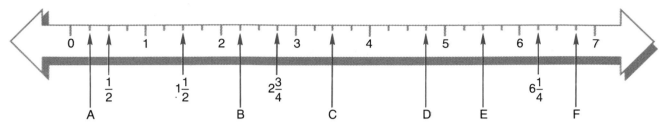

Write the fraction or mixed number which gives the location of each point.

1. A
2. B
3. C
4. D
5. E
6. F

Use the number line below to determine the greater number
in each question. Then write > or < for each ▣ .

7. $\dfrac{1}{8}$ ▣ $\dfrac{1}{4}$

8. $\dfrac{7}{8}$ ▣ $\dfrac{1}{2}$

9. $1\dfrac{1}{2}$ ▣ $\dfrac{7}{8}$

10. $2\dfrac{3}{4}$ ▣ $1\dfrac{7}{8}$

11. $2\dfrac{1}{4}$ ▣ $2\dfrac{1}{2}$

12. $2\dfrac{5}{8}$ ▣ $2\dfrac{3}{4}$

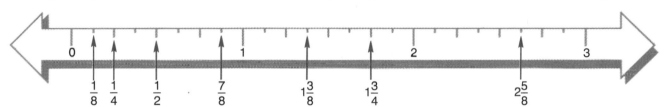

BITS AND BYTES

The symbol π (called "pi") stands for the
most famous number in mathematics.
The value of π to the first 6 decimal
places is 3.141 592....

For centuries people have used these
mixed numbers to approximate π.

$3\dfrac{1}{8}$ $3\dfrac{1}{7}$ $3\dfrac{16}{113}$ $3\dfrac{177}{1250}$

$$\pi = 3.141\ 592\ldots$$

1. Use your calculator to write each
   mixed number as a decimal number.

2. Which of these mixed numbers
   is closest to π?

377

The L.C.M. and the Least Common Denominator

The world's land area is shared among 7 continents. The table shows the areas of the 2 largest continents as a fraction of the world's total land area.

Into how many equal parts must we divide a circle to show this information on a circle graph?

Continent	Fraction of the World's Total Land Area
Asia	$\dfrac{3}{10}$
Africa	$\dfrac{1}{5}$

We think:

To show...	the number of equal parts must be...	Multiples
fifths	a multiple of 5	5, 10, 15, 20, ...
tenths	a multiple of 10	10, 20, 30, ...
fifths and tenths	a common multiple of 5 and 10	10, 20, ...

We say: 10 is the least common multiple (l.c.m.) of **5** and **10**, so

10 is the **least common denominator** (l.c.d.) of $\dfrac{1}{5}$ and $\dfrac{3}{10}$.

We write:

Continent	Fraction of World's Total Land Area	
	Simplest Form	Denominator 10
Asia	$\dfrac{3}{10}$	$\dfrac{3}{10}$
Africa	$\dfrac{1}{5}$	$\dfrac{2}{10}$

Equivalent Fractions

We graph:

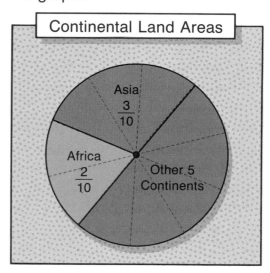

Continental Land Areas

Asia $\dfrac{3}{10}$

Africa $\dfrac{2}{10}$

Other 5 Continents

Find the l.c.m. of each pair of numbers.

1. 4, 8   2. 3, 4   3. 6, 8
4. 6, 10   5. 12, 30   6. 18, 24

Find the l.c.d. of each pair of fractions.

7. $\dfrac{1}{3}, \dfrac{2}{5}$ 8. $\dfrac{3}{8}, \dfrac{1}{4}$ 9. $\dfrac{5}{6}, \dfrac{7}{9}$ 10. $\dfrac{1}{12}, \dfrac{7}{8}$ 11. $\dfrac{3}{4}, \dfrac{5}{6}$

12. $\dfrac{1}{6}, \dfrac{1}{12}$ 13. $\dfrac{3}{5}, \dfrac{5}{12}$ 14. $\dfrac{7}{8}, \dfrac{5}{12}$ 15. $\dfrac{3}{10}, \dfrac{1}{6}$ 16. $\dfrac{1}{6}, \dfrac{5}{21}$

The table shows the areas of the 3 largest continents as fractions of the world's total land area.

Into how many equal parts must we divide a circle to show this information on a circle graph?

Continent	Fraction of the World's Total Land Area
Asia	$\frac{3}{10}$
Africa	$\frac{1}{5}$
North America	$\frac{1}{6}$

We think:

To show...	the number of equal parts must be...	Multiples
fifths	a multiple of 5	5, 10, 15, 20, 25, 30, ...
sixths	a multiple of 6	6, 12, 18, 24, 30, 36, ...
tenths	a multiple of 10	10, 20, 30, ...
fifths, sixths and tenths	a common multiple of 5, 6 and 10	30, ...

We say: 30 is the l.c.m. of 5, 6 and 10, so 30 is the l.c.d. of $\frac{1}{5}$, $\frac{1}{6}$, and $\frac{3}{10}$

We graph:

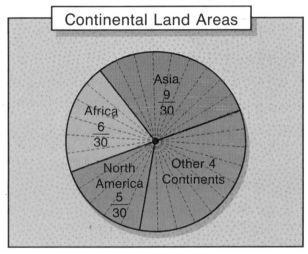

Continental Land Areas

We write:

Continent	Total Land Area
Asia	$\frac{3}{10} = \frac{9}{30}$
Africa	$\frac{1}{5} = \frac{6}{30}$
North America	$\frac{1}{6} = \frac{5}{30}$

Find the l.c.m. of each set of numbers.

1. 2, 3, 4
2. 3, 5, 7
3. 2, 4, 10
4. 3, 5, 10
5. 4, 6, 10
6. 5, 8, 10

Find the l.c.d. for each set of fractions.

7. $\frac{1}{2}$, $\frac{1}{3}$, $\frac{1}{4}$
8. $\frac{1}{2}$, $\frac{1}{4}$, $\frac{3}{10}$
9. $\frac{2}{5}$, $\frac{1}{3}$, $\frac{7}{10}$
10. $\frac{3}{4}$, $\frac{1}{6}$, $\frac{1}{10}$

11. Into how many equal parts must a circle be divided to show $\frac{1}{3}$, $\frac{1}{4}$, and $\frac{2}{5}$?

12. What fraction of the world's land area is contained in the 4 smallest continents? Use the graph above.

Comparing Fractions

This circle graph shows the areas of the largest continents as fractions of the world's total land area.

WHICH HAS THE GREATER AREA, ASIA OR THE 4 SMALLEST CONTINENTS COMBINED?

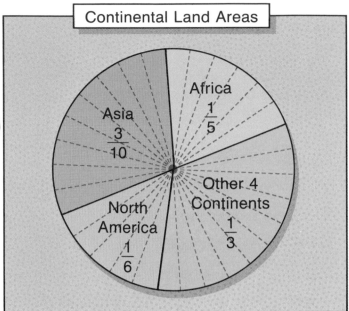

Continental Land Areas

Asia $\frac{3}{10}$

Africa $\frac{1}{5}$

North America $\frac{1}{6}$

Other 4 Continents $\frac{1}{3}$

To compare fractions of unlike denominators:	Find the l.c.d.	Write equivalent fractions with a common denominator.	Compare the numerators.
$\frac{3}{10}, \frac{1}{3}$	l.c.d. of $\frac{3}{10}$ and $\frac{1}{3}$ is l.c.m. of 10 and 3 or 30.	$\frac{3}{10} = \frac{9}{30}$ $\frac{1}{3} = \frac{10}{30}$	$10 > 9$ so $\frac{10}{30} > \frac{9}{30}$

That is $\frac{1}{3} > \frac{3}{10}$ so the 4 smallest continents have greater total land area than Asia.

Find equivalent fractions with like denominators.
Then compare the fractions by writing > or < for each 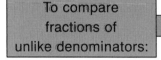.

1. $\frac{3}{4} \ \blacksquare \ \frac{5}{8}$

2. $\frac{4}{5} \ \blacksquare \ \frac{9}{10}$

3. $\frac{2}{3} \ \blacksquare \ \frac{3}{4}$

4. $\frac{1}{3} \ \blacksquare \ \frac{2}{5}$

5. $\frac{5}{6} \ \blacksquare \ \frac{8}{10}$

6. $\frac{1}{5} \ \blacksquare \ \frac{2}{9}$

7. $\frac{1}{5} \ \blacksquare \ \frac{1}{6}$

8. $\frac{5}{6} \ \blacksquare \ \frac{7}{8}$

9. $\frac{4}{5} \ \blacksquare \ \frac{5}{6}$

10. $\frac{7}{10} \ \blacksquare \ \frac{2}{3}$

11. $\frac{1}{10} \ \blacksquare \ \frac{1}{15}$

12. $\frac{3}{20} \ \blacksquare \ \frac{4}{15}$

BITS AND BYTES

This table lists alphabetically the continents and their approximate areas as fractions of the world's total land area.

Continent	Fraction of the World's Total Land Area
Africa	$\frac{1}{5}$
Antarctica	$\frac{1}{10}$
Asia	$\frac{3}{10}$
Australia	$\frac{1}{20}$
Europe	$\frac{1}{15}$
North America	$\frac{1}{6}$
South America	$\frac{1}{8}$

List the continents in order from least to greatest area.

To compare more than 2 or 3 fractions, it is sometimes impractical to look for a common denominator.

Find a path through the rain forest so that each fraction along the path is greater than the one before it.

Record the letters in your path.

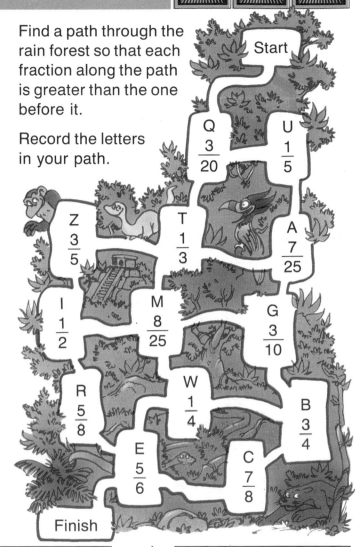

To order several fractions:	Express all the fractions as decimal numbers.	Display the fractions on a number line.

The continents are listed from left to right in order of increasing area.

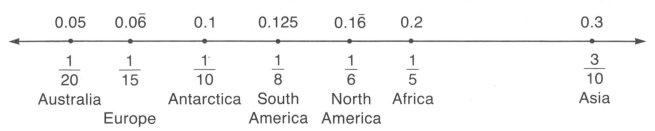

381

EXTENSIONS

The Concept of Percent

What fraction of the Canadian population is under 15 years of age?

We say: 23 out of 100 or 23 **percent** of Canadians are under 15 years of age.

We write: $\dfrac{23}{100}$ or 0.23 or 23%

Percents give us another way to name fractions with denominator 100.

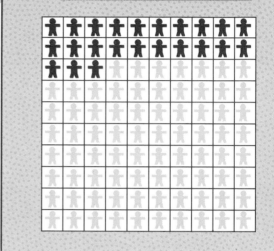

Fraction of Canadians under Age 15.

Write the shaded part of each 100-square as a common fraction, a decimal number and a percent.

1.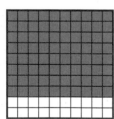

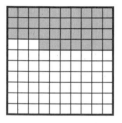

$\begin{array}{l} \text{1.} \quad \dfrac{37}{100} \\ \quad\ 0.37 \\ \quad\ 37\% \end{array}$

2.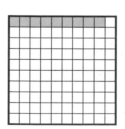

3.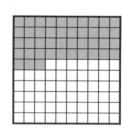

4.

5.

6.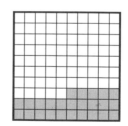

7.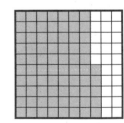

Estimate what percent of each square is shaded.

8.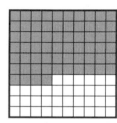

9.

10.

11.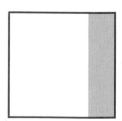

A group of 100 students were asked "What kind of movie do you like best: adventure, horror, or comedy?"

1. What kind of movie was the favorite of most students?

2. What percent of students preferred:
   a) adventure? b) horror? c) comedy?

The results of the survey are shown on the tally sheet.

Adventure	Horror	Comedy
￪￪￪￪ ￪￪￪￪	￪￪￪￪ ￪￪￪￪	￪￪￪￪ ￪￪￪￪
￪￪￪￪ ￪￪￪￪	￪￪￪	￪￪￪￪ ￪￪￪￪
￪￪￪￪ ￪￪￪￪		￪￪￪￪ ￪￪￪￪
￪￪￪￪ ￪￪￪￪		￪￪￪￪ ￪￪￪￪
		￪￪￪￪ ￪￪￪

3. Use the box graph to help you write the percent of Canadians who are:
   a) between 15 and 44 years old.
   b) over 44 years of age.
   c) under 45 years of age.
   d) over 14 years of age.
   e) under 200 years of age.

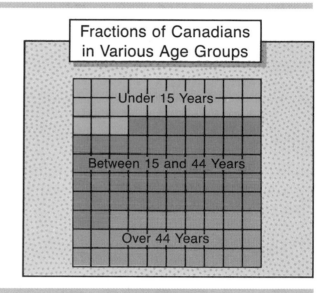

Fractions of Canadians in Various Age Groups

Under 15 Years

Between 15 and 44 Years

Over 44 Years

The circle graph shows the fraction of Canadians in each blood group.

4. Estimate the percent of Canadians who have
   a) type O blood.
   b) type A blood.
   c) type B blood.
   d) type AB blood.

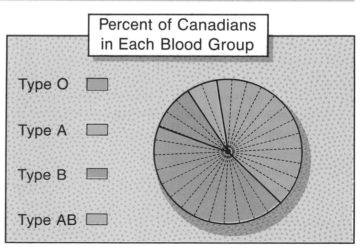

Percent of Canadians in Each Blood Group

Type O ▢

Type A ▢

Type B ▢

Type AB ▢

383

PROBLEM SOLVING

Making a Table

Membership at Sunnybrook Pool costs $10.00 per year. Each swim costs 50¢ for members and $1.50 for non-members. How many times would Sondra have to swim before it would be cheaper to be a member than a non-member?

To solve this problem, . . .

A. First, make sure you understand the problem.

Discuss:

- *What is the cost of membership?*
- *What is the cost of one swim for a member? a non-member?*
- *What are you asked to find?*
- *After one swim, how much would a member have paid? a non-member?*

B. Then, think of strategies.

- *Try making a table.*
- *Show the total amount paid after each swim.*

	1st swim	2nd swim	3rd swim
Member	$10.50	$11.00	$11.50
Non-member	$1.50	$3.00	$4.50

C. Solve the problem and answer the question.

Complete the table to find when a non-member begins paying more than a member.

D. Check your answer and discuss your solution.

- *What is the difference between the cost for a member and a non-member after one swim? After 2 swims?*
- *When is the difference 0?*
- *After what swim would a member have paid $10.00 less than a non-member?*

384

Solve each of these problems.

1. Bradley and Teresa each bought plants on the same day. Bradley's plant was 12 cm tall and it grew 2 cm per week. Teresa's plant was 3 cm tall but it grew 5 cm per week.
   a) After how many weeks were the plants the same height?
   b) In what week was Teresa's plant exactly twice the height of Bradley's plant?

2. About 2 out of every 5 people have blue eyes. Use this fact to estimate how many students in a class of 35 have blue eyes.

3. Bryan jogged 350 m in 2 minutes. At this rate, how long would it take him to jog 1400 m?

4. Kirsten bought 12 L of chocolate milk for her baseball team's parent night party. She allowed 2 L for every 7 people, and all the milk was drunk. How many people were at the party?

5. A cassette tape costs $8 at the Discount Tape Shop. If you join their Collectors Club, the cost of the first tape is $20, and each tape after that costs $4. Which is the cheaper way to buy 5 tapes?

EXTENSIONS

The Concept of Ratio

Ratios are used to compare
2 or more quantities.

We see:

We say:

The ratio of dogs to cats is 5 to 4.

We write:

The ratio of dogs to cats is 5:4.

Another example:

The ratio of:
blue to green pieces is 4:6.
knights to pawns is 3:4.
chess pieces to pawns is 10:4.

Rooks   Knights   Pawns

For the chess pieces above, write the following ratio.

1. pawns to rooks
2. knights to rooks
3. green rooks to chess pieces
4. rooks to chess pieces
5. green to blue pawns
6. blue knights to green pawns

For this sheet of wallpaper,
write the following ratios.

7. squares to circles
8. hexagons to circles
9. hexagons to squares
10. circles to all white figures
11. all white figures to squares
12. How many times as many
    squares as circles are there?

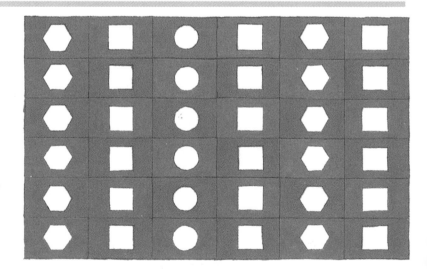

The ratio of water to concentrate is 3:1.

Tins of Concentrate	Tins of Water
1	3
2	6
3	
4	
5	
6	

1. Copy and complete the table to show how much water is needed for various amounts of concentrate.

2. How much water should be mixed with 9 tins of concentrate?

3. Write the ratio of concentrate to water.

4. How many tins of concentrate are needed to make 12 tins of orange juice?

5. How many tins of orange juice can be made from 5 tins of concentrate?

6. How many times the volume of the concentrate is the volume of the orange juice made from it?

7. What is the ratio of orange juice to concentrate in a proper mixture?

PROBLEM SOLVING

When a bicycle pedal makes 3 complete turns, its rear wheel makes 7 complete turns.

Each time the rear wheel makes a complete turn, the bicycle travels a distance of 2.2 m.

How many times does the pedal turn when the bicycle travels 77 m?

Tallying Outcomes of an Experiment

Follow these steps to make a spinner.

- Cut out a circle.
- Fold it into eighths.
- Draw in the fold lines.
- Colour as shown.

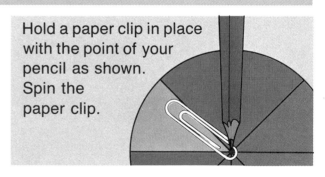

Hold a paper clip in place with the point of your pencil as shown. Spin the paper clip.

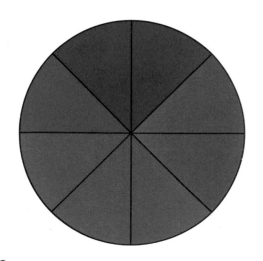

1. On which colour do you think the spinner is:
   a) most likely to stop?
   b) least likely to stop?

2. With a partner, spin the paper clip 100 times. Tally your results.

Blue	Green	Red	Yellow

3. Copy and complete this table.

Use the information from your tally on page 388.

Outcome	Fraction of Times It Occurred	Equivalent Decimal
Blue	▦	▦
Green	▦	▦
Red	▦	▦
Yellow	▦	▦

4. Make a box graph showing the outcome of your experiment.
   • Use a 100-square.
   • Colour a square blue for each time that your outcome was blue.
   • Repeat with the remaining colours.

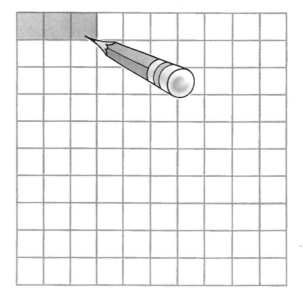

5. What fraction of the times was the outcome: **a)** blue? **b)** green?
   c) red? **d)** yellow?

6. Which outcome occurred:
   a) most often? **b)** least often?

7. Why do you think one outcome occurred more often than the others?

8. Repeat questions 1 to 7 using this spinner.

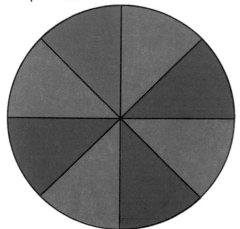

EXTENSIONS

Add all the fractions in the second column of your table in question 3. What do you discover?

Is the result the same with the table in your second experiment?

CHECK-UP

Write a fraction to tell what part is coloured.

1.

2.

Write 2 equivalent fractions for the coloured part of each set.

3.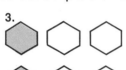

4.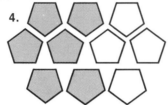

Copy and complete.

5. $\dfrac{1}{2} = \dfrac{\blacksquare}{10}$

6. $\dfrac{2}{3} = \dfrac{4}{\blacksquare}$

7. $\dfrac{7}{10} = \dfrac{\blacksquare}{20}$

8. $\dfrac{4}{5} = \dfrac{12}{\blacksquare}$

List the common factors and the greatest common factor of each pair of numbers.

9. 10, 12   10. 4, 20   11. 18, 30

Reduce each fraction to simplest form.

12. $\dfrac{10}{15}$ 13. $\dfrac{16}{20}$ 14. $\dfrac{5}{50}$ 15. $\dfrac{6}{24}$

Write each coloured part as a decimal number and as a fraction in simplest form.

16.

17.

Write as a fraction in simplest form.

18. 0.5   19. 0.15   20. 0.08   21. 0.75

Write as a decimal number.

22. $\dfrac{1}{5}$ 23. $\dfrac{11}{50}$ 24. $\dfrac{3}{4}$ 25. $\dfrac{5}{8}$

Write a mixed number for each picture.

26.

27.

Find the least common multiple of each pair of numbers.

28. 3, 8   29. 10, 12   30. 15, 18

Find equivalent fractions with like denominators. Then compare the fractions by writing > or < .

31. $\dfrac{1}{2} \ \blacksquare \ \dfrac{2}{3}$

32. $\dfrac{3}{5} \ \blacksquare \ \dfrac{3}{4}$

33. $\dfrac{7}{8} \ \blacksquare \ \dfrac{5}{6}$

34. $\dfrac{9}{10} \ \blacksquare \ \dfrac{4}{5}$

Solve.

35. Paul bought 3 apples for 53¢. How many apples can he buy with $2.12?

36. Paula receives $20 every 3 weeks for doing chores for her neighbour. How much money will she earn after 15 weeks?

390

Fox and Geese

This game was played in Iceland over 700 years ago. There, it was called Halatafl. Fox and Geese soon became popular throughout northern Europe. Records show that the Royal Household of King Edward IV of England purchased 2 sets of silver game pieces.

Artist's impression of a Fox and Geese game, 15th century England.

Adding and Subtracting Fractions: Like Denominators

This circle graph shows how Abbie spends her time on an average day.

ABBIE'S DAILY ACTIVITIES (24 h)

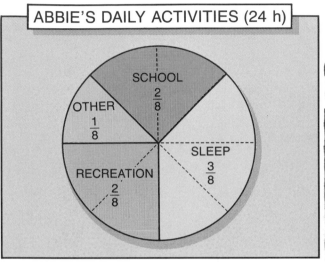

SCHOOL $\frac{2}{8}$

OTHER $\frac{1}{8}$

SLEEP $\frac{3}{8}$

RECREATION $\frac{2}{8}$

What fraction of Abbie's time is spent altogether on recreation and sleeping?

We think:

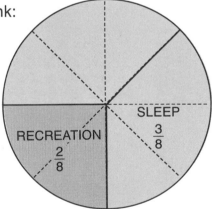

RECREATION $\frac{2}{8}$

SLEEP $\frac{3}{8}$

$$\frac{2}{8} + \frac{3}{8} = \frac{5}{8}$$

We write: $\frac{5}{8}$ of Abbie's time is used for sleeping and recreation.

During what fraction of her day is Abbie not sleeping?

We think:

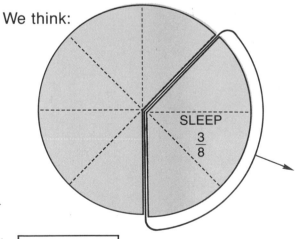

SLEEP $\frac{3}{8}$

$\frac{8}{8}$ is another name for 1

$$\frac{8}{8} - \frac{3}{8} = \frac{5}{8}$$

We write: Abbie is not sleeping $\frac{5}{8}$ of the time.

392

Complete each addition sentence to show what fraction is coloured.

1.

$$\frac{1}{5} + \frac{2}{5} = \rule{1cm}{0.4pt}$$

2.

$$\frac{1}{6} + \frac{3}{6} = \rule{1cm}{0.4pt}$$

3.

$$\frac{1}{7} + \frac{2}{7} = \rule{1cm}{0.4pt}$$

4.

$$\frac{2}{8} + \frac{3}{8} = \rule{1cm}{0.4pt}$$

5.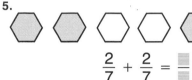

$$\frac{2}{7} + \frac{2}{7} = \rule{1cm}{0.4pt}$$

6.

$$\frac{3}{9} + \frac{4}{9} = \rule{1cm}{0.4pt}$$

Complete each subtraction sentence to show what fraction is left.

7.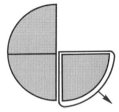

$$\frac{3}{4} - \frac{1}{4} = \rule{1cm}{0.4pt}$$

8.

$$\frac{5}{6} - \frac{2}{6} = \rule{1cm}{0.4pt}$$

9.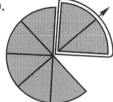

$$\frac{7}{8} - \frac{2}{8} = \rule{1cm}{0.4pt}$$

10.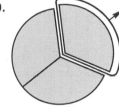

$$1 - \frac{1}{3} = \rule{1cm}{0.4pt}$$

11.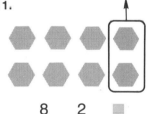

$$\frac{8}{8} - \frac{2}{8} = \rule{1cm}{0.4pt}$$

12.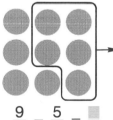

$$\frac{9}{9} - \frac{5}{9} = \rule{1cm}{0.4pt}$$

13.

$$\frac{5}{5} - \frac{2}{5} = \rule{1cm}{0.4pt}$$

14.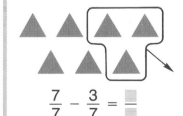

$$\frac{7}{7} - \frac{3}{7} = \rule{1cm}{0.4pt}$$

Add or subtract. Write your answers in simplest form.

15. $\frac{1}{4} + \frac{1}{4}$

16. $\frac{5}{8} - \frac{2}{8}$

17. $\frac{3}{7} + \frac{1}{7}$

18. $\frac{3}{10} + \frac{2}{10}$

19. $\frac{5}{8} + \frac{1}{8}$

20. $\frac{6}{7} - \frac{2}{7}$

21. $\frac{1}{3} + \frac{2}{3}$

22. $1 - \frac{1}{5}$

23. What fraction of Abbie's time is spent on school and recreation altogether?

24. What fraction of Abbie's time is spent out of school?

393

Mixed Numbers and Improper Fractions

Greg works at a pizza parlor and counts the pizza left at the end of the day.

He sees:

He thinks: If $\frac{1}{8}$ of one pizza was moved to make one whole pizza, there would be $\frac{5}{8}$ left over.

He writes: $\frac{13}{8}$ or $1\frac{5}{8}$

Fractions like $\frac{13}{8}$ that have a numerator greater than or equal to the denominator are called **improper fractions**.

Draw each picture as a whole and a fraction. Then write an improper fraction and a mixed number for each picture.

1.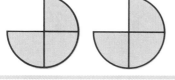

2.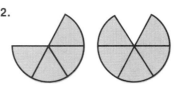

3.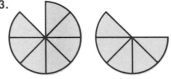

4.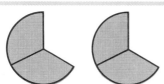

5.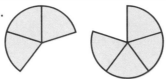

6.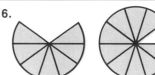

Write as a mixed number. Draw a picture if you wish.

7. $\frac{5}{3}$
8. $\frac{7}{4}$
9. $\frac{8}{6}$
10. $\frac{12}{8}$
11. $\frac{9}{6}$
12. $\frac{7}{2}$

13. $\frac{7}{3}$
14. $\frac{18}{5}$
15. $\frac{20}{6}$
16. $\frac{35}{6}$
17. $\frac{40}{9}$
18. $\frac{23}{3}$

Write as an improper fraction. Draw a picture if you wish.

19. $1\frac{4}{5}$
20. $1\frac{3}{4}$
21. $1\frac{2}{3}$
22. $2\frac{1}{4}$
23. $3\frac{1}{2}$
24. $2\frac{2}{5}$

25. $2\frac{1}{3}$
26. $3\frac{1}{4}$
27. $3\frac{3}{4}$
28. $4\frac{1}{2}$
29. $2\frac{3}{8}$
30. $5\frac{1}{6}$

Adding and Subtracting with Improper Fractions

How many cherry pies?

We see:

We think: If we moved $\frac{1}{6}$ of the pie on the right to make one whole pie, there would be $\frac{3}{6}$ left over.

We write: $\frac{5}{6} + \frac{4}{6} = \frac{9}{6}$ or $1\frac{3}{6}$ or $1\frac{1}{2}$

There are $1\frac{1}{2}$ cherry pies.

How much blueberry pie is left?

We see: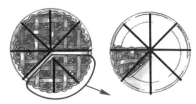

We think: $1\frac{1}{8}$ blueberry pie is the same as $\frac{9}{8}$ blueberry pie.

We write: $1\frac{1}{8} - \frac{3}{8}$

$= \frac{9}{8} - \frac{3}{8} = \frac{6}{8}$ or $\frac{3}{4}$

There is $\frac{3}{4}$ blueberry pie left.

Write an addition or subtraction sentence for each picture.
Write your answers in simplest form.

1.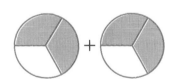

2.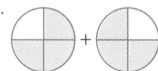

3.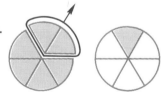

4.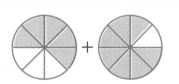

5.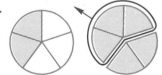

6.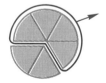

Add. Write your answer in simplest form. Draw a picture if you wish.

7. $\frac{3}{4} + \frac{3}{4}$

8. $\frac{5}{8} + \frac{7}{8}$

9. $\frac{3}{6} + \frac{5}{6}$

10. $\frac{3}{8} + \frac{7}{8}$

11. $\frac{4}{5} + \frac{3}{5}$

12. $\frac{3}{8} + \frac{5}{8}$

Subtract. Write your answer in simplest form. Draw a picture if you wish.

13. $1\frac{1}{4} - \frac{3}{4}$

14. $1\frac{5}{8} - \frac{7}{8}$

15. $1\frac{1}{5} - \frac{3}{5}$

16. $1\frac{2}{4} - \frac{2}{4}$

17. $1\frac{1}{6} - \frac{3}{6}$

18. $1\frac{2}{4} - \frac{3}{4}$

Adding Fractions: Unlike Denominators

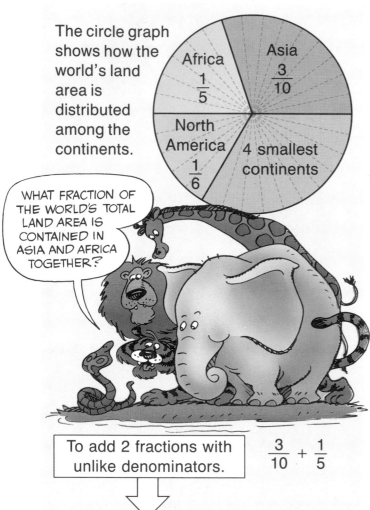

The circle graph shows how the world's land area is distributed among the continents.

Africa $\frac{1}{5}$

Asia $\frac{3}{10}$

North America $\frac{1}{6}$

4 smallest continents

WHAT FRACTION OF THE WORLD'S TOTAL LAND AREA IS CONTAINED IN ASIA AND AFRICA TOGETHER?

| To add 2 fractions with unlike denominators. | $\frac{3}{10} + \frac{1}{5}$ |

⬇

| Write equivalent fractions with a common denominator. | $= \frac{3}{10} + \frac{2}{10}$ |

⬇

| Add the fractions. | $= \frac{5}{10}$ or $\frac{1}{2}$ |

Asia and Africa together contain $\frac{1}{2}$ of the world's total land area.

Add. Write your answers in simplest form.

1. $\frac{1}{8} + \frac{3}{4}$ 2. $\frac{1}{5} + \frac{3}{4}$

3. $\frac{3}{10} + \frac{1}{5}$ 4. $\frac{1}{6} + \frac{2}{3}$

5. $\frac{1}{3} + \frac{1}{6}$ 6. $\frac{2}{3} + \frac{1}{5}$

7. $\frac{1}{3} + \frac{2}{5}$ 8. $\frac{3}{10} + \frac{1}{6}$

Add. Write your answers as mixed numbers.

9. $\frac{7}{8} + \frac{1}{4}$ 10. $\frac{2}{3} + \frac{5}{6}$

11. $\frac{4}{5} + \frac{3}{4}$ 12. $\frac{5}{6} + \frac{1}{2}$

13. $\frac{1}{3} + \frac{5}{6}$ 14. $\frac{7}{8} + \frac{1}{2}$

15. $\frac{5}{6} + \frac{2}{3}$ 16. $\frac{3}{5} + \frac{5}{6}$

17. What fraction of the world's total land area is contained in Africa and North America altogether?

EXTENSIONS

What fraction of the world's total land area is contained in Asia, Africa, and North America altogether?

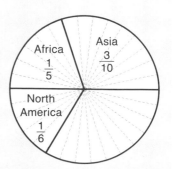

Africa $\frac{1}{5}$

Asia $\frac{3}{10}$

North America $\frac{1}{6}$

Subtracting Fractions: Unlike Denominators

North America and the 4 smallest continents contain about $\frac{1}{2}$ of the world's total land area.

WHAT FRACTION OF THE AREA IS CONTAINED IN THE 4 SMALLEST CONTINENTS?

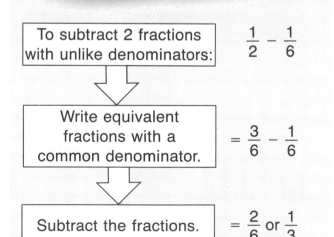

To subtract 2 fractions with unlike denominators:	$\frac{1}{2} - \frac{1}{6}$

⬇

Write equivalent fractions with a common denominator.	$= \frac{3}{6} - \frac{1}{6}$

⬇

Subtract the fractions.	$= \frac{2}{6}$ or $\frac{1}{3}$

The 4 smallest continents together contain $\frac{1}{3}$ of the world's total land area.

Subtract. Write your answer in simplest form.

1. $\frac{1}{3} - \frac{1}{4}$

2. $\frac{7}{10} - \frac{1}{5}$

3. $\frac{3}{4} - \frac{3}{8}$

4. $\frac{5}{8} - \frac{1}{4}$

5. $\frac{7}{10} - \frac{3}{5}$

6. $\frac{7}{8} - \frac{2}{3}$

7. $\frac{5}{6} - \frac{3}{8}$

8. $\frac{3}{4} - \frac{2}{5}$

Add or subtract.

9. $\frac{3}{5} + \frac{5}{6}$

10. $\frac{7}{8} - \frac{3}{5}$

11. $\frac{4}{5} - \frac{1}{10}$

12. $\frac{6}{8} + \frac{1}{3}$

13. $\frac{5}{8} + \frac{5}{12}$

14. $\frac{9}{10} - \frac{3}{4}$

15. $\frac{5}{6} - \frac{4}{5}$

16. $\frac{3}{4} + \frac{2}{5}$

17. What fraction of the world's total land area is not part of either North America or Africa?

18. What fraction of the world's total land area is not part of either Asia or North America?

EXTENSIONS

Write the difference between the land areas of Africa and North America as a fraction of the world's total land area.

The Product of a Whole Number and a Fraction

Clara practises the piano for $\frac{3}{4}$ h every day of the week.
How many hours per week does Clara practise the piano?
We think:

Sun. Mon. Tues. Wed. Thur. Fri. Sat.

$$\frac{3}{4} + \frac{3}{4} + \frac{3}{4} + \frac{3}{4} + \frac{3}{4} + \frac{3}{4} + \frac{3}{4} = 7 \times \frac{3}{4}$$

We say: 7 times 3 quarters is 21 quarters.

We write: $7 \times \frac{3}{4} = \frac{21}{4}$ or $5\frac{1}{4}$.

Clara practises the piano $5\frac{1}{4}$ h per week.

Write the multiplication sentence suggested by each picture.

1.

$$5 \times \frac{3}{4} = \frac{15}{4} \text{ or } 3\frac{3}{4}$$

2.

3.

4.

5.

6.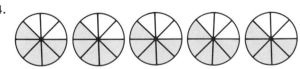

Draw a picture to match each multiplication sentence.

7. $5 \times \frac{1}{2} = 2\frac{1}{2}$

8. $3 \times \frac{3}{4} = 2\frac{1}{4}$

9. $4 \times \frac{5}{6} = 3\frac{1}{3}$

We can use this flow chart to multiply
a whole number and a fraction.

To multiply a fraction by a whole number:	⇒	Multiply the numerator by the whole number.	⇒	Express any improper fraction as a mixed number.

$$7 \times \frac{3}{4} \qquad\qquad 7 \times \frac{3}{4} = \frac{21}{4} \qquad\qquad \frac{21}{4} \text{ or } 5\frac{1}{4}$$

We can use the order property of
multiplication to multiply a whole number
by a fraction. That is, $7 \times \frac{3}{4} = \frac{3}{4} \times 7$

To multiply a whole number by a fraction:	⇒	Multiply the whole number by the numerator.	⇒	Express any improper fraction as a mixed number.

$$\frac{3}{4} \times 7 \qquad\qquad \frac{3}{4} \times 7 = \frac{21}{4} \qquad\qquad \frac{21}{4} \text{ or } 5\frac{1}{4}$$

Other examples:

$$2 \times \frac{3}{8} = \frac{6}{8} \text{ or } \frac{3}{4} \qquad\qquad 3 \times \frac{5}{8} = \frac{15}{8} \text{ or } 1\frac{7}{8} \qquad\qquad \frac{5}{6} \times 10 = \frac{50}{6} \text{ or } 8\frac{1}{3}$$

Multiply.

1. $4 \times \frac{2}{3}$ 2. $5 \times \frac{3}{8}$ 3. $9 \times \frac{2}{3}$ 4. $3 \times \frac{5}{6}$ 5. $7 \times \frac{1}{2}$

6. $\frac{3}{4} \times 8$ 7. $\frac{1}{2} \times 9$ 8. $\frac{5}{8} \times 7$ 9. $\frac{4}{5} \times 8$ 10. $\frac{2}{7} \times 6$

11. Three quarters are needed to play a video game. How much money is needed to play the game 9 times?

Express your answer in dollars and a fraction of a dollar.

PROBLEM SOLVING

Study these examples.

$\frac{1}{2}$ of $16 = 8$ $\frac{1}{3}$ of $12 = 4$ $\frac{3}{4}$ of $20 = 15$

What sign of operation, $+$, $-$, or $\times$, can be used in place of the word *of*?

A Fraction of a Whole Number

Della is 16 years old.

Kirk is $\frac{3}{4}$ of Della's age.

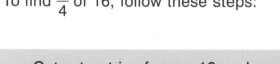

How old is Kirk?

To find $\frac{3}{4}$ of 16, follow these steps:

1. Cut out a strip of paper 16 cm long.
   Mark off lengths of 1 cm.

| 1 | 2 | 3 | 4 | 5 | 6 | 7 | 8 | 9 | 10 | 11 | 12 | 13 | 14 | 15 | 16 |

2. Fold the strip in half and then in half   Colour each quarter as shown below.
   again to divide it into quarters.

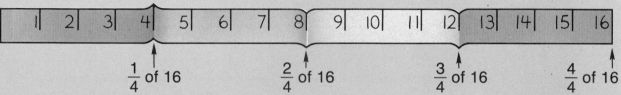

$\frac{1}{4}$ of 16 $\frac{2}{4}$ of 16 $\frac{3}{4}$ of 16 $\frac{4}{4}$ of 16

3. Use your paper strip to help $\frac{1}{4}$ of 16 = ▨ $\frac{2}{4}$ of 16 = ▨ $\frac{3}{4}$ of 16 = ▨
   you complete each sentence.

   Compare with the products. $\frac{1}{4} \times 16 =$ ▨ $\frac{2}{4} \times 16 =$ ▨ $\frac{3}{4} \times 16 =$ ▨

Kirk is $\frac{3}{4}$ of 16 or 12 years old.

The comparison in step 3 above suggests we can replace *of* with a multiplication sign, ×.

That is, $\frac{3}{5}$ of 20 means $\frac{3}{5} \times 20$.

We see:

We think: $\frac{3}{5}$ of 20 circles are red.

We write: $\frac{3}{5} \times 20 = \frac{60}{5}$ or 12

12 circles are red.

Use the picture to help you complete each sentence.
Then complete the matching product and compare.

1.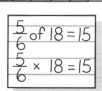

$\frac{3}{4}$ of 16 = 12

$\frac{3}{4}$ × 16 = 12

2.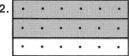

$\frac{2}{3}$ of 18 = ▦

$\frac{2}{3}$ × 18 = ▦

3.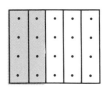

$\frac{2}{5}$ of 20 = ▦

$\frac{2}{5}$ × 20 = ▦

4.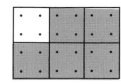

$\frac{5}{6}$ of 24 = ▦

$\frac{5}{6}$ × 24 = ▦

Copy and complete the statement to match the picture.
Then write the related multiplication sentence.

5.

$\frac{5}{6}$ of 18 = 15

$\frac{5}{6}$ × 18 = 15

6.

$\frac{1}{2}$ of ▦ = ▦

7.

$\frac{3}{5}$ of ▦ = ▦

8.

$\frac{1}{3}$ of ▦ = ▦

9.

$\frac{1}{4}$ of ▦ = ▦

10.

$\frac{▦}{8}$ of 16 = 6

11.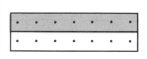

$\frac{▦}{▦}$ of ▦ = ▦

12.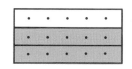

$\frac{▦}{▦}$ of ▦ = 10

Copy and complete. Draw a picture
to show your answer if you wish.

13. $\frac{1}{3}$ of 24 = ▦   14. $\frac{3}{5}$ of 20 = ▦

15. $\frac{1}{7}$ of 21 = ▦   16. $\frac{4}{5}$ of 10 = ▦

17. $\frac{1}{6}$ of 72 = ▦   18. $\frac{3}{4}$ of 64 = ▦

19. Use the circle graph on page 392 to
determine how many hours per day
Abbie spends: a) at recreation.
b) sleeping. c) on other activities.

401

Products of Fractions

To find $\frac{3}{4}$ of $\frac{1}{2}$, we follow these steps.

1. Fold the paper in half lengthwise and colour one half blue.

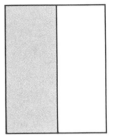

2. Open the paper, then fold in quarters in the other direction.

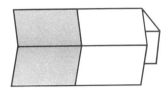

3. Unfold your paper and mark $\frac{3}{4}$ of the paper with stripes as shown.

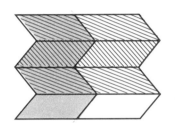

4. The part of the paper that is both blue and striped is $\frac{3}{4}$ of $\frac{1}{2}$.

We write: $\frac{3}{4}$ of $\frac{1}{2} = \frac{3}{8}$

or $\frac{3}{4} \times \frac{1}{2} = \frac{3}{8}$

Use the picture to help you complete the sentence.
Then complete the matching product.

1.
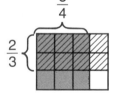

$$\frac{2}{3} \text{ of } \frac{3}{4} = \frac{6}{12}$$
$$\frac{2}{3} \times \frac{3}{4} = \frac{6}{12}$$

2.
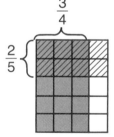

$\frac{2}{5}$ of $\frac{3}{4} = $ ■

$\frac{2}{5} \times \frac{3}{4} = $ ■

3.
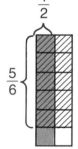

$\frac{5}{6}$ of $\frac{1}{2} = $ ■

$\frac{5}{6} \times \frac{1}{2} = $ ■

4.
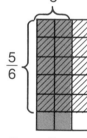

$\frac{5}{6}$ of $\frac{2}{3} = $ ■

$\frac{5}{6} \times \frac{2}{3} = $ ■

5.
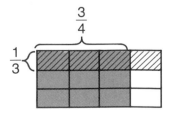

$\frac{1}{3}$ of $\frac{3}{4} = $ ■

$\frac{1}{3} \times \frac{3}{4} = $ ■

6.
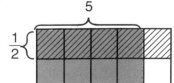

$\frac{1}{2}$ of $\frac{4}{5} = $ ■

$\frac{1}{2} \times \frac{4}{5} = $ ■

We can use a flow chart to multiply fractions.

We see: $\dfrac{5}{8} \times \dfrac{3}{10}$

We think: To multiply fractions:

Multiply the numerators.	$\dfrac{5}{8} \times \dfrac{3}{10} = \dfrac{15}{\blacksquare}$
Multiply the denominators.	$\dfrac{5}{8} \times \dfrac{3}{10} = \dfrac{15}{80}$
Write in simplest form.	$\dfrac{15}{80}$ or $\dfrac{3}{16}$

Write a multiplication sentence to show what fraction of the total area is coloured.

1.

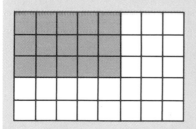

2.

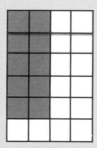

3.

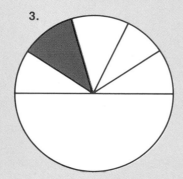

Multiply.

4. $\dfrac{1}{3} \times \dfrac{2}{5}$ 5. $\dfrac{1}{4} \times \dfrac{3}{8}$ 6. $\dfrac{2}{3} \times \dfrac{5}{6}$

7. $\dfrac{2}{5} \times \dfrac{5}{8}$ 8. $\dfrac{2}{3} \times \dfrac{4}{5}$ 9. $\dfrac{1}{6} \times \dfrac{1}{4}$

10. Asia and Africa together contain $\dfrac{1}{2}$ of all the land area on earth.

Asia contains $\dfrac{3}{5}$ of the combined area.

What fraction of the world's land area is contained in Asia?

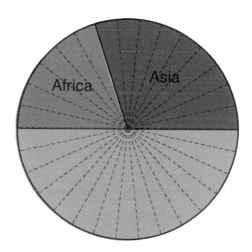

PROBLEM SOLVING

- $\dfrac{3}{4}$ of all the students in Amy's class can swim.
- Only $\dfrac{1}{3}$ of the swimmers can also dive.
- Of those who can dive and swim, exactly half are boys.

What fraction of the students in Amy's class are girls who can swim and dive?

403

Dividing a Whole Number by a Fraction

Complete the division sentence to answer each question.

1. How many quarters are in 5?

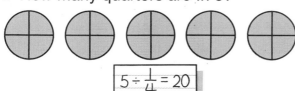

$$5 \div \frac{1}{4} = 20$$

2. How many thirds are in 4?

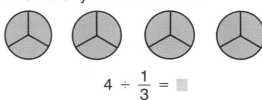

$$4 \div \frac{1}{3} = \blacksquare$$

3. How many halves are in 5?

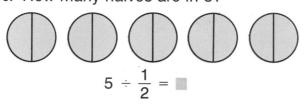

$$5 \div \frac{1}{2} = \blacksquare$$

4. How many sixths are in 4?

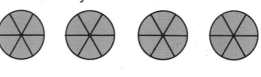

Draw figures divided into equal parts
to check each division sentence.

5. $3 \div \frac{1}{2} = 6$

6. $2 \div \frac{1}{4} = 8$

7. $4 \div \frac{1}{4} = 16$

8. $5 \div \frac{1}{3} = 15$

9. $1 \div \frac{1}{5} = 5$

10. $3 \div \frac{1}{6} = 18$

11. $2 \div \frac{1}{3} = 6$

12. $1 \div \frac{1}{8} = 8$

Write a division sentence to match each picture.

13.

14.

15.

16.

  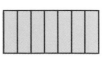

Divide. Draw a picture if you wish.

17. $8 \div \frac{1}{3}$

18. $5 \div \frac{1}{5}$

19. $6 \div \frac{1}{4}$

20. $4 \div \frac{1}{5}$

21. $9 \div \frac{1}{2}$

22. $8 \div \frac{1}{6}$

23. $3 \div \frac{1}{7}$

24. $5 \div \frac{1}{8}$

Quotients of Fractions

FRACTIONS HAVE MANY DISGUISES...

...SOMETIMES A FRACTION IS DISGUISED AS A DIVISION $\frac{3}{4} = 3 \div 4$

...SOMETIMES A FRACTION IS DISGUISED AS A MULTIPLICATION $\frac{3}{4} = 3 \times \frac{1}{4}$

...BUT UNDERNEATH THE DISGUISE IT IS ALWAYS THE SAME FRACTION.

$3 \div 4 = 3 \times \frac{1}{4}$

I SAY, MR. HOMELY, YOU HAVE JUST SHOWN THAT DIVIDING BY 4 IS THE SAME AS MULTIPLYING BY $\frac{1}{4}$.

ACTUALLY, MY DEAR PROFESSOR, I HAVE SHOWN MUCH MORE! DIVIDING BY ANY NUMBER IS THE SAME AS MULTIPLYING BY ITS RECIPROCAL!

$12 \div 5 = 12 \times \frac{1}{5}$
$20 \div 7 = 20 \times \frac{1}{7}$
$2 \div \frac{1}{3} = 2 \times 3$
$\frac{1}{4} \div 5 = \frac{1}{4} \times \frac{1}{5}$

WHAT'S A RECIPROCAL?

THE RECIPROCAL OF A FRACTION IS THE FRACTION YOU GET BY SWITCHING THE NUMERATOR AND DENOMINATOR!

NUMBER	RECIPROCAL
$\frac{2}{3}$	$\frac{3}{2}$
$\frac{1}{3}$	3
5	$\frac{1}{5}$

SHERLOCK HOMELY TURNS MY WORLD UPSIDE DOWN!

Sherlock Homely has discovered the following procedure for dividing by a fraction.

| To divide any number by a fraction. | $4 \div \dfrac{2}{3}$ |

⬇

| Multiply by the reciprocal of the fraction: | $4 \times \dfrac{3}{2} = \dfrac{12}{2}$ |

⬇

| Write your answer in simplest form. | $\dfrac{12}{2}$ or 6 |

Other examples:

$$\frac{2}{3} \div \frac{3}{4} = \frac{2}{3} \times \frac{4}{3} = \frac{8}{9}$$

$$\frac{1}{6} \div \frac{5}{8} = \frac{1}{6} \times \frac{8}{5} = \frac{8}{30} \text{ or } \frac{4}{15}$$

Write the reciprocal of each number.

1. $\dfrac{1}{6}$ 2. $\dfrac{3}{5}$ 3. $\dfrac{4}{7}$

4. $\dfrac{9}{10}$ 5. $\dfrac{1}{2}$ 6. $\dfrac{3}{7}$

7. $\dfrac{2}{5}$ 8. $\dfrac{5}{6}$ 9. $\dfrac{7}{2}$

10. $\dfrac{4}{3}$ 11. $\dfrac{5}{8}$ 12. $\dfrac{6}{10}$

Divide.

13. $4 \div \dfrac{2}{5}$ 14. $6 \div \dfrac{3}{4}$

15. $8 \div \dfrac{2}{3}$ 16. $3 \div \dfrac{2}{5}$

17. $\dfrac{1}{2} \div \dfrac{2}{3}$ 18. $\dfrac{3}{8} \div \dfrac{1}{4}$

19. $\dfrac{5}{8} \div \dfrac{2}{3}$ 20. $\dfrac{5}{6} \div \dfrac{3}{4}$

21. The school day at Oakdale Junior High School is 6 h long. The day is divided into periods which last $\dfrac{2}{3}$ h each. How many periods are in the day?

BITS AND BYTES 💾💾💾

Calculate these quotients. Then use your calculator to check your answers.

1. $6 \div \dfrac{3}{4}$ 2. $\dfrac{2}{5} \div \dfrac{1}{2}$ 3. $\dfrac{2}{3} \div \dfrac{1}{3}$

Selecting a Strategy

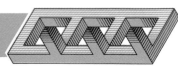

IF ONE STRATEGY DOESN'T WORK...

...TRY ANOTHER!

Each of these problems can be solved by one or more of the strategies you have studied.

1. The teacher said, "Your homework for tonight is on 2 facing pages of your textbook. The product of the page numbers is 702." What were the page numbers?

2. What is the unknown number?

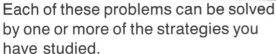

unknown number → − 6 → ×2 → 8

3. The fence around a rectangular garden has 40 posts. There are 16 posts on each of the long sides. How many posts are on each of the 2 short sides?

4. Robin's dresser drawer contains 10 identical blue socks and 20 identical black socks. How many socks must she pull from the drawer (without looking) to make sure she has a matching pair?

5. The section of Gridtown in which Mr. Descartes lives and works has all one-way streets. The streets shown by vertical line segments allow northbound travel only. The streets shown by horizontal line segments allow eastbound travel only. How many different ways can Mr. Descartes drive home from work?

HOME

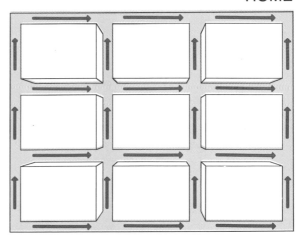

WORK

6. Mrs. Morrow has 44 ribbons to award the top 10 students on sports day. Can she give a different number of ribbons to each student?

7. If I multiply a number by itself and add 26, the result is 350. What is the number I started with?

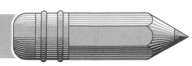

Add or subtract. Write answers in simplest form.

1. $\dfrac{1}{3} + \dfrac{1}{3}$ 2. $\dfrac{6}{8} - \dfrac{3}{8}$ 3. $\dfrac{3}{4} - \dfrac{1}{4}$

Write as a mixed number.

4. $\dfrac{7}{4}$ 5. $\dfrac{15}{10}$ 6. $\dfrac{8}{3}$

Write as an improper fraction.

7. $1\dfrac{1}{3}$ 8. $1\dfrac{2}{5}$ 9. $1\dfrac{7}{10}$

Add. Write answers in simplest form.

10. $\dfrac{4}{5} + \dfrac{3}{5}$ 11. $\dfrac{3}{8} + \dfrac{7}{8}$ 12. $\dfrac{5}{10} + \dfrac{9}{10}$

Subtract. Write answers in simplest form.

13. $1\dfrac{1}{5} - \dfrac{4}{5}$ 14. $1\dfrac{3}{8} - \dfrac{7}{8}$ 15. $1\dfrac{1}{4} - \dfrac{2}{4}$

16. Nelson's Café had $1\dfrac{5}{8}$ of a pizza. When Ms. Hancock came in, she and her friends ate $\dfrac{7}{8}$ of a pizza. How much pizza was left?

Add. Write answers in simplest form.

17. $\dfrac{1}{2} + \dfrac{1}{8}$ 18. $\dfrac{1}{3} + \dfrac{3}{8}$ 19. $\dfrac{3}{4} + \dfrac{2}{5}$

Subtract. Write answers in simplest form.

20. $\dfrac{3}{4} - \dfrac{1}{3}$ 21. $\dfrac{4}{5} - \dfrac{1}{4}$ 22. $\dfrac{7}{8} - \dfrac{1}{2}$

Write a multiplication sentence for the picture below.

23.

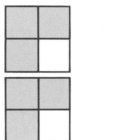

Multiply.

24. $5 \times \dfrac{1}{2}$ 25. $3 \times \dfrac{2}{3}$ 26. $\dfrac{2}{5} \times 4$

27. $\dfrac{1}{4} \times \dfrac{2}{3}$ 28. $\dfrac{7}{10} \times \dfrac{1}{2}$ 29. $\dfrac{3}{4} \times \dfrac{3}{10}$

30. How many halves are in 4?

Divide.

31. $3 \div \dfrac{1}{5}$ 32. $2 \div \dfrac{1}{10}$ 33. $4 \div \dfrac{1}{3}$

34. $5 \div \dfrac{1}{4}$ 35. $\dfrac{5}{6} \div \dfrac{1}{2}$ 36. $\dfrac{3}{8} \div \dfrac{1}{4}$

37. Kate had 4 granola bars. She broke each one in thirds. How many pieces did she have?

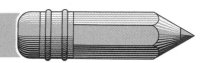

1. Write the ordered pair that locates each of these letters: a) D b) C c) F

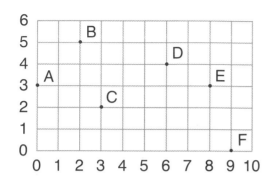

2. Write the letter for each ordered pair.
   a) (8,3)   b) (0,3)   c) (6,4)

3. Graph the quadrilateral with these vertices. Then graph its slide image.
   a) (2,3), (2,5), (4,5), (4,3)
      slide: 4 units right and 1 unit down
   b) (4,1), (5,3), (6,1), (7,2)
      slide: 4 units up

Copy each figure onto dot paper.

Then draw its image after a) $\frac{1}{4}$ turn,

b) $\frac{1}{2}$ turn, c) $\frac{3}{4}$ turn counterclockwise.

4.   5.

6. Which of these letters have:
   a) line symmetry?
   b) point symmetry?
   c) both?

Copy each figure onto dot paper. Then draw its flip image.

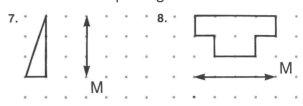

7.   8.

9. Write the numbers of the figures:
   a) congruent to A   b) similar to A

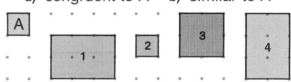

Copy and complete.

10. $\frac{1}{2} = \frac{\blacksquare}{6}$ 11. $\frac{8}{10} = \frac{16}{\blacksquare}$

Write each fraction in simplest form.

12. $\frac{4}{6}$ 13. $\frac{5}{10}$ 14. $\frac{8}{12}$ 15. $\frac{15}{25}$

Write as a fraction in simplest form.

16. 0.75   17. 0.8   18. 0.16   19. 0.05

Write as a decimal number.

20. $\frac{2}{5}$ 21. $\frac{1}{4}$ 22. $\frac{12}{25}$ 23. $\frac{7}{10}$

Write a mixed number for the picture below.

24.

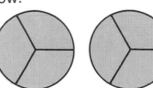
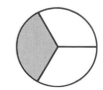

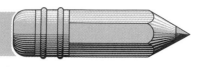

Find equivalent fractions with like denominators. Then compare the fractions by writing > or <.

25. $\frac{1}{2}$ ▦ $\frac{1}{3}$ 26. $\frac{3}{4}$ ▦ $\frac{5}{6}$ 27. $\frac{7}{8}$ ▦ $\frac{2}{3}$

28. A package of 7 pencils sells for 49¢. How many pencils could be bought with $2.50?

Add or subtract. Write answers in simplest form.

29. $\frac{3}{5} + \frac{1}{5}$ 30. $\frac{8}{10} - \frac{4}{10}$ 31. $\frac{5}{6} - \frac{3}{6}$

Write as a mixed number.

32. $\frac{13}{8}$ 33. $\frac{12}{10}$ 34. $\frac{9}{6}$

Write as an improper fraction.

35. $1\frac{1}{4}$ 36. $1\frac{3}{10}$ 37. $1\frac{4}{5}$

Add. Write answers in simplest form.

38. $\frac{2}{5} + \frac{4}{5}$ 39. $\frac{2}{3} + \frac{2}{3}$ 40. $\frac{9}{10} + \frac{8}{10}$

Subtract. Write answers in simplest form.

41. $1\frac{3}{8} - \frac{5}{8}$ 42. $1\frac{1}{5} - \frac{3}{5}$ 43. $1\frac{2}{6} - \frac{4}{6}$

Add or subtract. Write answers in simplest form.

44. $\frac{1}{2} - \frac{3}{8}$ 45. $\frac{4}{10} + \frac{2}{3}$ 46. $\frac{9}{10} - \frac{1}{6}$

47. Dotty had $1\frac{1}{6}$ apple pies for sale at noon. Mr. Whitworth bought $\frac{5}{6}$ of a pie for his family. How much pie did Dotty have left?

48. Write a multiplication sentence for the picture below.

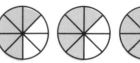

Multiply.

49. $3 \times \frac{2}{5}$ 50. $\frac{7}{10} \times 2$

51. $\frac{1}{3} \times \frac{3}{4}$ 52. $\frac{5}{6} \times \frac{1}{4}$

53. How many thirds are in 5?

Divide.

54. $3 \div \frac{1}{2}$ 55. $\frac{3}{10} \div \frac{1}{4}$

56. Charles and his 5 sisters each had $\frac{1}{4}$ of a candy bar. How many candy bars did they have altogether?

Add.

1. 2 036
   + 321

2. 678
   + 4 306

3. 1 435
   + 439

4. 6 596
   + 768

5. 502
   + 3 000

6. 9 468
   + 978

7. 1 729
   + 4 200

8. 2 985
   + 3 007

9. 5 084
   + 7 729

10. 1 926
    + 3 140

11. 3 310
    + 1 994

12. 7 665
    + 7 793

13. 61 592
    + 8 406

14. 5 840
    + 33 926

15. 48 174
    + 5 579

16. 20 681
    + 3 678

17. 91 514
    + 2 536

18. 1 021
    + 58 442

19. 36 633
    + 12 256

20. 60 520
    + 21 569

21. 44 386
    + 26 472

22. 22 370
    + 81 698

23. 98 771
    + 14 226

24. 24 276
    + 65 901

Subtract.

25. 7 818
    − 513

26. 3 639
    − 487

27. 2 670
    − 600

28. 7 862
    − 551

29. 6 496
    − 392

30. 4 374
    − 153

31. 8 087
    − 6 061

32. 8 996
    − 4 579

33. 2 662
    − 1 009

34. 5 100
    − 3 243

35. 7 682
    − 4 415

36. 1 667
    − 1 416

37. 72 343
    − 1 200

38. 66 761
    − 5 638

39. 34 746
    − 2 483

40. 12 385
    − 8 076

41. 78 719
    − 2 598

42. 91 834
    − 7 827

43. 48 222
    − 26 101

44. 96 062
    − 35 850

45. 47 001
    − 16 826

46. 25 394
    − 23 678

47. 99 343
    − 94 987

48. 49 413
    − 32 992

Add or subtract.

49. 6 792
    + 1 203

50. 48 239
    − 19 222

51. 6 792
    + 3 501

52. 35 827
    − 17 494

53. 2 176
    + 8 015

54. 6 645
    + 286

55. 21 928
    − 10 505

56. 23 785
    + 53 814

57. 15 280
    + 8 395

58. 49 143
    − 26 857

59. 21 800
    − 6 350

60. 1 318
    + 86 293

Multiply.

1. $\begin{array}{r} 16 \\ \times\ 4 \\ \hline \end{array}$ 2. $\begin{array}{r} 26 \\ \times\ 6 \\ \hline \end{array}$ 3. $\begin{array}{r} 57 \\ \times\ 8 \\ \hline \end{array}$ 4. $\begin{array}{r} 38 \\ \times\ 9 \\ \hline \end{array}$ 5. $\begin{array}{r} 94 \\ \times\ 2 \\ \hline \end{array}$ 6. $\begin{array}{r} 65 \\ \times\ 3 \\ \hline \end{array}$

7. $\begin{array}{r} 109 \\ \times\ 7 \\ \hline \end{array}$ 8. $\begin{array}{r} 971 \\ \times\ 5 \\ \hline \end{array}$ 9. $\begin{array}{r} 474 \\ \times\ 8 \\ \hline \end{array}$ 10. $\begin{array}{r} 1\ 701 \\ \times\ 6 \\ \hline \end{array}$ 11. $\begin{array}{r} 4\ 878 \\ \times\ 4 \\ \hline \end{array}$ 12. $\begin{array}{r} 3\ 841 \\ \times\ 9 \\ \hline \end{array}$

13. $\begin{array}{r} 23 \\ \times 13 \\ \hline \end{array}$ 14. $\begin{array}{r} 97 \\ \times 44 \\ \hline \end{array}$ 15. $\begin{array}{r} 626 \\ \times\ 35 \\ \hline \end{array}$ 16. $\begin{array}{r} 508 \\ \times\ 57 \\ \hline \end{array}$ 17. $\begin{array}{r} 4\ 172 \\ \times\ 26 \\ \hline \end{array}$ 18. $\begin{array}{r} 2\ 254 \\ \times\ 89 \\ \hline \end{array}$

19. $\begin{array}{r} 369 \\ \times 102 \\ \hline \end{array}$ 20. $\begin{array}{r} 192 \\ \times 210 \\ \hline \end{array}$ 21. $\begin{array}{r} 819 \\ \times 654 \\ \hline \end{array}$ 22. $\begin{array}{r} 2\ 862 \\ \times\ 139 \\ \hline \end{array}$ 23. $\begin{array}{r} 6\ 310 \\ \times\ 385 \\ \hline \end{array}$ 24. $\begin{array}{r} 1\ 597 \\ \times\ 861 \\ \hline \end{array}$

Divide.

25. $3\overline{)96}$ 26. $2\overline{)39}$ 27. $4\overline{)62}$ 28. $7\overline{)91}$ 29. $8\overline{)57}$ 30. $6\overline{)87}$

31. $5\overline{)497}$ 32. $4\overline{)559}$ 33. $8\overline{)389}$ 34. $6\overline{)1924}$ 35. $7\overline{)2868}$ 36. $4\overline{)1229}$

37. $2\overline{)819}$ 38. $4\overline{)830}$ 39. $2\overline{)806}$ 40. $3\overline{)623}$ 41. $5\overline{)3200}$ 42. $6\overline{)5406}$

43. $23\overline{)1569}$ 44. $18\overline{)1366}$ 45. $49\overline{)2793}$ 46. $51\overline{)6456}$ 47. $44\overline{)9284}$ 48. $28\overline{)5517}$

49. $26\overline{)7826}$ 50. $18\overline{)1880}$ 51. $49\overline{)3925}$ 52. $87\overline{)3496}$ 53. $53\overline{)3728}$ 54. $22\overline{)4510}$

Multiply or divide.

55. $\begin{array}{r} 39 \\ \times\ 5 \\ \hline \end{array}$ 56. $4\overline{)65}$ 57. $7\overline{)616}$ 58. $\begin{array}{r} 108 \\ \times\ 7 \\ \hline \end{array}$ 59. $\begin{array}{r} 4\ 284 \\ \times\ 6 \\ \hline \end{array}$ 60. $6\overline{)567}$

61. $8\overline{)648}$ 62. $\begin{array}{r} 55 \\ \times 58 \\ \hline \end{array}$ 63. $\begin{array}{r} 993 \\ \times\ 22 \\ \hline \end{array}$ 64. $\begin{array}{r} 762 \\ \times\ 47 \\ \hline \end{array}$ 65. $28\overline{)420}$ 66. $33\overline{)3399}$

Add.

1. 4.4
    +5.2

2. 3.6
    +8.5

3. 48.5
    +44.9

4. 96.6
    +17.7

5. 123.2
    + 37.9

6. 488.3
    + 56.8

7. 7.25
    +2.33

8. 4.92
    +6.07

9. 43.67
    +11.22

10. 21.66
     +39.34

11. $35.88
     + 94.25

12. $1.79
     + 8.57

13. 1.262
     +6.304

14. 3.243
     +1.108

15. 23.462
     +99.097

16. 2.3
     1.1
     +4.2

17. $6.62
     9.45
     3.22
     + 7.18

18. 96.9
     45.9
     +30.2

Subtract.

19. 6.2
     −4.1

20. 8.9
     −4.7

21. 5.2
     −2.9

22. 18.4
     − 6.3

23. 68.5
     −46.8

24. 93.6
     −81.5

25. 9.64
     −5.02

26. 3.82
     −2.54

27. 3.93
     −0.87

28. 27.06
     −15.01

29. 63.68
     −45.94

30. 84.94
     −22.76

31. $6.38
     − 5.11

32. $8.87
     − 7.20

33. $9.85
     − 2.69

34. $39.65
     − 14.15

35. $69.99
     − 30.00

36. $52.05
     − 49.90

Add or subtract.

37. 5.8
     −4.2

38. 23.6
     +16.7

39. 304.9
     +173.8

40. 95.78
     − 4.95

41. 9.92
     −7.62

42. $7.26
     + 3.29

43. $90.55
     − 40.30

44. 9.257
     +8.840

45. 8.092
     +2.459

46. 20.516
     − 6.809

47. 17.442
     −12.956

48. 93.160
     +46.385

Multiply.

1. 1.7
    × 6

2. 3.2
    × 7

3. 18.6
    × 4

4. 9.4
    × 5

5. 24.5
    × 8

6. 17.1
    × 9

7. 5.31
    × 3

8. 8.09
    × 2

9. 13.46
    × 5

10. 3.657
    × 7

11. 2.446
    × 6

12. 18.012
    × 8

13. 16
    ×3.2

14. 6.9
    ×28

15. 7.08
    × 52

16. 34
    ×5.66

17. 61
    ×2.105

18. 2.994
    × 80

19. 12.5
    × 66

20. 72.3
    × 87

21. 24.73
    × 43

22. 54.81
    × 17

23. 70.016
    × 22

24. 84.619
    × 93

25. 134
    ×8.5

26. 685
    ×6.3

27. 740
    ×14.38

28. 355
    ×9.82

29. 6.954
    × 271

30. 7.901
    × 147

Multiply.

31. 0.4
    ×0.3

32. 0.5
    ×0.6

33. 0.8
    ×0.6

34. 0.9
    ×0.2

35. 0.7
    ×0.4

36. 0.5
    ×0.3

37. 6.2
    ×1.8

38. 7.4
    ×3.6

39. 9.6
    ×2.4

40. 81.7
    × 0.8

41. 62.8
    × 2.9

42. 58.6
    × 4.3

43. 2.86
    × 9.1

44. 9.07
    × 6.8

45. 1.29
    × 7.9

46. 8.76
    × 6.2

47. 2.53
    × 1.8

48. 13.67
    × 2.5

49. 0.76
    ×0.13

50. 8.04
    ×2.92

51. 3.58
    ×2.15

52. 12.80
    × 3.97

53. 9.936
    × 1.08

54. 1.301
    × 1.67

55. 0.8
    ×0.1

56. 0.25
    × 0.2

57. 0.31
    × 0.3

58. 0.69
    ×0.24

59. 0.09
    ×0.06

60. 0.0018
    × 0.3

Divide.

1. 3)5.7

2. 2)9.7

3. 4)7.5

4. 8)6.4

5. 5)3.2

6. 4)4.86

7. 3)6.51

8. 5)5.75

9. 2)5.02

10. 5)6.82

11. 7)18.69

12. 6)19.26

13. 5)4.960

14. 4)55.64

15. 8)9.944

16. 26)239.2

17. 18)333

18. 14)4.2

19. 21)105

20. 32)243.2

21. 13)18.85

22. 24)87.36

23. 35)76.65

24. 42)949.20

25. 11)8.25

26. 2)6.8

27. 7)8.4

28. 9)9.27

29. 16)60.8

30. 24)67.84

Divide.

31. 0.4)7.2

32. 0.3)2.4

33. 0.6)6.6

34. 0.8)11.2

35. 0.9)10.8

36. 1.2)6.0

37. 3.4)173.4

38. 6.7)21.507

39. 8.1)51.03

40. 2.9)30.74

41. 23.6)99.12

42. 14.2)49.7

43. 18.3)16.47

44. 31.6)79.316

45. 40.5)243

46. 0.05)0.65

47. 0.09)1.8

48. 0.06)7.2

49. 0.03)0.09

50. 0.08)0.16

51. 1.12)8.288

52. 2.05)0.738

53. 3.65)5.475

54. 4.18)17.138

55. 11.32)32.828

56. 0.7)4.9

57. 2.4)0.384

58. 0.15)94.5

59. 2.19)23.871

60. 12.8)47.36

Add.

1. $\dfrac{1}{3} + \dfrac{1}{3}$ 2. $\dfrac{2}{4} + \dfrac{1}{4}$ 3. $\dfrac{3}{10} + \dfrac{4}{10}$ 4. $\dfrac{1}{5} + \dfrac{3}{5}$ 5. $\dfrac{4}{6} + \dfrac{1}{6}$ 6. $\dfrac{7}{10} + \dfrac{1}{10}$

7. $\dfrac{2}{5} + \dfrac{1}{4}$ 8. $\dfrac{1}{3} + \dfrac{1}{10}$ 9. $\dfrac{1}{6} + \dfrac{3}{4}$ 10. $\dfrac{1}{5} + \dfrac{1}{3}$ 11. $\dfrac{1}{2} + \dfrac{1}{4}$ 12. $\dfrac{3}{10} + \dfrac{2}{3}$

13. $\dfrac{2}{3} + \dfrac{4}{5}$ 14. $\dfrac{1}{2} + \dfrac{7}{10}$ 15. $\dfrac{3}{4} + \dfrac{1}{3}$ 16. $\dfrac{9}{10} + \dfrac{1}{5}$ 17. $\dfrac{3}{5} + \dfrac{1}{2}$ 18. $\dfrac{1}{4} + \dfrac{4}{5}$

Subtract.

19. $\dfrac{9}{10} - \dfrac{2}{10}$ 20. $\dfrac{2}{3} - \dfrac{1}{3}$ 21. $\dfrac{5}{6} - \dfrac{1}{6}$ 22. $\dfrac{3}{4} - \dfrac{1}{4}$ 23. $\dfrac{7}{10} - \dfrac{3}{10}$ 24. $\dfrac{4}{5} - \dfrac{1}{5}$

25. $\dfrac{4}{5} - \dfrac{1}{2}$ 26. $\dfrac{3}{4} - \dfrac{1}{3}$ 27. $\dfrac{9}{10} - \dfrac{2}{5}$ 28. $\dfrac{7}{10} - \dfrac{1}{6}$ 29. $\dfrac{2}{3} - \dfrac{1}{5}$ 30. $\dfrac{1}{4} - \dfrac{1}{6}$

Multiply.

31. $3 \times \dfrac{1}{4}$ 32. $8 \times \dfrac{1}{10}$ 33. $4 \times \dfrac{2}{5}$ 34. $2 \times \dfrac{2}{3}$ 35. $5 \times \dfrac{1}{6}$ 36. $6 \times \dfrac{3}{10}$

37. $\dfrac{1}{5} \times 7$ 38. $\dfrac{1}{4} \times 2$ 39. $\dfrac{1}{3} \times 2$ 40. $\dfrac{3}{10} \times 4$ 41. $\dfrac{5}{6} \times 3$ 42. $\dfrac{2}{3} \times 5$

43. $\dfrac{1}{2} \times \dfrac{2}{3}$ 44. $\dfrac{4}{5} \times \dfrac{1}{3}$ 45. $\dfrac{1}{10} \times \dfrac{3}{4}$ 46. $\dfrac{5}{6} \times \dfrac{1}{4}$ 47. $\dfrac{3}{10} \times \dfrac{1}{5}$ 48. $\dfrac{1}{6} \times \dfrac{1}{3}$

Divide.

49. $3 \div \dfrac{1}{2}$ 50. $6 \div \dfrac{1}{3}$ 51. $4 \div \dfrac{1}{10}$ 52. $7 \div \dfrac{1}{4}$ 53. $3 \div \dfrac{3}{5}$ 54. $2 \div \dfrac{7}{10}$

55. $\dfrac{3}{5} \div \dfrac{1}{4}$ 56. $\dfrac{2}{3} \div \dfrac{1}{2}$ 57. $\dfrac{1}{2} \div \dfrac{1}{10}$ 58. $\dfrac{9}{10} \div \dfrac{1}{3}$ 59. $\dfrac{2}{3} \div \dfrac{1}{4}$ 60. $\dfrac{3}{10} \div \dfrac{1}{6}$

INDEX